Making Mandated Addiction Treatment Work

Making Mandated Addiction Treatment Work

Barbara C. Wallace

JASON ARONSON
Lanham • Boulder • New York • Toronto • Oxford

Published in the United States of America
by Jason Aronson
An imprint of Rowman & Littlefield Publishers, Inc.

A wholly owned subsidiary of
The Rowman & Littlefield Publishing Group, Inc.
4501 Forbes Boulevard, Suite 200, Lanham, Maryland 20706
www.rowmanlittlefield.com

PO Box 317
Oxford
OX2 9RU, UK

British Library Cataloguing in Publication Information Available

Library of Congress Cataloging-in-Publication Data
Wallace, Barbara C.
  Making mandated addiction treatment work / Barbara C. Wallace.
     p. cm.
  Includes bibliographical references and index.
  ISBN 0-7657-0397-1 (cloth : alk. paper)—ISBN 0-7657-0398-X (pbk. : alk. paper)
1. Substance abuse—Treatment—United States. 2. Community mental health
services—United States. 3. Criminals—Substance use—United States.
4. Prisoners—Substance use—United States. I. Title.

  RC564.W355 2005
  362.29'0973—dc22   2005006949

Printed in the United States of America

∞™ The paper used in this publication meets the minimum requirements of
American National Standard for Information Sciences—Permanence of Paper
for Printed Library Materials, ANSI/NISO Z39.48-1992.

This book is dedicated to my parents, Uriel H. Wallace Jr. and Cynthia Comer Wallace.

You have served as role models for excellence in leadership, what it means to be a lifetime educator, the value of hard work, and the meaning of spiritual service. Because of the priority placed upon education, you made personal sacrifices in order for me to attend Princeton University and to pursue graduate and postgraduate training. Thus, I acknowledge you both for creating the very foundation for my personal growth and development. As you gracefully age and enjoy the golden years, please know that my eternal gratitude and love are yours.

Contents

Tables and Figures

TABLES

FIGURES

Preface

Community-based addiction treatment represents a national frontier for pioneering the adaptation of evidence-based addiction-treatment interventions with some of the most challenging, multiproblem clients who also bring a high risk of recidivism and relapse. Answers are being forged on the front lines and in the trenches of community-based addiction-treatment centers with regard to absolutely timely and essential questions: What works with heterogeneous clients who are diverse across a multitude of dimensions and who constitute some of the most difficult clients to ever be treated in the field of addiction in such high record numbers? How should evidence-based interventions be integrated, adapted, and tailored, given client backgrounds involving not only addiction, but also incarceration, ongoing criminal-justice-system supervision, performance of risky behaviors, histories of trauma across the lifespan, engagement in violence, psychiatric comorbidity, and a high risk of recidivism and relapse to more than one problem behavior? Moreover, how can practitioners successfully accomplish this work within a societal era characterized by conservative, moralistic, intolerant attitudes toward the drug involved, and the stigmatization of drug users?

In light of these questions and the urgent need for answers, there is great justification for a book on making mandated addiction treatment work. Quite simply, all that has been compiled through empirical research with regard to what works represents an important body of knowledge on evidence-based addiction-treatment interventions. However, what remains to be clearly articulated in the literature is how to adapt evidence-based addiction-treatment interventions and deliver multiple interventions within a unified model of care in the real world with contemporary multiproblem clients; this book seeks to move the field of addiction treatment toward a unified model and theory to guide treatment delivery. For, the real-world challenges inherent in working with varied clients who have idiosyncratic combinations of multiple problems, complex characteristics, and assorted needs requires a book that can serve as a practical guide in this important work. The massive influx of those being released from incarceration back into the community in the aftermath of the historically unprecedented use of mandatory minimum sentences and attainment in the United States of record numbers being incarcerated means that this work is of the highest importance. For, in the last decade of the twentieth century, the United States became the uncontested global leader in rates of imprisonment, relying on a policy of massive incarceration that mandated lengthy prison terms. Today we face the aftermath: an ongoing process involving the massive return of the incarcerated back into communities across the nation. The potential recidivism and relapse of those being released from incarceration, as well as their all-too-frequent risky behaviors, violent behaviors, health problems, and psychiatric symptoms, create real challenges. In addition, the resulting challenges include how those returning from incarceration will face obstacles to employment and difficulty reintegrating into family, community, and societal life. Thus, the contemporary phenomenon of massive reentry could have a devastating impact on communities across the United States. Hence, there is great urgency to the task of successfully addressing all of these clients' risk factors, characteristics, and needs through the provision of evidence-based addiction treatment that is appropriately adapted and tailored for contemporary clients.

Fortunately, the dawning of the new millennium has brought with it refreshing proposals for directing toward treatment those clients with addictive behavior who have been arrested for nonviolent crimes such as drug possession and drug sale. Consistent with this trend, drug courts, alternatives to incarceration, and mandates to drug treatment are on the rise. Those on probation and parole are being mandated to addiction treatment. Criminal-justice-system personnel are enforcing intensive supervision policies that include monitoring urine toxicology specimens for evidence of drug use in those under their supervision. These personnel then apply graduated sanctions for positive toxicology results, including mandates to addiction treatment and reincarceration.

Hopefully, the current conservative, moralistic, and intolerant era, which is promoting criminal sanctions and zero tolerance, is rapidly drawing to a close as an artifact of the twentieth century. This book seeks to promote the dawning and ascendance of a new era of rational and compassionate drug policy that restores the value of rehabilitation for drug offenders and that relies upon mandates to evidence-based addiction treatment. And the mandated addiction treatment to which drug offenders are sent must reflect the thoughtful integration and application of evidence-based addiction-treatment interventions, while the tailoring of interventions to meet client characteristics and needs must be valued as essential.

Because the largest and fastest-growing segment of the community-based addiction-treatment population includes those who are mandated, this book addresses the task of making mandated addiction treatment work. Also recognized are the needs of clients who are coerced into treatment. Still others involved with illicit drugs are concerned clients who volunteer for treatment for varied reasons, with many wanting to "get help before they get caught." The community-based addiction-treatment scene must meet the challenges inherent in the largest and fastest-growing segment of the client population being mandated, as well as the needs of all of those diverse clients engaging in treatment in our contemporary times.

Also, practitioners working in prison- and jail-based treatment services for addictive behaviors have been confronted with the reality that the incarcerated population includes those who bring the need for drug treatment with them into the criminal justice system. Hence, collectively, contemporary community-based and incarcerated clients are creating a great challenge to the overall field of addiction treatment.

In light of the contemporary challenge, the nature of the social context, and the reality that the new majority of clients in addiction treatment are mandated, there is a tremendous need for a book about making mandated addiction treatment work. The kind of book needed at this time of national crisis must be a practical guide for how to adapt evidence-based addiction treatment interventions, how to integrate them within a unified treatment model, and how to tailor treatment to individual client needs. Practitioners need a book that goes so far as to articulate what those working with contemporary clients in addiction treatment should say and do in their consultation rooms across the United States. This book serves as such a guide.

As a fellow in Division 50 (Addictions) within the American Psychological Association, and being a seasoned practitioner, I bring lengthy preparation to the tasks of moving the field of addiction toward a unified model and theory, and of articulating how to adapt evidence-based addiction treatment to contemporary clients in community-based addiction treatment. This includes twenty-two years of consultation in community-based addiction treatment, where I have worked on the front lines and in the trenches at the height of epidemics and in varied areas of drug treatment. Early preparation within postdoctoral training at NDRI (formerly Narcotic Drug Research Inc., now National Development Research Institutes) included working with Harry Wexler as he compiled early data on the Stay'n Out prison-based therapeutic community in New York (Wexler & Williams, 1986). This preparation encompassed a lengthy period engaged in clinical work and research in the New York City inpatient, residential therapeutic community (TC) and in outpatient addiction-treatment settings, including the period covering the onset, rise, and aftermath of the crack-cocaine epidemic (Wallace, 1987, 1989a, 1989b, 1990a, 1990b, 1990c, 1991a, 1991b, 1991c, 1992a, 1992b, 1992c, 1992d, 1992e, 1992f, 1992g, 1992h, 1992i). Learning much about the distinct challenges involved in community-based addiction treatment during the 1990s era of overlapping drug, HIV/AIDS, and violence epidemics was also vital preparation (Wallace, 1993a, 1993b, 1995, 1996a, 1996b, 2002). Other preparation involved forging a multicultural approach to addressing the histories of oppression, abuse, trauma, and violence in clients' lives, as well as fostering identity development in diverse clients (Wallace, 2000a, 2000b, 2003; Wallace & Carter, 2003; Wallace, Carter, Nanin, Keller, & Alleyne, 2003).

And the past seven years have involved striving to implement with fidelity the most recent evidence-based addiction-treatment interventions in the real-world context of community-based addiction treatment in New York City. This has meant pioneering rational adaptations of empirically proven interventions with heterogeneous clients who have multiple problems and complex characteristics, as treatment was tailored to meet client needs. Hence, what is offered is a timely, essential, and practical guide to making mandated addiction treatment work, as well as a unified model and theory for practitioners to use as a framework for service delivery.

INTENDED AUDIENCE

The intended audience for this book includes diverse practitioners, whether psychologists, social workers, psychiatrists, or counselors in the fields of addiction and mental health. The intended audience includes health educators, public-health officials, workers in the criminal-justice field, judges, policy makers, researchers, and community outreach workers—as all may attain deeper understanding and insight into the needs of those clients with whom they work. The book is also intended to assist those professionals and paraprofessionals working with this population at a variety of agencies within health, housing, employment, vocational, social, and welfare-service delivery systems. Indeed, the book is for all of those willing to accept the charge of learning how to engage empathically with a population that has been stigmatized, criminalized, and regarded with increasingly conservative, moralistic, and intolerant attitudes.

Directing this book to all those who work with or come in contact with the population of clients in addiction treatment, and placing an emphasis on learning how to effectively engage with them empathetically, is consistent with the remarks of Bandura (1997):

> Supportive social relationships not only reduce stress and compete with substance use but also strengthen self-regulatory efficacy by enabling those struggling with self control to weather adversities. Quality of social aid is a predictor of abstinence. . . . Environmental contributors involve much more than shoring up infirm self-regulation with social supports. Environmentally oriented ap-

proaches create social structures that enable people to exert satisfying proactive control over their familial, occupational, and recreational lives. (p. 294)

The environment that this book seeks to help create includes a social structure composed of members of the intended audience for this book who are capable of empathy when engaging with the population of mandated addiction-treatment clients. The ability to engage empathically with a client serves to further define what it means to provide a supportive social relationship that enables a client to exert proactive control over varied areas of his or her life. All of the mandated, coerced, and concerned clients need empathic engagement as a critical ingredient in making mandated addiction treatment work—whether with a practitioner within a community-based addiction-treatment center, a social-services worker, or a member of their community. Regardless of our formal or informal role in relation to a mandated client, when we give the gift of empathy from the heart, it transcends the moment and endures. When we give the gift of empathy, we have contributed one of the most important ingredients to the process of recovery.

Those willing to take on the contemporary challenge of making addiction treatment work with the growing population of mandated, coerced, or concerned clients need to know not only how to engage clients with genuine empathy, but also how to deploy research-based clinical techniques that have demonstrated efficacy. This book provides essential preparation for a diverse audience.

OVERVIEW OF THE BOOK

Part I provides guidelines for practitioners with regard to the overall task of making mandated addiction treatment work, in chapter 1 explaining how this is an age of evidence-based practice, and providing key standards and guiding definitions. Chapter 2 presents the characteristics, needs, and diversity commonly found among contemporary multiproblem clients. Chapter 3 presents the research on what works and examines the findings on mandated addiction treatment, and addiction treatment in general. Chapter 4 provides practitioners with a recommended menu of evidence-based options and state-of-the art practices to be adapted, integrated, and tailored to meet individual client needs, moving the field of addiction treatment toward a unified model and theory to guide service delivery. Chapter 5 discusses the correct timing for the delivery of interventions across phases of treatment and stages of change in light of client characteristics and needs.

Part II provides training for practitioners for the task of making mandated addiction treatment work, using a casebook approach. This training includes the following: (1) how to overcome negative countertransference (chapter 6), (2) how to conduct the initial psychological assessment/psychiatric screening (chapter 7), (3) how to conceptualize cases in order to meet short- and long-term treatment goals (chapter 8), and (4) how to create positive long-term treatment outcomes (chapter 9). Finally, chapter 10 concludes the book by underscoring the rationale for all that has been presented, and it cites that which we still do not know in the field of addiction treatment.

Acknowledgments

First, I must acknowledge with deep gratitude the many clients in community-based addiction treatment who opened up and trusted in the therapeutic process. The stories in this book reflect the pain, progress, and joy shared with clients in consultation rooms in community-based addiction treatment, even as I went to great lengths to change numerous details to maintain client anonymity, while preserving the essence of our work together. The resulting book is intended to serve as a tool for use by other practitioners and anyone who comes in contact with clients who are engaged in community-based addiction treatment—offering the hope that this practical guide produces more long-term positive treatment outcomes. This is only possible because of the clients.

Second, acknowledgements are also due my students at Teachers College, Columbia University, who offered enthusiasm when learning about integrated models and theory for preventing relapse and fostering change with regard to addictive/problem behavior. Their respect and attention helped me to move toward articulation of a unified model and theory in the field of addiction. Gratitude is due to both my students and the many other members of my Teachers College family.

Third, I must acknowledge with love and gratitude my immediate family, extended family, and spiritual family for vital support and encouragement throughout the writing process, especially Nana Korantemaa who also provided important editorial assistance.

Finally, I must acknowledge Dr. Janice Williams for being my colleague for nearly twenty years, providing intermittent peer supervision and unwavering support. Dr. Williams has truly proven to be a gift from God, as have all of those to whom I offer these acknowledgments.

I

GUIDELINES FOR MAKING MANDATED ADDICTION TREATMENT WORK

1

Mandated
Addiction Treatment

McLellan (2003a) asserts that there is no issue in the field of addiction treatment that is more timely and relevant than the one this book seeks to address: the management and disposition of those clients convicted of drug-related crimes who are flooding jails, prisons, probation/parole departments, and community-based addiction-treatment centers across the United States in historically unprecedented numbers. The successful treatment of this population also involves high stakes for society as a whole, given the risks to both public safety and public health if clients experience either relapse or recidivism. Public health concerns are especially valid, in light of how contemporary drug addiction overlaps with very real threats to public health: the risk of HIV/AIDS, varied sexually transmitted infections, hepatitis, and tuberculosis. There also may be no greater clinical challenge than for those practitioners who actually sit in their consultation rooms and seek to engage members of this population in treatment, given how the task involves multiproblem clients who may be among the very most difficult cases.

Most importantly, the context for addressing this issue is an age of evidence-based practice (Sammons, 2001). Contemporary times call for evidence-based guides for practitioners working with clients mandated to addiction treatment (Springer, McNeece, & Arnold, 2003). There is a need to narrow the gap between research findings on what works in addiction treatment and the actual work of practitioners in delivering treatment (Sorensen, Rawson, Guydish, & Zweben, 2003).

Practitioners need assistance translating what researchers disseminate as empirical evidence supporting specific addiction treatment interventions into what they actually say and do in their consultation rooms. This book provides practitioners with guidance with regard to what they should say and do in order to make mandated addiction treatment work. This book goes beyond summarizing what the research says works and conveys in considerable detail how any individual practitioner should proceed step-by-step, using case material to illustrate what is recommended. This kind of guide is important, given how the consultation rooms within the practice of community-based addiction treatment represent a national frontier for pioneering the adaptation of evidence-based addiction-treatment interventions in order to address the distinct characteristics and needs of contemporary clients in the real world. Given the heterogeneity of clients in the real world, evidence-based interventions also need to be thoughtfully integrated, and treatment must be tailored for individual clients.

The diversity inherent in the population necessitates training in multicultural sensitivity and competence (Bronstein & Quina, 2003; Carter, 2000; Howard, 2003; Rounds-Bryant, Motivans, & Pelissier, 2003; Sue, 2003; Sue & Sue, 2003; Sue et al., 1998; Wallace, 2003; Wallace & Carter, 2003) in order to avoid perpetrating racial/ethnic disparities in health (National Institute on Drug Abuse, 2003). And, where there is involvement in violence or a risk of recidivism and relapse involving violence, this, too, must be understood from a perspective that is multiculturally sensitive, given the history and dynamics of oppression in the United States (Wallace, 2003; Wallace & Carter, 2003). Despite the presence of multiple problems, also needed is an approach that builds upon clients' strengths as part of a positive psychological approach (Aspinwall & Staudinger, 2003; Lopez & Snyder, 2003; Seligman, 2002; van Wormer & Davis, 2003) that replaces the all-too-common stigma and disdain held for this population. The challenge of building upon clients' strengths is often complicated by histories of abuse, trauma, and resulting comorbid disorders of various kinds (Ouimette & Brown, 2003). So, an approach is needed that effectively addresses these factors and meets the state-of-the-art standards implicit in the work of these authors. This book strives to do so.

This first chapter of the book will introduce mandated addiction treatment in an age of evidence-based practice. As an introductory chapter, this first chapter presents justification for the assertion that the largest and fastest-growing segment of the addiction-treatment population is mandated, and it discusses what is driving this phenomenon. In addition, this chapter provides important definitions of what it means to be a mandated, coerced, or concerned client, along with the impact of each status. Discussion covers the impact of having the experience of external legal pressure to enter and complete treatment. Also covered is the practitioner task of enhancing a client's internal motivation.

CONTEMPORARY COMMUNITY-BASED ADDICTION TREATMENT AS PREDOMINANTLY MANDATED CARE

Perhaps van Wormer and Davis (2003) best articulate how contemporary times are essentially for the delivery of mandated addiction treatment:

"While many private, for-profit treatment centers, especially residential units, are closing their doors, there is a tremendous demand for services for the poly-drug addicted, often mentally ill clients for whom treatment is mandated by the courts" (p. 403). Margolis and Zweben (1998) report that the "greatest expansion of addiction treatment services is occurring in the criminal-justice sector, which is rapidly becoming a major employer of professionals" (p. 363). Farabee and Leukefeld (2001) assert that the "criminal justice system dominates the substance abuse treatment referral process in the United States" (p. 40). In addition, Farabee and Leukefeld (2001) cite a body of studies showing that the criminal justice system is responsible for "40 to 50% of referrals to community-based treatment programs" (p. 40). However, by the year 2003, the courts, probation, parole, and corrections system accounted for "40–60% of all those entering addiction treatment programs" in the United States (McLellan, 2003a, p. 187). Indeed, the work of others (Howard, 2003) supports the assertion that in outpatient addiction-treatment programs located in poorer communities, urban communities, or communities with large numbers of African-American clients, the percentage of clients who are court mandated or have been arrested for criminal offense is even higher. Also, a body of research shows that, among adolescents, roughly two-thirds to nine-tenths are mandated to community-based addiction treatment, and involvement with the criminal justice system is the norm (Dennis, 2002; Jainchill, 2002; Shane, 2002).

A variety of practitioners in varied settings are witnessing from the vantage point of their contemporary consultation rooms the tremendous influx of clients from criminal-justice-system referrals who are under criminal-justice-system supervision. Moreover, this book asserts that we have been living in a societal era of criminal sanctions, zero tolerance, and intensive supervision that has been driving this increase in mandated clients. The criminal justice system, corporations, agencies, public-housing authorities, and a variety of other governmental arms all reflect a pattern of increasingly embracing criminal sanctions, zero tolerance, and intensive supervision policies; this is part of a societal shift toward conservatism, moralism, and intolerance. For example, parents involved with child-protection agencies who test positive for illicit-drug use are being coerced into drug treatment in order to regain child custody and avoid the ultimate sanction of termination of parental rights. And, applicants for welfare found to be involved with illicit drugs or who have alcohol problems are being coerced into community-based addiction treatment in order to receive and maintain benefits.

Even where clients have not been mandated or coerced into addiction treatment, the reality of our living in this contemporary societal era means that other clients are harboring deep concerns about the prospects of their "getting caught" for having engaged in illicit-drug use or other criminal behavior. Many concerned clients have witnessed what has happened to those who were caught, and they want to avoid a host of negative consequences. The growing population of mandated, coerced, and concerned clients is entering addiction treatment at an unprecedented rate, reflecting the contemporary reality of our prevailing societal era. This justifies this book's timely presentation of the key ingredients for making mandated addiction treatment work in varied community-based settings, including the entire continuum of care both during and after incarceration.

The Massive Influx into the Community of the Supervised

Thus, it is impossible to separate what is happening in contemporary community-based addiction treatment from societal developments involving the arrest, threat of criminal prosecution, and actual criminal prosecution of those involved with illicit drugs. Indeed, we live in a historically unprecedented period in time in the United States.

Across the country, more African Americans, Hispanics, and women, as well as substance abusers of all races, religions, ethnicities, educational levels, and socioeconomic statuses, have become involved in the criminal justice system than ever before in our history as a nation. The social policy of the past thirty years "can be described only as mass imprisonment" (Mauer & Chesney-Lind, 2002, p. 1). Statistics bear out this proclamation, also highlighting how the greatest negative impact has been born by the most vulnerable in our society—women and communities of color.

The United States has surpassed all other countries in the Western world for per-capita incarceration rates (Glaze, 2002; Harlow, 2003). Relying on 2001 data from the Sentencing Project, Farmer (2002) asserts that in recent years, the "United States has surpassed Russia to become the uncontested world leader in detention. Of every 100,000 U.S. citizens, approximately 700 are in prison" (p. 243). Indeed, Harrison and Beck (2003) report the year-end 2002 statistics for the U.S., indicating that the rate of 701 inmates per 100,000 residents was up from 601 in 1995. In contrast, the rates are 685 per 100,000 for Russia, 125 for Britain, 129 for Canada, and 40 for Japan (Isralowitz, 2002). For prisoners with a sentence of more than 1 year per 100,000 in the U.S. resident population, Harrison and Beck (2003) report that the prison population increased 2.6 percent in 2002, the largest increase in three years, with this growth reflected most strongly in the federal system (163,528 or 11.5 percent increase); California (162,317 or 8.6 percent increase); Texas (162,003 or 7.9 percent increase); Florida (75,210 or 7.9 percent increase); and New York (67,065 or 7.9 percent increase).

Harrison and Beck (2003) elaborate on the categories in which this growth falls, emphasizing how sources of growth differ by gender, as well as by race and ethnicity. "The increasing number of violent offenders accounted for 64% of the total growth among male inmates and 49% among female inmates" (p. 10). The growth in violent offenders for "white State inmates (59%), black inmates (57%), and Hispanic inmates (82%)" may be contrasted with the growth in drug offenders at "23% of the total growth among black inmates and 18% of the growth among white inmates" (pp. 10–11). With regard to gender, while growth in the incarcerated population attributable to drug offenders has decreased from that of previous years, nonetheless, drug offenders accounted for 13 percent of total growth among female inmates and 15 percent of growth among male inmates from 1995 to 2001.

Springer, McNeece, and Arnold (2003) place these kinds of statistics in context:

> The extent of the drug problem is far worse than these statistics suggest. Anyone familiar with how the U.S. criminal justice system operates knows that the crime for which an offender is sentenced does not tell the full story. Plea bargaining results in many less serious drug charges simply being dropped. Many offenders are sentenced for a non-drug offense who also have a substance abuse problem, which may not appear in the official records. . . . [I]n 25 sites in 1998, between 59% to 79% (in Houston and Philadelphia, respectively) of adult arrestees tested positive for at least one illicit drug. . . . From January to September 2000, between 51% and 79% (in Des Moines and New York, respectively) of adult male arrestees in 27 sites tested positive. (p. 4)

In places such as New York City, those entering the criminal justice system as arrestees and voluntarily providing urine samples between 1987 and 1997 (n = 13,674) were diverse, as African Americans (54 percent), Caucasians (13 percent), Hispanics (30 percent), and women (28 percent)—testing positive for cocaine (66 percent), opiates (20 percent), marijuana (23 percent), and other drugs (8 percent), even when only 13 percent had been arrested for drug possession and 6 percent were arrested for drug sale (Johnson & Golub, 2002).

Other data show that more than 50 percent of violent crimes, 60 to 80 percent of child-abuse and neglect cases, and 50 to 70 percent of theft and property crimes involve drug use on the part of the perpetrator (Marlowe, 2003). Also, data show that a full 60 to 80 percent of prison and jail inmates, parolees, probationers, and arrestees were drug and/or alcohol involved (Marlowe, 2003). Nearly half of women arrested for domestic violence and court referred to batterer-intervention programs were hazardous drinkers, about one-quarter reported symptoms consistent with a drug-related diagnosis, and over one-half reported having partners who were hazardous drinkers (Stuart, Moore, Ramsey, & Kahler, 2003).

Thus, despite the tremendous growth in violent offenders, relative to that of drug offenders, the widespread use of illicit drugs among those ever arrested remains a reality. The massive influx back into the community of those once incarcerated for a variety of offenses does not mitigate the reality that community-based addiction treatment will be mandated and/or vitally needed for many.

The reaching of a historic high with regard to women's imprisonment in the United States has also been well documented. By 1999, there were more than

90,000 women incarcerated, increasing "more than sixfold" from the 1980 figure of 12,000 incarcerated (Chesney-Lind, 2002, p. 80). This suggests a rate of 66 women per 100,000 incarcerated in 2000, which is a rate "ten times greater than the number of women incarcerated in all of Western Europe," a region roughly equivalent to the United States in terms of population (Chesney-Lind, 2002, p. 81). By the end of 2002, there were 97,491 women in state or federal prisons, reflecting how the number of female prisoners increased by 4.9 percent, being double the rate of increase for men, at 2.4 percent (Harrison & Beck, 2003). Moreover, from 1995 to 2002, the average annual rate of growth for female inmates was 5.25 percent, surpassing the annual growth rate of 3.5 percent for male inmates (Harrison & Beck, 2003). Oklahoma, Mississippi, Louisiana, and Texas had the highest female incarceration rates, while Texas, the federal system, and California held more than a third of all female inmates (Harrison & Beck, 2003). There were, however, racial and ethnic disparities in female incarceration rates that were found to be consistent across all age groups (Harrison & Beck, 2003). "Black females (with an incarceration rate of 191 per 100,000) were more than twice as likely as Hispanic females (80 per 100,000) and 5 times more likely than white females (35 per 100,000) to be in prison on December 31, 2002" (Harrison & Beck, 2003).

Racial and ethnic disparities in male incarceration rates have also been well documented. With regard to African-American men, more than three-quarters of a million are incarcerated, and "nearly 2 million are under some form of correctional supervision, including probation and parole" (Mauer & Chesney-Lind, 2002, p. 2). Moreover, for those African-American men between the ages of twenty-five and thirty-four, "one of every eight is in prison or jail on any given day" (Mauer & Chesney-Lind, 2002, p. 2). Offering another figure, Harrison and Beck (2003, p. 9) report that "10.4% of black males age 25 to 29 were in prison on December 31, 2002, compared to 2.4% of Hispanic males and about 1.2% of white males in the same age group." Furthermore, "nearly 80 percent of inmates in state prison for drug offenses" are African American or Latino (Mauer & Chesney-Lind, 2002, p. 6). While African Americans "make up 13 percent of the nation's monthly drug users, they represent 35 percent of those persons arrested for drug crimes [and] 53 percent of drug convictions" (Rubinstein & Mukamal, 2002, p. 40). "Black inmates represented an estimated 45% of all inmates with sentences of more than 1 year, while white inmates accounted for 34%, and Hispanic inmates 18%" (Harrison & Beck, 2003).

Suggesting the nature of the growth in the prison population, and the consistent overrepresentation of African Americans and Hispanics, from 1995 to 2002, there was a 27 percent increase in the total number of sentenced inmates, with only small changes in the racial and ethnic composition of the inmate population (Harrison & Beck, 2003). Fueling racial and ethnic disparities is a pattern of excess rates of arrest, conviction, and incarceration, especially for African Americans (National Institute on Drug Abuse, 2003).

However, despite any disproportionate impact on women, African Americans, and poor communities, the nation as a whole bears the burden of the policy of mass imprisonment. Leukefeld, Farabee, and Tims (2002) report that more than 6 million people are under criminal-justice supervision, with 2 million in U.S. prisons and jails, at a cost of $40 billion per year, based upon statistics released in 1998. Communities across the United States are experiencing the massive return of the incarcerated. More specifically, by the end of the year 2001, the number of men and women in the United States under criminal-justice-system supervision in their communities attained a record high of 4,665,102—a substantial increase over the 1995 figure of 3,757,282 (Glaze, 2002), as well as the 1998 figure of 4.3 million. By the end of 2001, approximately 1 out of every 32 adults in the United States was under the supervision of the criminal justice system—whether in a state prison, federal prison, local jail, or on parole or probation (Glaze, 2002). The result is much larger supervision caseloads for probation and parole officers (Kinlock & Hanlon, 2002). Perhaps most telling, by the end of 2001, a full 1 in 5 probationers was a woman, and 1 in 3 was African American, while a quarter of probationers were convicted of a drug-law violation (Glaze, 2002).

Thus, the contemporary reality is that there is now an ongoing process involving a large influx into communities of individuals who are under some form of criminal-justice supervision. And, the largest impact of this return of the incarcerated to communities will be felt by African-American families and the children and families of the women under criminal-justice supervision. However, Hispanic families and communities will also experience a disproportionate impact.

The disproportionate impact of massive prisoner reentry upon poor families and communities of color will bring a considerable burden to these communities for several reasons. These reasons include not only the risk of relapse to addictive behaviors and recidivism to crime, but also the fact that the newly released from incarceration typically lack important resources, such as education, employment, health care, housing, and the right to vote (Mauer & Chesney-Lind, 2002). Also, there is a federal ban on eligibility for welfare and food stamps for those having a drug-felony conviction, even as states can opt out of the ban completely or narrow it (Rubinstein & Mukamal, 2002). In addition, federal laws require "public housing agencies to exclude individuals who engage in drug-related criminal activity" (Rubinstein & Mukamal, 2002, p. 39). It has been asserted that these are among the many "invisible punishments" constituting the collateral consequences of mass imprisonment (Mauer & Chesney-Lind, 2002).

The fact that the United States has reached a historical high in terms of the number of individuals incarcerated, and the reality that those incarcerated are reentering and destined to continue to reenter communities across this country in equally high numbers is cause for great concern. Indeed, the massive influx into communities of the supervised suggests both an opportunity and a great danger. This may be considered both a potential public-health crisis bringing great danger, and an opportunity to prevent relapse and recidivism—if community-based addiction treatment is adequate to the task of making mandated addiction treatment work.

What Does It Mean to Be a Mandated Client?

A mandated client may be defined as any individual who is under correctional supervision in the community and enters community-based addiction treatment with a legal status, having been referred to treatment by criminal-justice-system authorities. The mandated client is typically on probation or parole, or under supervision and monitoring by a judge or some agency personnel under contract with the criminal justice/judicial system. Typically, the completion of a course of community-based addiction treatment is one of many conditions of a client's probation, parole, or supervision. Those fulfilling this condition of probation/parole/supervision are effectively mandated clients within community-based addiction treatment.

What Does It Mean to Be a Coerced Client?

A coerced client may be defined as any individual who has been involuntarily committed to treatment or referred to treatment by criminal-justice authorities, while the remaining clients are defined as "voluntary" (Marlowe, Glass, et al., 2001, p. 208). Marlowe, Glass, et al. (2001) explain that coercion in substance-abuse treatment is "commonly viewed as being synonymous with a legal mandate to receive services" (p. 208). Thus, in some instances, the terms mandated and coerced may be used interchangeably.

In a related vein, capturing the vast number of criminal-justice-system referrals under the term "compulsory treatment," Farabee and Leukefeld (2001, p. 41) define this as "directly or indirectly applying legal coercion for an individual to enter substance abuse treatment." Yet this "does not necessarily mean that the client is entering treatment involuntarily," as some, for example, would have entered treatment voluntarily if given the choice (p. 41).

However, it is also possible that coercion is coming from a source other than a criminal-justice authority. Employers and agencies responsible for the distribution of welfare, supplemental income, and other benefits may deploy coercion. Also, agencies for child protection from parental abuse/ neglect may deploy coercion. Lawyers working with clients who are scheduled to go before judges may use coercion in getting clients to attend treatment. A level of coercion is present when preparing clients to go before parole boards or to get off of parole or probation, insofar as clients understand and follow what is strongly recommended to them by a paralegal or lawyer.

In terms of what it means to be a mandated or coerced client, research suggests that criminal-justice authority, mandatory treatment, civil commitment, and pressure from legal authorities enhance treatment retention, reduce relapse, and increase the likelihood of favorable outcomes (Hiller, Knight, Rao, & Simpson, 2002; Leukefeld, Tims, & Platt, 2001, p. 406; Marlowe, Glass, et al., 2001). The more recent findings of Gregoire and Burke (2004) represent an important addition to a body of evidence that coerced treatment produces positive benefits (Farabee, Prendergast, & Anglin, 1998; Hiller, Knight, Broome, & Simpson, 1998; Joe, Simpson, & Broome, 1999), as well as mixed results (Brecht, Anglin, & Wang, 1993; Watson, Brown, Tilleskjor, Jacobs, & Lucel, 1988). Gregoire and Burke (2004) found that clients' status of being legally coerced into treatment was associated with an increased motivation to change, even when controlling for problem severity at the time of admission, prior treatment history, and gender. Those clients who entered treatment due to legal coercion were over three times more likely to have engaged in recovery-oriented behavior in the month preceding admission to outpatient treatment.

However, this positive impact is not always uniform, given a host of variables that may involve either program or client factors. But, the positive impact may include enhancing readiness or motivation to change. A more complete discussion of treatment-outcome studies will be presented in chapter 3.

What Does It Mean to Be a Concerned Client?

A concerned client is a voluntary admission into an addiction-treatment program who is harboring and responding to internal pressure to change. Some clients have deep concerns about losing things that are highly valued, such as their freedom, a source of income, or family members such as children. They experience internal pressures to enter treatment, as only they may know about their personal danger of getting caught for violating either social norms or codes of conduct, having crossed the line into criminal behavior.

Society frequently operates on the hope that a new law, regulation, or policy will serve as an external source of pressure or motivation for individuals to change. Thus, external pressure from some new criminal sanctions, zero tolerance, or intensive supervision policy may mean the effective enhancement of motivation for change. For example, a prominent person in the public eye being made a spectacle, as well as an example of the application of criminal sanctions, may serve as a symbolic statement to all in society that certain behaviors are not tolerated and that negative criminal sanctions may follow. Or, those made an example may be more readily accessible as a member of one's family, workplace, social network, or community.

Thus, as a result of exposure to information about potential criminal sanctions, clients readily emerge as having concerns about getting caught, getting fired, or being prosecuted, as well as about facing potential forms of intensive supervision, such as the most intensive, incarceration. Thus, what starts as external pressure or an extrinsic source of motivation may transform into intrinsic motivation for change under some circumstances, as client's emerge with genuine concerns that they harbor inside themselves, spurring motivation to change. This may involve a cognitive process wherein an individual surmises that there is value in avoiding a negative consequence of their addictive behavior and decides to act on his or her own, wanting to avoid negative consequences and feeling that the choice to act or change is one they have made on their own, under their own volition.

Other clients often begin to develop concerns and internal motivation to change as a result of receiving health education, medical test results, assessment findings from a professional, or merely from being asked questions about their behavior. As a result of an assessment or interview process, clients may have their consciousness or awareness raised with regard to the extent to which they have a problem or may potentially suffer negative consequences from their behavior. They emerge as concerned about their behavior, which is typically addictive, compulsive, or high risk in nature, justifying their concerns.

More specifically, many clients become concerned clients as a consequence of having been exposed to motivational interviewing (Miller & Rollnick, 1991, 2002). Within motivational interviewing, clients are asked questions about any problems or concerns they have in relation to their behavior. They may emerge as concerned clients. Within motivational interviewing, it is also common to go beyond asking clients about their concerns with their behavior, or about any problems they are having that are related to their behavior— asking clients about any next steps they feel they should take. A common response to this question involves clients' responding that they think they should stop or alter their behavior, or that they should possibly enter treatment. Clinicians typically then offer a menu of options as to the types of treatment available to the client (Miller & Rollnick, 1991, 2002), often being based on the type of insurance the client has and what is available in that particular community with regard to addiction-treatment options. Clients who benefit from motivational interviewing and other adaptations of motivational interviewing (Rollnick et al., 2002), or who end up deciding to voluntarily enter treatment as a result of their own internal pressures to change are referred to as concerned clients in this book.

Being a concerned client means that internal motivation to pursue change is building and can be sustained, especially if the person continues to receive interventions tailored to "where the client is" in the change process. It is possible that ambivalence prevails, despite the client's being concerned, and tailored interventions could enhance motivation to change. The typical concerned client will enter treatment in a stage of change where they are contemplating change, are prepared to make a change, or are ready to take action toward change—following the stages of change articulated by DiClemente and Velasquez (2002). The status of being a concerned client usually means that the person is open and willing to pursue the next steps of entering treatment and/or working toward behavior change. Concerns tend to involve one's health, potential loss of family members, loss of family support, loss of employment, loss of housing, or loss of one's freedom, as with facing criminal sanctions, zero tolerance, and intensive supervision policies. Concerned clients experiencing these various types of internal pressures tend to have an internal motivation to pursue behavior change, but they may suffer from ambivalence, from a lack of confidence (self-efficacy), or from insufficient coping skills so that they are unable to consistently pursue and maintain behavior change. Thus, concerned clients may benefit from treatment interventions, such as motivational interviewing and relapse prevention with specific skills-training components, ensuring that these clients move across stages of change toward the successful maintenance of behavior change.

Table 1.1 provides a summary of the three main types of clients entering contemporary community-based addiction treatment. Along with the typology presented in this table, some of the key aspects of their statuses are identified.

De Leon, Melnick, and Tims (2001) specifically acknowledge how there are two types of motivation impacting on recovery from substance abuse— external and internal. "External motivation is generally defined as perceived outside pressures or coercion to change, or to enter and/or remain

Table 1.1. A Typology of Clients Entering Contemporary Community-Based Addiction Treatment

Typology of Clients	Key Issues	Main Motivation	Treatment Goal
Mandated clients	*Under criminal-justice-system supervision *On probation or parole *Forced to enter/attend treatment program *Mandate may enhance treatment retention	*Extrinsic motivation *Wants to avoid sanctions, violations *Responding to external pressures	*Enhance intrinsic motivation *Maximize impact of external pressures
Coerced clients	*Being coerced by an employer, family child-protection agency, welfare, lawyer, etc. into attending treatment *Coercion may enhance treatment retention	*Extrinsic motivation *Wants to avoid the loss of something valued *Responding to external pressures	*Enhance intrinsic motivation *Maximize impact of external pressures
Concerned clients	*Harbor internal concerns *Some readiness to change *Voluntarily enters treatment program *Retention rates vary for concerned clients	*Intrinsic motivation *Wants to avoid negative consequences *Responding to internal pressures	*Sustain and enhance intrinsic motivation *Resolve ambivalence

in treatment," typically coming from sources that involve legal, family, or employment pressures (p. 145). The mandated or coerced clients are responding to external pressure as they pursue addiction treatment.

On the other hand, internal motivation refers to "pressures to change that arise from within the individual," whether involving negative self-perceptions or desire for a new lifestyle (De Leon et al., 2001, p. 145). Thus, concerned clients are responding to internal pressure when they enter addiction treatment.

Most pertinent to this discussion, De Leon et al. (2001) report that research on extrinsic or external motivation has been confined to studies of legal coercion or pressure. And a large body of studies across the 1980s and 1990s supports the relationship between legal pressure and retention in therapeutic communities, showing external motivation to be an important predictor of treatment retention and outcomes (De Leon et al., 2001).

Farabee and Leukefeld (2001) similarly acknowledge research showing that clients referred to treatment through the criminal justice system remain in treatment longer than those not referred through the criminal justice system, but appreciate that the "long-term implications of external versus internal motivation as they relate to treatment outcome are still unclear" (p. 49). One problem involves the extent to which the increased application of external sources of motivation for treatment "may lead to misleading short-term treatment outcomes," especially if those referred by the criminal justice system "lack the internal motivation to readily engage themselves in the treatment process" (Farabee & Leukefeld, 2001, p. 49). For, "establishing long-term changes in substance abuse also requires internal motivation for change" (p. 53). On the other hand, a client's internal motivation for change at the time of program admission significantly predicted long-term post-treatment outcomes in research reported by Simpson, Joe, and Rowan-Szal (1997; see also Farabee & Leukefeld, 2001).

Clearly, both internal-motivation and external-motivation enhancements play a critical role in promoting long-term recovery and preventing relapse. Motivational interviewing (Miller & Rollnick, 1991, 2002) is an important tool for *enhancing the internal motivation* of clients to participate in treatment and to pursue behavior change. Deploying techniques within motivational interviewing may enhance internal motivation and move clients across stages of change (DiClemente & Velasquez, 2002), from not even thinking about change (*precontemplation stage*), toward thinking about change (*contemplation stage*), as well as toward preparing to change (*preparation stage*); in addition, the goal is for clients to move toward actually taking action to change (*action stage*, for up to 6 months), as well as toward seeking to maintain behavior change over time (*maintenance stage*, for greater than 6 months to a lifetime).

On the other hand, the criminal justice system (parole, probation) uses the legal mandate to treatment as an important tool for *enhancing external moti-*

vation to participate in treatment. Indeed, via the use of coercion, a number of authorities, such as employers, welfare agencies, and child-protection agencies, are also serving to enhance external motivation to participate in treatment, producing attendant benefits.

However, legal coercion, within itself, may enhance readiness or internal motivation to change. Gregoire and Burke (2004) state the following, in this regard:

> Evidence presented here that legal coercion is associated with greater readiness to change suggests that treatment retention resulting from legal coercion may, at least in part, reflect underlying change among coerced clients. . . . By enhancing readiness to change, legal coercion may ultimately improve outcomes for clients mandated to seek treatment for alcohol and other drug problems. . . . As the use of drug courts and other alternative sentencing schemes increase, these findings suggest that appropriate use of coercion may increase a client's readiness for treatment. (pp. 39–40)

In a similar vein, Maxwell (2000) has reported that for clients with a legal status, the effect on clients' compliance with treatment is not a direct one. Instead, the client's appraisal of the legal threat serves to mediate or moderate the effects of the legal status.

Thus, substantial hope emerges for the effective treatment of mandated clients. This hope may arise both from those instances where either a legal mandate or coercion operates, and from those instances where the use of motivational-interviewing techniques prevails. The experience of being delivered a legal mandate to attend treatment, or of receiving coercion to enter treatment, may lead an individual to develop and harbor substantial concerns. Appraisal of the legal threat may include a consideration of negative consequences that may follow from noncompliance. The resulting concerns may cover the negative consequences that may follow from violating the mandate or failing to meet certain requirements. A mandated client or coerced client may readily become a concerned client, once those applying external pressure spell out potential negative consequences for noncompliance, so that initial external pressure produces internal pressure to change. Clients may first experience external pressure to enter community-based addiction treatment, yet they can readily process the implications of positive urine toxicology results; these may include losing many things, whether losing their freedom through reincarceration or losing employment, child custody, housing, or welfare benefits. Facing such potential negative sanctions, mandated and coerced clients may readily become concerned, indeed.

Drieschner, Lammers, and van der Staak (2004) conceptualize motivation to engage in treatment as having several internal determinants—problem recognition, level of suffering, perceived external pressure, perceived costs of treatment, perceived suitability of treatment, and outcome expectancy. However, they emphasize how motivation to engage in treatment is also influenced by external factors such as the actual treatment, circumstances, and events, as well as client characteristics, including problems and demographics. In this manner, they hope to clarify the concept. However, a key point that Drieschner et al. (2004, p. 1117) make is that the term *motivation to change* is "adequate as long as change refers to well-defined problem behavior" such as an addictive behavior or a violent behavior, versus when it refers to something a client "wants to get rid of, rather than to a behavior." Examples of such a desire or wish to get rid of something might apply to depression or anxiety.

Additional hope comes from the promise that motivational-interviewing techniques (Miller & Rollnick, 2002) may foster movement across stages of change, serving to enhance internal motivation for change, despite mixed findings of efficacy (Miller, Yahne, & Tonigan, 2003). Motivational interviewing may *potentially transform an initial externally enhanced motivation (from a parole or probation mandate or other coercion into addiction treatment) into internal motivation.* This begins to suggest a strong rationale for the approach taken in this book for making mandated addiction treatment work.

CONCLUSION

This chapter served to introduce addiction treatment in an age of evidence-based practice. This chapter has provided support for the assertion that the largest and fastest-growing segment of the contemporary community-based addiction-treatment population is mandated. In addition, important factors in society and in the criminal justice system that are driving this phenomenon were identified. Guiding definitions were provided, serving to clarify what it means to be a mandated, coerced, or concerned client, while important aspects of each status were also discussed. The important function of external pressure to attend and complete treatment was underscored as operating for those who are mandated or coerced. In addition, the crucial task of also building internal motivation to change was highlighted.

The presence of such contemporary clients in community-based addiction treatment serves to challenge practitioners working on the front lines and in the trenches to pioneer adaptations of evidence-based addiction-treatment interventions. More specifically, the challenge of making mandated addiction treatment work in the real world requires that practitioners know the answers to the three basic questions that follow: (1) What are clients bringing into the treatment setting, as their characteristics, needs, and diversity? (2) As the course of treatment is conceptualized in terms of short- and long-term goals, what are the evidence-based interventions and recommended state-of-the-art options available for deployment across the course of addiction treatment? and (3) Given client characteristics, needs, and diversity, how should the practitioner proceed, in terms of those matters to be urgently addressed and those that can wait to be addressed once the client has stabilized? The remaining chapters in part I of this book will answer these questions.

2

Multiproblem Clients' Characteristics, Needs, and Diversity

The clients with both drug/alcohol and criminal involvement who are currently entering the consultation rooms of practitioners in community-based addiction treatment across this nation may be described as the very most challenging to treat. They are multiproblem clients, to say the least. But, what does it mean to be a multiproblem client? Or more specifically, what are the multiple problems, characteristics, and needs of clients, as well as the nature of that diversity to be found in the contemporary community-based addiction-treatment population? This chapter will answer these questions, and, in the process, present a compelling portrait of contemporary clients. Drawing upon the power of storytelling, twelve brief case vignettes have been chosen in order to convey the multiple problems, characteristics, and needs of clients who may be either mandated, coerced, or concerned—voluntarily entering treatment. The cases also convey the multitude of dimensions across which clients are diverse, suggesting the extreme degree of heterogeneity to be found within the contemporary population of clients entering community-based addiction treatment.

THE MANDATED

Case 1: Man Recently Released from Incarceration for Drug Dealing

A male client was mandated to outpatient community-based addiction treatment following his release from prison, after having served a mandatory minimum sentence for drug sale. He was coping with the stress of returning to a wife and family from which he had become estranged over many years of incarceration. The client was also struggling with impulses to relapse to drug-dealing behavior, given what he acknowledged to be his addiction to "fast money." He was also coping with the challenge of being trained for work to replace the drug-dealing income upon which he and his family had been dependent for so many years. He was unsure as to whether or not he would be able to resume a loving, intimate relationship with his wife, given her lack of sexual fidelity to him while he was away in prison—even as they had three children together. He recalled with great pain the severe depression with which he had to cope while in prison upon finding out that his wife had an affair. Initially, in treatment, he placed great emphasis upon his primary identity as a drug dealer who made good money, clearly differentiating himself from those with the stigmatized identity of being a "crack head" or a "hard drug user," and this created an obstacle to his successful engagement in treatment. However, over time, he admitted to his having had a regular pattern of marijuana and alcohol use during the time he was dealing drugs before his incarceration.

Case 2: Remorseful and Modest Man Who Committed Homicide

A man was mandated to outpatient substance-abuse treatment by parole. He is on parole for life. He had over two decades free from alcohol, cocaine, and marijuana use, given that he was incarcerated for twenty-two years for a homicide he committed as an adolescent while intoxicated and high off of drugs. He had deep remorse over this homicide and had difficulty talking about it, feeling he was nothing like the reckless adolescent who shot another youth. He also struggled with getting to know his young-adult twin daughters and grandchildren. He participated in a prison-based therapeutic community (TC) for his alcoholism and drug addiction. He was so successful in the TC that he assumed a peer-leadership position, conducting recovery groups. He was modest, polite, and eager to comply with all aspects of treatment, hoping to gain employment as soon as possible.

Case 3: Immigrant Refugee Woman with Comorbidity

Following her release from incarceration for a cocaine sale, a young immigrant woman was mandated to outpatient community-based addiction treatment for her alcohol and cocaine dependence. She had been abstinent from cocaine and alcohol for four years and was determined to avoid reincarceration. She was also mandated by parole to outpatient mental-health treatment for her mood disorder and post-traumatic stress disorder. She was plagued by painful memories of the war that reigned for years in her country when she was a young child. Being able to still hear the noises of bombing and screams of the injured, she suffered from flashbacks that included images of shootings and dead bodies. Arriving to the United States with her father and several other members of her family, she came to this country as a young child and refugee. Adolescent self-cutting and suicidal behavior preceded her young-adult use of alcohol and cocaine. More recent experiences of domestic violence led to her becoming suicidal at times, and she admitted to having angry and violent outbursts, suggesting the severity of her mood disorder and symptoms of post-traumatic stress disorder. She was also motivated for treatment, given her recent news of being pregnant.

Case 4: Adolescent Male Brought into Treatment by His Recovering Mother

An early-adolescent male was mandated into outpatient substance-abuse treatment, having been arrested as a juvenile for selling crack. He admitted to using marijuana. His mother accompanied him the first day he entered outpatient treatment. Having nine years of continuous abstinence from crack cocaine herself, this mother was distressed about her son's behavior. This mother struggled with recurrent symptoms of major depressive disorder and post-traumatic stress disorder from her own childhood experiences of sexual and physical abuse by her chemically dependent father and mother, respectively. Her mother, her son's grandmother, also physically abused the boy (now the adolescent seeking treatment) when he was in her temporary custody as a child. His grandmother beat him on his back to the point where he had blood in his urine. This was during the period of his mother's recovery from addiction before his reunification with her. In elementary school, this boy was frequently violent, even fighting the school principal, and he was placed in special education. Once his mother regained custody of him, she secured psychological treatment; they attended family therapy, and the mother also made progress in resolving her guilt, discontinuing overcompensating for her absence in his life during the period of her loss of custody. His mother also became actively involved in his school and witnessed his return to the regular classroom. However, as an early adolescent involved in truancy and drug dealing, he presented a conduct disorder and marijuana abuse.

Despite his mother's active role in his life, even taking him to the mandated outpatient treatment, he stopped attending the program. This young man was being sought for a technical violation involving noncompliance with the conditions established by his probation officer; he had absconded, and his whereabouts were unknown. He also dropped out of high school. His mother moved into a smaller apartment, away from the building location from which he was regularly selling drugs. She was determined to forbid him from living with her again and potentially dealing drugs from her new housing location, which would jeopardize her access to housing.

Case 5: Woman in Jeopardy of Losing Her Public Housing for Herself and Her Grown Children

A mother of three young-adult children, including one son with a disability, was arrested for crack possession. She spent two nights in jail and was mandated to outpatient community-based addiction treatment. She lived under intensive supervision in a residential program operating under contract with the criminal justice system. As a result of her arrest, she was no longer able to live in her public housing apartment and had lost her right to live in any public housing. She entered treatment tearful and hoping, perhaps unrealistically, to be able to stop the eviction of her four young-adult children from the apartment in public housing that was under lease to her. Also, potentially related to her nearly two decades of chronic crack-cocaine smoking, there were educational deficits and some neurocognitive impairment that affected her memory and language, negatively impacting the retention of information with regard to recovery and relapse prevention.

THE MANDATED AND/OR COERCED

Case 6: Male with Paranoid Schizophrenia

A man on parole was mandated into outpatient substance-abuse treatment, as well as to mental-health treatment. He had a psychiatric history that included multiple hospitalizations on several psychiatric units, having a history of paranoid schizophrenia. In addition, he had a history of having been homeless for nearly twenty years, living in the streets as an active heroin addict, and eventually being arrested for attempted sale and possession of heroin, for which he served three years in prison. After his release from incarceration, when he applied for welfare, he was also assessed as having a drug history sufficient for agency coercion into outpatient substance-abuse treatment. He mentioned both his parole officer and welfare as "forcing" him to come to the outpatient program.

Case 7: Woman Who Lost Child Custody of Her Sexually Abused Daughter

A child-protection agency coerced a woman to attend outpatient substance-abuse treatment as a condition for regaining custody of her child. This followed the woman's taking her daughter to the local hospital in an urban center, reporting suspicions of sexual abuse of her daughter by a neighbor, and requesting that her daughter be examined. As part of an assessment process within the investigation into the allegations of sexual abuse against this neighbor, the woman admitted to occasionally smoking marijuana. She was arrested for neglect of her child. Her daughter was immediately placed in foster care. A psychological assessment performed at the outpatient substance-abuse treatment program revealed the extent to which the mother herself was a survivor of physical abuse, sexual abuse, and domestic violence, and was suffering from a mood disorder, a personality disorder, and post-traumatic stress disorder. At an assessment performed at a welfare agency, her substance-abuse history was disclosed, and she was also coerced into attending outpatient substance-abuse treatment in order to remain eligible for welfare benefits.

Case 8: Late-Adolescent/Young-Adult Male Sent to Treatment by a Judge

A late-adolescent male entered into a contingency contract with a judge that specified case dismissal if the client completed six months of treatment and paid the hospital bill for a man he assaulted during an alcohol-induced blackout. He was initially resistant. He also felt coerced by his lawyer into entering outpatient alcoholism treatment, but he reluctantly did so. The client had a history of childhood sexual abuse and adolescent compulsive sexual behavior with which he continued to struggle. He considered himself lucky for not having any arrests for driving under the influence (DUI), but he admitted to reckless driving while intoxicated on alcohol and to having had several car accidents. Also, he had a great deal of difficulty accepting the goal of total abstinence. As a college-age youth accustomed to binge drinking at parties, he initially negotiated the harm-reduction goal of moderate drinking. However, once engaged in treatment, he shared concerns about his long adolescent history of committing serious offenses while intoxicated, even though he had rarely been caught for these criminal behaviors. He also had concerns about his own drinking, given that his mother was an active alcoholic for many years. As a result, he started to experiment with total abstinence from alcohol. He departed treatment at the end of the court-ordered 6-month period, eager to return to college and find part-time work. He left treatment without a plan for receipt of continuing aftercare, and he rejected Alcoholics Anonymous (AA) as a support system.

Case 9: Young Woman Arrested in a Dance-Club Drug Sweep

A late-adolescent female was arrested in a drug sweep at a downtown dance club known to be a place where cocaine and club drugs such as ecstasy, ketamine, methamphetamine, and Rohypnol were suspected of being sold. She had been arrested for suspected use and possession of an illicit drug. She was advised that if she entered community-based addiction treatment, remained compliant with treatment, and completed treatment, the charges against her would be dismissed. She had never been arrested before, and she feared having a criminal record. A Treatment Accountability for Safer Communities (TASC) program helped her find outpatient addiction treatment. Once in treatment, she admitted to using ecstasy.

Case 10: Gay Man Referred by a Drug Court

A gay man was offered an alternative to incarceration after he was arrested, having been observed by police purchasing crack on a street corner. His alternatives to an incarceration program included his being monitored by a drug court and his participation in an outpatient substance-abuse-treatment program, in which he would undergo intensive supervision through regular drug testing. His motivation to embrace recovery rested in the fact that he had a medical disability, and crack-cocaine smoking actually served to further jeopardize his health. In addition, after his expression of concerns, he responded well to interventions delivered to reduce his risk of acquiring HIV/AIDS and other sexually transmitted diseases.

THE CONCERNED

Case 11: Man Involved in Corporate Wrongdoing

A man concerned about possible prosecution for corporate wrongdoing voluntarily entered outpatient substance-abuse treatment. He reported a history of having worked on Wall Street at a prominent corporation at which he enjoyed great success. He admitted to creating fictitious companies and funneling money into bank accounts to which he and a group of coworkers had access, allowing him to enjoy great wealth. However, two coworkers with whom he shared profits, as well as long evenings engaged in heavy drinking and soliciting prostitutes, had already been arrested for corporate wrongdoing; thus, he secretly feared his own eventual prosecution. He believed that the pressures of working at the level of a workaholic, and especially the stress of fearing his own prosecution for corporate wrongdoing contributed to his disappearance from work and relapse to compulsive crack-cocaine smoking in the isolation of the basement of his suburban home.

Case 12: Bisexual Woman with a Trauma History and Comorbidity

A bisexual woman voluntarily entered outpatient substance-abuse treatment, having great concern about her possible arrest and incarceration for interpersonal violence. Her history included severe childhood physical abuse at the hands of her father, as well as witnessing her father violently assaulting many other people throughout her childhood and adolescence. She had several psychiatric diagnoses that largely stemmed from this traumatic history—a bipolar disorder, borderline personality disorder, and posttraumatic stress disorder. She saw a psychiatrist who prescribed her medication at an outpatient mental-health clinic. There was a risk of relapse to interpersonal violence, crack-cocaine smoking, and severe depression. She had attained substantial periods of abstinence from crack cocaine. Thus, of greatest concern was a continuing pattern of angry outbursts as well as physical aggression, suggesting her ongoing risk for committing serious interpersonal violence. Given her psychiatric disorders and this considerable risk, she successfully qualified for Social Security disability. Long-term psychological and psychiatric care was essential. Her concern with regard to avoiding incarceration for violence would likely sustain her active participation in this care, as might the recent birth of her son.

ANALYSIS OF CASES

As the case vignettes suggest, while the vast majority of clients in addiction treatment are mandated, others are there under coercion. Indeed, there are clients who are facing both a mandate to enter outpatient substance-abuse treatment from parole, as well as coercion from welfare. Other clients are being coerced into addiction treatment by a different combination of agencies, such as a child-protection agency and welfare. And there are yet other clients who are voluntarily seeking addiction treatment out of personal concerns rooted in the reality that they, too, may face criminal sanctions or end up under intensive supervision by some agency bound by the use of zero-tolerance policies for any drug involvement. Indeed, the cases effectively convey how contemporary clients may be classified as mostly mandated and/or coerced, while the remainder are concerned. However, what also emerges is the manner in which all clients, cutting across that typology, may be aptly and succinctly described as multiproblem.

What Do the Cases of Mandated Clients Illustrate?

The case of the former drug dealer who was recently released from prison (case 1) conveys the manner in which incarceration has contributed to the breakdown of the family. Incarceration serves as a tremendous source of stress when lengthy sentences take the incarcerated away from partners and children. Moreover, a history of incarceration makes the challenge of finding employment even more difficult, as many employers are hesitant about, or in fact barred from, hiring someone with a criminal background, especially a felony conviction. The temptation inherent in returning to a community where there are still active drug users and drug-dealing opportunities means that recidivism looms large as a potential risk. Meanwhile, the stress of coping with alienation from one's partner and children after a long period of separation, as well as the difficulty in finding employment, contribute to the risk of relapse to both depression and substance abuse.

The case of the remorseful and modest man who committed homicide (case 2) illustrates the manner in which those being released back into the community after lengthy periods of incarceration include those charged with violent crimes where states of drug and alcohol intoxication played a significant role in the commission of the crime. The case also shows how those who receive and benefit from prison-based treatment, such as a TC established in the prison setting, may emerge from prison substantially rehabilitated, but in need of a continuum of care beyond their incarceration. And such individuals are being mandated to community-based addiction treatment as a condition of their parole. Yet they still face the challenges involved in finding employment and adjusting to life back in the community after over two decades of incarceration and isolation from family and friends.

Suggesting the manner in which women have also been arrested, prosecuted, and incarcerated for criminal possession and sale of a controlled substance within the contemporary drug-prohibition era, there is the case of the immigrant refugee woman with distressing comorbidity from war trauma (case 3). Indeed, the criminal prosecution of women has occurred at historically unprecedented numbers within the crack-cocaine epidemic of the late 1980s and early 1990s, as well as in the aftermath of that epidemic, including up to the present day. And, the case reveals how those now living in the United States and left vulnerable to addiction include immigrants and refugees of war from distant lands, many of whom are suffering from mood disorders and post-traumatic stress disorder.

The effect and legacy of multiple generations of illicit drug use, as well as family violence, can be seen in the case of the adolescent male brought into treatment by his recovering mother (case 4). This adolescent male who was just a young boy when his mother was deeply immersed in her own crack-cocaine addiction, at the height of the late 1980s and early 1990s crack-cocaine epidemic, has now matured. He is no longer the child who was left yearning for his mother while she was mandated to community-based addiction treatment in a residential TC. He is no longer the child who faced physical abuse at the hands of his grandmother in whose care he was temporarily placed during his mother's addiction and recovery. He is now an adolescent drug dealer with a marijuana problem. Thus, the case also powerfully illustrates how so many individuals who end up involved in drug addiction and drug distribution have a childhood history of exposure to parental addiction, as well as violence and abuse. The case also shows the all-too-common history of placement in special education for acting-out behavior, as well as an early-adolescent diagnosis of conduct disorder. Also quite common is the manner in which an early juvenile period of incarceration has been rapidly followed by reimmersion in the drug-dealing lifestyle. Thus, his likelihood of facing reincarceration is great, given his status as having absconded and violated the conditions of his probation.

This case also shows how a recovering mother may want to do all she can to assist her son, being in danger of overcompensating out of feelings of guilt for what transpired during her period of active addiction, but there is a new reality in many housing settings. This reality involves how people can effectively jeopardize the stability of their housing. Housing stability is jeopardized if a relative, such as one's son, is arrested for a drug crime. This means that the mother is wisely protecting herself against this risk by having moved into a new, smaller apartment that cannot accommodate her son if he reappears.

Reflecting this very same reality of what it means to live in pubic housing and have criminal drug involvement is the case of another mother (case 5). In this instance, it is the mother who jeopardizes the public-housing apartment that she shares with her four adult children. Due to her arrest for crack-cocaine possession, she is now barred from living in public housing, and she is living under intensive supervision in a residential facility operating under contract with the criminal justice system. She is also adhering to a mandate to attend community-based addiction treatment. Her case highlights how there is, indeed, a stable cohort of crack-cocaine users who have been using crack since the early days of the crack-cocaine epidemic, and who now have histories of illicit-drug involvement spanning nearly two decades. And it is only because of a legal mandate that such individuals are entering community-based addiction treatment and complying with their treatment plans, given their fear of being violated, incarcerated, and separated from their children and families. Meanwhile, initially in recovery, her severe educational deficits and possible neurocognitive impairment are cause for concern. Her memory, speech, and personality functioning reflect either some stunted growth or deterioration from two decades of chronic crack-cocaine smoking. Thus, it is hard for her to retain information deemed vital to recovery and the prevention of relapse.

What Do the Cases of Mandated and/or Coerced Clients Illustrate?

There are clients who are both mandated by the criminal justice system and coerced into addiction-treatment participation by authorities from places such as welfare offices and child-protection agencies. Many contemporary clients have not only just left the confines of captivity in a correctional setting where many external pressures for compliance with supervision abounded, but they now face external pressure for compliance from more than one source in the outside world.

A case involving serious comorbidity in a man (case 6) illustrates how someone can be *both* mandated by parole *and* coerced by welfare into outpatient substance-abuse treatment. This case also serves to highlight a common pattern involving the prison system's gathering sufficient experience treating a client's long-standing psychiatric condition across a period of incarceration so that the decision is made that a mandate to both outpatient mental-health services *and* substance-abuse services is in order. For those who do make contact with a prison-based psychiatrist, this dual-mandate practice reflects the contemporary wisdom prevailing in the criminal justice system, given the work of these prison-based psychiatrists. For, it is clear that many clients present both the risk of relapse to illicit-drug and alcohol abuse, as well as a relapse to active psychosis or other problematic psychiatric symptoms, suggesting the need for a dual mandate to appropriate community-based treatment modalities to address each set of problems. Such multi-problem clients, or MICA clients (mentally ill chemical abusers), are well represented in large numbers within the contemporary population of clients entering community-based addiction treatment. Many clients differ from the case of the sixth client, insofar as they enter the prison setting with no clearly documented psychiatric history and are treated for the very first time for their psychiatric conditions in the prison setting. These clients also need the kind of dual mandate to both outpatient mental-health and addiction treatment illustrated in this case.

Showing how clients may be coerced into treatment by both a child-protection agency in order to regain custody of their child *and* by a welfare agency in order to remain eligible for benefits, there is the case of another severely distressed mother (case 7). This case also illustrates how a client entering into community-based addiction treatment under coercion has the experience of assessment for mental disorders for the very first time. In this case, a mood disorder, personality disorder, and post-traumatic stress disorder were uncovered, suggesting how there is a hidden population of clients with severe multiple mental disorders within the contemporary community-based addiction population. And, fortunately, if not also ironically, it is because of coercion into addiction treatment that such clients receive psychological and psychiatric treatment for the very first time in their lives.

Several cases (cases 4, 8, and 9) serve to highlight how a significant portion of the contemporary community-based addiction-treatment population are adolescents, late adolescents, or part of a college-age cohort of individuals who commonly engage in heavy alcohol drinking, binge drinking, and/or the use of club drugs such as ecstasy, as well as the use of ketamine, methamphetamine, and Rohypnol at places such as clubs, parties, and raves. However, the experience of blackouts and the violence and crime that may attend such overindulgence in alcohol suggests the severity of the problems that arise with the use of a legal substance such as alcohol (case 8).

Potential danger includes that inherent in driving under the influence (DUI), as illustrated in the case of an older adolescent/young man (case 8). Also, this case illustrates how those most vulnerable to alcohol dependence in late adolescence may also have traumatic childhood histories, just as this male has a history of sexual abuse. The case also demonstrates the willingness of judges to provide youth with opportunities for case dismissal if they comply with directives and receive necessary treatment across the specified period of time, while also avoiding any further involvement with the law.

Meanwhile, the case of a young woman (case 9) shows how the rise in drug sweeps of clubs suspected of being places where club drugs are sold means that many adolescents and young adults may face the choice between criminal prosecution with a permanent criminal record or attending a community-based addiction-treatment program. The ninth case also highlights how TASC programs are helping clients in having such a choice and in finding appropriate community-based addiction treatment.

The case of a gay man (case 10) further underscores the prominent and crucial role being played by TASC programs, as well as how TASC works in close association with drug courts. The case also illustrates the role of intensive supervision and regular urine testing, as clients are also closely monitored and assisted with regard to successfully competing an appropriate community-based addiction-treatment program.

What Do the Cases of Concerned Clients Illustrate?

The concerned enter community-based addiction treatment for a variety of reasons, voluntarily seeking help for their problems. The case of another older man (case 11) speaks to the reality that a significant portion of the contemporary community-based addiction-treatment population is voluntarily seeking care because of a concern that they may face criminal prosecution. The case demonstrates a concern about facing criminal prosecution as a consequence of a lengthy history of being involved in corporate wrongdoing. Heavy alcohol use likely contributed to initial and deepening involvement in corporate wrongdoing. A complex web, once woven, may then include heavy alcohol use, crack-cocaine smoking, and compulsive sexuality.

The case of the bisexual woman (case 12) clarifies the internal motivation of many concerned clients who find that it is not only their involvement with an illicit drug that may lead to criminal arrest and prosecution, but also their involvement in interpersonal violence. Although this is a case involving a woman, a large proportion of both men and women within the contemporary community-based addiction-treatment population struggle with the challenge of no longer readily releasing aggression and engaging in interpersonal violence. For many individuals who were involved in drug dealing, this aggression and violence is rooted in having to do whatever was necessary in the course of dealing drugs and protecting drug turf, as well as within the process of securing money for personal drug use. As in the twelfth case, for many clients, a substantial history of childhood exposure to severe physical abuse, parental domestic violence, and other parental interpersonal violence in the community goes far in establishing the client's current proclivity and risk for engagement in violence. With abstinence and improvement in reality testing and judgment, clients can themselves become deeply concerned about the risk of facing criminal arrest, prosecution, and incarceration for the commission of interpersonal violence. This concern allows them to embrace the goal of avoiding a relapse to violence and recidivism to violent crime. The case of this woman (case 12) also shows how many clients with such a proclivity to violence present mood disorders, such as a bipolar disorder, suggesting the need for psychiatric medication, such as Depakote or Zyprexa, given that states of agitation may involve violent activity. Meanwhile, ongoing psychological care is essential to address issues arising from such a client's other comorbid disorders of a borderline personality disorder and post-traumatic stress disorder that are rooted in childhood physical abuse and other exposure to parental violence.

MANDATED, COERCED, AND
CONCERNED CLIENTS AS A DIVERSE GROUP

Whether mandated, coerced, or concerned, the contemporary clients seeking addiction treatment are not only multiproblem, but they are also diverse across multiple dimensions. These dimensions span everything from basic demographics, to drug-use patterns, to addictive-behavior patterns, to psychiatric symptoms. The twelve case vignettes opening this chapter and analyzed with regard to what they illustrate about the characteristics and needs of contemporary clients entering community-based addiction treatment also suggest the kind of diversity to be found among the population. However, much more may be said about the various dimensions across which clients are diverse. Table 2.1 provides a summary of these dimensions of diversity.

Diverse Demographics

The mandated, coerced, or concerned addiction-treatment clients are coming from all walks of life. They represent all races, ethnicities, religions, educational levels, and socioeconomic statuses. In addition, the population includes clients of both genders, including the transgender, as well as those of all sexual orientations. This population comes from every geographic region. They are to be found in urban centers across America and in rural and suburban areas. They are early and late adolescents, adults, mothers, fathers, and members of families. They are Internet users at home, school, work, and in libraries, using computers to secure drug formulas and ingredients. They are part of diverse communities that are all negatively impacted when addiction and related destructive, compulsive, high-risk behaviors negatively affect the fabric of personal and social life.

Addiction treatment clients also come from all occupations, including blue collar, white collar, government, and corporate America, spanning all possibilities across the nation. In all of their work settings, those with addictive behaviors are increasingly being detected through drug-testing policies at work, where positive urine-toxicology results can mean being denied employment, terminated from work, court-martialed, prosecuted, and having one's reputation destroyed (Vereby, Buchan, & Turner, 1998, pp. 72–73).

Table 2.1. Contemporary Multiproblem Clients' Characteristics, Needs, and Diversity

Diverse demographics
  *Representing all races, ethnicities, and religions
  *Being of both genders, including the transgender, and all sexual orientations
  *Coming from all geographic regions—urban, rural, and suburban
  *Having all occupational and employment categories, including unemployment, welfare
  *Representing all socioeconomic statuses
  *Using varied types of insurance, including Medicaid and Medicare
Varied drug-use patterns
  *Alcohol
  *Crack cocaine, cocaine
  *Heroin
  *Marijuana
  *Methamphetamine
  *Ecstasy and club drugs (GHB/GLB, ketamine, Rohypnol)
  *Hallucinogens, phencyclidine (PCP)
  *Prescription opiods (Oxycodone, Percodan)
  *Over-the-counter medication (caffeine, ephedrine, phenylpropanolamine)
  *Poly-substance abuse/dependence
Varied multiple addictive and problem behaviors
  *Presence of more than one addictive behavior (e.g., alcohol, crack, and marijuana)
  *Presence of more than one problem behavior (e.g., violence and high-risk sex)
  *Combinations of multiple addictive and problem behaviors
Clients with challenging comorbidity/disability
  *Combined or multiple DSM IV-TR Axis I and Axis II mental disorders/disability
Varied health, disability, and medical conditions
  *HIV/AIDS and sexually transmitted diseases (STDs)
  *Hepatitis B and C virus (HBV and HCV, respectively)
  *Reproductive-health problems among women
  *Smoking-related disease (asthma, coronary heart disease, cancer)
  *Chronic disease (diabetes, hypertension, etc.), obesity
  *Problems associated with aging: visual and hearing impairments/disabilities
  *Lifelong disabilities: learning disabilities, speech impairments, etc.
Relationships among characteristics: the mental, behavioral, and physical health nexus
  *Mental health compromises behavioral health
  *Compromised behavioral health may lead to serious physical-health problems
Being in varied stages of change for multiple problems
  *Stage of change for any one problem behavior varies from precontemplation, to
    contemplation, preparation, action, or maintenance
  *A client may be in a different stage of change for each problem behavior
Histories of abuse, trauma, and violence across the lifespan
  *Childhood neglect, abuse (emotional, physical, sexual), parental domestic violence
  *Adolescent and adult rapes, battering/domestic violence, drug-culture violence
  *Varied patterns of both victimization from and perpetration of violence

The client population includes professional athletes who abuse drugs, as well as those conducting business, such as bankers and stockbrokers who handle investors' money. The population includes those with some of the highest rates of current and past-year illicit-drug use found in the 1990s, such as construction workers, those in food preparation, and waiters and waitresses. In addition, there are heavy alcohol users who are auto mechanics, vehicle repairers, and light-truck drivers and laborers, as well as personnel in the military services, in the regulated transportation industry, in nuclear industries, in federal and state agencies, and in private business and other industries (Verebey, Buchan, and Turner, 1998, p. 73). The manner in which alcohol use contributes to absenteeism from work for employees at large companies has also been well documented by McFarlin and Fals-Stewart (2002); these authors acknowledge the negative consequences that follow from substituting absent workers with their peers who are present at the job, creating hazardous work conditions and accidents. The accidents and errors at work that follow from alcohol and drug addiction, including errors in judgment and risk-taking behavior, may also contribute to corporate wrongdoing, as an opening case vignette suggests.

Client diversity also includes those who are not working, such as those who are recipients of welfare and other federal assistance programs. In this conservative era, federal guidelines for Temporary Assistance for Needy Families encourage states to deny cash assistance or food stamps to women with recent drug convictions (van Wormer & Davis, 2003), leading to varied state polices, including the use of coercion into alcohol and drug-treatment programs, the use of routine drug testing, and abstinence contracts. The result has been strong links between welfare departments and addiction-treatment programs (van Wormer & Davis, 2003). Several case vignettes opening this chapter illustrated this circumstance.

Given varied sources of income, there is also client diversity with regard to the varied means by which payment for addiction treatment occurs. There are clients who have the benefits, postincarceration financial standing, or health insurance necessary for receipt of treatment in an employee-assistance program; in an inpatient, outpatient, or private practice; or in a residential setting—even as this pool of clients may be shrinking due to the effects of managed care. Consistent with this, van Wormer and Davis (2003) explain how many working Americans are being moved over from traditional health-insurance coverage at their place of work to managed-care plans, essentially to manage costs, and this severely limits access to addiction and mental-health treatment. For example, there has been a pattern of severely restricting the use of inpatient detoxification, placing limits on outpatient addiction treatment via psychotherapy with the emphasis on brief treatment, yet allowing for psychiatric medication instead (van Wormer & Davis, 2003). As a result, many private, for-profit treatment centers, including residential settings, are closing (Johnson, 2002; van Wormer & Davis, 2003).

In order to receive treatment, other clients are accessing government-funded treatment using federal subsidies for alcohol and drug treatment (New York City Department of Mental Health, Mental Retardation, and Alcoholism Services, 1998). Because substance abuse and addiction are major public-health issues, a large portion of drug treatment is funded by local, state, and federal governments, even as private and employer-subsidized health plans may also provide coverage (National Institute on Drug Abuse, 1999). Clients are also using government benefits such as those that accompany being on welfare, such as Medicaid, or even Medicare. Fewer in number are those executive employees in top corporations who benefit from access to consulting psychologists in the corporate work setting, given the stress of mergers, buyouts, and concerns about corporate wrongdoing that lead corporations to hire professional consultants to address potential problems involving destructive, compulsive, high-risk behaviors, augmenting and going beyond the standard employee-assistance program.

Varied Drug-Use Patterns

Client diversity also includes the use of a variety of substances. This includes patterns of use, abuse, and dependence involving alcohol; cocaine/crack; heroin; marijuana; amphetamine/methamphetamine; ecstasy (methylene dioxymethamphetamine, MDMA); other club drugs (GHB/GLB, ketamine, Rohypnol); hallucinogens; phencyclidine (PCP), prescription medication (Oxycodone, Percodan); and over-the-counter medications (mixtures of caffeine, ephedrine from decongestants, and phenylpropanolamine from diet pills), as well as poly-substance abuse (Anderson & Larimer, 2002; Botvin, Scheier, & Griffin, 2002; Brecht, O'Brien, von Mayrhauser, & Anglin, 2004; Compton, 2002; Dennis, 2002; Earleywine, 2002; Freese, Miotto, & Reback, 2002; Haas, 2002; Herrell, 2002; Hester & Miller, 2003; Higgins & Abbott, 2001; Isralowitz, 2002; Johnson & Golub, 2002; Kandel, 2002; Kelly, Halford, & Young, 2002; Rawson, 2002a, 2002b; Riehman, Iguchi, & Anglin, 2002; Schuckit, 2000; Shane, 2002; Staton, Leukefeld, & Logan, 2002; Tucker, 1999; Wiscott, Kopera-Frye, & Begovic, 2002).

The case vignettes opening this chapter showed such client diversity, as clients were using anything from alcohol alone and in combination with other drugs (case 1—man recently released from incarceration for drug dealing; case 2—remorseful and modest man who committed homicide; case 3—immigrant refugee woman with comorbidity; case 8—late-adolescent/young-adult male sent to treatment by a judge; and case 11—man involved in corporate wrongdoing) to the primary use of other drugs such as crack cocaine (case 5—woman in jeopardy of losing her public housing for herself and her grown children; case 10—gay man referred by a drug court; and case 12—bisexual woman with a trauma history and comorbidity); heroin (case 6—male with paranoid schizophrenia); marijuana (case 4—adolescent male brought into treatment by his recovering mother; and case 7—woman who lost child custody of her sexually abused daughter); and ecstasy (case 9— young woman arrested in a dance-club drug sweep).

Multiple Addictive and Problem Behaviors

The manner in which contemporary clients are multiproblem may be best il-lustrated by the common co-occurrence of multiple addictive and problem be-haviors. The dimensions across which clients are diverse include the presen-tation of multiple addictions and problem behaviors. This dimension of diversity involves addictions and problem behavior involving gambling, sex-ual behavior, or other activities to rapidly accumulate money, whether hus-tling, drug dealing, shoplifting, prostitution, insider trading, compulsive high-risk monetary practices, or other forms of corporate wrongdoing (DeCou & Van Wright, 2002; Ignatius, 2002; Ladd & Petry, 2002; Levin, 2001; Marshall, Hudson, & Ward, 1992; Steenberg, Meyers, May, & Whelan, 2002; van Wormer & Davis, 2003; Wallace, 1996a; Winters, Stinchfield, Botzet, & Anderson, 2002). Another common combination involves alcohol and/or drug use and the problem behavior of driving a motor vehicle under the influence (DUI) or driving while intoxicated (DWI); the rise in courts and treatment/education programs addressing this problem constitutes a significant industry in the United States (McLellan, 2003a; National Institute on Drug Abuse, 2003).

Clients may also present the combination of having addictions to multiple substances, as well as multiple problem behaviors. Stories of overlapping problems with compulsive, destructive, and addictive behaviors of varied kinds are presented throughout this volume, as some of the opening case vi-gnettes began to suggest (case 1—man recently released from incarceration for drug dealing; case 8—late-adolescent/young-adult male sent to treat-ment by a judge; case 11—man involved in corporate wrongdoing; and case 12—bisexual woman with a trauma history and comorbidity). Just one client may reflect this diversity in having a severe addiction to cocaine, a pattern of heavy drinking with corporate-work peers, a history of engaging in com-pulsive sexual behavior, and a tendency to commit corporate wrongdoing, as one introductory case vignette (case 11—man involved in corporate wrongdoing) showed.

An addiction to fast money is common among clients in contemporary community-based addiction treatment, as another opening case illustrated (case 1—man recently released from incarceration for drug dealing). Fast money is acquired quickly relative to that income for which one typically labors across long hours while performing hard work within some standard legal-employment contract. The specific means and methods by which one acquires fast money may vary. Both corporate wrongdoing and an addiction to fast money may have common roots in the experience of reinforcement that comes from having money and being able to obtain desired possessions or a preferred lifestyle. This may include the experience of the rewards of being able to purchase expensive cars and fine jewelry, engage in frequent travel, send children to private schools, and live a privileged lifestyle. Through these sources of reinforcement, a client's behavior may have thereby been effectively shaped so that a compulsive, destructive, thrill-seeking problem behavior involving the goal of rapidly obtaining large sums of money evolved. Thus, in the case of a generic addiction to fast money, this may fuel the specific behaviors of corporate wrongdoing, insider trading, inaccurate accounting, tax fraud, drug dealing, gambling, and risk-taking behavior of many kinds that involve a potential to make money relatively quickly. These specific behaviors are present across a diverse group of clients, as two of the opening case vignettes (case 1—man recently released from incarceration for drug dealing; and case 11—man involved in corporate wrongdoing) serve to illustrate.

Clients with Challenging Comorbidity/Disability

For clients who may be generally described as multiproblem, among the most serious and challenging examples of this status are cases involving comorbidity that also constitutes having a disability. Thus, the diversity to be found in this population of clients also includes those who are MICA, having challenging comorbid conditions that even include multiple mental disorders. The range includes psychoactive substance abuse and psychoactive substance dependence. Following the *Diagnostic and Statistical Manual of Mental Disorders* (*DSM-IV-TR*), there are combinations of both Axis I and Axis II mental disorders (APA, 2000). For all clients, their substance abuse and/or dependence on one or many substances constitute Axis I mental disorders. But also commonly found are Axis I disorders such as mood disorders, especially bipolar disorder, as well as generalized anxiety disorders and schizophrenia, particularly paranoid schizophrenia. In addition, there are commonly found Axis II developmental and learning disorders, including personality disorders, attention deficit disorder with/without hyperactivity, and conduct disorder, for example. And many of these mental disorders are rooted in experiences of trauma across the lifespan (Broner, Borum, & Gawley, 2002; Brown, Stout, & Mueller, 1999; DeCou & Van Wright, 2002; De Leon, Sacks, & Wexler, 2002; Evans & Sullivan, 1994; Handmaker, Packard, & Conforti, 2002; Hegamin, Longshore, & Monahan, 2002; Landsberg, Rock, Berg, & Smiley, 2002; Molina, Bukstein, & Lynch, 2002; Newman, Leahy, Beck, Reilly-Harrington, & Gyulai, 2002; Ouimette & Brown, 2003; Wallace, 1996a; Young, 1995; Zweben, 1992). Some may be viewed as having a legitimate mental disability and many end up receiving benefits for this status.

Several case vignettes (case 3—immigrant refugee woman with comorbidity; case 4—adolescent male brought into treatment by his recovering mother; case 7—woman who lost child custody of her sexually abused daughter; and case 12—bisexual woman with a trauma history and comorbidity) opening this chapter suggested the potential link between experiences of abuse and trauma at various points across the lifespan and the manifestation of mental disorders consistent with the status of being a MICA client or of having comorbid psychiatric conditions. Indeed, a variety of combinations of these mental disorders/deficits may be found in the population, as suggested in some of the case vignettes opening this chapter. As a result of client diversity involving a MICA status or comorbidity, there is frequently a need for the use of combined treatments that include the integration of evidence-based pharmaceuticals, pharmacological adjuncts, and psychological and behavioral treatments (Carroll, 2001; Clark, Wood, Cornelius, Bukstein & Martin, 2003; Sammons & Schmidt, 2001).

There are also high rates of neuropsychological deficits that may have contributed to clients' diagnoses of attention deficit disorder with/without hyperactivity, while these deficits and specific patterns of neurocognitive impairment may significantly impact the course of addiction recovery and treatment outcome (Bates, Labouvie, & Voelbel, 2002). Special-education placements in school and other difficulties may follow for clients; one case vignette (case 4—adolescent male brought into treatment by his recovering mother) served to illustrate such potential problems at the beginning of this chapter.

Varied Health, Disability, and Medical Conditions

Beyond mental-health problems, there are substantial physical-health problems and/or biologically based conditions among the client population. And social, economic, environmental, and psychological factors may contribute to and/or exacerbate these health problems. Thus client diversity also includes the presentation of a wide range of health problems and engagement in behaviors that place them at risk for disease. These include HIV/AIDS; hepatitis B and C virus (HBV and HCV, respectively); sexually transmitted diseases; tuberculosis; reproductive-health problems; smoking-related disease (asthma, coronary heart disease, cancer); other chronic diseases (diabetes, hypertension, etc.); obesity; and problems associated with aging, as well as disabilities (visual, learning, speaking, hearing, etc.), some of which constitute serious medical conditions (Cropsey, Eldridge, & Ladner, 2004; Farabee & Leukefeld, 2002; Farmer, 2002; Freudenberg, 2001; Hegamin et al., 2002; National Institute on Drug Abuse, 1999, 2003; Palepu et al., 2003; Strathdee, 2003; Timpson, Williams, Bowen, & Keel, 2003). The high prevalence of cocaine use may be especially problematic, as cocaine use is associated with HIV, hepatitis, other sexually transmitted diseases, and a variety of infections; however, cocaine use may impair the immune system in the four hours following use, increasing the risk of infection, and helping to explain some of the associations with infectious diseases (Halpern et al., 2003).

One case vignette (case 10—gay man referred by a drug court) included issues related to having both a medical disability and engagement in high-risk sexual behavior that placed him at risk for HIV/AIDS and other sexually transmitted diseases. Although cases were not presented to convey this reality, it has been documented that high-risk sexual behavior, including the relatively extreme case of being HIV positive and failing to use condoms with multiple sexual partners, frequently occurs among heterosexuals, bisexuals, and homosexuals (Timpson et al., 2003).

Relationships among Characteristics: The Mental, Behavioral, and Physical Health Nexus

There are also relationships between level of psychopathology, or psychiatric symptoms such as depression, and engagement in the risky behavior of needle sharing (Johnson, Yep, Brem, Theno, & Fisher, 2002). Thus, mental health and behavioral health interact, impacting physical-health status.

This suggests a possible *mental-health, behavioral-health, and physical-health nexus* that is worthy of attention, as a connection between these factors further complicates the treatment challenge. Mental health can compromise behavioral health. Compromised behavioral health, such as engagement in risky behaviors, can compromise physical health. Addiction treatment must address each of these factors, as well as the interrelationships among them, while recognizing the unique combinations of specific mental-health, behavioral-health, and physical-health problems that clients present. Thus, client diversity includes individual clients possessing unique combinations of specific conditions for their particular mental-health, behavioral-health, and physical-health nexus; this requires tailoring treatment interventions to address a client's distinct mental, behavioral, and physical problems.

Being in Varied Stages of Change for Multiple Problems

Moreover, client diversity includes the reality that different clients are in different stages of change or states of readiness to address problems in any one of the three areas in this nexus. An individual may be in different stages of change for each of his or her mental, behavioral, or physical problems, even though they are all closely interrelated. A client may be in an action stage, ready to pursue steps involving seeing a psychiatrist, taking medication, and alleviating the symptoms of depression. With regard to one of the opening case vignettes (case 12—bisexual woman with a trauma history and comorbidity), early in her treatment, the client was in a maintenance stage for taking her psychiatric medication for her bipolar disorder, in an action stage for her crack-cocaine dependence, but in a contemplation stage for addressing her violence, being highly ambivalent about this problem behavior. Given her concerns about the risk of arrest and incarceration for violent acting out, as well as her involuntary psychiatric commitment, the client was successfully engaged in treatment interventions so that, over time, she entered an action stage and then a maintenance stage for working on violence.

Practitioners have to start where the client is and address that problem upon which the client feels ready to take action. However, it is often in the client's best interest and the most ethical course of action to prioritize the client's multiple problems and address the one that is posing the greatest overall risk to either the client or others in society, despite the client's level of willingness to take action and pursue change. For example, a risk of violent acting out, with either suicidality or homicidality, might justify what is prioritized as a focus of treatment.

Histories of Abuse, Trauma, and Violence across the Lifespan

In addition, client diversity includes histories of victimization and violence across the lifetime, spanning from childhood to adulthood. Patterns include childhood exposure to domestic violence, sexual abuse, physical abuse, verbal abuse, emotional abuse, and neglect, as well as adolescent and adult experiences of rape, domestic violence, battering by partners, and exposure to violence in the drug culture. Several cases illustrated such histories (case 3— immigrant refugee woman with comorbidity; case 4—adolescent male brought into treatment by his recovering mother; case 7—woman who lost custody of her sexually abused daughter; case 8—late-adolescent/young-adult male sent to treatment by a judge; and case 12—bisexual woman with a trauma history and comorbidity).

Together with their own personal vast experiences with varied forms of victimization and violence across their lifespan, the population has also engaged in violence themselves, whether in drug crime, interpersonal crime, relationship violence, domestic violence, childhood maltreatment, property crime, or physical violence (Acierno, Coffey, & Resnick, 2003; DeCou & Van Wright, 2002; Locke & Newcomb, 2003; Hegamin et al., 2002; Parrott, Drobes, Saladin, Coffey, & Dansky, 2003; Riggs, Rukstalis, Volpicelli, Kalmanson, & Foa, 2003; Salasin, 2002; Schewe, 2002; Stuart et al., 2003; Wallace, 1996a; Young, 1995). This was illustrated in one case (case 12—bisexual woman with a trauma history and comorbidity). There is a long history of examining the drug/violence nexus (Brownstein & Goldstein, 1990; Hoaken & Stewart, 2003).

Many drug users have engaged in violence to obtain money for drugs, robbing others, for example, or committing burglary. No cases presented illustrated this common pattern. But drug dealing is a primary way of obtaining money for many users, and two cases involved drug dealing (case

1—man recently released from incarceration for drug dealing; and case 4—adolescent male brought into treatment by his recovering mother).

Some violence is the result of merely being involved in the drug culture. For example, the day-to-day activities of drug dealers include either being directly involved themselves or having a crew with members who take on the responsibility of protecting drug territory, managing potential violence related to competition between drug dealers, and making sure all monies due are collected from crew members and drug users. Together with the influx of guns into the community, these factors contribute to the commission of violence that becomes routine within the drug culture. Although the most pertinent case (case 1—man recently released from incarceration for drug dealing) does not illustrate this, other cases do, for this particular client was not disclosing this kind of past history as troublesome, given that his focus was on much more present-day concerns.

Other violence and criminality may be the product of addiction and intoxication, particularly in the case of alcohol (Fals-Stewart, Golden, & Schumacher, 2003; Hoaken & Stewart, 2003; Lange, 2002; Quigley, Corbett, & Tedeschi, 2002); cocaine (Fals-Stewart et al., 2003); and amphetamines (Benda, Corwyn, & Rodell, 2001). This was powerfully illustrated in one case (case 2—remorseful and modest man who committed homicide).

In some instances, clients readily enact violence and victimize others, given the violence to which they were themselves exposed as children and adolescents, so that childhood physical abuse contributes to violent acting-out behavior. This was illustrated by two cases (case 4—adolescent male brought into treatment by his recovering mother; and case 12—bisexual woman with a trauma history and comorbidity).

Other violence intimately experienced by some segment of this population includes that associated with war, ethnic cleansing, refugee experiences, international violence, and the U.S. domestic experiences with terrorism (September 11, 2001). As a result of these kinds of experiences, many clients suffer from mental disorders that are directly linked to their experiences of victimization and violence, including post-traumatic stress disorder, depression, anxiety, and phobias (Kagee, 2003; Smith, 2003; La Greca, Silverman, Vernberg, & Roberts, 2002). These disorders frequently set the stage for alcohol and drug addiction, as one of the opening case vignettes (case 3—immigrant refugee woman with comorbidity) suggests. The course of treatment is complicated by the presence of psychopathology rooted in terror and violence.

CONCLUSION

This chapter began by drawing upon the power of storytelling, using twelve case vignettes in order to convey the characteristics and needs of contemporary clients entering community-based addiction treatment— whether they are mandated and/or coerced, or concerned, voluntarily entering treatment. The chapter also considered in depth the multitude of dimensions across which contemporary multiproblem clients are diverse, reviewing each of these dimensions and indicating where the opening case vignettes served to highlight a certain dimension of diversity. The emergent reality involves the extent to which there is tremendous heterogeneity to be found in the contemporary population of clients entering community-based addiction treatment.

Indeed, practitioners might be easily overwhelmed with the task of adapting evidence-based addiction-treatment interventions and utilizing recommended state-of-the-art practices with clients who are so very challenging, with so many multiple problems, challenging characteristics, pressing needs, and ways in which they are diverse. Hence, it is important to consider, in terms of available treatment interventions with empirical support, what seems to work with this multiproblem population. Chapter 3 will do so, examining available evidence from research on addiction treatment.

3

The Evidence

This chapter will review a large body of evidence in order to answer several questions: (1) Does mandated addiction treatment work? (2) Does addiction treatment, in general, work? and, given three decades of research in the field of addiction treatment, (3) What do we know or think we know? This discussion will allow us to go beyond an appreciation of the value of evidence-based addiction-treatment interventions to recognize the value in naturalistic longitudinal observations. What will emerge from discussion is the critical role of practitioners in community-based addiction treatment in making mandated addiction treatment work with contemporary multi-problem clients, as well as the nature of the challenge inherent in adapting evidence-based interventions in this vital work. Also underscored is the value of the expert opinions of practitioner researchers who suggest what constitutes the state of the art, given due consideration of both the body of empirical evidence and naturalistic longitudinal observations.

DOES MANDATED ADDICTION TREATMENT WORK?

Hiller et al. (2002) report that, in the case of clients mandated to addiction treatment, this pressure from legal authorities improves retention in community-based programs, and it serves to increase the likelihood of favorable outcomes. Donovan and Rosengren (1999) cite a growing body of research to debunk the belief that clients who are mandated to treatment by either the courts or an agency cannot be helped until they are intrinsically motivated. Instead, Donovan (1999) emphasizes how research shows no differences between those mandated or coerced into treatment and those who enter voluntarily, and how it shows differences that favor mandated clients in a sample of ethnic-minority-group members (Brecht et al., 1993; De Leon, 1988; Stitzer & McCaul, 1987; Watson et al., 1988; Wells-Parker, 1994).

Others assert that a body of research suggests that criminal-justice authority, mandatory treatment, and civil commitment enhance treatment retention and reduce relapse (Leukefeld et al., 2001, p. 406; Marlowe, Glass et al., 2001). Indeed, it has been found that the use of the legal mandate by parole or probation serves to increase the length of time a person remains in substance-abuse treatment, as well as to increase positive treatment outcomes that enhance recovery (Leukefeld et al., 2001, p. 402). Marlowe, Glass et al. (2001) acknowledge research showing that legal pressures are among those experienced by clients entering treatment, and perceived legal pressures are effective in maintaining such clients in treatment and in contributing to their maintenance of abstinence (Marlowe, Glass et al., 2001, p. 219).

Investigators also found that continuing care (typically outpatient) following more intensive interventions (typically inpatient) tends to produce a relatively higher level of attendance when it is presented as mandatory versus voluntary (Donovan, 1998, p. 323). Other research showed a better treatment outcome for clients who faced a greater likelihood of losing a valued outcome due to continued substance use, suggesting the impact of some contingency in their treatment outcome (Donovan, 1999; Mark, 1988). Thus, clients who risk losing employment, family, or a welfare check may benefit from being coerced or mandated into treatment and produce better treatment outcomes than those who are voluntary, self-referred, or referred by noncoercive agents such as friends, a physician, or a social-service agency (Donovan, 1999, pp. 140–42).

When examining treatment outcome, it is important to go beyond an investigation of retention with common findings of a direct relation between retention and positive posttreatment outcomes (Sung, Belenko, Feng, & Tabachnick, 2004). Treatment engagement and treatment compliance are also important factors. Sung et al. (2004, p. 24) acknowledge that, although "legal coercion may be sufficient extrinsic motivation to accept treatment, continued engagement in recovery" requires yet something more. And retention is "a complex product of organizational culture, program rules, and individual performances" (Sung et al., 2004, p. 24). Among clients mandated into residential treatment who were repeat nonviolent drug offenders arrested for felony drug-sale offenses, Sung et al. (2004) found that those categorized as noncompliant had certain characteristics: they tended to be in their late teens or early adult years, to lack social support by having impoverished friendship networks, and to lack an internal desire for change. Also, men were overrepresented among compliant clients, while the higher noncompliance rates among females in the residential setting may be explained by their "high rates of economic hardships, poor health, and histories of comorbid mental health disorders" (Sung et al., 2004, p. 24).

Drieschner et al. (2004) caution that treatment engagement, or degree of adequate performance of client behaviors in treatment, may not share a functional relationship with motivation for treatment. This is because situational factors may interfere with entering into, continuing with, or adhering to a treatment regime or strategy for change. Examples of situational factors include discovering a preference for another treatment regime and switching to it, as well as financial resources (transportation costs), time constraints, and even internal factors that are not under one's volitional control, such as cognitive capacity or neuropsychological factors. Finally, Drieschner et al. (2004) note that such preferences, experiences, and difficulties will vary for clients, yet they impact what might be summed up in noncompliance rates.

On the other hand, research in regard to the efficacy of mandating individuals to attend Alcoholics Anonymous (AA) meetings consistently shows that it does not improve treatment outcomes, even as courts and employee-assistance programs have regularly made such mandates (Miller, Andrews, Wilbourne, & Bennett, 1998, p. 213; Miller, Wilbourne, & Hettema, 2003, p. 35). However, research suggests that when clients with alcohol-use disorders did participate in AA for a period of four months or longer in the first year after seeking treatment, they had better one-year and eight-year alcohol-related outcomes when compared to those who did not participate in AA (Moos & Moos, 2004). Moreover, Moos and Moos (2004) found that clients who continued their participation in AA in years two through eight of their recovery, thereby having sustained participation in AA, had better eight-year outcomes when compared to those who did not participate in AA or who participated for a shorter duration of time.

The Integrated Approach: Community-Based Addiction Treatment and Criminal-Justice Supervision

Perhaps most importantly, there is research suggesting that the combination of community-based addiction treatment and ongoing criminal-justice supervision represents a promising approach. It has been called an integrated approach, given the manner in which it combines a public-health perspective and a public-safety viewpoint (Marlowe, 2003). Marlowe (2003) explains that practitioners often embrace a public-health perspective that focuses upon the delivery of treatment with minimal criminal-justice-system involvement. On the other hand, public-safety proponents tend to embrace the notion of criminal offenders being under constant criminal-justice-system supervision. Marlowe's (2003, p. 5) review of the research suggests that "neither the pure public safety nor an exclusively public health approach to the problem works fully; instead, it supports an integrated approach." Successful examples include drug courts and work-release therapeutic communities that provide the following key elements: treatment in the community, an opportunity to avoid incarceration or a criminal record, close supervision to ensure compliance, and responses to noncompliance with certain and immediate consequences (Belenko, 1999; Belenko & Logan, 2003; Gottfredson & Exum, 2002; Knight, Simpson, & Hiller, 1999; Marlowe, 2003; Wexler, 2003).

Within the most effective model of integration of criminal-justice and drug-treatment systems and services, the personnel within each system ideally work together on plans and implementation of screening, placement, testing, monitoring, and supervision, as well as on the systematic use of sanctions and rewards in the criminal justice system (NIDA, 1999). It is worth noting that the criminal justice system refers drug offenders into community-based addiction treatment using many different mechanisms: diverting nonviolent offenders to treatment; stipulating treatment as a condition of probation or pretrial release; convening specialized courts that handle cases for criminal offenses involving drugs; and using drug courts that are exclusively dedicated to the cases of drug offenders and that mandate and arrange for treatment as an alternative to incarceration, actively monitor progress of clients in treatment, and arrange for other services as needed (NIDA, 1999).

Evidence to Support Drug Courts

Drug courts originated with the Dade County, Miami, Florida, program in June 1989, evolving into the contemporary preferred mechanism for linking drug- and/or alcohol-involved offenders with community-based treatment and other needed services. In just eleven years, there was tremendous growth in the utilization of the drug court. By June 2000, there were 516 operational drug courts, with 281 planned for implementation, spanning all 50 states, the District of Columbia, Puerto Rico, Guam, and 54 Native American tribal courts—all of these courts claiming a total of 55,000 graduates (American University, 2000; Belenko, 2002). At the arrest/pretrial stage, the drug courts function to divert offenders with drug-use histories into community-based, court-monitored substance-abuse treatment (Prendergast & Burdon, 2002). The drug-court model includes several typical components: a dedicated courtroom reserved for drug-court participants, judicial supervision of structured community-based treatment, timely assessment and referral of eligible defendants to treatment and related services as soon as possible after arrest, regular status hearings to monitor treatment progress and compliance, increasing defendant accountability via graduated sanctions and rewards, mandatory periodic or random drug testing, establishment of specific treatment requirements, and either case dismissal or sentence reduction upon successful completion of treatment (Belenko, 2002).

The body of research on drug courts is in a relative state of infancy, yet it shows the following: they produce "relatively high retention rates; low recidivism and drug use rates while participants are in drug court programs; reduced recidivism in the year following program participation; and provide relatively close community supervision through drug testing and regular court hearings" (Belenko, 2002; Belenko & Logan, 2003, p. 202). On the other hand, some evaluations have found no postprogram impact on recidivism (Belenko, 2002). But, reviews of nearly one hundred drug-court evaluations showed that an average of 60 percent of drug-court clients completed a year or more in treatment with approximately 50 percent graduating from the program (Marlowe, Elwork, Festinger, & McLellan, 2003). The success of drug courts stands in stark contrast to the more typical retention rates found in community-based addiction treatment where approximately 70 percent of those on probation drop out of treatment or attend inconsistently within a two-to-six-month period (Marlowe et al., 2003).

Marlowe et al. (2003) assert that the success of the drug court is likely due to the judge. Research needs to investigate the differential impact of sanctions when administered by judges, corrections officers, or administrative review panels, in addition to the role of incentives in producing compliance and cooperation with treatment and testing requirements (Harrell & Kleiman, 2002, p. 171–72). For Marlowe et al. (2003), it seems that of all those within the criminal justice system who may provide supervision, it is the judge who has the most powerful impact in producing positive outcomes. Marlowe et al. (2003) speculate that it may be how the judge tends to have an aura of authority, impartiality, and a great deal of influence over clients, as well as the power to administer sanctions and rewards in a powerful way. Also, another factor in the success of drug courts may be the regular holding of client-status hearings so that the modification of client negative behavior includes the delivery of negative sanctions and positive rewards in a much more swift or immediate and consistent manner. In fact, the best available evidence suggests that weekly reports from treatment programs on client behavior, such as to a presiding judge in drug court (or to a probation or parole officer), work best; this is consistent with a body of research on contingency management showing that interventions have large treatment effects when target behaviors are monitored and responded to on a weekly basis (Marlow et al., 2003).

Marlowe et al. (2003) also succinctly summarize a large body of research findings on alternatives to standard incarceration in jail or prison that do not appear to work—as effectively as drug courts—as a way of contrasting the value of research support for how drug courts do work. For example, the use of intensive supervised probation and parole (ISP) involves more intensive monitoring of offenders, reducing caseload size, and increasing resources for probation and parole officers. ISP may include anklet monitoring, home detention, or shock incarceration. However, studies show that there may be worse outcomes for clients, in terms of there being more technical violations and a high level of return to incarceration, as greater monitoring means greater detection of infractions (Marlowe et al., 2003). Therefore, technically, ISP does not markedly reduce drug use or prison crowding (Kinlock & Hanlon, 2002). At the same time, research shows that shock incarceration, electronic monitoring, boot camps, and house arrest are associated with either no appreciable change in recidivism or a slight increase in recidivism (Marlowe et al., 2003).

Marlowe (2003) also contrasts drug courts with TASC, emphasizing how, despite early promising findings, TASC's latest long-term evaluations prevent declaring TASC as having firm empirical support. The program that began in the 1970s called Treatment Alternatives to Street Crime (TASC) and renamed Treatment Accountability for Safer Communities (TASC) proliferated across the country. The Special Action Office of Drug Abuse Prevention introduced the concept and model of TASC in 1972, and it became the basis for many effective programs and practices for managing drug-dependent adolescent and adult offenders who are either at the pretrial stage, are diverted offenders, or are already-sentenced offenders (Cook, 2002). Prendergast and Burdon (2002) primarily classify TASC as being for the presentencing stage, serving the needs of nonviolent substance-abusing offenders who benefit from this alternative to incarceration.

Regular drug testing and reporting of client progress/compliance to judges and other critical parties is also an important function of TASC, so that those in violation of the conditions of their TASC involvement are readily returned to the criminal justice system (Battjes & Carswell, 2002; Cook, 2002). Being subject to such intensive supervision often means that TASC clients who commit a technical violation, for example, submitting urines positive for illicit substances, are more likely to face arrest. But, in general, research suggests that TASC works effectively with diverse clients. Data show that TASC clients have reduced rearrest rates, receive significantly more treatment and other services than non-TASC clients, and show reductions in drug use and drug crimes (Anglin, Longshore, & Turner, 1999; Battjes & Carswell, 2002; Cook, 2002; Longshore, Turner, & Anglin, 1998). As of 1996, there were three hundred TASC programs operating in thirty states in the United States, and this number has grown since then (Anglin, Longshore, Turner, McBride, Inciardi, & Prendergast, 1996; Prendergast & Burdon, 2002). However, TASC also plays an important role for those who have already served time incarcerated and are now being released to the community. Such clients are in need of aftercare or community-based addiction treatment. And TASC effectively serves more than two hundred communities in this manner (Farabee & Leukefeld, 2001).

Most recently, it has been suggested that, despite these earlier evaluations, the most recent long-term evaluation of five TASC programs found that effects on drug use and recidivism were mixed; drug use was reduced for TASC clients in three of five sites, while criminal activity was reduced in only two of the five sites. Furthermore, positive findings were only modest and confined to the high-risk offenders. The concluding judgment on TASC is, therefore, that there is no empirical basis for determining the efficacy of this model. Hence, in contrast, the empirical support for the relatively new drug courts stands as quite impressive (Marlowe et al., 2003).

But, drug courts actually enjoy a natural and happy marriage with TASC programs. Drug courts rely upon either referral to multiple existing community-based substance-abuse treatment programs, or utilization of dedicated treatment slots purchased by the drug court or reserved for drug-using clients within treatment programs (Belenko, 2002). Drug courts serve to support client compliance with treatment goals within these programs, often as specified and monitored by TASC, suggesting the natural marriage between the two (Cook, 2002). Moreover, TASC provides drug courts with the essential structures necessary to ensure that clients receive the services that they need (Cook, 2002). Even the residential therapeutic community (TC) has enjoyed a long, happy marriage with TASC.

Evidence to Support Therapeutic Communities

The history, nature, supportive theory, overall model, treatment method, and efficacy of the residential TC have been described in great detail. TCs tend to have a planned length of stay of six to twelve months, and they focus on re-mobilization of the client, using the entire community as active components of treatment, including other residents, staff, and the social context. The TC model is known for being highly structured and, at times, confrontational when helping clients to examine negative beliefs, self-concepts, and behavioral patterns. These programs are also comprehensive, including employment training and other on-site support services (NIDA, 1999). A body of work shows how TCs produce positive outcomes of lower drug use (cocaine, heroin, alcohol); lower crime; less unemployment; and lower rates of depression/psychopathology. Moreover, those who stay longer in treatment have better outcomes (Cullen, Jones, & Woodward, 1997; De Leon, 2000; De Leon et al., 2002; Wexler, De Leon, Thomas, Kressel, & Peters, 1999). For example, the TC for drug offenders has been shown in research to result in 40 percent or greater reductions in arrests for violent and nonviolent criminal acts (NIDA, 1999).

Since the 1980s, the TC has been gaining favor for use in communities as well as in corrections institutions. Deitch, Carleton, Koustsenok, and Marsolais (2002) explain how, as early as 1980, the need for solutions to the crisis of prison expansion led to a search for treatment models best suited for a criminal population. The residential TC emerged as the model having the most experience with predatory criminals with little work history and substantial psychosocial problems. And TCs demonstrated success at three- and five-year follow-up in decreasing crime, increasing work productivity, and decreasing multiple types of drug taking (Deitch et al., 2002, pp. 131–32). The TC model also seemed well suited for the correctional mission, in light of the emphasis placed on prosocial values, hierarchical structure, and demand for compliance (Deitch et al., 2002). Moreover, TCs rely on the use of group therapy, community meetings, and encounter groups, while also providing for access to educational and vocational training activities (De Leon, 2000). Deitch et al. (2002) acknowledge problems in adapting the TC model to the criminal justice system, explaining that the process of blending the TC model with the prison setting has been bumpy, convoluted, and painful (p. 132).

Deitch et al. (2002) raise the pertinent question as to whether or not the same kind of positive results found in community-based TCs will be found over time in a criminal-justice custody setting (p. 135). However, De Leon et al. (2002) assert that there was not only evidence for early, positive prison TC outcomes produced as early as the 1980s (Wexler, Falkin, & Lipton, 1990), but also that there was substantial evidence supporting the feasibility and effectiveness of prison-based TCs, even in light of some modifications for that setting (Simpson, Wexler, & Inciardi, 1999; Inciardi, Surratt, Martin, & Hooper, 2002). Having firm empirical support and a long history covering some twenty-five years is the prison-based residential TC Stay'n Out in New York, which showed positive treatment outcomes, and over time the focus has shifted to include aftercare following prison-based treatment, which contributed further reductions to recidivism as shown in a large body of research conducted in many states (Wexler, 2003).

Given the variety of problems that are found among the incarcerated population, including dual diagnoses (Broner, Borum, & Gawley, 2002; DeCou & Van Wright, 2002; Hegamin et al., 2001), the modified prison TC has also been implemented, suggesting the extent to which it can be adapted successfully. This represents a new focus on meeting the needs of drug offenders with co-occurring mental illness and substance abuse disorders (COD), who are "multi-problem and impaired" (Wexler, 2003, p. 228). This is consistent with the needs of contemporary clients flooding community-based addiction treatment. De Leon et al. (2002) assert that the prison-based TC can form a part of a continuum of care for contemporary clients who will enter community-based addiction treatment.

One ideal continuum of care that is totally dependent on the incorporation of the TC model has been described in the literature (Inciardi et al., 2002). The model rests on a research-based strategy and involves long-term TC involvement across three stages. The first stage would involve a prison-based TC experience for at least nine to twelve months. Secondly, there should be a community-based residential TC experience during the work-release phase, as the initial exposure to freedom carries many risks, such as relapse to addiction and recidivism to crime; this would be a traditional TC experience. The third stage would constitute aftercare and would involve living in the free community under the supervision of parole or some other surveillance program. Such a comprehensive TC model has been implemented in Delaware (Inciardi et al., 2002, pp. 207–9).

TCs have long been used in communities as an alternative to incarceration, with offenders mandated to a residential TC in the community. Thus, TASC frequently refers clients to community-based residential TCs, and it has a long history of doing so since the 1970s. Indeed, it may be argued that it is because of the steady stream of referrals of drug offenders by TASC to the residential TC that the TC has been able to acquire the longest record of experience working with a large population of drug offenders in community-based addiction treatment. Thus, TASC referrals have played a key role in the community-based residential TC's being able to document treatment success. The external pressure of supervision by TASC personnel and the mandate to the TC may have a great deal to do with clients' remaining in treatment long enough to produce the findings that researchers cite as evidence of the success of TCs, especially as these findings clearly relate to length of stay in treatment (the longer the stay, the better the treatment outcomes). Such findings are a function of retention, and retention is often a function of having external/legal pressure. In this manner, the body of research showing that TCs work and that length of stay is key may actually largely reflect just how effective treatment may be when clients are under external/legal pressure to remain in treatment.

The best-known residential treatment model is the TC. However, there are other residential treatment programs that may employ other models, such as cognitive-behavioral therapy (NIDA, 1999).

Future Directions in Research

There has been criticism of the body of available research on what works in the field of addiction treatment, including what works for drug-involved offenders. Thus, more controlled studies of a variety of community-reentry strategies for drug-involved offenders are needed (Marlowe, 2003). The National Institute on Drug Abuse (NIDA) has launched the Criminal Justice Drug Abuse Treatment Studies (CJ-DATS) as a multisite five-year investigation (2002 through 2007) to identify key elements of prison-based treatment systems in the United States, with the goal of establishing integrated, evidence-based treatment models for service delivery within the criminal justice system (Simpson, 2002). Through seven regional centers and a coordinating center, there will be greater structured support for systematic studies on all aspects of treatment, essentially creating a national research infrastructure and setting the stage for major advances in treatment of this challenging population (Wexler, 2003).

Implications for Community-Based Practitioners

However, for those on parole or probation undergoing reentry into the community, at this point in time, the ideal continuum of care will include community-based addiction treatment under the care of those practitioners for whom this book is written. Contemporary practitioners have a key role to play in the research-supported integrated approach that combines criminal-justice supervision with participation in community-based addiction treatment. Those providing criminal-justice-system supervision, whether a judge in a drug court or a probation or parole officer, need practitioners in community-based addiction treatment to work with referred clients within the context of such ideal integrated models. In essence, this will be mandated addiction treatment.

In sum, in preparation for this work, practitioners need to know that there is evidence to suggest that mandated addiction treatment is effective. Moreover, there is a vital role for practitioners in delivering this care in community-based addiction-treatment settings. For, this area of work is not only very much needed, but it is also likely to expand in the new millennium. This is due to the fact that probation and parole populations are growing, the number of drug courts is growing, and the majority of those under criminal-justice supervision have drug and alcohol problems, necessitating reliance on community-based addiction treatment as a vital resource surely to be utilized by criminal-justice authorities (Hiller et al., 2002).

But, practitioners also need to know that the impact of being a mandated client may vary depending upon many factors: the length of retention in treatment; the amount of services received in the first three months of treatment; whether the treatment program was completed or not; the degree of engagement in treatment or of compliance while in treatment; client characteristics (age, gender, race/ethnicity, social support, economic status, health, comorbid mental-health disorders, etc.); the specific elements of the treatment program; and whether an integrated approach was used combining criminal-justice-system supervision with community-based addiction treatment. Research on these factors and their influence upon treatment has been conducted within more general studies on addiction treatment, as discussed in the next section.

DOES ADDICTION TREATMENT, IN GENERAL, WORK?

In support of the overall effectiveness of community-based addiction treatment, there is a body of supportive evidence that continues to grow. This includes national evaluations of drug-treatment outcomes and processes over the past thirty years. Simpson (2003) acknowledges that this real-world evidence may be more limited than experimental protocols in its capacity to

establish scientific causality, but it "excel[s] in documenting naturally occurring patterns of treatment and patient recovery" (p. 123). Of most rele-
vance are the three national evaluations of community-based treatment effectiveness funded by the National Institute on Drug Abuse: the 1970s Drug
Abuse Reporting Program (Simpson & Sells, 1982); the 1980s Treatment
Outcomes Prospective Study (Hubbard, Rachal, Craddock, & Cavanaugh,
1984); and the most recent 1990s Drug Abuse Treatment Outcome Studies
(DATOS), which are most pertinent at this time, with findings worthy of review. Nationwide samples include treatment programs and clients who
vary widely in demographic and diagnostic characteristics, as well as in the
severity and chronicity of their disorder, as Moos (2003) points out.

Using a nationally representative sample of outpatients and long-term residential drug-treatment programs, the DATOS data may also inform a discussion on the impact of having a legal status, of being mandated or coerced
into community-based addiction treatment, as well as what works when, or
under what conditions, in the real world. The DATOS data may inform such
a discussion, since it has been reported that approximately two-thirds of
clients in long-term residential drug-treatment programs, and one-half of
clients in outpatient-drug abuse treatment, are also on probation or parole
(Marlowe, 2003). Thus, findings on what works in addiction treatment, in
general, is most applicable to this book's focus.

With regard to retention data on this large nationally representative sample, Marlowe (2003) summarizes as follows:

> [Three] months of participation in drug treatment may be a minimum threshold
> for detecting dose-response effects for the interventions (Simpson et al., 1997).
> . . . It also appears that 6 to 12 months of treatment may be a further threshold
> for observing lasting reductions in drug use. . . . Approximately 50 percent of
> clients who complete 12 months or more of treatment remain abstinent for an
> additional year after completing treatment. . . . Approximately 70 percent of pro-
> bationers and parolees drop out of drug treatment or attend irregularly prior to
> a 3-month threshold, and 90 percent drop out prior to 12 months. . . . Compara-
> ble attrition rates are found for drug abuse patients in general (e.g., Stark, 1994).
> These figures suggest that, on average, only about 10 to 30 percent of clients, in
> or out of the criminal justice system, receive a minimally adequate dosage of
> drug treatment. Perhaps as few as 5 to 15 percent achieve extended abstinence.
> (p. 6)

Thus, those on probation and parole seem to require special interventions
that go above and beyond the standard care they received in community-
based addiction treatment during the critical first three months of treatment
in the 1990s, as data from DATOS show. In this vein, Marlowe (2003, p. 6) acknowledges how "these figures are national averages for treatment-as-usual
in community-based settings, and it is possible that particular regimens may
be more successful at retaining offenders in treatment." And, research has

yet to determine "whether some treatment interventions may be more acceptable to offender populations or superior for retaining offenders in treatment in noninstitutional settings" (Marlowe, 2003, p. 6).

Given the role of individual and program factors in impacting retention, NIDA (1999) specifies such factors. Individual factors related to engagement and retention in treatment include motivation to change drug-using behavior; degree of support from family and friends; and whether there is pressure to stay in treatment from the criminal justice system, child-protection services, employers, or the family. Program factors include the degree of success counselors attain in establishing a positive therapeutic relationship with the client; whether a treatment plan is established and followed so that a client knows what to expect during treatment; and whether medical, psychiatric, and social services are available to meet vital client needs.

Research has found differences across program types with regard to clients' receipt of services in the critical first three months in treatment. Fletcher, Broome, Delany, Shields, and Flynn (2003) found through data from DATOS that those clients in long-term residential programs received more services on average than did outpatients during this critical three-month period, while receipt of few services in the first three months of treatment was the general norm. Also, those with more service needs at the time of entry into treatment were more likely to relapse to drug use and reenter treatment, according to data from DATOS (Grella, Hser, & Hsieh, 2003). Specific client characteristics may also have contributed to relapse and treatment reentry, such as being an African American, having a prior history of being married, using cocaine at least weekly after treatment discharge (Grella, Hser, & Hsieh, 2003), and being a male with antisocial personality disorder (Grella, Joshi, & Hser, 2003).

Other analyses of DATOS data have examined outcomes with regard to cocaine use, employment, and illegal activity. Such multiproblem clients are in fact the focus of this book. However, there is a continuum of outpatient addiction-treatment programs in community-based settings, spanning from those that are low intensity and offer little more than drug education and admonition to those that provide intensive day treatment, being "comparable to residential programs in services and effectiveness, depending on individual patient's characteristics and needs" (NIDA, 1999, p. 27). Some even provide medical and mental-health services to meet clients' needs (NIDA, 1999). Thus, it is important to keep in mind the role of not only retention and duration, or how *extensive* treatment may be, but also how *intensive* treatment is designed to be, especially for challenging contemporary clients. But Moos (2003) supports the need to shift resources from intensive to extensive care, emphasizing the duration of care in light of research findings to support this shift.

Consistent with this, others caution that length of stay may be an incomplete predictor of successful treatment in such outcome studies

(Zarkin, Dunlap, Bray, & Wechsberg, 2002). For example, using data on clients in drug-free outpatient settings from the National Treatment Improvement Evaluation Study, it was found that, when holding length of stay constant, employment at follow-up for those clients who completed their planned treatment was almost two times that of clients who did not complete treatment (Zarkin et al., 2002). Similarly, in another study using a quasi-experimental design with a large sample from three states, it was found that those clients who completed treatment were 22 to 49 percent more likely than those who did not complete treatment to be employed and earning higher wages in the year following treatment, holding other variables constant (The TOPPS-II Interstate Cooperative Group, 2003). Thus, beyond retention alone, duration or degree of extensiveness of treatment appears to impact important client-treatment outcomes.

With regard to the "something more" that may be required to sustain recovery over time, data from DATOS with opiod-dependent clients in methadone-maintenance treatment programs who were considered to be effectively recovering at 5-year follow-up are informative. Flynn, Joe, Broome, Simpson, and Brown (2003) reported that the 28 percent who could be considered recovering indicated that their success was related to relying upon personal motivation, treatment experiences, religion/spirituality, a social-support network of family/friends, and their job/career.

McLellan et al. (1997) considered the available body of evidence as a whole, including both national evaluation studies and experimental protocols. They asserted that there was substantial supportive evidence that addiction treatment, in general, works, the data having been accumulated with regard to varied inpatient, outpatient, and residential settings, as well as for treatments for different addictions, whether to alcohol, cocaine, heroin, or methadone-maintenance treatments (Anglin & Hser, 1990; Ball & Ross, 1991; De Leon, 1984; Gerstein & Harwood, 1990; Hubbard & Marsden, 1986; Institute of Medicine, 1990; McLellan, Luborsky, Woody, & O'Brien, 1982; Miller & Hester, 1986; Saxe, 1983; Simpson & Savage, 1980). McLellan et al. (1997, p. 718) elaborate with regard to how addiction treatment "can be effective in reducing substance use and in bringing about improvements in the areas of employment, criminal activity, social adjustment and use of health care resources." NIDA (1999, p. 15) similarly concluded that, overall, the "treatment of addiction is as successful as treatment of other chronic diseases, such as diabetes, hypertension, and asthma." This conclusion is based on research studies showing that drug treatment reduces drug use by "40 to 60 percent and significantly decreases criminal activity during and after treatment" (NIDA, 1999, p. 15). Also, treatment can "improve prospects for employment, with gains of up to 40 percent after treatment" (NIDA, 1999, p. 16).

Worthy of consideration are the findings from Project MATCH (1997a, 1997b, 1998a, 1998b, 2001), commonly referred to as the largest and most expensive research study ever conducted in the alcoholism field (Marlatt, 1999). Project MATCH found that twelve-step facilitation (TSF), cognitive-behavioral therapy (CBT), and motivational-enhancement therapy (MET) were equally effective in reducing drinking rates from baseline to one-year posttreatment. TSF involved twelve weekly sessions with a professional who introduced clients to the first five steps of AA and encouraged involvement in AA; CBT involved a professional therapist teaching coping skills for use in high-risk situations and with emotional states associated with relapse, as well as promoting the practice of drink-refusal skills, coping with urges to drink, and learning to manage negative moods over twelve individual sessions; and MET involved four individual sessions with a professional who used principles of motivational psychology, encouraged reflection on the impact of alcohol on their lives, and helped the client develop a plan to stop drinking. The results of Project MATCH stimulated much controversy, especially as little support was found for the efficacy of matching treatments to subject characteristics, and insufficient criteria for a treatment-efficacy study were met, such as use of a control group, creating serious limitations (Marlatt, 1999).

Other findings of note include how clients low in psychiatric severity had more days of abstinence upon receipt of TSF, relative to receipt of CBT, with neither intervention being superior for those clients with higher levels of psychiatric severity (Marlatt, 1999). Others emphasize that the finding that MET works well for clients who are initially angry partly justifies the belief that motivational interviewing has application with the offender population and is adaptable for use in criminal-justice settings with deployment by a variety of professionals (Ginsburg, Mann, Rotgers, & Weekes, 2002, p. 339). But, MET was least effective for clients who had social-support networks that reinforced the problem behavior of drinking, such as in the case where a significant other may deflate motivation for change or is willing to engage in the problem behavior with the client (Burke, Vassilev, Kantchelov, & Zweben, 2002). And, some emphasize that the findings of support for MET are with what is considered an adaptation of motivational interviewing (Burke, Arkowitz, & Dunn, 2002).

Marlatt (1999) asserts that generalization of the results of Project MATCH to real-world treatment is limited, lending support to the views of Goldfried and Wolfe (1996), who critique the generalizability of results that are obtained from treatment-efficacy studies within the clinical-trial paradigm; this is partly due to the use of rigorous inclusion and exclusion criteria for the selection of research participants. As the number of inclusion and exclusion criteria increases, the generalizability of the findings from treatment-efficacy research decreases, and the differential effectiveness of different treatment orientations, if they exist, are less likely to emerge. Goldfried and Wolfe (1996) call this the interpretability/generalizability dilemma, thereby providing a possible explanation as to why no differences were found in the effectiveness of TSF, CBT, and MET when delivered in individual sessions by well-trained professionals to clients who met certain inclusion and exclusion criteria (Marlatt, 1999).

The extensive exclusion criteria in Project MATCH barred clients with the following characteristics: dependence on a sedative/hypnotic, stimulant, opiate, or cocaine; use of IV drugs in the previous six months; suicidality, homicidality, or acute psychosis or organic impairment; probation/parole requirements that might interfere with participation; chance of residential instability or lack of a "locator" person to assist in tracking for follow-up assessments; current or planned involvement with alternative alcohol treatment other than that provided as part of the study; and lack of transportation to individual therapy sessions (Marlatt, 1999; Project MATCH Research Group, 1997a). As Marlatt (1999) suggests, the result was an extremely homogenous sample of clients, one "very different from the known heterogeneity of the alcohol dependent population" (p. 58). The homogenous nature of the sample is also quite different from the characteristics, needs, and diversity to be found among the multiproblem clients that are the focus of this book. Of note, Sayre et al. (2004) emphasize how recruitment strategies and screening processes in outpatient substance-abuse-treatment trials can create selection bias in study recruitment, with resulting differences between research subjects and the overall population affecting generalizability of study findings. One result of exclusion criteria is the underrepresentation of clients who are African American, low income, or present comorbidity involving substance abuse and psychiatric problems (Humphreys & Weisner, 2000; Moos, 2003).

Nonetheless, Project MATCH's findings seem consistent with the assertion that treatment programs with diverse ideologies are effective in reducing substance abuse and improving psychosocial outcomes (Moos, 2003). Moos (2003) also addresses the common criticism of Project MATCH, that it lacked an untreated comparison group that might have had comparable outcomes had they remained untreated. Moos (2003) points toward a body of studies concluding that receipt of formal treatment interventions produces better outcomes than remaining untreated.

The Heterogeneity of Clients with Addictive Behaviors in the Real World: What Works?

But, Moos (2003) also emphasizes, after more than thirty years as a stellar researcher in the field of addiction treatment, how the findings of tightly controlled empirical studies may not generalize to the real-world contexts in which practitioners work, nor may the treatments studied necessarily work with diverse populations. Efficacy trials provide only one specific context for observation (Moos, 2003).

Isralowitz (2002, p. 177) similarly asserts that contemporary clients in addiction treatment "are not a homogenous group and, in theory, the needs of each client should be matched, preferably to a service system characterized by rational, flexible, responsive, well defined, short- and long-term integrated service plans." Isralowitz (2002) points out that such an approach would require dependable funding sources with ongoing monitoring and evaluation, something generally absent in the United States.

In a similar vein, Bandura (1997) suggests that, in light of "the heterogeneity of alcohol abuse and its multiform determinants, treatment goals and strategies must be tailored to the particular constellation of determinants operating in any given case" (p. 357). One must add to this consideration of those determinants operating in any given case, those that are operating at any particular point in time, in light of a client's stage of change (DiClemente & Velasquez, 2002) or a client's phase of treatment and recovery (Wallace, 1992e, 1996a, 1996b, 1996c).

Some envision an ideal world in which practitioners participate in a comprehensive and empirically sound chemical-dependency treatment system characterized by the implementation of interventions that have been found to be effective through empirical evaluation, while also systematically collecting data to evaluate program effectiveness (Adler, Richter, Lorenz, & Hochhausen, 2002). Given some isolated trends suggesting that this is happening in the United States under conditions of grant funding for research, some rejoice that it is not only in the ivory tower that empirically based treatments are being delivered (Larimer, 2002). However, the majority of community-based addiction-treatment centers lack funding to conduct evaluations of program effectiveness, even if they are able to deliver comprehensive services, including those that are empirically sound.

In light of the available body of data on empirically based treatment interventions, some even ask what is a new valid research question (Larimer, 2002): How much of the "ideal" do we need to implement in the field? This is especially the case when practitioners face constraints involving time, resources, and managed-care dictates with an emphasis on the delivery of brief interventions, which often translates into minimal contact time with clients.

WHAT DO WE KNOW OR THINK WE KNOW?

Moos (2003), on the other hand, is proud to derive principles of effective addiction treatment and recovery based on treatment-outcome studies with a diverse heterogeneous sample that included those of varied genders, races, marital statuses, education, employment, and treatment histories. Taking a vantage point examining the past thirty years of research, Moos (2003) articulates seven principles of effective treatment and recovery, summarized in table 3.1. These seven principles of effective treatment and recovery represent what we know or think we know. Moos (2003, p. 3) recognizes the manner in which progress has occurred in the addiction-treatment field, given

Table 3.1. Moos's (2003) Seven Principles: What Do We Know?

Principle 1: Treated or untreated, an addiction is not an island unto itself.
- Clients with addictive disorders exist in a complex web of social forces, and stable factors in clients' lives, such as ongoing social resources, play an enduring role.
- Clients who establish and maintain relatively positive social contexts are likely to recover; and treatment directed toward improving clients' life circumstances is likely helpful.

Principle 2: Common dynamics underlie the process of problem resolution that occurs in formal treatment, informal care, and natural recovery.
- Clients usually use informal help (family, friend, physician, AA) first; and, when that fails, formal help is especially needed when a client has few personal or social resources.
- There is no compelling reason to distinguish between the influence of informal (family, friend, spouse, AA sponsor, etc.) and formal (counselor, therapist, etc.) help; and any distinction between life-context and informal help or formal treatment is arbitrary.

Principle 3: The duration and continuity of care are more closely related to treatment outcome than is the amount or intensity of care.
- Duration of care is more important than amount of care, as longer duration of care is associated with better outcomes, and resources need to shift from intensive to extensive care.

Principle 4: Patients treated by substance-abuse or mental-health specialists experience better outcomes than do patients treated by primary-care or nonspecialty providers.
- Clients who receive specialty care (e.g., addiction counselors, social workers, etc.) receive more services, more appropriate care, are more satisfied with their care, and have better treatment outcomes than do comparable clients seen only in the general medical sector.

Principle 5: Treatment settings and counselors who establish a therapeutic alliance, are oriented toward personal growth goals, and are moderately structured tend to promote positive outcomes.
- Counselors who are more empathic and able to establish a therapeutic alliance enhance their clients' involvement in treatment and treatment outcomes; and, to motivate clients to improve, counselors need to set specific performance goals and to maintain an appropriate level of structure.
- The finding that a positive treatment alliance predicts good treatment outcome may be due in part to a relatively structured focus on clients' real-life social contexts and coping skills.

Principle 6: The common component of effective psychosocial interventions is the focus on helping clients shape and adapt to their life circumstances.
- Most effective psychosocial modalities are cognitive-behavioral interventions, social-skills training, stress management/relapse prevention, a community reinforcement approach, motivational interviewing, behavioral contracting, and behavioral marital therapy.
- All focus primarily on enhancing clients' coping with daily life, developing clients' social skills, improving matches between clients' abilities and environmental demands, and altering reinforcement patterns in clients' community settings.

Principle 7: Among individuals who recognize a problem and are willing or motivated to receive help, formal intervention or treatment leads to better outcomes than does remaining untreated.
- Whether brief interventions or formal treatment, treatment is better than no treatment.

how an integrated biopsychosocial orientation and a theoretical paradigm of evaluation research have "supplanted earlier adherence to an oversimplified biomedical model and reliance on a restrictive methodological approach to treatment evaluation."

Reflecting some overlap with the work of Moos (2003), the National Institute on Drug Abuse (NIDA, 1999) also put forth principles of drug-addiction treatment as a research-based guide. NIDA's principles also stand on three decades of scientific research and clinical practice.

NIDA's thirteen principles of effective treatment are presented in table 3.2. NIDA (1999) concludes that a body of research has yielded a variety of effective approaches to drug-addiction treatment.

SELECTING FROM THE MENU OF EVIDENCE-BASED OPTIONS

Examining the list of effective psychosocial modalities that Moos (2003) summarizes under principle 6 in table 3.1, one may perceive, in essence, a menu of effective alternatives or effective psychosocial modalities: cognitive-behavioral interventions, social-skills training, stress management and relapse prevention, a community-reinforcement approach, motivational interviewing, behavioral contracting, and behavioral marital therapy. Reflecting much overlap, NIDA (1999) similarly highlights for use with adults using illicit drugs and alcohol the following scientifically based approaches to addiction treatment: relapse prevention, supportive-expressive psychotherapy, individualized drug counseling, motivational-enhancement therapy, the community-reinforcement approach (CRA) plus vouchers, day treatment with abstinence contingencies and vouchers, and the Matrix Model. The identified interventions reflect how treatment approaches derived from diverse ideologies are all effective in reducing substance use and improving psychosocial outcomes, all helping clients to understand, adapt to, and alter their life circumstances (Moos, 2003).

The reality is that practitioners now have "an array of alternatives with reasonable empirical support, offering a choice among promising options" (Miller & Hester, 2003, p. 1). An important guide for practitioners in deciding what treatments to use from the menu of available options comes from Miller, Wilbourne, and Hettema (2003), who offer the analogy of facing a life-threatening physical illness. Given a substantial treatment-outcome literature in a field such as alcoholism, would anyone want one's doctor to select the treatment most likely to give the best chance for recovery, or would one accept a doctor saying, "I really don't pay much attention to that scientific stuff" (p. 13)? Clearly, contemporary practitioners must know which treatments have a body of empirical support for their use and learn how to deploy evidence-based addiction-treatment interventions, adapting them as needed given client characteristics, needs, and preferences.

Table 3.2. NIDA's (1999) Thirteen Principles of Effective Drug Treatment

Principle 1. No single treatment is appropriate for all individuals.
- Matching treatment settings, interventions, and services to each individual's problems and needs is critical.

Principle 2. Treatment needs to be readily available.
- Potential treatment applicants can be lost if treatment is not immediately available or is not readily accessible.

Principle 3: Effective treatment attends to multiple needs of the individual, not just his or her drug use.
- Associated medical, psychological, social, vocational, and legal problems must be addressed.

Principle 4: An individual's treatment and services plan must be assessed continually and modified as necessary to ensure that the plan meets the person's changing needs.
- Varying combinations of services and treatment components may be needed during the course of treatment and recovery (e.g., medical, family, parenting, vocational, social, legal).

Principle 5: Remaining in treatment for an adequate period of time is critical for treatment effectiveness.
- Research suggests a minimum of three months in treatment, and additional time can produce further progress in treatment, suggesting the importance of retention strategies.

Principle 6: Counseling (individual and/or group) and other behavioral therapies are critical components of effective treatment for addiction.
- Therapy addresses motivation, skills building, replacing drug activities, and problem solving.
- Behavioral therapy facilitates interpersonal relationships and family/community functioning.

Principle 7: Medications are an important element of treatment for many patients, especially when combined with counseling and other behavioral therapies.
- For example, methadone, levo-alpha-acetylmethadol (LAAM), naltrexone, psychiatric medications.

Principle 8: Addicted or drug-abusing individuals with coexisting mental disorders should have both disorders treated in an integrated way.
- Clients presenting for either condition should be assessed and treated for comorbidity.

Principle 9: Medical detoxification is only the first stage of addiction treatment and by itself does little to change long-term drug use.
- Medical detoxification safely manages acute physical symptoms of withdrawal where needed.

Principle 10: Treatment does not need to be voluntary to be effective.
- Sanctions, enticements, coercion, and mandates can increase significantly both treatment entry and retention rates, as well as the success of treatment interventions.

Principle 11: Possible drug use during treatment must be monitored continuously.
- Urinalysis or other tests detect lapses, help clients withstand urges to use drugs, permit changes in the treatment plan, and require feedback to clients testing positive.

Principle 12: Treatment programs should provide assessment for HIV/AIDS, hepatitis B and C, tuberculosis and other infectious diseases, and counseling to help patients modify or change behaviors that place themselves or others at risk of infection.
- Counseling helps clients to avoid high-risk behavior, or helps those infected manage illness.

Principle 13: Recovery from drug addiction can be a long-term process and frequently requires multiple episodes of treatment.
- As with other chronic illnesses, relapse can occur, necessitating multiple treatment episodes.

Some practitioners may be in danger of being "uninformed and undisciplined eclectic therapist[s]" (Miller & Hester, 2003, p.1). Miller, Wilbourne, and Hettema (2003) acknowledge that there "does not seem to be any one treatment approach adequate to the task of treating all individuals with alcohol problems" (p. 41). Thus, consistent with the recommendations of the Institute of Medicine (1990), Miller, Wilbourne, and Hettema (2003) find hope in focusing on a menu of effective alternatives and selecting what seems most appropriate in order to meet individual client needs, characteristics, and preferences. And the challenge of treating multiproblem clients in the real world may mean assembling from the choices therein an appropriate combination of elements for each individual client.

It is important to take what Miller, Wilbourne, and Hettema (2003) refer to as evidence-based treatments or effective alternatives, and what Moos (2003) calls effective psychosocial modalities, as the practitioner's starting point. Metaphorically, holding menu in hand, practitioners should carefully review and become familiar with what is on the menu, following appropriate recommendations. But, in the case of alcoholism treatment, there is a gap between science and practice, with little overlap between what is actually employed in the United States in alcoholism-treatment programs and what the research demonstrates to be effective. There is a similar gap between research and practice in the field of substance abuse (Sorenson, Guydish, Rawson, & Zweben, 2003). Practitioners may also be impacted by what is realistically available in their social context for placement in the menu of options they hold in hand. Nonetheless, practitioners must be both informed and disciplined, relinquishing views and practices that do not stand up to the test of evidence (Miller, Wilbourne, & Hettema, 2003, p. 41).

The Need for Practitioner Fidelity and Flexibility When Selecting from the Menu of Evidence-Based Options

Practitioners, holding the menu of evidence-based options in hand, and selecting from that menu those that are best suited for meeting individual client needs, characteristics, and preferences, also contend with issues of fidelity and flexibility. Moos (2002) discusses the issue of fidelity versus flexibility. This involves real-world practitioners' fidelity to what is recommended to them, given findings of what treatments are empirically supported, what is recommended via expert-consensus guidelines, and what is written in manual-guided interventions, versus practitioners exercising flexibility in the real-world treatment context.

Practitioner flexibility may also be essential, given the lack of the kind of resources available to those conducting grant-funded empirical research. Flexibility is also required when working with diverse multiproblem clients with complex needs.

For example, Riggs et al. (2003) found that clients with comorbid post-traumatic stress disorder (PTSD) and alcohol dependence (AD) had more unemployment, lower income, and less social support—living without the support of a spouse or intimate—when compared to those with either PTSD alone or AD alone, creating a risk for premature termination from treatment focusing on alleviation of PTSD symptoms. Riggs et al. (2003, p. 1726) suggest that practitioners may need to be "flexible with regard to scheduling or rescheduling appointments and managing" those who arrive late for appointments due to practical barriers such as lack of money, transportation, or childcare, for example. Thus, clients with such extreme functional difficulties may also need practitioners who attend to the "emotional difficulties arising from these functional deficits" (Riggs et al., 2003, pp. 1726, 1727). Such difficulties are frequently found among contemporary multiproblem clients entering community-based addiction treatment.

Other requisite practitioner flexibilities follow from viewing and respecting clients as consumers. As consumers, clients also have the ability to select from a menu of viable treatment options that practitioners, peers, or advocates share with them, versus being assigned to a particular treatment by professionals following treatment-matching criteria (Marlatt, 1999, p. 45). In this regard, Moos (2003) points to the advocacy principle of "nothing about us without us," and speculates on what providers are to do when clients prefer an emphasis on personal growth and quality of life over an evidence-based symptom-reduction approach, all of which is consistent with the reemerging humanitarian, recovery-based model that values clients' personal experiences, responsibility, choice, and empowerment (e.g., Frese, Stanley, Kress, & Vogel-Scibilia, 2001). Therefore, practitioners face a new valid question: How can we implement evidence-based practices and yet fully incorporate clients' preferences into clinical decision making (Moos, 2003)? Clearly, the task of practitioners balancing fidelity and flexibility is a critical, ongoing one.

What Is the Value of Naturalistic Longitudinal Observations?

Through the method of naturalistic longitudinal observation, practitioners may offer invaluable insights regarding what happens in real-world contexts when they deploy empirically proven interventions, and regarding the kind of flexibility that is often required of practitioners in order to meet client characteristics, needs, and preferences. Moos (2002) values the research tradition involving naturalistic longitudinal observation of treatment as an alternative valid research tradition, aside from tightly controlled empirical evaluations of addiction treatments. The results of naturalistic longitudinal observation, as reported by practitioners, can create a vital feedback loop to empirical researchers regarding the manner in which flexibility versus fidelity gets played out with numerous clients over time. For example, practitioners may discover what works or seems to work with clients who differ demographically from those clients in empirical trials of treatment interventions. Practitioners who provide naturalistic longitudinal observations may be able to transmit important information, such as the nuances involved in forming therapeutic alliances and cultivating relationships based on the effective deployment of empathy with those most difficult clients with challenging characteristics such as having incarceration, mental disorders, homelessness, violence, or victimization in their histories, making them poor candidates for successful engagement and follow-up in empirical trials of treatment. Consistent with Moos's (2002) emphasis upon how not only individual but community health is impacted by these clients and their experiences in treatment, as well as his emphasis upon the essential role of the social context and extra treatment factors in the recovery process, practitioners engaged in naturalistic longitudinal observation may also provide a more complete picture of real-world recovery than is attainable in tightly controlled empirical studies. (See the case of Mr. K. X. in chapter 9.)

Tucker (1999) provides support for the views of Moos (2002) with regard to the value of longitudinal naturalistic observation. Tucker (1999) challenges the assumption that efficacy studies using randomized trials are the best research strategy for evaluating behavior-change initiatives such as psychotherapy, given that they search for true effects of the intervention and view patient and contextual variables as error variance (pp. 13, 22). Thus, randomized clinical trials seek to reduce error variance "by studying homogenous patient groups and by standardizing their research experiences except for variations that are the focus of the investigation" (p. 22). However, the variables and processes that randomized clinical trials treat as error variance or nuisance factors, such as compliance patterns, client expectations, helping processes, and behavior change over time in the absence of interventions, should actually be understood as key elements in behavior change and the delivery of psychotherapy and addiction treatment (p. 23). Thus, Tucker (1999) argues that it is highly inappropriate for the field of addiction to follow the medical model's use of the randomized clinical trial as the gold standard for efficacy research, given that behavior "change is a process, not a discrete event, that typically unfolds over time and depends to a large degree on the surrounding context" (p. 23). Tucker (1999) concludes that research on behavior change should be expanded to include "naturalistic studies of behavior change among persons with a range of help-seeking experiences, including studies of treatment effectiveness when clients self-select their interventions" (p. 24). And, if findings from randomized clinical trials and naturalistic studies of behavior change converge on similar inferences, then confidence in generalizations about behavior change will increase (p. 24).

The kind of changes in research of addiction-treatment efficacy that Tucker (1999) proposes are of vital importance, helping to move the field away from a paternalistic approach wherein the dissemination of research findings to practitioners occurs in a top-down fashion, largely from empirical researchers. Instead, following the recommendations of Moos (2002) and Tucker (1999) will foster the implementation of research strategies that tend to "operate within the worldview of practitioners and health care consumers" and yield more easily applied research findings (Tucker, 1999, p. 25). It is important to study situations in which clients experience treatment being "adjusted as consumer needs, preferences, and resources change over the course of treatment," versus treatment being "standardized within treatment conditions and not adjusted based on recipient responses, except when life-threatening developments occur" (Tucker, 1999, p. 25). Tucker (1999) concludes that, despite skepticism about the accuracy and value of naturalistic research in general, "it is a bias the field must set aside in an expanded perspective on addictive behavior change" (p. 26).

In support of this, Bandura (1997) offers the following views:

> The self-efficacy of regulation of refractory behavior over extended intervals is poorly elucidated by the static investigation procedure that is routinely used. It is a method of convenience rather than of explanatory merit. The behavior of interest is simply measured at a few arbitrary follow-up points, but the factors that supposedly regulate it at those times are not studied. The behavior is thus disembodied from its current determinants and is instead linked to past determinants. Maintenance processes are best clarified by microanalysis of ongoing self-regulation, rather than by changing behavior and then merely reassessing it weeks, months, or years later. . . . Diverse changes can and often do occur during those prolonged intervals. Some people maintain steadfast control, others lapse but recover quickly, others escalate lapses into prolonged relapses, and still others may have cycled from relapse to abstinence one or more times. The status at any point in time in this fluctuating dynamic process may or may not be representative of the self-regulatory attainments. Repeated analysis of covariance of behavior and its postulated determinants sheds light on how self-regulatory mechanisms operate and the conditions under which they malfunction, either temporarily or more enduringly. (p. 294)

Following Institute of Medicine (1990) recommendations, practitioners may engage in simple outcome monitoring in search of associations between some particular variable and a successful outcome, a methodology readily implemented in clinical treatment settings, versus relying on the randomized clinical trial as the sole criterion for conducting treatment-matching studies (Marlatt, 1999).

For example, when clients with the characteristics of severe psychiatric symptoms refuse to take their prescribed medication, the likely outcome is a greater risk of relapse. A practitioner who observes this pattern with regard to a determinant of relapse on several occasions may embrace a strategy associated with a successful outcome. This might involve clients with comorbidity entering into a formal contingency contract at intake, specifying how their admission to and retention within community-based addiction treatment is contingent upon their agreeing to take their prescribed medication. No randomized clinical trial within a community-based addiction-treatment program is necessary to formally endorse the practitioner's finding that the client characteristic or variable of severe psychiatric symptoms is associated with a successful outcome when clients adhere to prescribed medication regimes. However, this observation might lead to research investigating the value of such a contingency contract at intake evaluation.

As this example shows, practitioners who engage in naturalistic longitudinal observation of clients and their processes and progress over time are poised to engage in a microanalysis of ongoing self-regulation. Such a microanalysis may make an invaluable contribution to an understanding of the current determinants of behavior as they operate in real-world contexts, as well as lead to valuable treatment practices.

Practitioners collecting longitudinal naturalistic observations in their work with multiple cases over time may offer findings of what works prior to empirical researchers' seeking to demonstrate efficacy of that technique or intervention through empirical investigation. Indeed, this is the history of the origin of most evidence-based addiction treatments. First there were findings in the field that led to a good cause for empirical investigation as to whether an intervention did indeed work under the conditions of tight controls. And, regardless of which comes first—the practitioner's field observation or empirical results—when findings from randomized clinical trials and naturalistic studies of behavior change converge, one may declare that this is indeed what may be recommended for practical use. Thus, it is in the real world with challenging, complex, multiproblem clients that the actual art is practiced of both discovering (perhaps tentatively) what works, as well as forging real-world adaptations of evidence-based addiction-treatment interventions found to be effective under the tight controls of a clinical trial.

CONCLUSION

This chapter presented a large body of research to establish that mandated addiction treatment, and addiction treatment in general, work, systematically presenting what is known in the addiction-treatment field at this point in time. A critical finding was that an integrated approach that combines criminal-justice supervision and involvement in community-based addiction treatment is ideal, insofar as it addresses both concerns about public safety and public health. Moreover, the recommended integrated model contains an important role for contemporary practitioners within community-based addiction treatment, as this book seeks to underscore. In addition, discussion went on to suggest that there is indeed a menu of options containing a variety of treatment interventions with empirical support. These are effective alternatives or effective psychosocial modalities derived from diverse ideologies, all of which focus upon enhancing clients' competence in coping with daily life, developing clients' social skills, improving the match between clients' abilities and environmental demands, and altering reinforcement patterns in clients' community settings.

Contemporary practitioners may need to practice both fidelity and flexibility when selecting from this available menu of options or menu of effective alternatives or menu of effective psychosocial modalities that they metaphorically hold in hand. There are many reasons for this requisite fidelity and flexibility, including the need to integrate and tailor treatment to meet an individual client's distinct pattern of multiple problems, characteristics, needs, and preferences. There is also a valuable role for practitioners in offering feedback to researchers, as practitioners deploy recommended practice guidelines that follow from research, in addition to contributing practitioner findings from naturalistic longitudinal observations in the real world with heterogeneous clients.

4

◆

The Recommended Menu of Options for Practitioners

Making mandated addiction treatment work with a diverse and growing population of mandated, coerced, and concerned clients means both having knowledge of evidence-based addiction-treatment interventions (Carroll, 1997; Khantzian, Halliday, & McAuliffe, 1990; Marlatt, 1999; Marlowe et al., 2003; Miller, Brown, et al., 1995; Miller & Heather, 1998; Miller, Wilbourne, & Hettema, 2003; Moos, 2003; NIDA, 1999; Sorenson et al., 2003) and recommended state-of-the-art practices rooted in naturalistic longitudinal observation (Levin, 1999, 2001; Miller & Rollnick, 1991; Tatarsky, 2003; Wallace, 1991b, 1996a, 1996b, 1996c; Wurmser, 1992; Yalisove, 1997). These evidence-based addiction-treatment interventions and recommended state-of-the-art practices may be thought of as that which is on the contemporary menu of options held in hand by practitioners working in community-based addiction treatment. Just as in the field of alcoholism treatment, those in the field of addiction treatment may follow Miller, Wilbourne, and Hettema (2003) and find hope in focusing on a menu of effective alternatives and selecting what seems most appropriate in order to meet individual client needs, characteristics, and preferences.

As we saw in chapter 3, Moos (2003) considered a number of reviews of research in concluding that the most effective psychosocial modalities for the effective treatment of addictive disorders are the following: cognitive-behavioral interventions, stress management and relapse prevention (RP), social-skills training (SST), a community-reinforcement approach (CRA), behavioral contracting, and behavioral marital therapy. With the exception of behavioral marital therapy, this chapter will recommend a menu of evidence-based options that reflects the use of all of these, or the adaptation of each of these evidence-based psychosocial modalities. Similarly, as reviewed in chapter 3, NIDA (1999) cited the following as scientifically based approaches to drug-addiction treatment with adults: RP, supportive-expressive psychotherapy, individualized drug counseling, motivational-enhancement therapy (MET), the CRA plus vouchers, day treatment with abstinence contingencies and vouchers, and the Matrix Model. Again, nearly all of these, with the exception of any use of vouchers, will be placed on the menu of evidence-based options, reflecting overlap between what is deemed effective by Moos (2003) and NIDA (1999). And, in addition, to what appears on these two overlapping lists of effective treatments, another evidence-based intervention is added: building a strong positive therapeutic alliance with clients and helping clients develop a strong, enduring social-support network; this is added as an evidence-based intervention, in and of itself, given Moos's (2003) summary of research on the importance of the social context, supportive social networks, and formal and informal helping relationships.

This book embraces the goal of describing an adaptation of evidence-based interventions to multiproblem clients in the real world, emphasizing the need to integrate interventions as needed in order to forge a comprehensive treatment approach and tailor treatment for individual clients. Also, the goal is to empower practitioners in community-based addiction treatment to work effectively with contemporary multiproblem clients who are mandated, coerced, or concerned about their illicit-drug and/or alcohol involvement. In order to achieve these goals, this chapter presents the final recommended menu of options or effective alternatives, containing seven selections on the menu, discussed as interventions falling under category 1. Meanwhile, given the value of what practitioners have learned from longitudinal naturalistic observation, also recommended are state-of-the-art practices, including the integration of approaches arising from diverse theories, models, and ideologies; these are presented as seven selections on the menu that fall under category 2. Thus, a total of fourteen selections on the menu of what is recommended to practitioners as evidence-based addiction-treatment interventions and state-of-the-art practices will be presented and discussed in this chapter.

THE SEVEN MENU ITEMS UNDER CATEGORY 1: EVIDENCE-BASED ADDICTION TREATMENT

The seven recommended evidence-based addiction-treatment interventions, or menu items available for selection, are listed in table 4.1 within category 1. These will each be discussed in greater detail in this section, presenting both a brief review of supportive evidence and the key elements of the intervention.

Table 4.1.   Practitioner's Menu of Options: Effective Alternatives Available for Selection in the Social Context

Category 1: Seven evidence-based addiction treatments
   1. Special focus on building a strong therapeutic alliance/social-support network (TASS)
   2. Motivational interviewing/motivational-enhancement therapy (MET)/brief interventions
   3. Cognitive-behavioral therapy (CBT)/relapse prevention (RP)/social-skills training (SST)
   4. Twelve-step facilitation (TSF)/guidance using Alcoholics and/or Narcotics Anonymous
   5. Individual drug counseling (IDC) and/or supportive-expressive psychotherapy (SEP)
   6. Community reinforcement approach (CRA)/vouchers: contingency management (CM)
   7. The Matrix Model—or, a day-treatment approach, or an IEC outpatient model that is *I* for intensive (4–5 days per week), *E* for extensive (6–12 months), and *C* for comprehensive (TASS, CBT/RP, IDC, group drug counseling [GDC], drug testing, etc.)
Category 2: Seven recommended state-of-the-art practices
   1. Integration of motivational interviewing and stages of change
   2. Integration of stages of change and phases of treatment and recovery
   3. Integration of harm reduction, moderation approaches, and abstinence models
   4. Integration of psychoanalytic and cognitive-behavioral theories and techniques
   5. Acquisition of affective, behavioral, and cognitive coping skills—learning new ABCs
   6. Integration of motivational interviewing, stages of change, and identity development theory for a diverse identity involving race, sexual orientation, and/or disability
   7. Incorporating contemporary trends in psychology: Multiculturalism, positive psychology, the strengths-based approach, and optimistic thinking/learned optimism

1. Special Focus on Building a Strong Therapeutic Alliance/Social-Support Network (TASS)

Following the analysis of Moos (2003), there is justification for raising to the level of an evidence-based intervention, practitioners' placing a special focus on helping clients to build a strong therapeutic alliance and social-support network (TASS). Further support for this strategy comes from the work of Lebow, Moos, Kelly, and Knobloch-Fedders (2002). Lebow et al. (2002) go beyond what has been codified in treatment manuals for empirically based treatments (e.g., Budney & Higgins, 1998; Carroll, 1998; Daley & Mercer, 2002; Mercer & Woody, 1999) and identify key ingredients in effective alcohol and drug treatment. Lebow et al. (2002) reviewed the research literature on addiction treatment in search of any findings that relate relationship factors to outcome. As part of their search they had to go beyond findings in randomized clinical trials and examined many correlational studies, articulating these findings as sixteen principles that codify what is "probably efficacious" in fostering good treatment outcomes. As a consequence of their research analysis, Lebow et al. (2002) highlight key relationship factors, as well as the impact of these factors on treatment outcome. Table 4.2 presents the sixteen principles.

What emerges from the work of Lebow et al. (2002) is an evidence-based approach for placing a special focus on helping clients to build the kind of

Table 4.2.   Lebow et al.'s (2002) Sixteen Principles for Producing Positive Treatment Outcomes

Principle 1—When a stronger helping relationship is established at the initial intake or assessment interview, the client is more likely to enter treatment.

Principle 2—When a stronger alliance is established, the client is likely to remain in treatment longer and to complete the treatment episode.

Principle 3—When a stronger alliance is established, the client is more likely to explore problems in treatment. Yet, when the therapist is more confrontational, the client is more likely to show negative in-treatment behavior.

Principle 4—When a stronger alliance is established, the client tends to experience less distress and more pleasant mood during treatment.

Principle 5—When the therapist establishes a stronger alliance with the client, the client is more likely to abstain from alcohol and drugs during treatment and show more improvement in patterns of use of other substances.

Principle 6—When the therapist establishes a stronger alliance with the client, the client tends to experience better outcomes related to substance use.

Principle 7—A strong treatment alliance may have an especially beneficial influence on specific subgroups of clients, such as those who have an antisocial personality or have high levels of anger.

Principle 8—When treatment programs create a stronger alliance with clients (that is, are involving, supportive, and expressive), patients are more likely to remain in treatment and to have better in-program outcomes.

Principle 9—When treatment programs create a stronger alliance with clients (that is, are involving, supportive, and expressive), clients are more likely to have more positive discharge and postprogram outcomes.

Principle 10—Clients who indicate they receive general social support and support for reduced substance use during the time of treatment experience better treatment outcomes.

Principle 11—Clients who are part of non-substance-abusing networks have better treatment outcomes.

Principle 12—Spouse and family involvement in treatment may help engage the client in treatment, and the effects are particularly pronounced when that client is not initially ready to participate in treatment.

Principle 13—Spouse and family involvement in treatment may help produce better outcomes.

Principle 14—The impact of family involvement in treatment may be complex, and greatly affected by the interaction of client, therapy, and family variables.

Principle 15—Involving a supportive sponsor peer in treatment results in better outcomes.

Principle 16—Peer and family involvement in programs of formal and informal care and relapse prevention may increase the likelihood of stable remission, while stabilizing and enhancing clients' community support systems can help to maintain psychosocial functioning and enhance the likelihood of stable remission.

strong therapeutic alliance with a practitioner and the kind of social-support network associated with positive treatment outcome. Indeed, following the assertions of Lebow et al. (2002), these sixteen principles may be thought of as an evidence-based guide for practitioners with regard to producing positive treatment outcome by focusing on important relationship factors. TASS, or this special focus on helping clients to build a strong TASS network, is consistent with a body of research suggesting that those clients who are able to establish and maintain relatively positive social contexts are likely to recover, and treatment that facilitates improvement in this aspect of a client's life circumstances is likely to be helpful; and it is consistent with the conclusion that there is no compelling conceptual reason to distinguish between the influence of an AA sponsor, a spouse/ partner, relatives, or friends, versus that of a counselor or psychotherapist (Moos, 2003).

Discussion of a case in chapter 9, in particular, highlights the value of the sixteen principles Lebow et al. (2002) advance, and exactly what a practitioner can say and do to establish a strong therapeutic alliance and assist a client in building a social-support network. However, in literally every case to be presented, this special emphasis on helping clients to build a strong TASS network will be presented. And, no matter the intervention used from the recommended menu of options, item 1, *Special Focus on Building a Strong Therapeutic Alliance/Social-Support Network (TASS)*, will be an important key component from the onset of treatment and throughout service delivery.

2. Motivational Interviewing/Motivational Enhancement Therapy (MET)/ Brief Interventions

MET is "a client-centered counseling approach for initiating behavior change by helping clients to resolve ambivalence about engaging in treatment and stopping drug use" (NIDA, 1999, p. 38). Moreover, emphasis is placed upon employing "strategies to evoke rapid and internally motivated change in the client," typically accomplishing this in two to four individual-treatment sessions with a therapist (p. 38). Principles of motivational interviewing are used to strengthen motivation and assist a client in building a plan for change, even as some attention is paid to coping strategies for high-risk situations, suggesting a somewhat broader focus. As MET sessions progress, the therapist monitors change, reviews the cessation strategies being used, and continues to encourage client commitment to change (NIDA, 1999). NIDA (1999) based its declaration of MET as being a science-based approach to drug addiction on findings of success with clients using alcohol and marijuana.

Indeed, for over a decade, there has been an accumulation of a body of supportive research with regard to the efficacy of what is typically called MET, as in the most popular case involving Project MATCH (1997a, 1997b, 1998a, 1998b, 2001). Thus, the empathic clinical style of motivational interviewing emerges as an evidence-based approach for evoking internally motivated change and increasing client retention in treatment (Miller, Wilbourne, & Hettema, 2003, p. 23).

A rationale exists for practitioners' deploying motivational interviewing techniques with contemporary clients entering community-based addiction treatment, even as Miller, Yahne, and Tonigan (2003) present evidence that the addition of a single session of manual-guided motivational interviewing showed no effect on drug outcomes when added to inpatient or outpatient treatment within a randomized trial. Miller, Yahne, and Tonigan (2003) wonder to what extent clinicians delivering the standard-care intervention may have also been exposed to and incorporated in their work the motivational interviewing style, possibly impacting results. Yet, despite these findings, several randomized trials have reported improved retention, motivation, and outcomes when a single session of motivational interviewing was added to standard substance-abuse treatment (Aubrey, 1998; Bien, Miller, & Boroughs, 1993; Brown & Miller, 1993). And, a host of studies support the positive benefits of motivational interviewing within the context of addiction treatment (Aubrey, 1998; Baker, Boggs, & Lewin, 2001; Barrowclough et al., 2001; Carey et al., 1997, 2000; Daley, Salloum, Zuckoff, Kirisci, & Thase, 1998; Daley & Zuckoff, 1998; Lincourt, Kuettel, & Bombardier, 2002; Longshore, Grills, & Annon, 1999; Martino, Carroll, O'Malley, & Rounsaville, 2000; Saunders, Wilkinson, & Phillips, 1995; Stephens, Roffman, & Curtin, 2000; Stotts, Schmitz, Rhoades, & Grabowski, 2000; Swanson, Pantalon, & Cohen, 1999). Moyers (2003, pp. 143, 147) concludes that the evidence for using motivational interviewing in drug-abuse treatment is "promising, but inconclusive," even though motivational interviewing may be considered "an empirically validated treatment for substance abuse."

Miller and Rollnick (2002) have come to view most of the work using motivational interviewing techniques, accomplished over the course of more than a decade (Miller & Rollnick, 1991), as actually involving adaptations of motivational interviewing (Rollnick, Allison, et al., 2002). In a related vein, Rollnick, Allison, et al. (2002) discuss the goal of protecting motivational interviewing. "For example, an adaptation with a strong technical orientation might place too little emphasis on empathic listening to bear much resemblance to motivational interviewing" (p. 272). Thus, practitioners and researchers are left to reconcile the goal of protecting motivational interviewing versus the recommendation by Miller and Rollnick (2002) to integrate motivational interviewing with other interventions, perhaps using it as a prelude to another intervention, as a permeating counseling/communication style, and as a fallback option.

Rollnick, Allison, et al. (2002, p. 282) recommend that researchers consider the following questions: "How well have practitioners acquired competence in training? What training methods were used? Were practitioners able to transfer skills into real consultations?" and, "Was the delivery of the method adequately monitored with reliable and valid measurement tools?"

Resnicow et al. (2002) have found that motivational interviewing has been able to produce significant findings with regard to behavior change in

research subjects even where "analysis of tape-recorded motivational interviewing sessions indicated only moderate fidelity" to the "spirit and techniques of motivational interviewing" (p. 259). On the other hand, at least
two other studies found that "higher dose motivational interviewing failed
to produce greater treatment effects" (p. 260). Resnicow et al. (2002) also recognize how brief adaptations of motivational interviewing are distinguished
from full-blown motivational interviewing, given how, for example, when
there is limited client contact, "either in terms of duration or frequency, it is
generally not feasible to employ the full range of motivational interviewing
techniques nor is it possible to build the depth of rapport that may be needed
to maximize therapeutic effect" (p. 252). They also recognize that training
those in the addiction field in motivational interviewing interventions "often
represents only a moderate refinement of skills" (p. 254).

Perhaps most importantly, the work of Resnicow et al. (2002) establishes
how over a decade of research, as well as a host of ongoing grant-funded
studies, have gone forward with what are now being called adaptations of
motivational interviewing, even as Rollnick, Allison, et al. (2002) now seek
to protect what is the actual implementation of motivational interviewing
with fidelity. Practitioners in the field of addiction who work in real-world
community-based addiction-treatment settings may, nonetheless, proceed
with adapting motivational interviewing in their work with their multiproblem, diverse clients outside of the realm where tight controls govern experimental evaluations of motivational interviewing.

Motivational interviewing (Miller and Rollnick, 2002) is now emphasized
as being based on four general principles: the expression of empathy by the
counselor with a client, the development of discrepancy between present
problem behavior and client goals, rolling with resistance or avoiding directly opposing resistance, and supporting self-efficacy by enhancing the
client's belief in his or her ability to succeed with a specific task. In addition,
there are five early strategies recommended for use: asking open questions
as opposed to questions that result in a simple yes-or-no response from the
client, affirming clients to build rapport and as reinforcement, using reflection or reflective listening, summarizing what clients have stated to link together and reinforce material discussed by the client, and eliciting *change talk*
from clients. Other noteworthy elements include asking evocative questions
or using a decisional balance (i.e., pros and cons or costs and benefits of
change). Through change talk, a client may thereby state personal reasons for
and advantages of change, likely covering either disadvantages of the status
quo, advantages of change, optimism for change, or intention to change.
Other related techniques and details are provided by Miller and Rollnick
(2002), emphasizing adherence to the techniques they describe when the goal
is for motivational interviewing to be either directive or nondirective.

Motivational-enhancement approaches are also strongly supported as
brief interventions, although they are often utilized with alcohol-using

populations with somewhat less severe problems, typically identified via a screening procedure (Miller, Wilbourne, & Hettema, 2003, p. 21). With regard to alcohol treatment, in general, such brief interventions emerge as having the largest and most positive supportive base of research (Miller, Wilbourne, & Hettema, 2003, p. 21).

Several studies show that "clients who receive motivational interviewing at the beginning of treatment are likely to stay in treatment longer, work harder, adhere more closely to treatment recommendations, and experience substantially better outcomes than those who receive the same treatment program without motivational interviewing" (Miller & Rollnick, 2002, p. 27). The "most obvious integration" of motivational interviewing with other possible interventions is to "offer motivational interviewing as a first consultation, as a prelude to other services" (p. 27). Miller and Rollnick (2002) point out how the use of motivational interviewing will likely increase the chances that clients will return for other services. However, motivational interviewing should also be thought of as being readily integrated with the use of other treatment approaches, as a highly valued counseling or communication style, whenever motivational issues emerge. In sum, motivational interviewing may be used "as a prelude, a permeating style, and a fall-back option" (pp. 28). Thus, practitioners are advised to discern the best possible use(s) of MET in their work with contemporary multiproblem clients, given that it is item 2 (*Motivational Interviewing/Motivational Enhancement Therapy (MET)/Brief Interventions*) on the recommended menu of options.

3. Relapse Prevention (RP), Cognitive-Behavioral Therapy (CBT), and Social-Skills Training (SST)

RP, a cognitive-behavioral therapy (CBT), is also considered a scientifically based approach to addiction treatment. There is justification in speaking alternatively about CBT—as so designated in Project MATCH (1997a, 1997b, 1998a, 1998b, 2001)—or RP or SST. There is wide consensus that clients need exposure to viable techniques for overcoming the problems of relapse to varied addictive and problem behaviors (Carroll, 1997; Marlatt & Gordon, 1985; Wilson, 1992). Miller, Wilbourne, and Hettema (2003, p. 32) clarify that "the efficacy of relapse prevention appears to vary widely, depending on its content and focus," while social-skills training, also called RP, has a stronger track record.

Marlatt and Witkiewitz (2002) describe RP as CBT that is often based on identification of high-risk situations and the development of cognitive and behavioral coping strategies for dealing with these situations. There is often the inclusion of self-monitoring exercises; skills training; cue exposure; and exercises to enhance motivation, increase self-efficacy, and decrease positive-outcome expectancies.

In sum, the strategies are designed to enhance a client's self-control. And what is key within RP is "anticipating the problems patients are likely to meet and helping them develop effective coping strategies" (NIDA, 1999, p. 35). Also, research indicates that the "skills individuals learn through relapse prevention therapy remain after the completion of treatment," and one study found that clients maintained the gains made in RP throughout the year following treatment (p. 35). Hence, there is justification for asserting that RP is a scientifically based approach to drug-addiction treatment.

Carroll (1997) reviews a body of evidence with regard to the efficacy of RP, pointing out that RP may reduce the intensity of relapse episodes when they do occur. There is also evidence of sustained main effects or delayed emergence of effects that appear over time, as "sustained or continuing improvement may be associated with the implementation of generalizable coping skills conferred through RP treatment" (p. 710). Other findings support the effectiveness of RP for more impaired substance abusers, such as those with more severe levels of substance use, greater levels of negative affect, and greater perceived deficits in coping skills (Carroll, 1997).

There are also other considerations that may impact the results of controlled clinical trials of RP (Carroll, 1997). These include the fact that there "appeared to be a great deal of variability across the studies in terms of what relapse prevention actually consisted of" (p. 712). Also, problems of small sample size prevailed. There was no empirical evaluation of the optimal dose of RP treatment, nor the extent to which the "dose of relapse prevention treatment may be associated with robustness of durability of effects" (p. 713). Nor has there been sufficient investigation regarding therapist adherence to treatment manuals, or treatment discriminability, leaving uncertainty regarding the extent to which there was actual implementation of RP treatment (p. 713). In a related vein, "therapists' level of experience and training tended to vary widely" across studies, including having therapists at the predoctoral-trainee level (p. 713). Research also needs to address the effects of the "specific components of relapse-prevention treatment, and there is a need for more prospective matching studies to define types of patients who are best suited for this approach" (p. 713). Nonetheless, there is excellent cause for RP, CBT, and SST being item 3—*Cognitive-Behavioral Therapy (CBT)/Relapse Prevention (RP)/Social-Skills Training (SST)*—on the menu of evidence-based options.

4. Twelve-Step Facilitation (TSF)/Guidance Using Alcoholics or Narcotics Anonymous

There is a great deal of evidence to support the value of supporting and assisting clients in using self-help groups, or twelve-step groups—more specifically, Alcoholics Anonymous (AA) and/or Narcotics Anonymous (NA)—as one key component of comprehensive community-based addiction treatment. Practitioners are justified in assisting clients in this manner (Derby, 1992a), given the importance of helping clients to build a strong social-support network, and given how both informal and formal sources of social support are important and helpful for clients (and given that any distinction between these sources and the social context may be arbitrary), according to Moos (2003). Practitioners find justification in helping clients to get involved in AA and NA based on findings from Project MATCH (1997a, 1997b, 1998a, 1998b, 2001). TSF, CBT, and MET were found to be equally effective in reducing drinking rates. The TSF intervention involved twelve weekly sessions with a practitioner who introduced clients to the first five steps of AA and encouraged involvement in AA. Also, clients low in psychiatric severity had more days of abstinence upon receipt of TSF, relative to receipt of CBT, with neither intervention being superior for those clients with higher levels of psychiatric severity (Marlatt, 1999).

Moos and Moos (2004) present research suggesting that when clients with alcohol-use disorders participated in AA for a period of four months or longer in the first year after seeking treatment, they had better one-year and eight-year alcohol-related outcomes versus clients who did not participate in AA. Regarding the impact of extensive AA participation, or duration effects, Moos and Moos (2004) found that clients who continued their participation in AA in years two through eight of their recovery had better eight-year outcomes versus clients who did not participate in AA or who participated for a shorter duration of time.

Combining Twelve-Step Groups (AA/NA), Group Drug Counseling (GDC), and Individual Drug Counseling (IDC)

The scientifically based intervention of individual drug counseling (IDC) includes the twelve-step philosophy, and AA/NA participation is a central component of the overall treatment model (Mercer & Woody, 1999). Similarly, Daley and Mercer (2002) recognize the value of AA and NA participation for clients receiving the scientifically based intervention of group drug counseling (GDC). For example, in GDC, a session is devoted to introducing clients to the serenity prayer and the twelve steps of recovery. In addition, Daley and Mercer (2002) explain how GDC encourages clients to get support from people, such as friends and sponsors in AA and NA, who may help them cope with relapse warning signs. GDC includes introducing clients to the AA/NA philosophy; the different types of AA/NA meetings (e.g., open, closed); the typical format of meetings; the recommended frequency of attending meetings; the important techniques in attending AA/NA, such as sharing telephone numbers; and common barriers to participation. The GDC emphasis on managing cravings and on how people, places, events, and things may potentially serve as triggers that can lead to drug use is also similar to the AA/NA focus on avoiding such people, places, and things.

Daley and Mercer's (2002) GDC is a twelve-session intervention, with treatment actually beginning in a stabilization phase during which detoxification occurs, lasting up to two weeks and involving frequent contact with a counselor. Next, there is a phase lasting across weeks one through twelve, with a focus on clients' acquiring pertinent information on addiction. Clients then enter a group phase, called the problem-solving group, that covers weeks thirteen through twenty-four. Also discussed in groups in this phase are problems related to twelve-step-group participation.

The incorporation of such elements and encouragement of AA/NA involvement may partly explain the manner in which GDC helped clients with cocaine problems to improve, even as the combination of IDC and GDC produced the best results, while all other treatments (individual supportive-expressive psychotherapy [SEP] and individual cognitive therapy [CT] with GDC) also helped clients to improve (Crits-Christoph et al., 1999; Daley & Mercer, 2002; NIDA, 1999).

Thus, there is a rationale for recommending not only the combination of GDC and AA/NA participation, but also combinations that include IDC and GDC along with AA/NA. The use of a combination of addiction-treatment interventions—whether GDC and involvement in AA/NA, along with IDC—is consistent with what occurs within comprehensive programs in the field of addiction, including that used in the Matrix Model to be discussed below as item 7 on the menu of options. Thus, it is for good reason that item 4 (*Twelve-Step Facilitation (TSF)/Guidance Using Alcoholics and/or Narcotics Anonymous*) appears on the menu of evidence-based options, especially as it is a key component of any comprehensive approach within community-based addiction treatment.

5. Individual Drug Counseling (IDC) and/or Supportive-Expressive Psychotherapy (SEP)—Even Incorporating Some Principles of Psychoanalytic Psychotherapy

The history of research with IDC in outpatient community-based addiction treatment goes back to work with opiate addicts, comparing those receiving only methadone to those receiving methadone and IDC; the combination of methadone and IDC produced significantly more improvement, and adding other services on-site (e.g., medical/psychiatric components, employment, family services) further improved treatment outcomes (McLellan, Arndt, Metzger, Woody, & O'Brien, 1993; NIDA, 1999). Given the need for an effective cocaine treatment, IDC was found to be effective, but once again the combination of IDC and group drug counseling (GDC) produced the best results (Crits-Cristoph et al., 1999; NIDA, 1999).

Mercer and Woody (1999) detail the elements of and procedures to be followed within this scientifically supported therapy for addiction (i.e., IDC). IDC is just one component of comprehensive treatment that spans up to six months, including booster sessions that extend up to month eight. Within IDC, the practitioner provides support, education, and nonjudgmental confrontation, establishing good rapport with the client. IDC is seen as fitting well with many other treatments, given how it was designed to be just one component of a comprehensive treatment package. IDC can be coordinated with pharmacotherapy approaches for comorbid psychiatric disorders, but those dually diagnosed with significant psychopathology often require more attention to their psychopathology than IDC provides.

According to Mercer and Woody (1999), IDC was developed for research and is conceptualized for delivery in thirty-six sessions over six months, with four main stages (stage 1 as treatment initiation in two initial sessions, stage 2 as early abstinence, stage 3 as maintenance of abstinence, and stage 4 as advanced recovery), where up until month eight there are infrequent booster sessions. The structure of each session is to first check urine-test results, recall themes from the previous session, and prepare to discuss the topics appropriate to the client's phase in treatment. An important part of early-abstinence work, which includes a focus on participation in twelve-step groups, involves recognizing the medical and psychological aspects of cocaine withdrawal, identifying triggers to use and developing avoidance-of-triggers techniques, and learning to handle craving without using. The next stage of recovery, maintaining abstinence, begins at about the fourth month of treatment, depending upon when abstinence was achieved by the client. The maintaining-abstinence stage involves working to continue abstinent behavior, including ongoing avoidance, recognizing personal psychosocial and emotional triggers, anger management, use of relaxation and leisure time, employment and money management, relationships in recovery, and developing healthy behaviors to handle life stress. Finally, advanced recovery, which is to continue for life, is a stage that is just beginning when the six months of treatment is ending, even as there are infrequent booster sessions up into month eight. But, Mercer and Woody (1999, p. 61) acknowledge how, "in reality, patients will be terminating at different points in their recovery process," which is quite different from a research model where "tailoring the length of treatment to the individual's needs" is not possible. In the real world of community-based addiction treatment, working with multiproblem clients, such tailoring of the length of treatment so that it extends in time is quite likely, especially for clients with comorbidity.

Mercer and Woody (1999) emphasize that IDC, as addiction counseling, focuses upon short-term goals, behavioral goals, and goals directly related to addiction, and it maintains a focus on the present. However, Mercer and Woody (1999, p. 8) admit that in "clinical practice, however, the boundary between addiction counseling and psychotherapy often is blurred." They therefore point out how, in contrast, psychotherapy focuses on the following: short- and long-term goals; cognitive, emotional, and behavioral goals; goals related to all areas of recovery; and both the past and the present (Mercer & Woody, 1999). However, IDC also addresses other areas of impaired functioning, including employment, criminal activity, and family/social relations (NIDA, 1999). Mercer and Woody (1999, p. 9) also assert that IDC is dissimilar in both philosophy and content to "any psychotherapy model that does not focus primarily and specifically on changing addictive behavior, such as psychoanalytic or psychodynamic therapies, including supportive-expressive therapy." On the other hand, key modifications in psychoanalytic technique have been described for work with the chemically dependent (Derby, 1992b; Rothschild, 1992; Tatarsky, 2002, 2003; Wurmser, 1992; Yalisove, 1992).

The way in which the principles of psychoanalytic psychotherapy are inherent in SEP has been clearly articulated (Luborsky, 1984). A body of scientific evidence supports this approach to addiction treatment with the cocaine, heroin, and methadone dependent, especially where clients have greater psychiatric severity; and, when individual psychotherapy (i.e., SEP) is added to drug counseling, it produces better results (Woody, Luborsky et al., 1983; Woody, Luborsky, & O'Brien, 1987, 1995). A key finding was that clients who received SEP, versus clients receiving only drug counseling, had lower cocaine use and required less methadone, while both groups' opiate use were similar; and those receiving SEP tended to maintain their gains (NIDA, 1999).

SEP is a time-limited, focused form of psychotherapy that has a history of being successfully adapted for heroin- and cocaine-dependent clients (NIDA, 1999). SEP has two main components: (1) the use of supportive techniques that help clients feel comfortable in discussing their personal experiences and (2) expressive techniques that help clients identify and work through interpersonal-relationship issues. SEP pays special attention to the relationship between drug use and problematic feelings (i.e., affects) and behaviors (NIDA, 1999).

With regard to alcohol treatment, controlled studies of insight-oriented and exploratory psychotherapies (individual or group) have consistently produced negative findings, while many specific forms of psychotherapy have too few studies to permit drawing conclusions. One exception, producing positive findings, involves Rogers's (1951) client-centered therapy, having an emphasis on an empathic counseling style (Miller, Wilbourne, & Hettema, 2003, pp. 33–34). Also of note, confrontational counseling styles produce some of the worst treatment-outcome research findings, as do educational approaches using lectures and films (Miller, Wilbourne, & Hettema, 2003, p. 34).

Research evidence also points to the importance of factors beyond the specific treatment techniques that are used, such as nonspecific or common factors "that are present in many different kinds of psychotherapy, regardless of their theoretical rationale," and that may "exert a stronger influence on outcome than do the specific differences among techniques" (Miller, Wilbourne, & Hettema, 2003, p. 38). For example, therapist empathy may be among the most important of these, involving "the ability to listen reflectively and develop an accurate understanding of the client's experience" (Miller, Wilbourne, & Hettema, 2003, p. 39); this is consistent with the goal of developing a strong therapeutic alliance, discussed under item 1 on the recommended menu—TASS.

It may be asserted that psychoanalytic theory and training provides for some of the very best preparation for effective empathic engagement with clients, as well as for addressing the aftermath of trauma, problems in affect regulation, and deficits in ego functioning (Derby, 1992b; Dodes & Khantzian, 1998; Khantzian, Halliday, & McAuliffe, 1990; Luborsky, 1984; Rothschild, 1992; Tatarsky, 2002; Wallace, 1996a; Wurmser, 1992; Yalisove, 1992). Perhaps most importantly, to date, SEP is the only form of psychoanalytically derived individual psychotherapy with research support.

Is There a Role for Both IDC and SEP?

Because of the contemporary challenge inherent in meeting the needs of multiproblem clients entering community-based addiction treatment, there is a place for using both IDC and SEP, especially for those clients presenting comorbidity. While not all clients will require this combination, many will. Indeed, clients' needs also change in treatment. What is not initially indicated as needing to be a part of a comprehensive treatment practice in the first month of treatment may need to be added later, and vice versa (i.e., what was needed early in treatment may not be needed later in treatment).

In sum, the presence of item 5 on the menu of options—*Individual Drug Counseling (IDC) and/or Supportive-Expressive Psychotherapy (SEP)*—finds support.

6. Community Reinforcement Approach (CRA)/Vouchers: Contingency Management (CM)

Both the CRA alone and when used in combination with contingency management (CM) represent scientifically based approaches to addiction treatment. Starting with the premise that individuals use alcohol and drugs because it is reinforcing, CRA seeks to change the individual's social environment so that abstinence becomes more reinforcing than continued alcohol and drug use (Miller, Wilbourne, & Hettema, 2003, p. 27). Of note, operant conditioning lies at the root of CRA, and CRA illustrates the therapeutic power of CM therapies (Bigelow & Silverman, 1999).

Initially, CRA plus vouchers was described as a twenty-four-week (six month) outpatient treatment developed initially for cocaine dependence, and it had two goals: (1) the achievement of abstinence for a sufficiently long period of time so that clients learn new life skills that will assist them in sustaining abstinence and (2) the reduction of alcohol consumption for clients whose drinking is associated with cocaine use (NIDA, 1999). Treatment components included the following: one or two individual counseling sessions per week, a focus in counseling sessions on improving family relations and on learning skills to minimize drug use, vocational counseling, the development of new recreational activities and social networks, disulfiram (Antabuse) for those who use alcohol, urine testing two to three times per week, and receipt of vouchers for urines negative for cocaine (NIDA, 1999). This intervention is seen as facilitating client engagement in treatment and the achievement of substantial periods of cocaine abstinence, and it is used in both urban and rural areas (NIDA, 1999).

However, relatively few programs use CRA, despite many studies showing efficacy (Meyers & Miller, 2001, p. 165). Most pertinent is how CRA has been utilized in the treatment of not only cocaine but also opiod dependence, and also how it is being used in combination with CM interventions in which vouchers are delivered as positive reinforcement for urines negative for illicit-drug use (Higgins & Abbot, 2001; Higgins & Silverman, 1999).

Bigelow and Silverman (1999) are hopeful that CM can gain acceptance in the drug-abuse treatment field despite a contemporary preference among practitioners for conducting verbal therapy. However, Bigelow and Silverman admit that, outside of a research protocol, the task of disseminating CM programs that use reinforcers (e.g., money, vouchers redeemable for valued goods) involves the hard work of surmounting many obstacles. Kirby, Amass, and McLellan (1999) cite as an additional prohibitive factor the expensive nature of reinforcers, the cost of urine testing three to four times per week, and workload issues involving the time it takes for practitioners to implement a CM program. And there often is also community and political opposition to the concept of giving out reinforcers such as money to drug abusers.

A weakness of CM research involves a lack of sufficient evidence that the gain of establishing abstinence translates into maintenance of behavior change over time (Kirby, Amass, & McLellan, 1999). Silverman, Preston, Stitzer, and Schuster (1999, p. 163) explain how there is a need for "more effective and versatile interventions. No type of drug abuse treatment, including CM interventions, has been shown to be universally effective." Indeed, Silverman et al. (1999, p. 177) explain how the use of voucher-based reinforcement interventions "are not effective in all patients, and their effects do not fully persist after the intervention is discontinued." Maintenance of behavior change is therefore key. However, the use of voucher-based reinforcement interventions has been shown to be effective with some of the most challenging populations, such as the substance-abusing homeless, especially when combined with a comprehensive set of interventions, including, for example, relapse prevention (Milby et al., 1996).

Following the recommendations of Kirby et al. (1999), there may be a role for the use of reinforcement contingency, as well as for the use of punishment or response-cost contingency involving aversive consequences for positive drug-test results. One practical application involves the use of contingency contracting.

Contingency Management (CM): A Practical Application
Involving Contingency Contracting

In support of the use of contingency contracting, Donovan (1999) summarizes research showing that addiction-treatment clients produce better treatment outcomes when they faced a greater likelihood of losing a valued outcome due to continued substance use, suggesting the positive impact of some contingency in their treatment outcome. Examples of things of value that clients could risk losing as part of a contingency contract—where negative consequences followed from what was under the control of clients (i.e., their own behavior)—were employment, family support, or a welfare check.

With regard to drug offenders who may be on either probation or parole or in drug courts, what has been emphasized is the importance that drug offenders understand *in advance* the sanctions they face, or the contingency contract into which they enter with a judge. Harrell and Kleiman (2002) explain how this understanding of the contingencies they may face effectively makes drug offenders accountable for participating in treatment and complying with a known set of rules. What is key is that there is a known set of rules to which there are attached both sanctions (negative consequences) and incentives (positive consequences) that clients can control through their behavior (Harrell & Kleiman, 2002, p. 167). The timing of the delivery of sanctions (as well as rewards) is also important, with Harrell and Kleiman (2002) recommending what is supported by research showing that the application of sanctions should ideally be "certain, swift, and appropriate to the offense" (p. 169).

Further support for the use of contingencies comes from decades of research in the behavioral sciences using laboratory animals in tightly controlled experiments, with many studies being repeated with humans, documenting the efficacy of using CM approaches (Seligman, 1998, 2002). In this regard, Seligman (2002) asserts the following:

> In our learned helplessness experiment more than thirty years ago, we found that animals who received inescapable shock learned that nothing they did mattered, and they became passive and depressed. They even died prematurely. In contrast, animals and people that received exactly the same shock, but under

their control (that is, their actions turned it off), showed just the opposite results: activity, good affect, and enhanced health. The crucial variable is contingency— learning that your actions matter, that they control outcomes that are important. There is a direct implication . . . : learning mastery, control over important outcomes, should be all to the good. (p. 215)

Other research confirms how the crucial variable in the whole process of contingency management and contingency contracting is that of contingency itself—learning that your actions matter, that they control outcomes that are important. Below, Higgins and Abbott (2001) summarize research in which the goal was to assess the effects of contingent vouchers on cocaine abstinence separate from their effects on treatment retention:

To experimentally examine this matter, 70 cocaine-dependent adults were randomly assigned to receive CRA plus vouchers contingent on cocaine abstinence or CRA plus vouchers delivered independent of urinalysis results. The intention of making vouchers available to both treatment groups was to keep retention rates comparable between them. Making voucher availability contingent on cocaine-negative urinalysis results in one group but not the other permitted experimental isolation of the contribution of contingent reinforcement to cocaine abstinence.

As intended, there were no significant differences in treatment retention rates, or follow-up rates, between the two treatment groups. Nevertheless, cocaine abstinence differed significantly between the two groups, with, for example, threefold more subjects (36% versus 12%) in the contingent than the noncontingent groups achieving 12 or more weeks of continuous cocaine abstinence during treatment. Moreover, the point prevalence of cocaine abstinence at the end of treatment and at each of the follow-up assessments conducted 9, 12, 15, and 18 months after treatment entry was greater in the contingent group than in the noncontingent group (average differences = 16%). Those results demonstrate that contingent vouchers are capable of directly reinforcing cocaine abstinence and that those effects can remain discernable for up to 12 months following the end of the CRA plus vouchers treatment and for up to 15 months following the end of the contingent voucher component of that intervention. (p. 135)

Further work extending the use of CRA plus vouchers and comparing contingent versus noncontingent conditions supports the assertion that for diverse clients who are also on methadone maintenance, are opiod dependent, or are cocaine/stimulant abusers, there is support for efficacy (Higgins & Abbott, 2001; Rawson et al., 1995; Silverman et al., 1998). Indeed, a body of research evidence has now emerged with regard to how the use of CM interventions served the important function of motivation enhancement, producing substantial behavior change within the population of clients in community-based addiction treatment. However, as discussed earlier, this approach has many problems (Higgins & Silverman, 1999), suggesting the need for the creation of practical applications (Silverman et al., 1999).

For example, practitioners and treatment programs have many options involving the use of both rewards and sanctions as they seek to creatively apply contingency contracting in real-world settings, as Higgins (1999) explains below:

> Contingency management interventions almost always involve one or more of the following generic contingencies to motivate increases and decreases in the frequency of a therapeutically desirable and undesirable behavior: (a) Positive reinforcement involves delivery of a desired consequence (e.g., a voucher exchangeable for retail items), contingent on the individual meeting a therapeutic goal (e.g., negative urinalysis test results); (b) negative reinforcement involves removing an aversive or confining circumstance (e.g., intense criminal justice supervision), contingent on meeting a target therapeutic goal (e.g., attending counseling sessions); (c) positive punishment involves delivery of a punishing consequence (e.g., a professional reprimand), contingent on evidence of undesirable behavior (e.g., positive urinalysis test results); and (d) negative punishment involves removal of a positive condition (e.g., the monetary value of a voucher to be earned is reduced), contingent on evidence of the occurrence of an undesirable behavior (e.g., missing a scheduled counseling session).
>
> Reinforcement and punishment contingencies can be effective in motivating change, but the former generally are preferred over the latter by patients and therapists alike. (pp. 4–5)

In terms of creative, practical applications, the best that real-world practitioners may be able to do in most community-based addiction-treatment centers, in response to clients' negative urine-toxicology-test results and consistent attendance records, is to offer rewards (positive reinforcement) such as computer-generated certificates with the director's signature and a gold seal, or rewards such as being advanced to the next, higher phase of treatment, as well as verbal and pictorial descriptions of the client's eventual graduation, as the next reward for which the client works hard in treatment.

Other positive-punishment contingencies that may be offered in response to urine-test results positive for the use of illicit substances are common to the criminal justice system and ideally include the application of swift, certain, and appropriate graduated sanctions. In community-based outpatient addiction treatment, when urine-test results are repeatedly positive, graduated sanctions that are applied include clients' attending a five- to seven-day inpatient detoxification, a twenty-eight- to forty-five-day rehabilitation program, or eventual referral to a longer-term residential therapeutic-community-treatment program. Or, for a client who has emitted aggressive verbal behavior or made threats of physical violence in a residential program, there is the delivery of sanctions involving loss of weekend-pass privileges, being confined to the residence for a longer period of time, or the more graduated sanction of termination from the program.

Principles to Guide the Process of Contingency Contracting

For those who seek to implement creative or practical adaptations of CRA and/or CM, the first step involves contingency contracting. Four principles are offered to guide the process of contingency contracting. These appear in table 4.3.

Integrating Contingency Management with Relapse Prevention

Marlatt (2001) suggests that the benefits of CM could be further enhanced if clients are provided with coping-skills training for RP, given the empirical support for the use of cognitive and behavioral coping-skills training in enhancing long-term maintenance. The rationale for this suggestion follows from the criticism of contingency management that there is the possibility of relapse once the contingency period is over and there is no longer any reinforcement for client provision of clean urines. The integrated treatment approach combining contingency management with RP would enhance the extent to which one would attain to the goal of having a comprehensive behavioral-treatment program (Marlatt, 2001). However, whether alone—in whole or in part—or in combination with other addiction-treatment interventions with which it is integrated, or as part of a comprehensive treatment package, there is a rationale for recommending item 6, the evidence-based *Community Reinforcement Approach (CRA)/Vouchers: Contingency Management (CM)*.

Table 4.3. The Four Principles of Contingency Contracting

Establishment of a contingency contract

Principle 1—Establish contingency contracts with clients, at the onset of the relationship, ideally when contact is first made with the client, responding to individual client needs and characteristics.

Principle 2—Clearly explain to the client how contingencies function in response to behavior a client performs that is under the client's own personal control, and obtain client oral consent to the contract.

The contingency management phase

Principle 3—During the contingency management phase, when a client produces an outcome that the client controls through his or her own personal behavior, consequences follow through the application of sanctions or rewards that are certain, swift, and appropriate.

Principle 4—The sanctions and rewards applied over time increase or are graduated, increasing in value (rewards) or response cost (sanctions), as an appropriate response to a client's ongoing pattern of producing outcomes that the client controls through his or her own personal behavior.

7. The Matrix Model—Or, a Day-Treatment Approach, or an IEC Outpatient Model That Is *I* for Intensive (4–5 Days per Week), *E* for Extensive (6–12 Months), and *C* for Comprehensive (TASS, CBT/RP, IDC, GDC, Drug Testing, Etc.)

There is also a body of scientific evidence that suggests that the use of integrated- or combined-treatment approaches is effective in treating a variety of addictive disorders, including the cocaine, heroin, and methamphetamine dependent. The Matrix Model is one example of such a scientifically supported integrated-treatment approach, combining interventions such as individual sessions with a trained therapist who engages clients into treatment and provides support, encouragement, and reinforcement for behavior change, including the delivery of education in individual sessions that is facilitated by the use of a detailed treatment manual with work sheets; as well as involvement with a variety of groups such as early-recovery skills-training groups, social-support/weekend-leisure planning groups, relapse-prevention groups, and twelve-step groups (Rawson, Shoptaw, et al., 1995). Clients also become familiar with self-help groups (e.g., AA, NA), as the therapist serves as both an educator and a coach, fostering a positive relationship without the use of confrontation, and promoting the client's self-esteem, worth, and dignity (NIDA, 1999). In this manner, the Matrix Model integrates the use of numerous other tested approaches, such as RP, family and group therapies, drug education, and self-help (AA, NA) involvement, while codifying this in detailed manuals and work sheets (NIDA, 1999). The nature of the success of the Matrix Model is such that there have been significant reductions among stimulant users in their drug and alcohol use, as well as improvements in psychological indicators and reduced risky sexual behaviors associated with HIV transmission. As well, the Matrix Model is comparable to other treatments for stimulant users, also enhancing naltrexone treatment of opiate addicts (NIDA, 1999).

The Matrix Model has been analyzed as being (1) intensive, requiring patients to participate at a level that involves contacts several times per week with the treatment program, often having clients attend an outpatient program four to five days per week (Rawson, Shoptaw, et al., 1995; Wallace, 1991); (2) comprehensive, addressing the drug problem via a number of interventions, such as education, urine testing, individual sessions, family/couples sessions, education for family members, varied group sessions, and RP (Wallace, 1991); and (3) multifaceted, so that professionals utilize educational, cognitive, behavioral, and psychodynamic interventions, or techniques derived from a rationale that involves cognitive, behavioral, or psychodynamic theory (Wallace, 1991b). Indeed, the Matrix Model may best approximate that "ideal world" described by Adler et al. (2002). This is one in which clinicians participate in a comprehensive and empirically sound chemical-dependency-treatment system characterized by the implementation of interventions that have been found to be effective through empirical evaluation, while also systematically collecting data to evaluate program effectiveness (Adler et al., 2002).

However, within this context, and given more recent findings on the important role of the duration of treatment, and therefore the extent to which it is extensive (see chapter 3), the following characteristics of the Matrix Model are emphasized: (1) intensiveness, (2) extensiveness, and (3) comprehensiveness—or IEC. The Matrix Model is extensive in having phases of treatment that span as much as six months, as well as twelve months. Given the fact that the intensity of the Matrix Model program includes nearly five-day-per-week participation, it is asserted in this book that the Matrix Model shares some features in common with day treatment.

However, in day treatment, as it was developed for homeless crack-cocaine-dependent clients, for the first two months clients are required to spend 5.5 hours per day in the program, benefiting from lunch and transportation to and from shelters (NIDA, 1999). Pertinent interventions include once-per-week individual counseling; three-times-per-week group counseling; varied psychoeducational groups (e.g., on community resources, housing, cocaine, HIV/AIDS prevention, RP, weekend-leisure planning, and rehabilitation goals); and client-governed community meetings. After the initial two months, and if clients achieve two weeks of abstinence, clients graduate to a four-month work component, earning wages that may be used for housing; also, a voucher system rewards drug-free social and recreational activities. This model of day treatment plus vouchers was found to be more effective than another intervention (combining individual counseling, twelve-step groups, medical examinations and treatment, and referral to community resources for housing and vocational services) in terms of alcohol use, cocaine use, and days homeless (Milby et al., 1996; NIDA, 1999).

Many community-based programs may be characterized as being comparable to the Matrix Model and/or the day-treatment-program model, insofar as they may be characterized as being IEC—intensive, extensive, and comprehensive. Thus, in recognition of these features, item 7 on the menu of evidence-based options includes what is described as *The Matrix Model—Or, a Day-Treatment Approach, or an IEC Outpatient Model That Is I for Intensive (4–5 Days per Week), E for Extensive (6–12 months), and C for Comprehensive (TASS, CBT/RP, IDC, GDC, Drug Testing, etc.).*

THE SEVEN ITEMS ON THE MENU UNDER CATEGORY 2: RECOMMENDED STATE-OF-THE-ART PRACTICES

There are seven recommended state-of-the art practices under category 2. These will be discussed in this section.

1. The Integration of Motivational Interviewing and Stages of Change

There has also been an integration of the evidence-based motivational interviewing model (Miller & Rollnick, 2002) and the evidence-based transtheoretical model that specifies stages of change (DiClemente & Velasquez, 2002). Early on, the introduction of motivational interviewing and the task of preparing people for change included integration with stages of change (Miller & Rollnick, 1991). Miller and Rollnick (2002) now place greater emphasis on specifying exactly what constitutes the technique of motivational interviewing. However, DiClemente and Velasquez (2002) emphasize the natural marriage that continues to exist between motivational interviewing and stages of change.

Some research on the stages of change and transtheoretical model has been controversial, leading to some criticism (Breslin & Skinner, 1999). However, it has also been asserted that research has isolated the stages of change across a range of health behaviors, while the stages play a critical role in tailoring interventions to a client's state of readiness to change (DiClemente & Velasquez, 2002). Generally, clinical interventions need to be applied to where the client is in the change process, recognizing the client's stage of change for his or her problem behavior, whether precontemplation (not thinking about change), contemplation (thinking about change), preparation (preparing to change), action (taking action to change for up to six months), or maintenance (engaged in a change process for greater than six months); possibilities for entering a stage of relapse are also recognized (Connors, Donovan, & DiClemente, 2001; Prochaska & DiClemente, 1983; Prochaska, DiClemente, & Norcross, 1992).

Motivational interviewing may be deployed to move clients across stages of change, for example, from a state of precontemplation, to a state of contemplation about change, to a state of preparation to change, and to a state of taking action to change. Moreover, motivational interviewing may be used to address one problem behavior and then another, and then another, as needed and deemed appropriate by the client and the practitioner. Such is the reality of working with clients with multiple addictive and problem behaviors who may be in different stages of change for each one. Typically, motivational interviewing is thought of as most appropriate for application in the early stages of change, such as in the precontemplation, contemplation, and preparation stages, although it also plays an important role in the action and maintenance stages (DiClemente & Velasquez, 2002; Miller & Rollnick, 1991, 2002). Thus, a rationale exists for including the state-of-the-art practice involving an *Integration of Motivational Interviewing and Stages of Change* as item 1 under category 2 in table 4.1.

2. Integration of Stages of Change and Phases of Treatment and Recovery

The integration of the concept of stages of change and the concept of phases of treatment and recovery has been presented (Wallace, 1996b),

allowing for considerations of both a client's phase of treatment and recovery, and the implications of this for the correct timing for addressing a
client's addictive behaviors, problem behaviors, and other characteristics
or needs. First, it is important to determine whether or not the client is in
one of the following three phases of treatment and recovery: (1) a *withdrawal phase*, wherein the client has been engaged in active drug use in recent days, such as within the prior two-week period; (2) a *phase of prolonging abstinence*, wherein the client has only weeks, months, or less than six
months of actively pursuing change of addictive and problem behaviors,
and in which the main goal is preventing relapse, even as this is the equivalent of an action stage; or (3) a *phase of pursuing lifetime recovery*, wherein
the client has greater than six months or even one to several years of maintaining behavior change, also being the equivalent of a maintenance stage
(Wallace, 1996b).

Lending support to this conceptualization is the work of many others. For
example, closely paralleling Wallace's (1996b) three phases of treatment and
recovery (withdrawal phase, phase of prolonging abstinence, and phase of
pursuing lifetime recovery) are McLellan's (2003a, p. 170) "three usual stages
of care within the substance abuse specialty treatment field": (1) the *detoxifi-
cation/stabilization stage of care*, which is several days in duration; (2) the
intermediate stage of care, which is several weeks to months in duration; and
(3) the *continuing care stage*, which is one or more years in duration.

Also lending support to the use of phases and/or stages is the work of
Daley and Mercer (2002) in the area of GDC. They suggest a brief stabilization phase of treatment that lasts up to two weeks, allowing for stabilization of the client, including the completion of detoxification, whether as
an outpatient or in a hospital addiction-rehabilitation program from which
the client enters outpatient care. Next, within their GDC model, when outpatient GDC actually begins there is then a phase 1 of psychoeducational
group sessions, lasting ninety minutes each and spanning twelve weeks
(three months). After this, there is then a phase 2 of problem-solving group
sessions of ninety minutes each across another twelve consecutive weeks,
covering weeks thirteen through twenty-four (up to six months). An emphasis is placed in phase 2 on helping clients develop strategies to cope
with identified problems.

Similarly, in presenting their IDC model, Mercer and Woody (1999) identified the following stages: stage 1, or treatment initiation, covering the first
two sessions; stage 2, or early abstinence, where the identification of triggers
for drug use is key; stage 3, or maintaining abstinence, which begins around
month four in treatment; and stage 4, or advanced recovery, which begins
when treatment is ending around month six, even though there are infrequent booster sessions up to month eight. Advanced recovery is considered
to continue throughout one's life, as recovery is a lifelong process (Mercer &
Woody, 1999).

This consensus on the importance of the kinds of phases that Wallace (1996a) clearly articulated as an important development in the field of addiction treatment justifies an integration that can further guide practitioners with regard to when to do what. Wallace (1996b) proposed an integration of the phases of treatment and recovery with the stages of change of Prochaska and DiClemente (1983, 1992; also see DiClemente & Velasquez, 2002). The result is that the phases of withdrawal and prolonging abstinence are commensurate with that period of time when clients may be in either a stage of precontemplation, contemplation, preparation, or action (that spans the first six months in recovery). In this book, this period will be called an *early phase of treatment*, lasting six months. Beyond the period of the first six months in recovery, a person may be considered to be in both a phase of pursuing lifetime recovery and a maintenance stage that may last for many years up to a lifetime. In this book, this period will be called *the middle-to-late phase of treatment and recovery*.

In terms of which one of a client's addictions, problem behaviors, characteristics, or needs to address when, specific examples may provide clarification. A client in a withdrawal phase or early phase of treatment who is not in an acute psychiatric crisis may not yet clearly reveal the severity of problems with depression, paranoia, anxiety, or hallucinations; thus, it may not be the correct time to prescribe certain psychiatric medications. By the fourth week of abstinence, a much clearer picture will emerge, allowing for a better determination of the client's need for ongoing psychiatric medication for what now appears to be a valid mental disorder and not just symptoms of withdrawal. These are important considerations for a client with only days or a week since the last drug use, being in an early phase of treatment, or specifically, in a withdrawal phase, as well as in either a precontemplation, contemplation, preparation, or action stage (Wallace, 1996b).

Similarly, a client in a phase of prolonging abstinence, with anywhere from three weeks to up to six months working on an addiction or behavior change (still also constituting the early phase of treatment), but also having a history of sexual abuse that is now creating a mood disorder, may have specific treatment needs. Such a client presents challenging comorbidity. The phase of prolonging abstinence might only be successfully negotiated across six months if it is recognized that the client needs to become stabilized on appropriate psychiatric medication. This process may involve the client's gradually learning medication-adherence skills and communication skills with a psychiatrist to cover symptoms and medication side effects, allowing the psychiatrist to find an appropriate medication or combination of medications to address all of the client's psychiatric symptoms. These are vital considerations for clients in a phase of prolonging abstinence or in an early phase of treatment, spanning up to six months in the action stage (Wallace, 1996b).

*The Value of Integrating Phases of Treatment and Stages of Change in the Case
of Treating SUD-PTSD Comorbidity*

The value of integrating phases of treatment and recovery and stages of
change as a guide for practitioners is supported by the latest research and
recommendations for how to proceed with those clients who present the
most common form of comorbidity to be found in this population: both post-
traumatic stress disorder (PTSD) and substance use disorders (SUD) of either abuse or dependence upon a psychoactive drug. There are extraordi-
narily high rates of comorbidity involving SUD and PTSD in the target
population (Ouimette & Brown, 2003). The central issue involves how to
proceed with this large segment of the population in community-based addiction treatment.

Ouimette, Moos, and Brown (2003) suggest that empirically based SUD-
PTSD practice should include the following elements: (1) SUD patients
should be routinely screened for traumatic stress experiences and PTSD; (2)
SUD-PTSD patients should be referred for concurrent trauma/PTSD treatment for psychological treatment with the recommendation that trauma/
PTSD issues be addressed; (3) SUD-PTSD patients should be referred for
concurrent participation in self-help groups and, when indicated, for family
treatment; and (4) providers should offer SUD-PTSD patients continuing
outpatient mental-health care after SUD treatment has been completed,
ideally involving weekly individual sessions for a period of three months
or longer, or until the client stabilizes (Ouimette, Moos, & Brown, 2003,
pp. 109–10). For the purposes of screening and assessment, several instruments have been recommended (Read, Bollinger, & Sharkansky, 2003).

Stewart and Conrod (2003, p. 47) discuss findings that "suggest that SUD-
specific treatment possesses poor efficacy in reducing PTSD symptoms and
that untreated PTSD symptoms may place comorbid patients at increased
risk for posttreatment relapse." Also, research suggests that "deficits in specific coping strategies, namely, emotional discharge, account for the relatively poor response to SUD treatment by SUD-PTSD" clients (Stewart &
Conrod, 2003, p. 54). But, the "efficacy of combined SUD-PTSD treatment for
dually diagnosed patients suggests that those who complete such programs
are able to achieve significant improvement on a variety of variables, including psychopathology" (Stewart & Conrod, 2003, p. 54). Stewart and
Conrod (2003) recommend that future research explore the efficacy of brief
motivational interventions for SUD in combination with PTSD treatment.

Najavits (2003) acknowledges that several treatments have been devel-
oped and have undergone pilot testing for patients with SUD and PTSD (e.g.,
Back, Dansky, Carroll, Foa, & Brady, 2001; Donovan, Padin-Rivera, &
Kowaliw, 2001; Triffleman, Carroll, & Kellogg, 1999), including her own (e.g.,
Seeking Safety). But, the available empirically supported PTSD-treatment
option of exposure therapy, using either exposure through imagery or in

vivo exposure, is contraindicated for individuals with "numerous traumas that occurred many years prior to treatment (e.g., severe childhood sexual abuse)," especially where there may be "a large number of traumatic memories" (Coffey, Dansky, & Brady, 2003, p. 133). There are also reasons to avoid or postpone exposure therapy for PTSD, for example, in situations where extreme anger or intense anger is commonly experienced by a client (Coffey, et al., 2003). Also, if clients tend to experience dissociation, given the nature of their trauma, then exposure therapy may be problematic. Thus, Coffey et al. (2003) conclude that exposure-based techniques are best for those clients with the following characteristics: a history of single trauma or multiple discrete trauma; relatively clear memories of the trauma(s); traumas that did not occur before age fifteen, in the case of multiple trauma; relatively minor dissociation during exposure-therapy techniques; the ability to develop vivid images; and the experience primarily of intrusive memories, flashbacks, fear avoidance, or hyperarousal as the most prominent symptoms. However, Riggs et al. (2003) emphasize that the Coffey et al. (2003) guidelines have not been empirically tested, and some of his recent work with colleagues has shown that exposure therapy could be successful with clients who do not meet these guidelines, such as those having histories of child abuse.

On the other hand, there is support for Najavit's (2003) model, which emphasizes how clients may learn to cope in safe ways while explicitly avoiding any actual processing of the trauma, as the practitioner prioritizes stabilizing the client, teaching coping skills, and reducing the most destructive symptoms. Thus, this program is an example of a combined SUD-PTSD treatment that emphasizes how it was designed to "continually integrate attention to both disorders; that is, both are treated at the same time by the same clinician" as an "*integrated* model," versus those models that are sequential or parallel in nature (Najavits, 2003, p. 152). A body of research is identified as supporting the use of an integrated model, even as a survey of clients indicates that such a model is their preference. This contrasts with the norm in which clients are told "they need to become abstinent from substances before working on PTSD" (Najavits, 2003, p. 152).

Najavits (2003, p. 155) acknowledges a body of experts who have "recommended that such work not begin for substance abusers until they have achieved a period of stable abstinence and functionality." Also, interpretive psychodynamic work is explicitly omitted, including exploration of intrapsychic motives or dynamic insights, although it is acknowledged that "these powerful interventions can be helpful in later stages of treatment," but "they are believed too potentially upsetting for patients at this stage" (p. 156).

Najavits (2003, pp. 149–51) recognizes that her integrated treatment is best described as "first-stage therapy" for each of the SUD and PTSD disorders, consistent with experts in the fields of SUD and PTSD, as many have independently described a similar first stage that "prioritizes stabilizing the patient, teaching coping skills, and reducing the most destructive symptoms." She calls her first stage "safety."

Brown, Read, and Kahler (2003, p. 186) recognize how "most clinical researchers advocate the need for simultaneous treatment for patients suffering from comorbid SUDs and PTSD," and research evidence suggests that they "cannot be treated as independent, unrelated problems." They also warn practitioners "against viewing PTSD as secondary to SUDs" and against assuming that successfully treating the alcohol-drug problem alone will "somehow result in improved PTSD symptoms" (p. 186). But, with regard to the critical issue of the "correct timing" of the delivery of treatment interventions, Brown et al. (2003, p. 186) conclude that "the most effective focus and timing of such trauma/PTSD treatment remains to be determined."

Ouimette, Moos, and Finney (2003) report data on a sample of one hundred male veterans with SUD-PTSD comorbidity who completed inpatient SUD treatment and were followed at one, two, and five years, using a naturalistic treatment-effectiveness research design, with no random assignment to participation in PTSD treatment. Those men who completed all three follow-ups were more likely to be white, with 27 percent of the client sample being in remission (abstinent from illicit-drug use and either abstinent from or with nonproblem use of alcohol) at five-year follow-up. The odds of being in remission at five-year follow-up were 3.7 times higher for those clients who received PTSD treatment in the first year than for those who did not receive PTSD treatment. The odds of being in remission at five-year follow-up were 1.5 times higher for those who attended twelve-step groups in the first year than they were for those who did not. Moreover, after controlling for first- and second-year intervention variables, the odds of being in remission at the five-year follow-up were 4.6 times higher for those clients who received PTSD treatment in the fifth year than for those who did not receive PTSD treatment. Ouimette, Moos, and Finney then divided the first year following inpatient SUD treatment into four quarters and sought to predict five-year remission, finding that the odds of being in remission at the five-year follow-up were 3.6 times higher for those who received PTSD treatment in the first three months after discharge from inpatient Veterans Affairs (VA) treatment.

Duration of treatment was also examined by Ouimett, Moos, and Finney, comparing those with less than three months of treatment, those with three to six months of treatment, and those with seven to twelve months of treatment, finding that clients who received more consistent PTSD care (53 percent of those who received three to six months of PTSD treatment and 36 percent of those who received seven to twelve months of PTSD treatment) over the first year were more likely to be in remission at five years; but, the number of subjects in each cell was very small, and findings are considered only preliminary. Ouimette, Moos, and Finney (2003) state that evidence of change in PTSD symptoms may be the more important factor in the remission of both disorders. And, future research needs to determine the mechanisms that explain why PTSD treatment and twelve-step-group participation are help-ful for SUD remission. Ouimette, Moos, and Finney (2003) also admit that the VA databases do not reveal the interventions applied, whether cognitive-behavioral-skills training, exposure therapy, or supportive psychotherapy. They conclude by suggesting that, while simultaneous treatment of SUD and PTSD has been recommended in recent practice guidelines and research re-views, their data suggest the need for SUD practitioners to consider early (af-ter completion of inpatient care) and regular (ongoing) receipt of PTSD care in the treatment of SUD providers.

Research findings suggest that there is a "complex, dynamic relationship between SUD-PTSD comorbidity" and that this relationship is affected by the key variable of coping (Brown et al., 2003, p. 183). Of note, research shows that clients with PTSD may enter treatment with poorer coping skills. Clients in substance-abuse treatment experience changes in coping from baseline to follow-up assessment, and these changes are associated with bet-ter substance-use outcomes. Brown et al. (2003, p. 187) conclude that a "fo-cus on coping approaches may facilitate enhanced outcomes for both sub-stance abuse and PTSD." And, practitioners should focus on helping their SUD-PTSD clients "decrease their maladaptive coping approaches and learn or master more adaptive coping strategies as part of a comprehensive ap-proach to the treatment of these comorbid disorders" (p. 187).

Hence, the work of several researchers and the case of SUD-PTSD comor-bidity serve to illustrate the usefulness of this book's integration of phases of treatment and recovery and stages of change in order to emphasize the im-portance of correct timing. (See more discussion in chapter 5 and table 5.2.) A strong rationale exists for including, as a recommended state-of-the-art practice, an *Integration of Stages of Change and Phases of Treatment and Recovery* as item 2 under category 2 in table 4.1.

3. Integration of Harm Reduction, Moderation Approaches, and Abstinence Models

There is also a need for the integration of harm reduction, moderation ap-proaches, and abstinence models when tailoring an integrated treatment for many contemporary clients. Regarding the question as to whether to apply a harm-reduction or abstinence model (Tatarsky, 2002), in many cases the an-swer is to apply both. However, there is a need for evaluation of such inte-grated models (Tatarsky, 2003). Majoor and Rivera (2003) call for not only close collaboration between innovative researchers (i.e., those comfortable with quantitative, qualitative, and quasi-experimental methods) and harm-reduction programs, but also the full integration of harm-reduction ap-proaches into the overall field of addiction treatment. Research shows that contemporary treatment providers in the United States show considerable acceptance of harm-reduction interventions, even though they are not widely available (Rosenberg & Phillips, 2003). Other data suggest that even brief education provided to practitioners can serve to change practitioner attitudes toward harm reduction, suggesting this may be an essential preliminary step before the availability of harm-reduction interventions increases (Goddard, 2003). Kellogg (2003) makes a distinction between approaches that seek to integrate harm reduction in abstinence-oriented settings, citing the exemplary work of Denning (2001) and of Marlatt, Blume, and Parks (2001) in this genre, versus his focus on the goal of integrating abstinence into harm-reduction endeavors. Thus, there are varied ways in which the integration of harm reduction and abstinence approaches is being promoted to practitioners.

McLellan (2003b) acknowledges both the need for empirical evaluation and the recurrent theme of integration of abstinence into harm-reduction models, explaining the emergent model of gradualism as follows:

> "Gradualism" seeks to create a continuum in which people who are using alcohol or substances in a dangerous or destructive manner are gradually led through a channel that first seeks to reduce the destructiveness of their use, and then seeks to help them attain a life free of addictive behavior. The continuum would also serve as a safety net in the case of relapse. (p. 239)

The integration of harm reduction, moderation approaches, and abstinence models is needed in the real world, especially if practitioners are to meet clients where they are. For example, a probation or parole officer, judge, employer, agency, or corporate or governmental regulatory authority may be calling for the immediate cessation of some problem behavior, suggesting that total abstinence is the goal. However, practitioners often learn in the privacy of the consultation room how the client is still engaging in a forbidden addictive or problem behavior. This typically means that practitioners must initially work within a harm-reduction model.

As Marlatt (1998b) suggests, harm reduction is a "path between the polarized opposites of the moral and medical models—a path that promises to provide humane and practical help for drug users, their families, and our communities" (p. 3), even if critics "reject it as being overly permissive in its rejection of strict 'zero tolerance' policies and its promotion of alternatives to abstinence" (p. 3). As Marlatt (1998a) informs us, the Harm Reduction Coalition (1996) promotes principles of harm reduction that include accepting, for better and for worse, that licit and illicit drug use is part of our world, emphasizing working to minimize its harmful effects rather than simply ignoring or condemning them.

Weingart and Marlatt (1998) critique the U.S. treatment establishment, as it "perceives total abstinence as the only acceptable treatment outcome; consequently, treatment centers routinely discharge clients who can't stop using, as well as those who resume use after a period of abstinence" (p. 366). Thus, Weingart and Marlatt (1998) explain how addiction treatment in the United

States is a high-threshold endeavor, partly because of insufficient treatment slots available, and also because of the common requirement of complete abstinence. They recommend acknowledging how some individuals will inevitably be unwilling or unable to reduce their levels of drug use. This is especially the case early in treatment, when clients have as yet to be exposed to addiction-treatment techniques, such as RP.

There is also a place for moderation approaches. Sobell and Sobell (2002) provide support for moderate alcohol drinking, indicating that there is convincing evidence in support of moderation. They recognize how the belief that alcohol problems are "progressive and irreversible" has served as an obstacle to the wider acceptance of moderation goals. Similarly, the belief that continued drinking by those who develop an alcohol problem will serve to worsen their problem, creating a downward progression until the person dies, has created an obstacle to moderation goals (p. vii). Sobell and Sobell (2002) assert that there is a "plethora of evidence" that contradicts the "progressivity assumption." This is partly due to the fact that alcohol abuse predicts a less persistent, milder disorder that does not usually progress to dependence, following the research of Schuckit, Smith, Danko, Bucholz, and Reich (2001). But, they also recognize research findings that, without receipt of treatment, once alcohol problems become serious, they are likely to worsen (Sobell & Sobell, 2002).

Similarly, Rotgers, Kern, and Hoeltzel (2002) emphasize the central concept of moderation, explaining how moderation is a reasonable and attainable goal for many clients with less severe drinking problems. Rotgers et al. (2002) offer the following, in this regard:

> The choice of moderation or abstinence for each person should be a considered one, based on looking at the pros and cons of each, and taking full responsibility for one's own actions. Personal choice and empowerment are critical for success, and success in moderation will further build self-efficacy. (p. 1)

Miller (2001) explains how the thought of never drinking alcohol again can be overwhelming for some clients. Some clients fear entering treatment programs because they will face a firm insistence that they immediately become sober, along with other rigid expectations. Marlatt, Tucker, Donovan, and Vuchinich (1997) concur that the punitive nature of interventions deters help seeking.

Miller (2001, p. 23) discusses how, in response to this, clients are typically "asked to consider the possibility of staying abstinent from alcohol for an agreed-upon, limited period of time, prior to making a more informed decision about any drinking in the future." Thus, there are also much gentler, less threatening ways to approach the goal of sobriety. This technique is called "sobriety sampling" within the context of the CRA (Miller, 2001, p. 23).

Because practitioners must start where the client is, a rationale exists for the recommended state-of-the-art practice involving *Integration of Harm Reduction, Moderation Approaches, and Abstinence Models*. This is listed as item 3 in table 4.1, under category 2.

4. Integration of Psychoanalytic and Cognitive-Behavioral Theories and Techniques

Others not only integrate the use of harm-reduction and abstinence models, but also include the integration of both psychoanalytic theory and cognitive-behavioral interventions (Tatarsky, 2002, 2003; Wallace, 1996a). The presumption underlying this integration is that clients need to not only acquire adequate ego functioning and affect regulation, but must also acquire patterns of cognitive and behavioral functioning that are adaptive. A hallmark feature of the chemically dependent involves poor self-regulation of not only affects, but also of impulses, self-esteem, and interpersonal behavior, as well as poor self-care (Khantzian et al., 1990; Wallace, 1996a). Typically, these problems are rooted in poor early object relations, growing up in dysfunctional families, and experiences of trauma (Wallace, 1991b, 1993b, 1996a; Wurmser, 1992). Traumas frequently found in the population include high rates of childhood sexual abuse, especially in women, as well as experiences of physical abuse, exposure to domestic violence, and emotional abuse and neglect (Hegamin et al., 2001; Hiller et al., 2002; Staton et al., 2001; Wallace, 1991b, 1993b, 1996a). The result is that clients bring deficits in ego functioning, usually presenting problems in reality testing, judgment, and the exercise of defenses (Derby, 1992b; Rothschild, 1992; Yalisove, 1992), in addition to well-hidden phobias (Wallace, 1996a; Wurmser, 1992). Clients' functioning necessitates that clinicians acquire facility in the area of trauma resolution, including short-term (i.e., largely educational) and long-term (i.e., working through and integration of memories) trauma-resolution techniques (Wallace, 1996a), as well as in techniques that improve clients' self-regulation of affects, impulses, self-esteem, and interpersonal behavior (Khantzian et al., 1990; Wallace, 1996a). Again, this often includes providing clients with a way of understanding their functioning via the active delivery of education or psychoeducation (Derby, 1992b; Dodes & Khantzian, 1998; Rothschild, 1992; Wallace, 1996a; Yalisove, 1992).

In order to guide a focus on the production of adaptive affective, cognitive, and behavioral patterns of functioning, there is great logic in drawing upon psychoanalytic theory to foster understanding of affective functioning, as well as upon CBT to foster understanding of cognitive and behavioral functioning. And the corresponding clinical techniques for the accomplishment of this work may logically come from psychoanalytic and CBTs. Hence, there is great logic in recommending the state-of-the-art practice of

Integration of Psychoanalytic and Cognitive-Behavioral Theories and Techniques,
listed as item 4 under category 2 in table 4.1.

5. Acquisition of Affective, Behavioral, and Cognitive Coping Skills— Learning New ABCs

The integration of the four schools of psychoanalytic thought (i.e., drive, ego, self psychology, and object relations theory) with CBT has also given rise to a very practical emphasis on fostering in clients the acquisition of *af-fective, behavioral,* and *cognitive* coping skills, or the learning of new *ABCs* (Wallace, 1996a). Relapse frequently occurs in response to one of the most frequently encountered high-risk situations; this involves the challenge of coping with negative emotion or painful affective states (Marlatt & Gordon, 1985; Wallace, 1991b, 1996a). Thus, the learning of affective coping is crucial. And psychoanalytic or psychodynamic individual psychotherapy is the domain in which the greatest strides have been made in fostering the acquisition of affective coping skills—given the problems of alexythymia (the inability to recognize, label, or process feelings) and poor regulation of affect that are so common in clients (Derby, 1992b; Khantzian et al., 1990; Levin, 1999, 2001; Rothschild, 1992; Wallace, 1991b, 1992e, 1996a; Yalisove, 1992, 1997).

Moreover, cognitive-behavioral techniques typically foster the acquisition of cognitive and behavioral coping skills (Marlatt & Gordon, 1985). In order to be comprehensive, the goal of fostering in clients the acquisition of affective, behavioral, and cognitive coping skills is put forward, thereby reflecting the integration of both psychoanalytic and CBTs and techniques.

A focus is also placed upon fostering in clients acquisition of adaptive coping responses to replace maladaptive coping responses. For example, a maladaptive coping response may involve aggressive behavior, including violence or verbal abuse. Initially, an adaptive coping response may include walking away or sitting in silence and achieving a state of inner calm. Technically, this may qualify as avoidant coping. And, ideally, active coping is considered the most adaptive response, such as being able to deliver a positive, assertive verbal response (Wallace, 2005). However, for some clients, until this higher-order form of adaptive coping—involving a positive, assertive verbal response—has been learned, practiced, and has undergone successful generalization to a variety of situations, clients are encouraged to deploy avoidant forms of coping, such as walking away or remaining silent. Such avoidant coping is still relatively adaptive when compared to maladaptive responses of aggression (verbal abuse, violent behavior) or drug/alcohol use. Adaptive cognitive coping also includes a client's learning to discern when it is best to do what (i.e., whether the situation requires the execution of the higher-order response of a positive, assertive verbal response or, instead, walking away or sitting in silence). Clients must learn that there may be different times when certain responses are most appropriate. Skills for coping undergo not only generalization, but also increasing sophistication as clients acquire flexibility by learning when it is best to do what. This signals tremendous improvement over what may have been a prior rigid or overlearned pattern of consistently responding with the same maladaptive coping response (e.g., getting high, violence). In this manner, there is a very important process that occurs over time as clients acquire adaptive coping responses.

The focus on fostering in clients the acquisition of affective, behavioral, and cognitive coping skills is also consistent with the recommendations of Brown et al. (2003, p. 187) with regard to the specific needs of clients presenting comorbidity, such as PTSD along with a substance-abuse disorder. Brown et al. (2003) underscore just how important it is for practitioners to focus on helping such clients decrease their maladaptive coping approaches and learn or master more adaptive coping strategies; moreover, this is considered a comprehensive approach to comorbidity. However, Wallace (1991b, 1996a) argues that even where clients do not meet diagnostic criteria for an additional mental disorder beyond substance abuse/dependence, clients tend to have problems in self-regulation of affects, impulses, and interpersonal behavior. Problems in self-regulation may also be seen as involving maladaptive coping responses that need to be replaced with adaptive affective, behavioral, and cognitive coping responses.

Hence, there is a rationale for including in table 4.1 the recommended state-of-the-art practice involving practitioners fostering in clients the *Acquisition of Affective, Behavioral, and Cognitive Coping Skills—Learning New ABCs* as item 5 in category 2.

6. Integration of Motivational Interviewing, Stages of Change, and Identity Development Theory for a Diverse Identity Involving Race, Sexual Orientation, and/or Disability

There has also been a recent integration of motivational interviewing, stages-of-change theory, and stages of identity development for race (Blacks, Whites, and People of Color—Africans, Latinos, Asians, etc.); sexual orientation; and disability (Wallace et al., 2003). Motivational interviewing, as a brief intervention, is viewed as having great value in moving clients across stages of change for identity development. In the aftermath of any experiences of trauma or oppression in the U.S. culture of violence (Wallace, 2003), clients may benefit from empathic engagement with practitioners who are able to foster progressive movement in clients across stages of change toward the highest, most differentiated, and most mature identity statuses. Often, clients will stop working on their identity development as a Black, White, person of color, gay, lesbian, bisexual, transgender, or person with a disability, especially after a violent encounter in which they have been harassed, condemned, or verbally or physically attacked because of their identity. To stop working on one's identity may mean to attempt to pass as not having that identity, or to hide one's identity. This is not necessarily desirable or psychologically healthy, even though such a strategy may temporarily, intermittently, or occasionally allow for avoiding any further harassment or attacks, depending upon the prevailing social climate (Wallace et al., 2003).

An alternative involves the receipt of therapeutic interventions that assist an individual in continuing to make progress in claiming and expressing his or her identity. The goal is to promote the movement of clients toward reaching their highest potential, as clients move across stages of identity development and stages of change, rehearsing and deploying increasingly more sophisticated, generalized, and refined affective, behavioral, and cognitive coping strategies (Wallace, 2003).

In this manner, through the integration of motivational interviewing, stages of change, and identity development theory, practitioners may have the tools necessary to assist contemporary diverse clients with their identity development. This includes the possibility of fostering progressive movement toward the attainment of the highest, most differentiated, and most mature identity statuses for those who are not only working on a new identity as an alcoholic or addict, but also on an identity as a Black man, or as a Hispanic woman, or as a gay Jewish man with the disability of HIV/AIDS, or as a White man who is an ex-con with a learning disability and a mental disability.

In this manner, there is justification in recommending the state-of-the-art practice involving *Integration of Motivational Interviewing, Stages of Change, and Identity Development Theory for a Diverse Identity Involving Race, Sexual Orientation, and/or Disability*, listed as item 6 in category 2 in table 4.1.

7. Incorporating Contemporary Trends in Psychology: Multiculturalism, Positive Psychology, the Strengths-Based Approach, and Optimistic Thinking/Learned Optimism

Practitioners should also incorporate some of the latest developments in the field of psychology within community-based addiction treatment. The result may be practitioners incorporating multiculturalism (Bronstein & Quina, 2003; Carter, 2000; Sue et al., 1998; Wallace & Carter, 2003; Wallace, 2003); positive psychology (Lopez & Snyder, 2003; Seligman, 2002); the strengths-based approach (Aspinwall & Staudinger, 2003; van Wormer & Davis, 2003); and optimistic thinking/learned optimism (Seligman, 1998, 2002; Vaughan, 2001). There are many good reasons for practitioners to learn how to be multiculturally sensitive and competent, to practice a positive psychology and focus on clients' strengths, as well as to both acquire optimistic thinking/learned optimism and to teach such thinking to clients.

Contemporary multiculturalism offers the goal of ensuring that practitioners are free from any biases, prejudices, or social conditioning with regard to negative stereotypes that they may unconsciously and unwittingly harbor toward diverse and different others, perhaps projecting negative and low expectations upon clients (Wallace, 2003; Wallace & Carter, 2003). The projection of negative and low expectations might involve beliefs about certain clients having a tendency toward relapse and recidivism (Wallace, 1993a, 1995). The result may be negative countertransference.

Potentially exerting a stronger influence on treatment outcomes than do the specific differences among treatment techniques, there are also nonspecific or common factors such as hope and faith. These include the practitioner's expectation that the client will change (as a powerful self-fulfilling prophecy), as well as the client's own levels of hope or optimism about change (sometimes called self-efficacy) (Miller, Wilbourne, & Hettema, 2003, p. 39).

Another goal is to train practitioners to focus upon and to reinforce client strengths, resilience, and an amazing ability to endure, rebound, and grow (Aspinwall & Staudinger, 2003), despite absolutely astounding prior histories of pain, trauma, torture, and suffering through varied developmental eras of their lives (Ouimette & Brown, 2003), as well as through their traumatic addiction (Wallace, 1996a) and incarceration (Haney & Zimbardo, 1998). In addition, among the cognitive coping strategies to be taught to clients (and practitioners) is learned optimism (Vaughan, 2001). This includes, specifically, the skills of optimistic thinking and action so that clients can dispute cognitive distortions, such as catastrophic thinking, and be able to search for and acknowledge evidence of any fallacies in their thinking through credible disputation (Seligman, 1998, 2002).

Thus, *Incorporating Contemporary Trends in Psychology: Multiculturalism, Positive Psychology, the Strengths-Based Approach, and Optimistic Thinking/ Learned Optimism* is listed as item 7 in table 4.1, as a recommended state-of-the-art practice.

A STANDARD OF CARE FOR PRACTITIONERS TO FOLLOW

When metaphorically holding in hand the menu with seven evidence-based treatment interventions and seven state-of-the-art practices to choose from, practitioners should exercise both fidelity to what is recommended to them, as well as flexibility when working in the real world with limited resources and diverse, multiproblem clients with complex needs. This fidelity means deploying an evidence-based intervention, in particular, according to practitioners' best understanding of the key, essential elements that are associated

Table 4.4.   A Standard of Care for Practitioners to Follow

Selecting from the menu of options of evidence-based addiction treatment interventions
  and recommended state-of-the-art practices available in the social context, practitioners
  may create an integrated and tailored intervention for individual clients given where the
  client is, what the client needs, and what the client is willing to do or prefers to do when
  in a particular stage of change and phase of treatment and recovery.

with the efficacy of that intervention, or by maintaining the integrity of the
essential ingredients of that intervention. This should reflect practitioners'
acquisition of adequate reading materials, training, and supervision with regard to the deployment of that particular evidence-based intervention. But
then, going beyond this body of understanding, responding to ongoing assessments of clients, and acknowledging available resources in the overall
treatment setting, practitioners must also exercise flexibility and adapt
evidence-based interventions as needed. This adaptation may include integrating just some aspects of different evidence-based interventions or using
them just at certain points in time during the overall treatment, tailoring
what is delivered to meet individual client needs, characteristics, and diversity. Finally, as consumers, client preferences must be taken into account. A
resultant standard of care can be stated even more succinctly, as appears in
table 4.4.

CONCLUSION

This chapter presented the menu of evidence-based options, along with recommended state-of-the-art practices, that are available for use by practitioners, given the task of making mandated addiction treatment work. In the
process, practitioners were cautioned both with regard to the exercise of fidelity in adhering to recommended evidence-based addiction treatment, as
well as with regard to exercising flexibility in the real world, far away from
the environment of clinical trials, where tight controls and strict exclusion
and inclusion criteria reign.

This chapter also suggested a contemporary standard of care to be followed by practitioners when they are adapting evidence-based addiction-
treatment interventions and state-of-the-art practices, as well as when integrating them and tailoring them in light of client-assessment findings:
practitioners need to consider not only where the client is, but also what the
client needs, as well as what the client is willing to do or prefers to do when
in a particular phase of treatment/stage of change.

In many cases, the process of adapting evidence-based interventions and
tailoring treatment for individual clients will include the use of more than one
intervention having empirical support, suggesting a process of integrating

scientifically proven and state-of-the-art interventions. This may actually involve deployment of what can be described as a unified treatment model rooted in unified theory. Moos (2003) suggested the need for the field of addiction treatment to develop more unified models that encompass the role of life-context factors and of formal and informal care. The reality of the menu of evidence-based options presented in this chapter suggests that there are seven items that might be key elements of a unified model for the field of addiction treatment. The seven recommended state-of-the-art practices presented in this chapter as part of the menu of options suggests how there are also many integrated theories that might be key elements of a unified theory to guide the work of practitioners and researchers within the field of addiction treatment. Future chapters in part 2 of this book will move the field of addiction treatment toward a unified model and theory via detailed discussion of cases illustrating how the treatment model and theory operate in actual case conceptualization and service delivery.

5

The Correct Timing for Delivery of Interventions

When practitioners begin to work with multiproblem clients who present varied characteristics, needs, and diversity, it may be easy for practitioners to become overwhelmed. Practitioners need to consider when to do what, weighing and exploring the following: (1) what seems to be most urgent and most pressing, essential to address immediately in order to stabilize the client and increase the chances of forging a successful, positive long-term treatment outcome for a particular client; and (2) what seems to be less urgent and less pressing, possibly to be delayed until later, when the client is more stable and does not seem at risk of immediate relapse/recidivism. Issues to be addressed immediately are conceptualized as short-term goals, while issues to be addressed later constitute long-term goals. The correct timing for starting work pursuing long-term goals depends upon how long it takes to first accomplish short-term goals. And the time to accomplish short-term goals varies from individual client to client. Also, the answer to the practitioner question as to when to do what undergoes further modification based on considerations of where the client is, what the client needs, and what the client is willing to do or prefers to do when in a particular phase of treatment/stage of change.

A travel metaphor may also be helpful. It is as if the practitioner is attempting to first assist a client in arriving at destination A (short-term goals). And, if the client does not arrive at destination A, what is the value in actively working to help the client arrive at destination B (long-term goals)? Meanwhile, practitioners remain fully cognizant of the value, and in fact absolute necessity, of clients' successfully arriving at both destinations A and B. But a metaphoric map or guide is needed that sets out a suggested route to be followed in assisting clients in arriving at both destinations A and B. For sake of simplicity, the task of getting to destination A is discussed in terms of issues to be addressed in an early phase of treatment/action stage, spanning the first six months a client is actively working on changing addictive behavior in the real world. The task of getting to destination B is discussed in terms of issues to be addressed in a middle-to-late phase of treatment/ maintenance stage, spanning beyond six months of active work on changing addictive behavior, up to many years or a lifetime. As with all destinations, there is more than one way to get there, and the amount of time it takes to get to point A or B can vary because of many individual- and environmental-level factors. Thus, both a rough guide and an approximate estimate of correct timing result. These are presented in this chapter, and practitioners are urged to repeatedly consider ongoing assessment findings and to be flexible given these findings. For, where the client is today may not be where the client is tomorrow, or one month from now, or three months down the road. Only ongoing assessment findings can determine when to do what as the client moves across stages of change and phases of treatment.

Thus, a guiding logic and theory for framing discussion in this chapter is found in the concept of phases of treatment and recovery, with emphasis on the correct timing for the delivery of treatment interventions that are ideally suited for a particular phase (Wallace, 1992d, 1996a). Guidance also comes from the concept of stages of change (DiClemente & Velasquez, 2002). And there has also been an integration of the concept of phases of treatment and recovery with the concept of stages of change (Wallace, 1996b), serving to provide guidance with regard to how to correctly time the delivery of treatment interventions. This discussion in this chapter will therefore refer to phases of treatment/stages of change, reflecting this integration.

It is important to remember that clients are indeed moving across phases of treatment/stages of change as time passes, even if, for purposes of training, this book finds value in emphasizing a simple dichotomy of destination, A and B. It must be kept in mind, however, that arriving at destination A is akin to moving across the continuum of time for an initial six-month period of an early phase of treatment/action stage. And, arriving at destination B is akin to moving beyond a six-month marker on the time continuum in what is then a middle-to-late phase of treatment/maintenance stage. But, there can be a danger in such dichotomous thinking and simplification (i.e., over-simplification). Thus, practitioners are repeatedly reminded to address clients' multitude of problems, needs, and diversity with flexibility, paying attention to ongoing assessment findings and tailoring treatment to meet individual client needs.

Specifically, this chapter answers the following question: Given client characteristics, needs, and diversity, how should the practitioner proceed in terms of those matters to be urgently addressed and those that can wait to be addressed until the client has substantially stabilized beyond six months in treatment?

A GUIDE FOR PRACTITIONERS: WHEN TO DO WHAT TO ADDRESS MULTIPROBLEM CLIENTS' CHARACTERISTICS, NEEDS, AND DIVERSITY

Table 5.1 provides a summary description of the characteristics and needs commonly found among the contemporary population of clients in community-based addiction treatment, as well as a guide for when to do what. What this table (5.1) and this chapter provide may be considered a rough guide, and considerations in the case of individual clients will guide practitioners in how to proceed as they tailor treatment for clients, given where clients are and what they need, are willing to do, and prefer.

Client characteristics and needs are organized under two major headings in table 5.1. The first heading in table 5.1, "Urgent Issues to be Addressed Immediately," suggests that to which practitioners should attend early in treatment, ideally from day one of contact with clients, up to the first six months; this includes the point at which clients start working on actively changing addictive behavior, thereby also constituting the period of an action stage. Some clients may be in either a precontemplation, contemplation, preparation, or action stage with regard to working on addictive/problem behavior; all of these stages are encompassed by an early phase of treatment. (See the * note in table 5.1.) This early phase of treatment includes clients who must now work on their addictive behavior in the real world outside of a correctional setting. And, since clients may present more than one addictive or problem behavior, they may be in more than one stage of change for each addictive or problem behavior. Motivational enhancement techniques or motivational interviewing may be utilized in order to help a client move across stages of change toward an action stage. The goal is to enhance clients' readiness to actively work on changing their varied addictive and problem behaviors so that they enter an action stage and spend six months learning how to initiate, sustain, and solidify behavior change. Thus, it is important to prioritize that to which practitioners should attend in addiction treatment, suggesting the value of what is prioritized in table 5.1 as urgent issues to be addressed immediately.

The second heading in table 5.1, "Less Urgent Issues to Be Addressed Later," acknowledges that to which practitioners should attend once clients have attained a certain amount of stability. Although a rough guide, the correct timing for addressing these issues later may encompass the middle-to-late phase of treatment/maintenance stage, extending from a period of greater than six months actively working on changing addictive and/or other problem behavior, and lasting up to many years and, indeed, one's entire lifetime. Also included in table 5.1 are those issues to which practitioners need to attend in order for clients to achieve productivity as citizens and to enjoy a stable long-term recovery. These issues are also usually less urgent, but important nonetheless.

Table 5.1. When to Do What: Correct Timing for Addressing Multiproblem Clients' Needs, Characteristics, and Diversity

I. Urgent issues to be addressed immediately*

(* Clients may be in a precontemplation, contemplation, preparation, or action stage. But, the goal is to promote entrance into an action stage, so clients begin to actively work on changing addictive behavior. The first six months of active work on change also constitutes an early phase of treatment.)

   A. Urgent contemporary needs and characteristics: "First things first"
      1) The need for assistance in understanding and complying with mandates, contingency contracts, and intensive supervision requirements
      2) A characteristic high risk of recidivism and relapse to more than one problematic or addictive behavior
      3) The need for assistance in reintegrating back into family and community life
   B. Urgent need for psychiatric/mental-health services: Mental and emotional stability as essential
      1) Characteristic psychiatric symptoms, mental disorders, and MICA/comorbidity status: Education on trauma, strengthening the ego, and fostering coping
      2) Characteristic adjustment disorders/mental disorders from the stress of incarceration or release after lengthy incarceration
      3) Characteristic histories of violence and the urgent need for help in surrendering violent behavior

II. Less urgent issues to be addressed later**

(**Clients are likely in a maintenance stage after they have been actively working on changing addictive behavior for a period greater than six months. This period also constitutes the middle-to-late phase of treatment.)

   A. Need to address historical factors contributing to a high risk of relapse and recidivism
      1) Characteristic histories involving generational cycles of addiction, abuse, trauma, violence, and incarceration
      2) Characteristic histories of parental separation and/or foster-care placements: Client experiences of neglect, abuse, and trauma
   B. A need to address contemporary factors contributing to a high risk of relapse and recidivism
      1) Characteristic parental guilt and negative compensatory behaviors
      2) Parental trauma over termination of parental rights or loss of contact with children
   C. A need to foster successful long-term recovery in the community as a productive citizen
      1) Characteristic neuro-cognitive deficits: Evidence of stunted growth or deterioration in cognitive, intellectual, and personality functioning
      2) Characteristic learning problems, learning disabilities, educational deficits, and/or criminal background: Limited job-training and employment opportunities
      3) Characteristic homelessness and the goal of securing adequate stable housing for clients

In this manner, practitioners may follow individual-assessment findings and decide for each client when to do what, whether to address multiproblem clients' characteristics, needs, and diversity immediately or later; or practitioners can avoid becoming overwhelmed and draw upon the concept of phases of treatment and recovery and the concept of stages of change (even integrating them, following Wallace, 1996b). Practitioners are hereby being given a rough guide for how to prioritize clients' treatment issues from those that are absolutely urgent, to those that require a certain amount of stability in the client in order to be addressed. Through the performance of thorough individualized ongoing assessments, practitioners will determine exactly how to tailor addiction treatment to individual client characteristics and needs, setting short- and long-term goals.

Guidance may also be offered with regard to solving ongoing questions in the field of addiction treatment that have not yet been resolved through research. Moos (2003) suggested that more information is needed about how to address the role of life-context factors in clients' lives and with regard to recommended client-treatment matching strategies. For example, more needs to be known about the effectiveness of matching strategies based on a client's cognitive and psychosocial functioning, including the need to potentially target services to address a client's specific problems. Moos (2003) also identified the need for greater understanding in the field of addiction treatment with regard to how to organize and sequence treatment for clients with dual disorders, or comorbidity. Specific recommendations are offered in regard to these issues.

I. URGENT ISSUES TO BE ADDRESSED IMMEDIATELY

As shown in table 5.1, there are a number of urgent issues to be addressed immediately, typically in the early phase of treatment. Examples of urgent contemporary needs and characteristics will be discussed in this section. These may be considered short-term goals.

A. Urgent Contemporary Needs and Characteristics: "First Things First"

Clients have a number of more urgent needs and characteristics that need to be addressed immediately as opposed to later. It is vital that practitioners help clients with certain urgent, immediate matters in this early phase of treatment. If these urgent, immediate matters are not adequately addressed, clients may not be able to successfully participate in or complete treatment. They may never make it to a middle-to-late phase of treatment. Hence, practitioners must address certain immediate and urgent client issues, following the rationale of "first things first," or what needs attention immediately? Nothing else may go well, and treatment may not even be able to proceed, if the logic inherent in addressing first things first or immediately is not respected.

1. The Need for Assistance in Understanding and Complying with Mandates, Contingency Contracts, and Intensive Supervision Requirements

Clients need assistance in fully understanding and abiding by the terms and conditions of any mandates given out by parole, probation, a judge, a drug court, or a Treatment Accountability for Safer Communities (TASC) program. Clients must also understand the contingencies spelled out by a child-protection, welfare, or other agency coercing them into treatment. Even if clients are voluntary or concerned, the treatment program they are entering may have certain rules, regulations, and contingency contracts into which clients must enter. In all cases, this means that clients need to fully understand the kind of graduated sanctions they may face when urine-test results are positive for drug use. Clients need assistance in developing good judgment and reality testing, and in learning to engage in consequential thinking and problem solving, despite, for example, having a long history of impulsive behavior and acting without thinking about negative consequences when chronically high or intoxicated.

Also, clients accustomed to just doing what they are told, given social conditioning during incarceration, must learn how to think and act proactively. Clients need to understand that many consequences will follow for them in the real world, consequences that are contingent on behaviors that they, as clients, either perform or fail to perform. Clients need help adjusting to this reality, involving-life context factors of absolute importance. Errors and mistakes in judgment, or failure to engage in consequential thinking or problem solving, can have a long-lasting negative impact; these include clients being violated and sent back to prison, losing welfare benefits, losing child custody, or being asked to leave a treatment program for violation of rules, regulations, or contingency contracts.

2. A Characteristic High Risk of Recidivism and Relapse to More Than One Problematic or Addictive Behavior

Among first things first, there is the primary treatment task of preventing recidivism and relapse. This is the essence of the work to be accomplished immediately in the early phase of treatment, or across the action stage. For, if clients are not able to avoid recidivism and relapse, they may be violated and returned to incarceration by criminal-justice-system authorities, and they will no longer be available to attend community-based addiction treatment. Or they may face sanctions from other authorities in those agencies where they are under intensive supervision. This could lead to even more problems and difficulties arising for clients. For, clients who relapse may face graduated sanctions that have devastating emotional consequences, such as loss of child custody, loss of benefits, or loss of housing. The emotional pain, trauma, and stress from graduated sanctions may only further increase the risk of relapse and recidivism.

Clients who find that there are so many problems inherent in negotiating life in the real world, now that they are either free from incarceration or are facing life without states of intoxication, may resort to old coping patterns involving the use of drugs/alcohol or criminal behaviors. Thus, clients need help adapting to and coping within the larger social context in order to avoid relapse/recidivism. Clients need interventions that directly address their risk of resorting to old coping behaviors. This means the receipt of relapse prevention (RP). RP must cover the teaching of coping skills for anything from a relapse to a specific drug, to relapse to alcohol, to relapse to drug dealing, to relapse to other behaviors typically performed once clients are reimmersed in an addictive lifestyle, such as compulsive sexuality or hustling behaviors for acquiring money. Because many clients are polysubstance users, there may be a risk of relapse to several substances. The presence of multiple addictions may include an addiction to fast money, or rapidly accumulating wealth, as well as to gambling and the like. Clients may also relapse to such varied problem behaviors as high-risk sexual behavior, exchanging sex for drugs or money, and intravenous drug use with needle sharing, as well as violent interpersonal behavior to get money for drugs, to name a few examples.

Given the characteristic presence of multiple addictions and multiple problem behaviors, clients may be in varied states of readiness or different stages of change for each addiction and behavior. Clients, therefore, need treatment that enhances motivation for change and accepts that progress needs to be made with each addiction and each behavior. It becomes important to address the client's state of readiness for change, or stage of change, when it comes to each separate addiction and each separate behavior. Treatment may have to proceed methodically as each addiction and each behavior is systematically addressed over time. Consistent with the principle of first things first, clients must be engaged in treatment and assessed with regard to what they are facing or experiencing at the present time. This should lead practitioners to address that particular risk factor or problem behavior posing the greatest immediate danger to a client. In this manner, by starting where the client is, practitioners will be able to prioritize the area in which the client needs the most immediate help coping, teaching, and enhancing coping skills for that with which the client is currently confronted. This may involve, for example, a family member who is urging and inviting a client to use drugs, or a client's experiencing pressure from a drug dealer to sell drugs once again, and it is tempting, given lack of employment. Or this might involve teaching adaptive coping skills for use in response to the emergence of painful affect arising within a client, such as anger that might lead to violence.

Addressing first things first might include teaching a client how to execute an avoidant coping strategy of walking away in order to avoid relapse/recidivism. An avoidant coping response (walking away or sitting in silence) may be a vast improvement over maladaptive responses of relapse to drug/alcohol use, verbal abuse, or violence, for example. However, over time, practitioners should support clients in the acquisition of higher-order adaptive-coping responses, such as deployment of a positive, assertive verbal response as a form of active coping. The process of learning skills for coping, or adaptive affective, behavioral, and cognitive coping responses, represents an important short-term goal for an early phase of treatment/action stage. Important ongoing life-context factors may be addressed in this manner.

3. The Need for Assistance in Reintegrating Back into Family and Community Life

Clients who feel unable to reintegrate back into family and community life may set themselves up for relapse, recidivism, and a return to institutional life within a correctional facility. They may indeed feel that it is easier to manage in the controlled environment of a correctional facility, especially if life on the outside just seems entirely too hard to manage and face. Their interactions with family and community members in the outside world are very important, suggesting the value of practitioners' addressing in treatment these pertinent life-context factors. The creation of a supportive social network of family and close friends is essential to recovery. It matters a great deal if family or peer interactions are extremely stressful, are disappointing, and are a source of conflict.

For, there may be a greater risk of relapse and recidivism if valued interpersonal interactions are persistently difficult. It is vital that clients receive assistance in learning how to cope with this stress and conflict. Clients need to learn how to cope affectively, behaviorally, and cognitively in interpersonal situations involving family stress and conflict. They need to know how to cope with feelings that are no longer being medicated or escaped through alcohol and drug use. They need to know how to behave in high-risk and stressful situations. And they need to know how to think and process information, including how to engage in problem solving and consequential thinking, and how to exercise good judgment and reality testing. Such interpersonal-skills training and learning of adaptive coping responses constitutes vital work to be accomplished in an early phase of treatment/action stage. If these skills are not learned, clients may never make it to a middle-to-late phase of treatment/maintenance stage, and they may never attain greater than six months in community-based addiction treatment.

Clients need treatment that addresses their family problems stemming from the stress of enduring lengthy periods of incarceration, leading to the risk of family dissolution, including separation and divorce. There is also a risk of family violence and domestic violence. Help in reintegrating back into family life is the first step in negotiating clients' overall adjustment to community life, something for which they also need assistance. The importance of this work is underscored by research findings on the role of social support in enhancing the chances of successful recovery (see chapter 4). Lack of success in establishing a social-support network can have devastating consequences, as it may reduce the chances of positive long-term treatment outcome. Together with the role of family and community members, the use of twelve-step groups is vital in helping clients build new social-support networks in the community. In some cases, the social-support network found through twelve-step groups may be even more important than reconnecting with family and other community members, especially if they are actively involved in alcohol use, illicit-drug use, drug dealing, or other criminality. But, even here, clients have to be able to get along and cope with the normal stress of interacting with people in the real world. This includes learning how to interact with people in the community who may also be stressed out and have problems. Again, the learning of affective, behavioral, and cognitive coping skills is of vital importance.

B. Urgent Need for Psychiatric/Mental-Health Services: Mental and Emotional Stability as Essential

In terms of achieving success in coping in the real world, in avoiding relapse and recidivism, and in meeting addiction-treatment goals, the chances of having good outcomes in all of these areas are significantly compromised by mental and emotional instability. Addressing clients' psychiatric and mental-health problems in the early phase of treatment/action stage is seen as an urgent need. Indeed, some clients can take no action in addressing any issues or problem behaviors they may have if they are not first stabilized. Thus, the attainment of mental and emotional stability is of the highest priority as an urgent need in the early phase of treatment/action stage, and it is a vital short-term treatment goal requiring immediate attention. Mental and emotional stabilization is, therefore, an urgent need to be addressed across an early phase of treatment/action stage. These issues may now be elaborated upon.

1. Characteristic Psychiatric Symptoms, Mental Disorders, and MICA/Comorbidity Status: Education on Trauma, Strengthening the Ego, and Fostering Coping

Psychiatric symptoms and mental disorders that are often rooted in childhood abuse, trauma, and exposure to violence characterize this population.

This includes a variety of mood disorders, anxiety disorders such as post-traumatic stress disorder, and personality disorders, for example. There is an urgent need for psychiatric and mental-health treatment, frequently involving the task of becoming stabilized on appropriate psychiatric medications. There is also the challenge of clients' needing to learn how to regularly take their medications and dutifully report any side effects to their psychiatrist. All too often, clients tend to discontinue psychiatric medication and stop attending their appointments with a psychiatrist, given their discomfort with a certain dose of medication or its side effects. Many clients are totally new to this entire process. They may hold negative personal or cultural beliefs about taking medication, preferring to avoid it altogether. Motivation to engage in medication compliance needs to be systematically enhanced, and recurrent relapses to medication noncompliance need to be effectively managed. Education on medication purposes and compliance becomes essential. Also, clients desperately need assistance in learning how to report medication side effects to psychiatrists and in being assertive in discussing the potential need for a change in dose and/or medication. They also need assistance in understanding the importance of taking psychiatric medication and the negative consequences of discontinuing medication. This includes clients' fully understanding how psychiatric symptoms may reemerge or how problem behaviors may reappear.

Clients' mental disorders may have manifested at any point across their lifespan, but they all too frequently go undetected and untreated. Clients who are MICAs (mentally ill chemical abusers) or who present comorbid disorders are frequently a hidden population within the larger group of those entering community-based addiction treatment. The New York City Department of Mental Health, Mental Retardation and Alcoholism Services (NYCDMHMRAS, 1998, p. 41) explains how the New York State Office of Alcoholism and Substance Abuse Services (OASAS) has identified MICAs "based, primarily, on duration of psychiatric hospitalization. A substance abuser with a previous psychiatric hospitalization of more than 30 days duration has fit the definition" across the decade of the 1990s. However, clients with addictive behaviors who lead chaotic lives, end up in the criminal justice system, and never receive adequate psychiatric treatment may never have undergone a lengthy hospitalization but present problematic comorbidity. Also consider how the limited number of appropriate MICA programs and insufficient treatment slots typically meant that such programs needed all of their quite limited (especially in the 1980s and early 1990s) available slots for severely ill psychotic clients, as well as for other clients for whom the mental illness was clearly the primary diagnosis.

Moreover, to fill these slots, clients needed a well-documented primary psychiatric diagnosis, a picture quite difficult to attain with sufficient clarity when chronic addictive behaviors are predominating and making many new lifetime diagnoses somewhat tentative. Thus, those without clear psychiatric diagnoses were not appropriate for MICA settings and were not referred to them by mental-health professionals. Fortunately, things have changed, and there are now many more inpatient, residential, and outpatient MICA programs available in places such as New York State. Today, the hidden population of clients with comorbid disorders may experience the good fortune of finally having their conditions uncovered for the very first time by a psychiatrist working within a correctional facility or by a practitioner, such as a psychologist, working in a community-based addiction-treatment program. In the ideal situation, clients discovered to have a MICA status or comorbidity will receive integrated treatment providing both mental-health and addiction-treatment interventions at the same time, on the same site.

Research suggests that substance-abusing patients with schizophrenia have better functioning, better prognoses, and milder forms of schizophrenia than other patients with schizophrenia. However, they also have periods of substance abuse that involve serious illness and symptoms that are very difficult to manage (Shaner, Tucker, Roberts, & Eckman, 1999).

Many clients have severe multiple mental disorders, posing special challenges. And there is also a risk of relapse to depression, mania, active psychosis, or the manifestation of other psychiatric symptoms, such as suicidal or homicidal acting-out behavior, creating a special need for both ongoing monitoring and receipt of psychiatric and mental-health services in addition to treatment for addiction. Ideally, integrated treatment providing both mental-health and addiction-treatment interventions is available on-site. Some of these clients need assistance in applying for Social Security disability, given the serious nature of their mental disability.

The presence of psychiatric disorders and comorbidity often includes a history of trauma. With regard to addressing trauma, there is a general rule of thumb to follow: the strengthening of the ego and learning of adaptive coping responses tends to always precede any in-depth processing of traumatic memories with attendant emergence of painful affect states (Wallace, 1996a). Thus, there is the short-term goal of strengthening the ego and learning adaptive coping. And there is the long-term goal of processing traumatic memories and associated painful affect. However, the urgent goal to be accomplished more immediately is client mental and emotional stability, and the achievement of this short-term goal in an early phase of treatment/ action stage typically requires that clients acquire skills for coping or adaptive affective, behavioral, and cognitive coping responses.

Specifically, with regard to trauma, clients in the early phase of treatment (encompassing Wallace's [1996a] withdrawal phase, across weeks one and two, and Prochaska and DiClemente's [1983] precontemplation, contemplation, preparation, and action stages) receive primarily the delivery of psychoeducation (e.g., cognitive reframing) to strengthen the ego and facilitate acquisition of coping skills. Practitioners seek to cultivate the capacity of the ego for self-observation/self-monitoring; this involves the ability of the ego to observe the moment when certain affects or images arise within the self, the moment when the client enacts certain behaviors, or the moment when cravings or the thought to use drugs/alcohol arises.

Also in the early phase of treatment (specifically encompassing Wallace's [1996a] phase of prolonging abstinence, across week three to month six, and ideally Prochaska and DiClemente's [1983] action stage for the primary addictive/problem behavior of focus), the short-term goal is still to strengthen the ego. And any work on trauma is still largely educational and geared toward further enhancement of client coping skills. A client's ego should learn, practice, and effectively begin to master self-observation/ self-monitoring during this period. The client is further supported in learning how to first observe and then interrupt/stop the process of being triggered by a cue that leads to a relapse or provokes a maladaptive affective, behavioral, or cognitive response. Indeed, by the end of month six, the client has ideally gained substantial experience practicing and strengthening adaptive affective, behavioral, and cognitive coping responses across a variety of situations; and, because the client's ego has been substantially strengthened, he or she has ideally learned to engage in good self-observation/self-monitoring and has learned to replace old patterns of defense with more adaptive ego functions, and overall client functioning has substantially improved.

A client possessing such skills will be able to self-observe/self-monitor and report to a practitioner or peer what is arising within them (whether a painful affect, memory of trauma, craving, or a thought to use drugs/ alcohol) and execute adaptive coping responses. Thus, reaching short-term goals via a largely educational approach to trauma that is geared toward enhancing client coping skills establishes a foundation for accomplishing several long-term goals, whether future more-in-depth discussion of traumatic memories or having lifelong skills for avoiding relapse by being able to recognize and cope with any new triggers/cues.

Finally, during the middle-to-late phase of treatment (encompassing Wallace's [1996a, 1996b] phase of pursuing lifetime recovery, beyond month six, and ideally Prochaska and DiClemente's [1983] maintenance stage for the primary addictive/problem behavior of focus), the successful establishment of a substantially strengthened ego with capacity to engage in self-observation/ self-monitoring may permit a therapeutically guided regression to fixation points of past trauma (Wallace, 1996a). A qualitatively different kind of trauma-resolution work may proceed, going beyond the prior focus on delivering education and enhancing coping skills. A client may then both articulate and emotionally process painful affects from the moment of original trauma if it is deemed a worthwhile task likely to bring further benefits to the client. This follows an individual client's ongoing assessment findings.

Finally, it should be remembered that often the answer as to what constitutes the correct timing for addressing a particular addiction or problem behavior arises from the reality of what the client is willing, ready, and able to do.

2. Characteristic Adjustment Disorders/Mental Disorders from the Stress of Incarceration or Release after Lengthy Incarceration

Adjustment disorders involving disturbances in mood or anxiety also require urgent attention, as related symptoms may compromise a client's ability to cope with the challenge of living in the real world. An adjustment disorder that emerged in the past during a traumatic incarceration may or may not have led to psychiatric treatment during incarceration. A common characteristic of clients includes a history of an adjustment disorder with symptoms such as depression and anxiety. This disorder is a common response to the stressful experience of incarceration, separation from family, or to being placed in isolation ("the hole") in prison after a fight or violent behavior; some clients are placed in isolation for weeks or months, and others keep fighting over and over again and return to the hole repeatedly. Thus, many adjustment disorders with depression and/or anxiety first appear during incarceration. Problems with depression and/or anxiety may arise once again after release from incarceration, given the stress of coping with life on the outside.

Also commonly found are adjustment disorders with symptoms of depression, anxiety, and phobias that follow from the stress of adjusting to life outside of a correctional setting, especially after many years of being incarcerated. These disorders usually first appear after release from incarceration.

A *prison institutionalization syndrome* also appears in many clients with lengthy histories of incarceration. This involves those released from lengthy incarceration having an unconscious tendency to repeat and re-create in their lives the conditions of social isolation that they experienced while incarcerated or while in the hole. Some suffer from feelings of anxiety or actual social phobias as a consequence of the traumatic experience of imprisonment and isolation. Some exhibit the behavior of spending an inordinate amount of time alone, in small rooms or apartments, allowing themselves only limited mobility in the outside world. This is one way of re-creating and repeating the prison isolation experience as an attempt at mastery of what was once traumatic (i.e., isolation) when forcibly imposed by the criminal justice system. Yet this isolation and confinement was something to which the client adapted. Another way of repeating and re-creating the experience of isolation is to unconsciously or unwittingly engage in criminal or risk-taking behavior that is likely to lead to actual physical reincarceration. This represents a strange but understandable way of mastering the trauma of incarceration and isolation; one is now in control, having caused oneself to reexperience placement in a restrictive environment. Being incarcerated again also solves the problem of suffering from anxiety and social phobias in the outside world.

Thus, in some cases, practitioners should consider it a rather urgent need when clients seem to be setting themselves up for reincarceration. Clients

need to understand the possibility that they are suffering from an adjustment disorder, or prison institutionalization syndrome, allowing them to
avoid unwittingly acting in such a way that they experience actual physical
reincarceration. Unfortunately, many clients never survive the first six
months of recovery in the real world. They sabotage themselves, relapse, become recidivist, and reenter a correctional facility. However, this pattern can
be avoided if practitioners either secure for clients much-needed mental-
health and/or psychiatric services or deliver appropriate intervention in
their work with clients. If such issues are not addressed in the early phase of
treatment/action stage, or immediately as a rather urgent matter, then
clients may end up reincarcerated.

3. Characteristic Histories of Violence and the Urgent Need for Help
in Surrendering Violent Behavior

Clients typically need help coping with a history of violence or the commission of a violent crime. Many clients also need treatment that addresses any
current risk for violent acting-out behavior. This is indeed most urgent, and
it needs to be addressed immediately. The goal of preventing a relapse to violence may emerge as primary, given the risk of potential arrest, criminal
prosecution, and incarceration for violence. The need to surrender violent
behavior may be quite urgent, given that this, too, may be a common response to stress and a way of coping in the real world. Violence may be a
deeply engrained behavior for those who were immersed in the drug culture
and in drug dealing. For other clients, violence literally rises to the level of
being a way of life. Violent behavior must be surrendered if there is any realistic hope that a client will even be able to remain in a treatment program,
let alone receive needed addiction-treatment services. Quite simply, violence
is not an option in community-based addiction-treatment programs. Both
staff and other clients need to feel safe and remain protected.

Some violent clients have a psychiatric condition or mental disorder that
has never been uncovered, such as a bipolar disorder. The receipt of varied
psychiatric medications such as Depakote, Seroquel, or Zyprexa may be vital in order for clients to be able to contain violent behavior. If clients are
not stabilized on appropriate medications, not only is the attainment of
treatment goals quite difficult, but there is also a greater risk of relapse to
self-medication strategies with illicit drugs and alcohol. There is also a
greater risk of recidivism, especially when problems regulating aggressive
impulses persist.

The goal of learning to regulate aggressive impulses becomes a central
priority in clients' mental-health treatment. There are clients who do not
need psychiatric medication to enhance regulation of their aggressive impulses or to contain them. Instead, they need affective-skills coping training and anger management as important treatment components. In the case

of other clients, it is after they are stabilized on psychiatric medication that they may still need to learn affective coping skills and anger-management techniques. Indeed, anger management includes the learning of affective, behavioral, and cognitive coping strategies for use in situations with a high risk of relapse to violence and recidivism. Options include walking away (often a highly recommended avoidant coping response), sitting in silence, performing a self-talk/self-calming exercise, or making a positive, assertive verbal response (the ideal active coping response that often takes clients some time to master). Much may be accomplished in teaching such coping skills in both long-term mental-health treatment or through psychoeducation delivered in individual and group sessions within addiction treatment. Clients may also need to examine the underlying factors behind their violent behavior and overall high risk for relapse and recidivism, as discussed in the next section.

II. LESS URGENT ISSUES TO BE ADDRESSED LATER

A review of table 5.1 shows how there are issues to be addressed in treatment once clients are stable, perhaps in a middle-to-late phase of treatment/ maintenance stage, when clients have spent more than six months working to change addictive behavior in a community-based addiction-treatment setting, or perhaps earlier. Once again, this is a rough guide, and it is possible that an individual client has a pressing need or preference for addressing these issues at some point across months one through six in treatment; practitioners are advised to tailor treatment for individual clients based on assessment findings. However, as a rough guide that allows practitioners to avoid becoming overwhelmed by multiproblem clients and their many characteristics and needs, this section provides a map of how to correctly time the delivery of interventions, and three categories of issues will be discussed. These may be considered long-term goals.

A. Need to Address Historical Factors Contributing a High Risk of Relapse and Recidivism

It is not an urgent matter but a valuable task to provide clients with opportunities to understand some of their underlying risk factors and background issues that have played a role in their having such a challenging time in life. Of course these underlying risk factors and background issues serve to contribute to an ongoing risk of relapse and recidivism, so they, too, should be addressed at some point in treatment. After the essential initial tasks of mental/emotional stabilization and prevention of relapse/recidivism, such issues can be dealt with later. As a rough guide requiring practitioner flexibility, it is suggested that the middle-to-late phase of treatment/maintenance stage represents a good time to address certain factors later, such as the two factors discussed in this section.

1. Characteristic Histories Involving Generational Cycles of Addiction, Abuse, Trauma, Violence, and Incarceration

There are matters involving generational cycles of addiction, abuse, trauma, violence, and incarceration that should, in general, be addressed later, only after clients have become stabilized and all their urgent, more immediate needs have been addressed. While a generic rough guide for the correct timing for addressing these histories is in a middle-to-late phase of treatment/ maintenance stage, practitioner-assessment findings in individual cases are the ideal guide regarding how to proceed.

Some clients may seem to be sufficiently stable so that past trauma can be addressed as early as months one to six into treatment. A case in the forthcoming chapter 7, that of Mr. F. T., serves to illustrate how a multiproblem client presenting challenging comorbidity can become sufficiently stable after first pursuing eight weeks of outpatient psychiatric care, and then engaging in three months of community-based addiction treatment, to begin to address some of his past trauma. He had five months since his last marijuana and alcohol use when he began trauma work, but he was still in an early phase of treatment/action stage. Moreover, this trauma work largely sought to provide the client with a cognitive and intellectual framework for understanding what had happened to him, as well as the potential impact upon him up to the present day; this impact usually leads to a focus on resultant patterns of coping and the need to improve coping skills.

On the other hand, a forthcoming case in chapter 8 (Ms. M. T.) serves to illustrate how, by the end of three months in treatment, sufficient stability had not been achieved to justify trauma-resolution work. In this second case, the young woman's experience of obstacles and delays in becoming stable on psychiatric medication and her tendency to present recurrent states of suicidality and homicidality illustrates how three months in treatment was too soon to address past trauma. In fact, the case shows how even talking about the trauma of domestic violence served to create states of agitation, with a risk of relapse and acting out anger and aggression, either against herself or against her batterer. The task of improving her coping skills had to occur independently of her engaging in any discussion of her recent trauma. Thus, ongoing individual-assessment findings are crucial in determining the best approach to be taken by a practitioner.

Both of these cases, and many contemporary clients in general, however, share the legacy of past trauma. Characteristic problems among child, adolescent, and adult family members are often related to a historical legacy in which multiple generations in a family have experienced addiction, abuse, trauma, violence, and incarceration, and these generational cycles and patterns persist up to the present. Clients need help breaking generational cycles and personally changing their own problem behaviors. This includes the need to receive treatment that helps clients end their involvement in drug use, drug dealing, crime, violence, and other related problem behaviors.

The fact that clients once observed parental role models engaged in behaviors that clients promised to never repeat, yet did end up repeating once they grew up, causes great emotional pain for clients. Hence, practitioners must carefully consider the correct timing for work in treatment that addresses these generational cycles and the attendant pain, shame, and trauma, with this work ideally occurring at some point in the middle-to-late phase of treatment/maintenance stage.

Table 5.2 also presents a rough guide for the correct timing for addressing trauma across the phases of treatment of Wallace (1996a) and stages of change of Prochaska and DiClemente (1983). The various phases of treatment and recovery and stages of change are subsumed under an early phase of treatment and a middle-to-late phase of treatment, for simplicity (see box at far left in table 5.2).

2. Characteristic Histories of Parental Separation and/or Foster-Care Placements: Client Experiences of Neglect, Abuse, and Trauma

Many characteristics and problems among contemporary adolescents and adults stem from having endured across their childhood long periods of separation from parents due, for example, to factors such as parental incarceration, parental addiction, parental illness (HIV/AIDS), and resultant foster-care placements. Typically, there was also neglect and abuse when in the care of both biological parents and other court-appointed guardians. There may be many, many associated traumas. Clients may need treatment that helps them to resolve their profound disappointment, anger, bitterness, resentment, unresolved grief, and depression. They may also need treatment that addresses any associated experiences of neglect, abuse, violence, or trauma. Again, the ideal time for this work, if it is correctly timed, following the rough guide offered in this chapter, is likely during the middle-to-late phase of treatment/maintenance stage. Individual variations in when it is best to address this kind of trauma will be found, suggesting the role of practitioners in conducting assessments and tailoring treatment for clients.

B. A Need to Address Contemporary Factors Contributing to a High Risk of Relapse and Recidivism

While there are those clients who were once children suffering pain and trauma, on the other hand, there are also those clients who become the parents inflicting damage on their own children in a new generation. And, in fact, most clients fall into both categories. Given intimate knowledge of their

Table 5.2. Correct Timing of Interventions for Trauma Survivors

Time	Phase	Stage of change	Practitioner tasks
E A R L Y * Weeks 1 to 2	* In a withdrawal phase from drugs, or early initial work to change problem behavior(s), following Wallace (1996a).	* In a precontemplation, contemplation, preparation, or action stage, following Prochaska & DiClemente (1983) and DiClemente & Velasquez (2002) for one or more problem behaviors. Focus is placed on main problem behavior, striving to move client across stages of change into action stage. Other problem behaviors are focused upon, as appropriate.	* Use Psycho-education. * Strengthen ego. * Teach self-observation. * Assess clients for traumas. * Teach clients about triggers and cues for their affective, behavioral, and cognitive patterns of response/relapse. * Select from menu evidence-based interventions and state-of-the-art practices, integrating and tailoring them, given where clients are, what they need, and what they prefer.
P H A S E * Week 3 to month 6	* In a phase of prolonging abstinence from drugs, or preventing relapse, wherein clients learn how to change and sustain behavioral change (Wallace, 1996a).	* In a precontemplation, contemplation, preparation, or action stage for one or more problem behaviors. Usually in an action stage for main problem behavior, as time goes by. Focus on preventing relapse to main problem behavior, moving client toward action for other problem behavior(s), also preventing relapse for these behavior(s).	* Strengthen ego further, as clients master self-observation/ interruption of being triggered by cues for relapse or maladaptive responses (affects, behaviors, cognitions) and perform adaptive coping. * Select from menu evidence-based interventions and state-of-the-art practices, integrating and tailoring them, given where clients are, what they need, and what they prefer.

MIDDLE TO LATE PHASE	* Beyond month 6	* In a phase of pursuing lifetime recovery from problem behavior(s), wherein clients refine and generalize coping skills to prevent relapse so that behavior change is successfully maintained over time (Wallace, 1996a).	* In a precontemplation, contemplation, preparation, or action stage for one or more problem behaviors. Usually in a maintenance stage for main problem behavior. Focus on fostering progress toward action for other problem behavior(s), and avoiding relapse for all these behaviors.	* Because of a strong self-observing ego, option exists for working through and integrating traumatic memories with processing of painful affect; some clients need engage in the work earlier/later. * Select from menu evidence-based interventions and state-of-the-art practices, integrating and tailoring them, given where clients are, what they need, and what they prefer.

Table 5.2 shows the *early phase of treatment* (encompassing a *withdrawal phase*, a *phase of prolonging abstinence*, and an *action stage*) and the *middle-to-late phase of treatment* (encompassing a *phase of pursing lifetime recovery* and a *maintenance stage*). Correct timing for when and how practitioners should address trauma is also shown.

own childhood experiences of trauma, contemporary parents suffer emotionally when their own children have had to negotiate active parental addiction, parental incarceration, and foster-care placements. Two sets of factors typically plaguing parents as they suffer emotionally are discussed in this section, and these factors usually require attention in the middle-to-late phase of treatment/maintenance stage.

1. Characteristic Parental Guilt and Negative Compensatory Behaviors

There are characteristic feelings of guilt on the part of parents, especially mothers, and negative compensatory behaviors (e.g., spoiling; overindulging; giving out money; buying expensive clothing, toys, and gifts) due to a prior period of parental active addiction, incarceration, or loss of child custody. Clients need help in resolving their feelings of guilt, in coming to appreciate the potential damage that may be done through the performance of compensatory behaviors, in ending the enactment of compensatory behaviors, and in avoiding a relapse to such behaviors. Clients may also need help in coping with feelings of guilt so that they do not relapse to drug use. Pressure to have and obtain money in order to perform compensatory behaviors can also lead to recidivism. For example, a parent who successfully enters a middle-to-late phase of treatment/maintenance stage and has acquired a substantial period of abstinence from drug use may nonetheless contemplate, for example, selling drugs, hustling, shoplifting, or engaging in credit-card fraud in order to acquire expensive items for his or her children as a compensatory behavior. Interventions are essential to help clients resolve their guilt and to avoid compensatory behaviors and their attendant risks, such as recidivism.

This characteristic parental guilt and negative compensatory behaviors also underscores the role of practitioner flexibility as to when to address such issues. While this chapter provides a rough guide as to when to correctly time the delivery of interventions to address these issues, practitioners must follow what emerges from ongoing assessments with clients. When material emerges about what clients are purchasing for their children, or when other evidence of parental guilt arises, that is the ideal time to deliver interventions. However, as it turns out, usually this kind of material does not emerge when entire sessions are taken up by more urgent issues, such as the risk of relapse or problems with mental and emotional instability/ psychiatric symptoms. Typically, it is only when more urgent matters have been addressed in treatment that clients then shift their focus and begin to talk more freely about time spent with their children, allowing the practitioner to also shift focus and attend to issues such as parental guilt. When practitioner-assessment findings suggest that a parent may be at immediate risk of relapse to drug dealing or other criminality because of guilt driving them to indulge their children with expensive items, then this topic, too, becomes an urgent matter to be addressed immediately. In some cases, it may then have to be addressed in month one of treatment, in an early phase of treatment/action stage, if this is when such material arises. Thus, this underscores how what is presented in this chapter is a rough guide, and practitioner flexibility includes using ongoing assessment findings to decide when to do what, whether immediately or later.

2. Parental Trauma Over Termination of Parental Rights or Loss of Contact with Children

Both mothers and fathers can suffer parental trauma over termination of parental rights or loss of contact with children. This can go beyond merely suffering from intense feelings of guilt. Unresolved guilt can lead to problems with depression and anxiety, as well as to something as extreme as a psychotic depression: guilt, in particular, can exacerbate a depression and lead to the emergence of auditory hallucinations in which voices chastise, criticize, or berate the client. In fact, many parents use defenses that seem to protect them from intense guilt and any feelings associated with separation from their children or with contemplating what happened to their children during the period of parental addiction or incarceration. Often it is better to leave these defenses in place and allow clients to avoid detailed discussion of their guilt and emotional pain over separation from children or over the neglect and abuse of their children, especially in the early phase of treatment or in the action stage. However, by the time clients are in a middle-to-late phase of treatment/maintenance stage for drug use, it is possible that clients are ready and that it is the correct time to address their guilt, shame, emotional pain, and trauma caused by separation from children, loss of custody, and/or termination of parental rights. Clients have usually gained experience coping with the emergence of painful affect without relapsing to chemical use across the six months of the early phase of treatment/action stage. With such experiences with coping with painful affect, and with substantial time since last drug use suggesting a lower risk of relapse, practitioners may support clients in addressing emotional pain and trauma caused by separation from children. Individual clients may have different needs in this regard, and some clients may address these issues much earlier, such as across months one through six in treatment, in the early phase of treatment/action stage, following practitioner flexibility in light of ongoing assessment findings.

The deepest feelings of guilt and the greatest trauma typically involve cases in which clients have had their parental rights terminated. Some parents have had parental rights terminated for an entire family of children, including as many as four to six children, for example, and they suffer some of the most intense guilt and serious depression. In all cases, practitioners must discern the best time to address this pain, guilt, and depression, especially if the use of defenses is allowing a person to function by keeping certain issues in isolation from all the other ones they are addressing in their recovery. For some clients, even after one or two years in treatment, the fragility of the stability they have worked so hard to attain is not worth jeopardizing because of unresolved issues of guilt and emotional pain. Individual decisions must be made in the cases of such clients, given an assessment of their situation. In some cases it may be best to let sleeping dogs lie, or to leave defenses intact, allowing feelings of guilt and other emotional pain to be defended against until the overuse of those defenses becomes problematic, if they ever do. Other clients are so debilitated by the pain, guilt, and depression associated with termination of parental rights that they relapse to self-medication strategies with chemicals, finding chronic intoxication to be effective in helping them defend against their overwhelming pain. In unraveling cases of relapse to chronic drug use, the reality of a history of termination of parental rights is often the key to an explanation.

There will also be some cases wherein the issue of pain from loss of child custody/separation/termination of parental rights must be at least briefly addressed in the early phase of treatment/action stage, or whenever the issue arises. It may be the case that a client cannot make any initial progress at all in treatment, or any further progress after some time in treatment, unless they receive interventions that lessen their guilt and emotional pain about what happened to their children. This could be at the time of initial assessment/screening, during month one in treatment, during month six, or at literally any crisis point that might arise at any time. At all such times, what is helpful is for the practitioner to deliver for the very first time, or to reiterate, education about the role of brain-based cravings, neurochemical compulsions to secure and use drugs, and how drug users do what they have to do, pointing out how addiction came to dominate the client's life. The goal is to help clients appreciate how the biological nature of the disease of addiction tends to override any innate motherly or parental instincts they had, leading to the neglect and abuse of children, and/or to an inability to readily terminate drug use on one's own. Quite simply, the goal is to explain to clients again and again how the nature of addiction is such that drug use continues despite knowledge of negative consequences such as the risk of incarceration or loss of child custody. Until such education is received and repeatedly reinforced, clients may not be able to move forward in pursuing their treatment goals. But, in the early phase of treatment/ action stage, this education merely aims to give clients a cognitive and intellectual understanding of what happened to them during their active addiction; it is not about creating an opportunity for in-depth emotional processing of their feelings of guilt—work typically relegated until clients have attained considerable stability, learned adaptive coping responses, and have a considerably strengthened ego (usually by the middle-to-late phase of treatment/maintenance stage). Of course individual assessment findings are key in making a determination in terms of when to do what.

In some cases, guilt has led to a serious depression that now plagues clients to the point of being associated with a chronic pattern of relapse or inability to terminate drug use. Active drug use or chronic relapse poses a risk of recidivism as well. Again, receipt of psychiatric and mental-health treatment may be essential to stabilize such clients. However, in nearly all cases, any detailed processing of their feelings of guilt and the trauma of having been separated from their children, or having neglected or abused their children, ideally occurs in a middle-to-late phase of treatment/maintenance stage, when clients have had greater than six months actively working on addictive behavior. Thus, the point at which work on these issues occurs, if at all, may vary depending on individual-assessment findings, underscoring the role of practitioner flexibility.

C. A Need to Foster Successful Long-Term Recovery in the Community as a Productive Citizen

There are other issues in the middle-to-late phase of treatment/maintenance stage that are pertinent to long-term recovery. These issues, once addressed, can ensure client's long-term success in recovery as productive citizens, and they are usually relegated until later for practitioner attention in a middle-to-late phase of treatment/maintenance stage. Three such issues are discussed in this section.

1. Characteristic Neurocognitive Deficits: Evidence of Stunted Growth or Deterioration in Cognitive, Intellectual, and Personality Functioning

The neurochemical and biological changes that occurred in clients' brains during their active addiction may also have left clients with neurocognitive deficits. Neurocognitive deficits may therefore characterize many clients, especially those with deeply entrenched chronic drug/alcohol-use patterns that spanned as much as two or more decades. There may also be a stunting or deterioration in cognitive, memory, speech, intellectual, and personality functioning because of a long-standing lifestyle centered on the daily use of drugs and/or alcohol. Stunting of growth is especially likely when chronic, long-term drug/alcohol-use patterns started in adolescence, while all clients may present substantial deterioration in functioning. Within the ongoing assessment process, clients may also be asked about their experiences of forgetting and about problems with comprehension, retention, or merely understanding what is being discussed in their group sessions, for example. Clients can also be asked what they perceive to be the cause of their problems and what they feel they need. All of this information may impact practitioner decisions about when to do what, to assist clients with such problems.

Neurocognitive deficits may also be related to HIV/AIDS or histories of head injury, stroke, brain tumors, or nutritional deficiencies. The aging population of the incarcerated and the presence of long-term drug and alcohol users increase the chances that clients with these kinds of deficits may enter treatment. Collectively, a host of clients may not be able to comprehend standard written materials or memorize key tenets of recovery and relapse prevention for a variety of reasons. Such clients must have treatment adapted to meet their needs. Again, the role of practitioner flexibility emerges as pertinent. Starting from the very first assessment/screening session, first individual drug-counseling session, or first group drug-counseling session, modifications may have to be made for such clients. A shift to oral presentation of material in simple language with use of repetition may be required, suggesting another aspect of practitioner flexibility. While such steps involving modifications may be made in an early phase of treatment/action stage, other steps may be delayed until a middle-to-late phase of treatment/ maintenance stage for a variety of reasons.

Clients' insurance plans and the prohibitive cost of neurological testing may mean that the performance of formal testing and diagnosis does not regularly occur when clients are suspected of having substantial neurocognitive deficits. Other clients will have appropriate insurance and/or sufficiently serious deficits to substantiate attention and referral in an early phase of treatment/action stage. Practitioners should always proceed with any referral they feel is necessary at any point in treatment, regardless of what they think may or may not happen because of a client's insurance plan. A common response is to pursue standard vocational testing and to modify clients' treatment plans so that they include appropriate and realistic goals in the area of vocational training and employment, including the possibility of a client's applying for Social Security disability.

Regarding the correct timing for addressing clients' neurocognitive deficits and evidence of impaired cognitive functioning, assessments performed in the first month of treatment or when clients are in a withdrawal phase from chronic alcohol/chemical use may not reflect an accurate picture of functioning. Also, many clients show improvements with six months of abstinence from chronic alcohol/illicit-chemical use. For practitioners who have expected to see improvements by six months since last chronic alcohol/ chemical use but do not observe this, client entrance into the middle-to-late phase of treatment/maintenance stage (reaching over six months since last alcohol/chemical use) marks another important time to consider and act on referrals for assessment, appropriate services, and Social Security disability. Meanwhile, practitioner flexibility is urged once again.

2. Characteristic Learning Problems, Learning Disabilities, Educational Deficits, and/or Criminal Background: Limited Job-Training and Employment Opportunities

There is also the characteristic presence of continuing learning problems related to educational deficits and/or childhood diagnoses such as attention deficit disorder with/without hyperactivity or a learning disability. There is often a history of placement in special education and of school dropout. Together with educational deficits, there is the reality of what it means to have a criminal background. Many clients have never worked or have never maintained employment for more than several months or a year, while others have only engaged in drug distribution to earn money. Educational deficits, learning problems, severely limited or no work history, and a criminal background, in turn, impact the range of vocational-training, job-training, and employment opportunities that may be pursued. Clients need help securing appropriate and realistic job-training and employment opportunities. They also need help coping with any frustration that might contribute to reinvolvement in drug distribution or other criminality. Clients may need special assistance, given such problems, as well as help adjusting to their limitations without resorting to recidivism or relapse.

In some cases, it is so clear that Social Security disability for life is a much more likely possibility than ever being able to maintain employment, that application for these benefits is made in an early phase of treatment/action stage at the urging of and/or with the support of practitioners. In other cases, time is needed to determine whether the attainment of six months or more in recovery allows for some improvement in cognitive and intellectual functioning that could end up reflecting childhood/adolescent learning problems, learning disabilities, and educational deficits. Practitioners wait to observe the extent to which addiction treatment and elapsed time since chronic alcohol/illicit-drug use help to improve a client's apparent cognitive level of functioning. Thus, quite often, it is not until a middle-to-late phase of treatment/maintenance stage that practitioners feel confident that there are indeed persistent cognitive deficits that limit vocational-training and employment opportunities. Practitioner flexibility in responding to individual-assessment findings is vital once again.

3. Characteristic Homelessness and the Goal of Securing Adequate Stable Housing for Clients

Contemporary multiproblem clients need help securing and maintaining stable housing. Many clients leaving incarceration are sent to shelters. They are literally homeless. Applications for housing, which may require many, many months of processing, are typically filed in the early phase of treatment/action stage. Practitioners need to refer clients as soon as possible for such assistance, or offer it themselves, filling out the appropriate paperwork. However, because of typical delays in processing paperwork for single-room-occupancy slots and apartments, the actual search for housing will usually occur for most clients in a middle-to-late phase of treatment/maintenance stage. There are then substantial problems finding housing in places like New York City, as well as across the country, in contemporary times. Both urban and some rural/suburban areas suffer from limited low-income-housing stock for multiproblem clients who may also still be unemployed or pursing education/training/vocational goals. This makes the eventual search for housing in the community most challenging.

Because homelessness is very common among multiproblem clients, especially in places such as New York City, homelessness is frequently seen as commonplace and less urgent a problem than other issues. Addressing homelessness may rank below many problems in importance, being deemed as appropriate for attention later.

It is now routine for parole to refer newly released homeless clients to shelters. Homelessness is not only the plight of the poor who lack social-support networks. Some clients with felony convictions may no longer live with family who reside in public housing. There is the risk of jeopardizing the housing of other family members with whom one lives if there is a relapse to drug use and/or recidivism to drug crime. Police may seize cars, houses, and boats when arresting suspected drug offenders. Many family members are hesitant to accommodate drug offenders in their housing, given this risk. Even clients of high socioeconomic status with luxurious homes often have partners/family who will no longer allow them to live in that home after incarceration, necessitating that they find alternative living arrangements, too. Other employed, middle-income clients have been evicted from their housing because of a pattern of using their income on drugs instead of for regularly paying their bills and rent. Some clients enter community-based addiction treatment in a residential therapeutic-community (TC) setting, apply for housing outside the residence, and they also have to wait months for their new housing to be secured.

Practitioner flexibility should be exercised in deciding when to do what with regard to clients' need for housing, in light of overall ongoing assessment findings. For example, a client's psychiatric symptoms in an early phase of treatment/action stage may be rooted in the stress of living in a shelter or related to experiences transpiring there, suggesting the need for urgent action—perhaps a transfer to a residential therapeutic community for a six-to-twelve-month stay as paperwork for independent housing is being processed. A practitioner should therefore use what is presented in this chapter and summarized in table 5.1 only as a guide, staying on top of the latest developments in their region with regard to housing procedures and practices.

CONCLUSION

This chapter discussed the common characteristics and needs of the diverse group of contemporary multiproblem clients, focusing on the correct timing for addressing client issues within addiction treatment. The concept of correct timing led to an emphasis regarding, quite simply, how practitioners need to consider when to do what. Providing further simplification, the chapter suggested that the pertinent options for practitioners included weighing and exploring what seems to be most urgent and most pressing to address immediately as short-term goals, versus what seems to be less urgent and less pressing to address later as long-term goals. Meanwhile, the larger context of when to do what included practitioner considerations of where the client is, what the client needs, and what the client is willing to do or prefers to do in a particular phase of treatment/stage of change.

The resulting discussion in this chapter and table 5.1 provided a rough guide showing how the appropriate time for a practitioner to address certain urgent client characteristics and needs is immediate, or in the early phase of treatment/action stage, when clients are stabilizing and actively working to change addictive/problem behavior across their first six months within a community-based addiction-treatment program. And other, less urgent issues could be addressed later, once clients are stable and in the middle-to-late phase of treatment/maintenance stage, having greater than six months of working to change addictive/problem behavior.

Given the potential risk that practitioners may become overwhelmed by the multitude of problematic characteristics and needs that clients bring with them into community-based addiction treatment, the rough guide for the correct timing of the delivery of interventions offered in this chapter has great value. This practical guide helps practitioners to prioritize client issues, yet it also requires flexibility on the part of practitioners. Practitioners may emerge with a better understanding of how to organize and sequence treatment, especially for clients presenting dual diagnoses/comorbidity. Guidance was also provided with regard to how to match clients to treatment interventions, creating tailored care, basing these decisions on client characteristics such as their cognitive and psychosocial functioning, as well as on ongoing life-context factors. Practitioners must perform the kinds of thorough individualized assessments (see chapter 7), as well as ongoing assessments across phases of treatment/stages of change (see Wallace, 1991b, 1996a), that can guide the process of tailoring treatment for individual clients.

Given the foundation of knowledge provided in part 1 of this book, part 2 will provide overall training for making mandated addiction treatment work, using a casebook approach. Cases briefly mentioned in this chapter will be presented in full within chapters in part 2.

II

TRAINING

6

◆

Overcoming Negative Countertransference

There are social-conditioning processes operating in our society that lead to the stigmatization of those with a drug addiction, as well as those with criminal behavior. These processes of stigmatization operate as a social-control tactic (Des Jarlais, 1995; Tucker, 1999). Those with the "stigmatized characteristics (the 'marks') as members of a social out-group" are denied advantages of the dominant in-group, while "stigmatization seeks to maintain the dominant social order and to promote greater cohesiveness among the in-group" (Tucker, 1999, p. 32). In addition, stigmatization seeks to promote "identification of the marks, thus allowing them to be segregated in stigma-defined groups that are sufficiently visible, so that they can be monitored and controlled by the dominant group" (Tucker, 1999, p. 32).

The National Institute on Drug Abuse (NIDA) convened experts in public health, academia, and government at Chantilly, Virginia, in November 1995, in order to decide whether or not drug addiction should be declared a disease of the brain, arriving at the decision to do so (Satel, 2002). The declaration of addiction as being a chronic brain disease, as well as a chronic and relapsing disorder—like diabetes, asthma, and high blood pressure—was intended to destigmatize compulsive drug taking (Satel, 2002). In addition, the intent was to "shift the commonly held perception of addicts from 'bad people' to be dealt with by the criminal justice system to 'chronic illness sufferers' to be triaged to medical care" (Satel, 2002, p. 58), that is, to the perception of addiction as being a medical disorder and not something self-induced or reflecting a failure of will. A full-blown public-health campaign by NIDA followed, showing pictures of addicts' brains that were "lit up" on PET scans as an "image of desire" (Satel, 2002, p. 55).

Satel (2002) views efforts to neutralize the stigma of addiction by convincing the public that the addict has a brain disease as understandable. However, those having the experience of actually treating those with addictive behaviors find cause for therapeutic optimism, viewing clients as capable of self-control, whereas the brain-disease model "leads us down a narrow clinical path" (Satel, 2002, pp. 55–56). "The addiction as brain disease" model means that compulsive addictive behaviors are driven by drug-induced brain changes, and pharmacological imperatives follow as the narrow path to pursue with regard to treatment. However, the reality is that no pharmacological treatment for cocaine dependence has been found. Most importantly, locating addiction in the brain and not in the person fails to acknowledge the reality that people can be "agents of their own recovery . . . or non-recovery" (pp. 55–62).

Satel (2002) suggests that combating the stigma of addiction might work better by promoting conditions within treatment settings and society at large that foster the development of self-discipline, self-respect, and self-control in addicts. And, positive expectations of change and self-control on the part of addicts, as well as the placement of reasonable demands for change upon addicts—including the use of consequences and coercion—may play a vital role in fostering the recovery of addicts (Satel, 2002, p. 62).

In a similar vein, Marlatt (1997) discusses the role of choice of terminology and the potential resulting optimism as being critical for overcoming the effects of stigma. In explaining why psychologists prefer the term *addictive behavior*, Marlatt (1997) emphasizes how psychology is often defined as the study of behavior, and psychologists prefer to focus on what people do—whether drinking, smoking, or ingesting various substances—rather than placing people in fixed diagnostic categories. In addition, there is typically a focus on the determinants of addictive behavior, elucidating how it is acquired and how it can be modified through prevention and treatment procedures. As a result, the focus shifts to an emphasis upon an optimistic potential for behavior change. Marlatt (1997) also explains how this is very different from defining *addiction* as a "progressive, chronic disease," concluding as follows: "Choice of terminology is an important one for both therapists and clients, given the stigma and shame often associated with these 'taboo' behaviors" (Marlatt, 1997, pp. xiii–xiv).

This introductory discussion suggests how terminology or cognitions may make a tremendous difference in how one feels and behaves toward those with addictive and criminal behaviors. Ideally, these cognitions are not stigmatizing of clients, do not lead to feelings of disdain for clients, and do not lead to behaviors of discrimination against clients. But, because of how social-control tactics have long operated in this society, there is the current challenge of shifting focus from stigmatizing, disdaining, and discriminating against those with addictive and criminal behaviors to placing emphasis upon an optimistic potential for behavior change.

Practitioners' expectations may operate as powerful self-fulfilling prophecies for clients, impacting client self-efficacy or confidence in their ability to cope in specific challenging situations (Miller, Wilbourne, & Hettema, 2003). Ideally, practitioners' expectations reflect learned optimism/optimistic thinking with regard to clients' potential for behavior change, and this approach is also taught to clients as a cognitive coping strategy (Seligman, 1998, 2002; Vaughan, 2001). Also, both practitioners and clients may need to learn to dispute cognitive distortions, such as catastrophic thinking (Seligman, 1998, 2002) about future treatment outcomes, as well as to dispute those cognitive distortions that lie at the root of stigmatization. Practitioners may also focus on client strengths (Aspinwall & Staudinger, 2003; van Wormer & Davis, 2003) as a way to shift away from any negative impact caused by the view that clients necessarily have a progressive, chronic disease; practitioners may go on to appreciate those strengths and attributes that clients are actually demonstrating that justify the practitioner's attaining an optimistic view of that client's potential for behavior change.

To the extent that practitioners and members of clients' social-support networks shift toward an optimistic view of clients' potential for behavior change, they may be contributing influential variables in treatment. This may include a focus on clients' strengths (Aspinwall & Staudinger, 2003). Most importantly, these nonspecific or common factors (such as practitioner optimism and empathy versus negative countertransference of disdain and negative, low expectations for clients) may exert a stronger influence on treatment outcome than do the specific differences among treatment techniques (Miller, Wilbourne, & Hettema, 2003). Thus, the role of nonspecific factors in individual and group work is both discussed and demonstrated through a case example in this chapter.

This chapter will provide training in overcoming negative countertransference. The chapter will present the case of Ms. F. W., covering her first two months in outpatient community-based addiction treatment, and detailed commentary. Case discussion will highlight the many kinds of negative countertransference reactions a practitioner may have toward a contemporary client, as well as the goals of practitioners' attaining adaptive cognitive, affective, and behavioral responses—such as optimism and empathy—and their engaging in fidelity in service delivery without discriminating against clients. A table (table 6.2) summarizes the process by which practitioners may move across stages of change toward the attainment of adaptive cognitive, affective, and behavioral coping responses to the challenge of treating clients they may have been socially conditioned to stigmatize, disdain, and discriminate against.

This chapter will also discuss the process of clients' learning how to cope with the stress of encountering negative countertransference reactions toward them, as well as their learning new adaptive cognitive, affective, and behavioral responses to this stress and other more general life stress. In addition, the chapter will illustrate how contemporary community-based addiction treatment routinely incorporates some evidence-based addiction interventions. The chapter also elucidates how practitioners must regularly thoughtfully select from a menu of evidence-based addiction treatments and recommended state-of-the-art practices those treatments and practices that should be integrated and adapted for use in the process of tailoring treatment for an individual client, given the client's characteristics, needs, and diversity. The chapter presents a table (table 6.1) that shows how, from among all possible evidence-based interventions and recommended state-of-the-art practices discussed at length in chapter 2, those interventions and practices marked with an *X* were utilized in the case of Ms. F. W. across her two months of treatment reviewed in this chapter. In this manner, the chapter will illustrate the essential work of making mandated addiction treatment work by adapting evidence-based addiction treatments in the real world with heterogeneous clients.

Table 6.1.   Options from the Menu Used (*X*) in the Case of Ms. F. W.: Evidence-Based Interventions and State-of-the-Art Practices

Selections (*X*) for Ms. F. W. from category 1: Evidence-based addiction treatments
   X * Special focus on building a strong therapeutic alliance/social-support network (TASS)
   X * Motivational interviewing/motivational enhancement therapy (MET)/brief interventions
   X * Cognitive-behavioral therapy (CBT)/relapse prevention (RP)/social-skills training (SST)
   X * Twelve-step facilitation (TSF)/guidance using Alcoholics and/or Narcotics Anonymous
   X * Individual drug counseling (IDC) and/or supportive-expressive psychotherapy (SEP)
   X * Community reinforcement approach (CRA)/vouchers: Contingency management (CM)
   X * The Matrix Model—or, a day-treatment approach, or IEC outpatient model that is *I* for intensive (4–5 days per week), *E* for extensive (6–12 months), and *C* for comprehensive (TASS, CBT/RP, IDC, group drug counseling [GDC], drug testing, etc.)
Selections (*X*) for Ms. F. W. from category 2: Recommended state-of-the-art practices
     * Integration of motivational interviewing and stages of change**
   X * Integration of stages of change and phases of treatment and recovery
     * Integration of harm reduction, moderation approaches, and abstinence models
   X * Integration of psychoanalytic and cognitive-behavioral theories and techniques
   X * Acquisition of affective, behavioral, and cognitive coping skills—learning new ABCs
   X * Integration of motivational interviewing, stages of change, and identity development theory for a diverse identity involving race, sexual orientation, and/or disability
   X * Incorporating contemporary trends in psychology: Multiculturalism, positive psychology, the strengths-based approach, and optimistic thinking/learned optimism

---

**Motivational interviewing was used, but not integrated with stages of change, as the client was already in an action stage, and the case only extends over a period of two months.

THE CASE OF MS. F. W. AND SESSION 1
IN THE MENTAL-HEALTH GROUP

Ms. F. W. is a thirty-four-year-old woman who was just released from eight months in jail for criminal sale of marijuana. Having two toddlers, a common negative countertransference reaction toward her might include affects of disdain and stigmatization of her as a "drug addict," a "drug dealer," and a "bad mother."

Despite any "clean time" she accumulated in jail, Narcotics Anonymous peers view her as having to start counting her days clean in the real world. She may also be considered as entering an early phase of treatment or action stage, given the task of actively changing old conditioned responses of smoking marijuana in the real world outside of jail in response to old classically conditioned cues or triggers. This conceptualization of the case reflects the recommended state-of-the-art practice of *Integration of Stages of Change and Phases of Treatment and Recovery* (see table 6.1) and may guide the selection of interventions that are most appropriate for the early phase of treatment or action stage.

KEY BACKGROUND INFORMATION ON MS. F. W.

Key background involves how her husband of many years was also arrested. Using his home as a base of operation, it was actually his active involvement in drug distribution that led to charges being filed against the client. Ms. F. W. admits to smoking marijuana on a regular basis within her home.

As a result of her arrest, Ms. F. W. lost custody of her three-year-old son and two-year-old daughter; they are now in the custody of their paternal grandmother. Ms. F. W. is on probation and is mandated to a residential facility for women, as she is under the supervision of a judge in drug court.

MS. F. W.'S PARTICIPATION IN MANDATED
COMMUNITY-BASED ADDICTION TREATMENT

Ms. F. W. also received outpatient substance-abuse treatment five days per week, participating in a comprehensive program including random urine testing, relapse prevention (RP), individual sessions, and varied group sessions, to list just a few elements. This was consistent with the recommendation that clients be involved in an evidence-based program such as *The Matrix Model—Or, a Day-Treatment Approach, or an IEC Outpatient Model That Is*

I *for Intensive (4–5 days per week),* E *for Extensive (6–12 months), and* C *for Comprehensive (TASS, CBT/RP, IDC, GDC, drug testing, etc.)* (see table 6.1). Her primary substance-abuse counselor delivered individual drug counseling (IDC). In some of her varied groups, discussion covered both why and how to utilize Narcotics and Alcoholics Anonymous meetings in the community, suggesting use of the evidence-based *Twelve-Step Facilitation (TSF)/Guidance Using Alcoholics and/or Narcotics Anonymous* (also listed in table 6.1).

SESSION 1 IN THE MENTAL-HEALTH GROUP

I conducted one group, mental health (MH), as one of the many groups in the program that Ms. F. W. attended, and it was held once per week. When she attended the mental-health group for the very first time, Ms. F. W. talked spontaneously and at great length about her experience of incarceration and the impact upon her. Becoming tearful, yet continuing to talk loudly, clearly, and passionately despite her tears, the client described the conditions in the female jail as "absolutely horrendous. You wouldn't want your dog to live like that. The conditions are horrible. The women's section is much worse than the men's section. And they talk to you and treat you so badly. It was enough for me to decide that I will never do anything to end up in a place like that again!"

The client also spoke eloquently in the mental-health group about how her traumatic incarceration experience motivated her to rapidly change her behavior. This included not only acceptance of the goal of total abstinence from alcohol and all illicit chemicals, but also abandonment of many other behaviors, such as being verbally aggressive and domineering, doing whatever she wanted, and acting out violently at times.

Ms. F. W. elaborated on her old ways before her incarceration experience as follows: "You see how we are sitting around this table here. Eight months ago, I would have gotten angry and flipped this table over. Yes, I would have. But today, I am learning a different way." This last statement reflected how she was in an action stage with regard to addressing her violent, aggressive behavior, actively learning new adaptive behaviors to replace old maladaptive behaviors.

KEY INTERVENTIONS DELIVERED IN
SESSION 1 IN THE MENTAL-HEALTH GROUP

Deploying the evidence-based *Motivational Interviewing/Motivational Enhancement Therapy (MET)/Brief Interventions* (see table 6.1), motivational interviewing techniques emphasized the following: the delivery of positive verbal reinforcement after she made a statement about an intention to change, which is called client "change talk." So, after Ms. F. W.'s last statement, or change talk, I stated the following: "Very good. It's wonderful that you were able to change so quickly."

The evidence-based *Cognitive-Behavioral Therapy (CBT)/Relapse Prevention (RP)/Social Skills Training (SST)* listed in table 6.1 was also deployed with Ms. F. W. in the mental-health group. I sought to foster her ability to cope with the stress she would inevitably encounter during social interactions in the real world. The goal was for Ms. F. W. to avoid relapse to violence or marijuana use, as well as to support good interpersonal coping. Consistent with both the classic difficulty among chemically dependent clients with regard to processing their affective experience, and how stressful interpersonal interactions typically give rise to distressing affects, a decision was made to also use a recommended state-of-the-art practice, supporting client *Acquisition of Affective, Behavioral, and Cognitive Coping Skills—Learning New ABCs* (see table 6.1). The pertinent treatment goal was to foster Ms. F. W.'s learning adaptive affective, behavioral, and cognitive coping responses to stress. The most important active adaptive coping strategy involves learning how to talk about feelings instead of potentially acting them out. Again, in the case of Ms. F. W., this potential acting out of distressing affect was likely to involve either a display of violence or a relapse to marijuana use.

In recognition of the treatment goal of Ms. F. W.'s learning to talk about her feelings in this early phase of treatment/action stage, her overall cognitive-behavioral/relapse prevention/social-skills training included the following brief education: "Now that you are no longer in jail, it is important that you learn to talk about your feelings so that you do not act them out. And it's great that you did that today in group, sharing your feelings about all that you went through in jail."

THE IMPORTANT ROLE OF PEER FEEDBACK IN THE MENTAL-HEALTH GROUP

With regard to all that she had shared in this mental-health group, some of her peers expressed open surprise at her description of past violent tendencies, as they stood in contrast to how she was now sitting at the table and talking. Other peers expressed gratitude that she was no longer aggressive, even appearing a bit shocked and frightened by her description of her prior violent behavior. Indeed, the fear in the eyes of one group member served to create a moment of *silent knowing* among all group members. It was as though several of us had the exact same realization at the same time: if Ms. F. W. was acting out violently in front of her children, then maybe all that had transpired involving her arrest and incarceration was some kind of blessing in disguise. Maybe she, in fact, needed a temporary separation from her children and this external pressure from a mandate in order to change her addictive and violent behavior. It seemed as though Ms. F. W. also came into this new awareness at the very same moment.

Perceiving fear in the eyes of some group members in response to her story, Ms. F. W. was apparently reminded of the fear she had seen in the eyes of her own children in the past when she had acted out violently. In this manner, the mental-health group allowed Ms. F. W. to receive some honest, objective feedback from her peers about maladaptive behavior she had performed in the real world, where no one ever dared to criticize her or give her feedback, knowing how she would likely respond: with violence. In this case, the honest objective feedback given to her in the group by her peers was nonverbal, yet it was powerfully conveyed in the eyes of group members who were left feeling genuine affects of fear. But now, in the group setting, Ms. F. W. was not high off of marijuana, and the full impact of her past maladaptive behavior and the truth of how she created fear in her children seemed to hit her. And the feedback of her peers—both verbal and nonverbal—played a vital role in her progress.

A SHIFT FROM EXTRINSIC TO INTRINSIC MOTIVATION IN SESSION 1 IN THE MENTAL-HEALTH GROUP

At this moment, Ms. F. W.'s motivation to change her violent behavior progressed further in shifting from being largely extrinsic to being intrinsic. Instead of external pressure from the criminal justice system being her main source of motivation to change, as with so many mandated clients, she now found a new reason to change involving her children. She arrived at her own inner personal concerns with regard to her violent behavior and was now shifting toward being intrinsically motivated to make sure she did not exhibit violent behavior in front of her children. As evidence of this, Ms. F. W. spoke in the following manner: "I needed to change, especially because my children are getting older. They don't need to see me act like that."

Using motivational-interviewing techniques, the client was given yet more positive verbal reinforcement for having this major realization, for experiencing a shift to being internally motivated to change, and for engaging in change talk. I stated, "Yes, it's really important that we don't expose children to things that can be frightening and traumatic for them. That's also how they learn to be violent, by watching other people act out violently."

THE PURPOSE OF OTHER INTERVENTIONS IN SESSION 1 IN THE MENTAL-HEALTH GROUP

This intervention was also planting the seed for Ms. F. W.'s learning how to engage in more sophisticated cognitive coping strategies involving problem solving and consequential thinking. The point was that serious consequences follow from behaviors performed impulsively without forethought, or while high on marijuana. The intervention included the straightforward provision of education with the conscious use of the word *we*, thereby including myself, Ms. F. W., and every other group member. The implication was that any of us might be at risk for committing violence in front of children, and there was no finger-pointing going on implying that she was the only one with a violence problem.

In this manner, the intervention served to avoid increasing or exacerbating any feelings of guilt or shame on the part of Ms. F. W. For, this was also a moment in which I felt empathy for Ms. F. W., sensing how she felt naked and exposed in front of the group, as well as ashamed about her behavior. In this moment wherein I was feeling empathy for her inner affective state of guilt and shame, I chose not to reflect back to her what I sensed she was feeling; to do so would have risked Ms. F. W.'s feeling further exposed in front of the group. Instead, my empathy for her led to an intervention that served to shift the focus specifically away from Ms. F. W.'s violence in front of her children and placed the focus on moving any and all of us in the group at risk for violent acting out in front of children to a new place of understanding via the delivery of brief education. The intent was to prevent such things from ever happening again in the future.

This intervention also reflected my implicit respect for Ms. F. W., as I did not want to embarrass her in the group setting. And the intervention also reflected my implicit acceptance of where she was in the change process, having just had the realization herself that her behavior of acting out violently in front of her children was problematic, as it likely terrified her children. Collectively, my affective responses of empathy, respect, and acceptance were key to Ms. F. W.'s feeling comfortable in the group and continuing to work on her issues in that setting. These affective responses, especially practitioner empathy, were consistent with the evidence-based deployment of a *Special Focus on Building a Strong Therapeutic Alliance/Social-Support Network (TASS)* (see table 6.1).

After my intervention, Ms. F. W. became quiet and calm, seeming to fully absorb her new realization, my comment, the experience of practitioner empathy/respect/acceptance extended to her, and the importance of her changing her addictive and violent behavior. In this quiet, calm state, she also seemed to be solidifying the new personal gain of shifting her motivation to terminate the use of marijuana from being extrinsic—following her arrest and incarceration and ongoing criminal-justice-system-supervision—to now being intrinsic. For, marijuana likely prevented her from fully seeing and accurately interpreting the fear in her children's eyes and the impact of her own impulsive violent behavior upon them. Seemingly making all of these connections on her own and fully grasping them during this moment of silence, Ms. F. W. finally verbally responded to my last comment: "I'm never going to act like that again. But now I have to do everything to get my children back." She again received positive verbal reinforcement for making this statement, which constituted more change talk, a verbal statement of an intent to change and get her children back into her custody. This positive reinforcement involved my replying, "Great. It's really important to do that."

Ms. F. W. also seemed to have made progress in surrendering her old identity as one who did whatever she wanted to do, all too often engaging in maladaptive coping responses to any stress. She seemed to have made progress in developing a new identity as one who was learning and refining adaptive coping responses (following from use of interventions reflecting an *Integration of Motivational Interviewing, Stages of Change, and Identity Development Theory for a Diverse Identity Involving Race, Sexual Orientation, and/or Disability* in table 6.1).

THE IMPACT OF INTERVENTIONS ON GROUP MEMBERS AS A WHOLE

Other peers in the mental-health group had their own personal material stimulated by Ms. F. W.'s raw expression of intense emotion, graphic storytelling, and frank honesty. These other group members proceeded to talk about their own feelings and struggles, moving the group to a new focus. But they had all witnessed something that helped them to open up and honestly share their stories in the mental-health group. The group members saw how, even when Ms. F. W. was metaphorically naked and exposed, having shared something that made her feel vulnerable, guilty, and ashamed, as the practitioner in charge of the group, I had interacted with Ms. F. W. with empathy, respect, and acceptance.

As the practitioner conducting the group, my displays of empathy, respect, and acceptance collectively served to inspire a number of group members to engage in the group process and to also develop a therapeutic alliance with me. This meant that the group was a safe place for them to share, also. And, when solutions to their problems were needed, perhaps I would just talk about what *we* needed to do in order to prevent negative outcomes in life, making all feel safe and protected. Somehow, we were all learning together. A feeling of equality prevailed in the group, and there were no "ones up" pounding information into the "ones down," nor was the practitioner in charge talking down to anyone and creating feelings of inferiority. And, as the practitioner, no negative countertransference reactions were leading to the expression of affective disdain, cognitions suggestive of stigmatization, or behavioral discrimination. Instead, quite simply, as the practitioner conducting the group, I seemed to have a lot of good information to share, but so did other group members. In fact, the group members whose eyes reflected inner feelings of fear offered the most powerful and telling information in this particular group session.

FIRST COMMENTARY ON CASE OF MS. F. W.

Ms. F. W.'s initial introduction of herself to the mental-health group might produce negative countertransference reactions in a practitioner. Her story might readily evoke any socially conditioned cognitive, affective, or behavioral responses one might have as a societal member living in contemporary times. One might readily stigmatize her, having typical socially conditioned cognitive responses, and likely thinking as follows: "She is just another addict involved in immoral and criminal behavior, and she is deserving of the punishment of incarceration and loss of child custody." Apparently, one of the things that made her experiences in jail so torturous and traumatic involved being constantly talked down to by correctional staff who embodied what it means to stigmatize drug offenders. While such a response is very common in our contemporary society, for anyone who seeks to be a practitioner in addiction treatment, or a potential member of her social-support network, these would all represent maladaptive cognitive coping responses to the challenge of treating Ms. F. W.

Maladaptive Cognitive, Affective, and Behavioral Responses: Negative Countertransference Reactions

Maladaptive cognitive responses might lead to common conditioned affective responses of disdain. There might also follow socially conditioned behavioral responses that are also consistent with disrespecting, devaluing, or discriminating against a client like Ms. F. W. This might involve behaviors of cutting her off when she is talking, talking down to her, ending a session abruptly before the requisite time has passed, forgetting about a scheduled session made with her, or discriminating against her by not providing her with standard care or routine services. In a similar fashion, members of her social-support network might provide less than they normally would.

What has been described all constitutes maladaptive cognitive, affective, and behavioral coping responses to a contemporary client, or negative countertransference reactions. An alternative response to hearing her story would involve adaptive cognitive, affective, and behavioral responses. Such adaptive responses are recommended, particularly on the part of practitioners or those who seek to harness the power of those nonspecific or common factors that may potentially exert a strong influence on treatment outcome. In fact, practitioners may anticipate, envision, and embrace the process of moving across stages of change from not even having thought about these issues (precontemplation); to thinking about them (contemplation); to making a determination to change maladaptive cognitive, affective, and behavioral responses (preparation); to actively working to change them over the next six months (action); to seeking greater sophistication in deploying new adaptive cognitive, affective, and behavioral responses that one will likely use for life (maintenance). This includes the possibility of potential relapse to what was maladaptive. Table 6.2 presents these stages of change, also suggesting how they represent progressively more mature and differentiated identity statuses, as practitioners move toward a new stable identity as one who is free from negative countertransference and old socialization processes to stigmatize, disdain, and unwittingly discriminate against clients with addictive and criminal behavior.

Positive Psychology, the Strengths-Based Approach, and Optimistic Thinking/Learned Optimism: Recommended State-of-the-Art Practices

A practitioner's adaptive cognitive responses to all that Ms. F. W. shared in her first mental-health group might focus on this client's strengths and positive attributes. A practitioner might have positive internal cognitive responses or think how "she is remarkably strong, resilient, and determined." Other adaptive cognitive responses on the part of practitioners might involve having positive expectations about this client's ability to change and maintain behavioral change over time so that it is enduring; such cognitive responses on the part of the practitioner might translate into a positive prophecy the client might fulfill. This might involve the practitioner engaging in optimistic thinking or having cognitions reflecting a learned optimism. For example, the practitioner might both observe a strength possessed by the client and optimistically think as follows: "She is working so hard in group. If she continues to work this hard, her chances of success are excellent." In this manner, a practitioner would be combining the recommended state-of-the-art practices of drawing upon *Positive Psychology, the Strengths-Based Approach, and Optimistic Thinking/Learned Optimism* in work with Ms. F. W., as listed in table 6.1.

Adaptive Affective Coping: Empathy as a Key Nonspecific Factor in Treatment

A practitioner's adaptive affective coping responses to the challenge of treating Ms. F. W. would include feeling empathy. Practitioner empathy may be the most important nonspecific factor influencing treatment outcome, and it is absolutely critical to the technically correct deployment of motivational interviewing within the evidence-based option of *Motivational Interviewing/ Motivational Enhancement Therapy (MET)/Brief Interventions* included in table 6.1. Empathy is likely the key ingredient or most important common/nonspecific factor for determining the success of any treatment intervention, following the use of the evidence-based intervention of placing a *Special Focus on Building a Strong Therapeutic Alliance/Social-Support Network (TASS)*, also listed in table 6.1.

Table 6.2. Stages of Change/Identity Status for Acquiring Adaptive Affective, Behavioral, and Cognitive Coping Responses (CRs)

Stage/Status	Cognitive CRs		Affective CRs		Behavioral CRs
Precontemplation Identity as one not thinking about changing one's coping responses (CRs)	Stigmatization Maladaptive cognitive coping responses (CRs)	↑	Disdain Maladaptive affective CRs	↑	Discrimination Maladaptive behavioral CRs
Contemplation Identity as one thinking about changing one's CRs	Confusion Questioning with regard to one's maladaptive cognitive CRs	↑	Ambivalence Conflict about maladaptive affective CRs	↑	Resistance Still performing maladaptive behavioral CRs
Preparation Identity as one preparing to work on changing one's CRs	Determination. Decision to replace maladaptive cognitive CRs with new adaptive CRs	↑	Desire Wish to attain adaptive affective CRs	↑	Preparation Steps taken to learn new adaptive behavioral CRs
Action Identity as one actively engaged in changing one's CRs for up to six months	Optimistic thinking, focus on strengths Actively learning, rehearsing, generalizing adaptive cognitive CRs	↑	Empathy, respect, acceptance Actively learning, rehearsing, generalizing adaptive affective CRs	↑	Fidelity in service delivery Actively learning, rehearsing, generalizing adaptive behavioral CRs
Maintenance Identity as one maintaining new CRs for more than six months and throughout one's life	Acquiring greater sophistication in thinking Refining, generalizing adaptive cognitive CRs	↑	Acquiring greater sophistication in feeling Refining, generalizing adaptive affective CRs	↑	Acquiring greater sophistication in behavior and service delivery Refining, generalizing adaptive behavioral CRs
Relapse A lapse/return to maladaptive CRs	Maladaptive cognitive CRs reappear	↑	Maladaptive affective CRs reappear	↑	Maladaptive behavioral CRs reappear

Empathy Defined

Empathy may be defined as an affective state attained by successfully using one's own capacity to feel in order to sense and sort out another individual's inner affective experience. Empathy includes coming to accurately understand the meaning of another's inner affective experience. To successfully achieve the affective state of empathy with another human being may constitute a powerful experience that is uniquely affirming and validating for the one whose private internal affective state has now become a shared reality with another human being. Thus, attaining the affective state of genuine empathy, alone, may constitute not only a vitally important practitioner skill, but also an important nonspecific/common factor helping to create a positive treatment outcome.

As shown in the first mental-health-group session, a key moment of empathy with Ms. F. W.'s inner affective experiences of guilt, shame, and feeling naked and exposed in front of the group was essentially a silent moment of both feeling and knowing the meaning of what Ms. F. W. was experiencing emotionally inside. There was no overt reflection or mirroring of Ms. F. W.'s inner affects back to her in this case of silent feeling and knowing. But, because of this state of empathy, an intervention was delivered that served to protect Ms. F. W. from any further exacerbation of her feelings of guilt, shame, and being naked and exposed. The intervention also served to deflect attention away from her as the only one possibly having this problem, given that I, the practitioner, used the word *we* in going on to deliver brief education about the negative impact of exposing children to violence.

Adaptive Affective Coping: Respect and Acceptance as Key Nonspecific Factors in Treatment

There is justification in viewing respect and acceptance as adaptive affective responses on the part of the practitioner that are also key nonspecific factors operating in treatment and impacting outcome. Moreover, it may be asserted that respect and acceptance are adaptive affective responses to the diversity commonly found among contemporary clients in community-based addiction treatment. In the case of Ms. F. W., the mental-health group included members who were diverse, including those who were poor; African American; Hispanic; Irish; gay; lesbian; and people with disabilities such as HIV/AIDS, learning disabilities, and mental disabilities/disorders, following the broad disability classification scheme of Linton (1998). Because such individuals have experienced stigmatization, disdain, and discrimination for not only their addictive and criminal behavior, but also for their race, ethnicity, sexual orientation, or disabilities, they are especially sensitive to moments when they are being disrespected and not accepted. Hence, experiences of being genuinely respected and accepted are of extreme importance to such clients. Moments of feeling genuinely respected and accepted are novel and go a long way in engaging clients in treatment, as well as in fostering a therapeutic alliance. This focus on respect is consistent with both the evidence-based intervention involving placing a *Special Focus on Building a Strong Therapeutic Alliance/Social-Support Network (TASS)* and the recommended state-of-the-art practice of *Incorporating Contemporary Trends in Psychology: Multiculturalism, Positive Psychology, the Strengths-Based Approach, and Optimistic Thinking/Learned Optimism*, especially by avoiding disdain/ stigmatization via multicultural sensitivity/competence with regard to diversity. Both are checked off (*X*) in table 6.1.

Respect Defined

Respect may be defined as an affective state that follows from acknowledgment of another's experience as valid, real, and worthy of recognition. Respect tends to be mutual and reciprocal, holding sway during interpersonal interactions. Thus, respect may also be seen as involving an experience of reciprocal recognition on the part of two individuals. Even as there may be degrees of respect, often there is also an either-or reality that prevails. The prevailing reality either involves respect and recognition or disrespect and nonrecognition. Thus, the opposite of respect and recognition, or disrespect and nonrecognition, may lead to an experience of invisibility (Ellison, 1952; Franklin, 2004; Wallace, 2003) or lack of any validation for even existing. Experiences of disrespect, nonrecognition, invisibility, and lack of any validation for even existing may damage identity. Hence, many who are diverse in our society have suffered damage to their identity (Wallace, 2003; Wallace et al., 2003). Typically, the perpetrators of this damage to identity have been those who presume themselves to be superior, and those they disrespect are presumed to be inferior (Wallace, 2003). Some of these dynamics are triggered by the perception of the overt marks associated with being diverse or stigmatized.

Respect precedes and allows for the experience of acceptance on the part of the practitioner with regard to a client. Especially in work with clients who are diverse, the first step is to respect them. Actually, this is what they demand and want.

Respect Relative to Acceptance

It is a much more rare and higher-order experience to actually be accepted. In fact, many diverse individuals do not expect to be accepted, especially after long histories of suffering stigmatization, disdain, and discrimination. But, at the very least, they want to be respected. For contemporary clients, whether those who have only suffered stigmatization for addictive and/or criminal behavior, or those who have also suffered stigmatization for their other diverse characteristics, it is a rare privilege and honor to be accepted. Ideally, any practitioner electing to work with the contemporary population of clients in community-based addiction treatment must also be willing to pursue the attainment of the adaptive affective response of acceptance. This focus on acceptance is also consistent with the recommended state-of-the-art practice involving a focus on *Incorporating Contemporary Trends in Psychology: Multiculturalism, Positive Psychology, the Strengths-Based Approach, and Optimistic Thinking/Learned Optimism* and, more specifically, multiculturalism with acceptance of diversity. So, what is acceptance? How may it be defined?

Acceptance Defined

Acceptance may be defined as an affective state that results from embracing where another person is, what is going on with the person, and the nature of the person's experience, while remaining free of harsh judgment, criticism, or condemnation. When accepting a person for where he or she is, this includes accepting the stage of change the person is currently negotiating, the person's level of readiness to change, and the phase of treatment and recovery in which the person may be found, as well as the person's diversity, characteristics, needs, and preferences. Accepting what is going on with a person means being open to whatever the person may be experiencing in any given moment on any given day, even if the person is engaging in defenses such as splitting, or is highly ambivalent, presenting alternating sides to his or her self or conflict. And, accepting the nature of the person's experience means withholding any judgment, criticism, or condemnation about the person's affects, values, behavioral practices, cultural traditions, or cognitive approach to his or her experiences in reality, even though one may not share any of these. One may personally judge the nature of the other person's experience as something that is not suitable or appropriate for oneself, but this is very different from engaging in harsh judgment, criticism, or condemnation.

Acceptance also includes embracing clients' possession of strengths, positive attributes, apparent potential, and evidence of resiliency, consistent with the recommended state-of-the-art practice involving *Incorporating Contemporary Trends in Psychology: Multiculturalism, Positive Psychology, the Strengths-Based Approach, and Optimistic Thinking/Learned Optimism* and, in particular, a focus on strengths.

Affects of Hope

Other adaptive affective responses include feeling hope about a client's ability to change, following from *Incorporating Contemporary Trends in Psychology: Multiculturalism, Positive Psychology, the Strengths-Based Approach, and Optimistic Thinking/Learned Optimism*. There might even be feelings of admiration and pride that a client is working so hard to change, or has accomplished change. For example, in the case of Ms. F. W., the fact that she was changing so rapidly and working so hard in treatment justified a feeling of hope, as well as of pride. Affects of hope may influence a client, supporting eventual fulfillment of a positive prophecy. An affective response of hope may also impact the development of a strong therapeutic alliance.

Multiculturalism: Going Beyond Respect, Acceptance, and Optimism in Order to Attain Multicultural Sensitivity and Multicultural Competence

The diversity among clients in the mental-health group that Ms. F. W. had just joined reflects that which is commonly found in community-based addiction treatment. Hence, there is a need for training in multicultural sensitivity and competence (Bronstein & Quina, 2003; Carter, 2000; Sue, 2003; Sue & Sue, 2002; Sue et al., 1998; Wallace, 2003; Wallace & Carter, 2003). Wallace (2000a) offers two definitions that are helpful in this regard:

> *Multicultural sensitivity* involves awareness of multiple cultural influences, and the ability to be able to adopt an attitude and stance of inquiry regarding what is appropriate in interacting and communicating with diverse others. An individual with multicultural sensitivity understands that all prior conditioned affective responses (for example, . . . hate), assumptions (all conditioned cognitions), and automatic conditioned behaviors should be questioned or suspended, as one seeks to discover what is appropriate interpersonal behavior. Often this requires entering the worldview of the individual . . . and coming to understand the values, traditions, expectations, and behaviors that are a part of that culture. This involves observation, empathic listening, asking well-timed and appropriate questions, or entering into an ongoing dialogue with an individual member of a cultural group. New affective, cognitive, and behavioral responses may be established to replace the old conditioned ones.
>
>   *Multicultural competence* involves an individual going beyond the mere possession of multicultural sensitivity to also attain an acceptable level of knowledge, a sufficient shift in attitude, and the production of a repertoire of behaviors consistent with successfully interacting with diverse populations in multicultural settings. The ability to convey genuine respect and acceptance is a part of multicultural competence. (p. 1101)

Thus, multicultural competence means going way beyond tolerance of those who are diverse and different, including as it does genuine respect and acceptance. If a practitioner has successfully shifted away from cognitions consistent with stigmatization, shifted toward positive optimistic thinking, and shifted toward affects of respect and acceptance, then there should be success in developing a repertoire of behaviors consistent with successfully interacting with diverse clients. The desired repertoire of behaviors may be described as adaptive behavioral coping.

Becoming multiculturally competent is a process that can take time. However, there are steps by which any practitioner may become free of maladaptive cognitive responses of stigmatizing clients, maladaptive affective responses of disdaining addict criminals, and maladaptive behavioral responses of discriminating against clients via infidelity in service delivery (i.e., failing to adequately perform the task of deploying evidence-based addiction treatments and recommended state-of-the-art practices). This process has already been depicted, in effect, in table 6.2, which shows the stages of change a practitioner transverses, as well as how these are actually progressively more mature identity statuses. However, three practical steps may also be recommended in this process: (1) learn to observe oneself in the act of deploying maladaptive responses, and ideally right before one is about to deploy them; (2) proceed to stop or interrupt these maladaptive responses, perhaps literally stating silently the word *stop*; and (3) replace the maladaptive response with any of the recommended adaptive responses presented in this chapter (e.g., focus on strengths, optimistic thinking, respect, acceptance, fidelity in service delivery by deploying an evidence-based intervention), doing this repeatedly over time so that these adaptive responses become increasingly refined and sophisticated with use.

Adaptive Behavioral Coping: Deploying Evidence-Based Interventions from a Menu of Options and Recommended State-of-the-Art Practices

In the case of Ms. F. W., adaptive behavioral responses on the part of myself, as the practitioner, included seeking to carefully integrate the interventions selected (*X*) from table 6.1, thereby tailoring treatment for her. This involved adapting these selected evidence-based addiction-treatment interventions and recommended state-of-the-art practices in work with her in the real world.

Of note, practitioners must appreciate the role of other, more subtle, yet specific adaptive behavioral responses that operated in the case of Ms. F. W. These involved my actively listening to her, looking directly into her eyes, nodding my head while she was speaking, asking questions, and making appropriate supportive verbal comments. All of these were used, starting in the first mental-health group with Ms. F. W.

Use of the Evidence-Based Intervention of Motivational Interviewing

Given that Ms. F. W. entered the first mental-health group in an action stage for working on her marijuana dependence and violence in the real world outside of jail, as the practitioner, I used the evidence-based intervention of *Motivational Interviewing/Motivational Enhancement Therapy (MET)/Brief Interventions*; motivational interviewing was deemed ideally suited for use with Ms. F. W. in her first session in the mental-health group and across the four weeks of treatment described in this chapter. Given that she was already in an action stage during our short period of therapeutic work, it was not necessary to use an *Integration of Motivational Interviewing and Stages of Change* (not marked with an X in table 6.1) in order to move her across stages of change (for example, from precontemplation, to contemplation, to preparation, to action).

Nonetheless, many of my adaptive behavioral responses included the deployment of many elements of motivational interviewing, serving to sustain and strengthen her resolve to take action to change. Most importantly, and consistent with motivational interviewing, it was important to use the delivery of supportive verbal comments as positive reinforcement for Ms. F. W.'s engagement in change talk, or talk expressing her intention to change or maintain change; this change talk is also the opposite of resistance talk, or talk about not intending to or not wanting to change (Miller & Rollnick, 2002). And, within motivational interviewing, if practitioners reinforce change talk, resistance talk will decrease, and change talk will further increase.

In the case example, the practitioner's use of the motivational-interviewing technique involving the provision of positive reinforcement for the client's engaging in change talk served to further enhance Ms. F. W.'s internal motivation for change. The result typically involves an enhancement of internal motivation, usually serving to further build upon, augment, and potentially replace the external motivation coming from a criminal justice system's mandate or other coercion, such as that from child-protection authorities. The first mental-health-group session contained the critical set of moments when Ms. F. W.'s motivation to change her violent behavior became something that was now deeply rooted in intrinsic motivation, or an internal desire to not expose her children to her violent outbursts. Even once this occurs for a client, as was seen in the first mental-health group with Ms. F. W., the practitioner should continue to use motivational-interviewing techniques in order to further enhance, strengthen, and sustain what is now primarily an internal motivation to change. Practitioners who continue to use motivational interviewing in this manner across the entire period that a client is in an action stage will further strengthen and enhance a client's internal motivation to change so that it is enduring over time. Hopefully, the strength of the client's internal motivation to change is such that it will be sustained beyond any crises of ambivalence that may come way down the road, as well as beyond the period when probation is over, intensive supervision is over, child custody has been regained, and a client is free to do what he or she wants to do again.

Integration of Motivational Interviewing, Stages of Change, and Identity Development Theory for a Diverse Identity Involving Race, Sexual Orientation, and/or Disability

In fact, the goal is for change to become so enduring that it is reflected in the development of a new identity that constitutes a fundamental part of Ms.

F. W.'s personality. This follows, at least partially, some of what is emphasized in the state-of-the-art practice involving an *Integration of Motivational Interviewing, Stages of Change, and Identity Development Theory for a Diverse Identity Involving Race, Sexual Orientation, and/or Disability*. In this case, the diverse identity fostered is that involving one who is progressively moving across stages of change toward the establishment of an identity as one who does not engage in overt displays of violence, using adaptive coping responses instead. Thus, table 6.2 can be seen in a more generic light, describing not only the process for practitioners in acquiring adaptive coping responses, but also those stages of change and statuses for identity development across which a client may progress in acquiring adaptive coping responses (see Wallace et al., 2003, for a more detailed discussion).

Use of the Evidence-Based Intervention of Cognitive-Behavioral Therapy/Relapse Prevention/Social-Skills Training

Also suitable for use in the case of Ms. F. W. was the evidence-based addiction-treatment intervention of *Cognitive-Behavioral Therapy (CBT)/Relapse Prevention (RP)/Social-Skills Training (SST)*, as listed in table 6.1. CBT/RP/SST techniques were viewed as appropriate for enhancing Ms. F. W.'s ability to cope with stress in social interactions. Specifically, she needed to focus on one of the most important tasks for the early phase of treatment or action stage, given the classic difficulty clients have with being able to process affect: she needed to learn how to talk about her feelings, especially those that might come up in stressful interpersonal interactions and might place her at risk of relapse to marijuana use or violent acting out. Thus, the brief education Ms. F. W. received was consistent with social-skills training involving being able to talk about one's feelings to others, as opposed to violently acting them out or relapsing to drug use as maladaptive ways to cope.

Acquisition of Affective, Behavioral, and Cognitive Coping Skills— Learning New ABCs

The use of *Cognitive Behavioral Therapy (CBT)/Relapse Prevention (RP)/Social-Skills Training (SST)* may also be conceived of as seeking to foster the acquisition of adaptive coping responses to both interpersonal stress and general life stress. Specifically, this involves use of the state-of-the-art practice of practitioners' fostering *Acquisition of Affective, Behavioral, and Cognitive Coping Skills—Learning New ABCs*, as listed in table 6.1.

The reality is that a client such as Ms. F. W. will inevitably face others in the social environment capable of having negative countertransference reactions toward her at any given time. The goal is to equip a client such as Ms. F. W. to cope in the face of any stressful responses on the part of others who may be in the process of stigmatizing, disdaining, or discriminating against her. This might include the stress involved in interacting with, for example, the following: a probation officer, residential-facility supervisors who are under contract to the criminal justice system, and child-protection-agency staff. Adaptive cognitive, affective, and behavioral responses are vital in order for Ms. F. W. to cope with her overall life stress, particularly without relapsing to her old coping behaviors of smoking marijuana or engaging in violence.

Other sessions held during the early phase of her treatment while she was in an action stage for working on her marijuana addiction and violent behavior highlighted the goal of further shaping her adaptive responses to stress. A goal involved successful generalization of her coping responses to varied circumstances in the real world.

THE CASE OF MS. F. W. AND SESSION 2 IN THE MENTAL-HEALTH GROUP

Ms. F. W. returned to the outpatient mental-health group for a second time one week later. Because of what had transpired in the first group, she seemed comfortable and readily shared.

MS. F. W.'S FOCUS ON LEARNING ADAPTIVE COPING SKILLS

Ms. F. W. shared how she was learning to talk about her feelings and cope with all of the rules in the residential facility. "I'm learning to talk to the other women in the facility, as well as my counselors. I have to. I can't keep my feelings all stuffed up."

This seemed to be Ms. F. W.'s way of sharing with me that she had followed my recommendation from the previous group: that she learn to talk about her feelings instead of acting out violently. Her internal motivation to learn to talk about her feelings also seemed to have become further enhanced, stronger.

One possibility was that her own internal motivation had been enhanced by her recollection in the prior group of the fear in her children's eyes when she acted out violently in front of them, likely unwittingly. But, she now had the new awareness of how her violent behavior was potentially frightening and traumatic for her children, for she was now perceiving and recollecting events in reality without the filter of the marijuana high. Perhaps Ms. F. W. had further processed this material on her own or in her other groups and counseling sessions, thereby achieving even stronger internal motivation to change as other practitioners and peers provided further positive reinforcement for her new behavior of talking about her feelings instead of acting them out. Practitioners and peers also likely kept reminding her and encouraging her to talk about her feelings.

Another possibility was that she had actually started talking more and more about her feelings, sharing them with her other female peers in the residential facility where she lived, as well as with the counselors, and found this to be reinforcing because it felt good and provided her with relief. The practice of new adaptive coping responses would likely produce rewards such as this in the real world, and could readily undergo generalization to many different situations. In this manner, her internal motivation to continue this practice may have naturally increased.

Regardless of the reasons, apparently Ms. F. W. was actively working on the goal of learning new adaptive affective, behavioral, and cognitive coping skills, specifically, practicing the adaptive coping response of talking about her feelings. Her repeated practice and rehearsal of new adaptive coping strategies served as a good sign that she was developing the relapse prevention/ social skills essential for success in treatment. This was in keeping with how such skills are typically slated for acquisition, practice, and refinement across the early phase of treatment/action stage. This allowed my feelings of hope and optimism about her case to increase (*Incorporating Contemporary Trends in Psychology: Multiculturalism, Positive Psychology, the Strengths-Based Approach, and Optimistic Thinking/Learned Optimism* as listed in table 6.1).

USING ADAPTIVE COPING: PASSING A KEY TEST

With enhanced motivation to avoid acting out violently, and learning how to talk about her feelings more and more, Ms. F. W. was now bringing to the mental-health group reports of every incident where she struggled with distressing affects. Ms. F. W. shared as follows:

> The program director is not always fair. She was yelling and screaming at me the other day, even cursing at me. She was talking down to me. But I sat there and I took it. I don't have a choice. I want my babies back. I'm going to do whatever they tell me to do so I can get my children back. And I promise you—I will never do anything again to put custody of my children in jeopardy. I am never going back to that women's jail.

It seemed possible that the program director was not exempt from having negative countertransference reactions to her clients. But, without focusing on this possibility, as it was something Ms. F. W. could not change, what was focused upon was what the client could change: her own affective, behavioral, and cognitive coping responses to the stress of being talked down to. Reinforcement of any signs of adaptive coping responses was vital to accomplish such a goal.

Thus, given Ms. F. W.'s active production of change talk, she received positive reinforcement, specifically, verbal praise and encouragement. I said, "Congratulations. You did a good job. Sometimes we don't have a choice. Sometimes it is better to just sit there silently instead of getting loud or violent. Sometimes a person does not want to hear what we think or feel. And we have to just sit there. In situations that involve a peer, sometimes it is better to just walk away. But you were in a meeting with the program director, and you did the right thing. Why risk getting kicked out of the program, getting arrested, having to deal with your probation officer, or going back to jail? We have to think, 'what will happen if I do X, Y, or Z?' Then we make a decision. You made the right decision to sit there and be silent." Finally, I said, "There are tests in life that we all face. Some are harder than others. It sounds like you faced a really hard test, but you did very well. You passed."

The intervention was also intended to further refine her cognitive coping strategies by teaching her problem solving and consequential thinking. In the past, her cognitive coping response to stress might have been, "I do what I want to do," being clearly maladaptive and supporting her old identity.

BENEFITS TO ALL GROUP MEMBERS AND PEER FEEDBACK

Beyond helping Ms. F. W. in the process of learning new adaptive responses to replace her old maladaptive cognitions, all members of the group effectively received brief education. Similarly, both Ms. F. W. and all group members were also being taught through this intervention the use of the adaptive behavioral responses of walking away or remaining silent, instead of violently acting out. All group members were progressing in developing identities as individuals who coped with stress via performance of adaptive coping responses.

Other peers in the group proceeded to give Ms. F. W. feedback and positive reinforcement, telling her how good it was that she didn't risk going back to jail. Some group members speculated on how the program director might have been having a bad day. The client was open and respectful, taking in all the feedback she was given. She also remained attentive when other group members went on to talk about their own issues, problems, and experiences.

SECOND COMMENTARY ON THE CASE OF MS. F. W.

Whereas criminal-justice-system involvement initially provided a powerful source of external motivation to change, by the second mental-health group, Ms. F. W. was now consistently manifesting a deep, genuine internal motivation to change and to sustain that change over time. This included accepting the treatment goal of mastering tasks vital to successful SST and RP, such as learning how to talk about her feelings, even generalizing this new adaptive coping response to many different stressful situations. However, she demonstrated how she had learned even more. This involved learning when it was both appropriate and inappropriate to openly express her feelings, as in the meeting with the program director. This reflected the development in Ms. F. W. of something that was likely clouded over and compromised by marijuana use in the period of her life prior to her incarceration: how to use good judgment in reality, or how to adaptively cognitively cope in stressful interpersonal interactions. She was, in effect, learning how to cope with ongoing life-context factors, many of which were a source of stress. Ms. F. W. was showing her ability to adaptively cognitively cope with stress by telling herself in an internal dialogue (likely both silently within and aloud in conversation with others) that she could not risk being discharged from her mandated residential facility. Consistent with the ongoing use of motivational-interviewing techniques, the client was positively reinforced for this change talk.

She was also sharing evidence of her ability to adaptively cope with stress by talking to her peers and counselors after the incident with the program director occurred, as well as by talking with those of us in that mental-health group that day. She freely shared her feelings of hurt and anger, given how she was talked down to. Indeed, her behavior of sitting quietly in the group meeting with the program director and choosing to talk with other people after the group about her experience also reflected her new ability to engage in adaptive behavioral coping, for the adaptive behavioral response of sitting quietly and listening is an essential social skill. Meanwhile, she was reminded, along with all of the other group members, of another adaptive behavioral response and essential social skill for use in preventing interpersonal interactions from escalating into exchanges of verbal aggression or actual physical violence—walking away. For Ms. F. W., in particular, such training within the group context is of primary importance during the early phase of treatment/action stage for changing her marijuana dependence and violent behavior, and her failure to deploy the adaptive behaviors of either sitting still or walking away could potentially lead to a serious relapse to violence, and perhaps even to marijuana smoking if she were expelled from the residence and waiting to face consequences from her probation officer. In this manner, the second mental-health-group session with Ms. F. W. provided an important opportunity for the practitioner to continue to deliver vital *Cognitive Behavioral Therapy (CBT)/Relapse Prevention (RP)/Social-Skills Training (SST)*, and the recommended state-of-the-art practice of fostering *Acquisition of Affective, Behavioral, and Cognitive Coping Skills—Learning New ABCs* was an important part of this task.

◀━━

THE CASE OF MS. F. W.: AN INDIVIDUAL SESSION
AND SESSIONS 3 AND 4 IN THE MENTAL-HEALTH GROUP

Because of her experiences of empathy, respect, and acceptance when inter-acting with me in the mental-health group, Ms. F. W. was open and receptive to receiving an individual psychotherapy session when the opportunity arose. In this manner, she also received another evidence-based intervention falling under *Individual Drug Counseling (IDC) and/or Supportive-Expressive Psychotherapy (SEP)*, in particular SEP, including an *Integration of Psychoana-lytic and Cognitive-Behavioral Theories and Techniques* (see table 6.1).

AN INDIVIDUAL PSYCHOTHERAPY SESSION

Ms. F. W. entered the consultation room smiling. She sat down, making her-self comfortable in the available chair. She wore a loose-fitting dress of dark color. Ms. F. W. was able to elaborate on some of the issues causing her the greatest emotional distress. These included her learning to cope with having little money and a limited supply of appropriate donated clothing to choose from at her residence. This was due to her having an unusually tall and thin stature. She stated as follows: "This dress and a couple of others are all I have. I just keep washing them out and wearing them." Clearly, she was experiencing some feelings of shame and embarrassment. In response, Ms. F. W. received genuine displays of empathy, understanding, and encourage-ment to continue to cope as best she could. My conscious intent was to cre-ate for her yet another experience of feeling my genuine empathy, now in the privacy of an individual session (in keeping with a *Special Focus on Building a Strong Therapeutic Alliance/Social-Support Network (TASS)* listed in table 6.1). Positive reinforcement was also offered to her; after listening intently to her story, I stated, "It's not easy, but you're coping very well with your situation. Keep doing what you're doing."

Ms. F. W. also talked about learning to cope with having little or no free-dom to move about autonomously, given the intensive supervision under which she functioned. This included limited freedom to autonomously at-tend Narcotics Anonymous meetings in the community, at least at this point in her treatment. The reality of what it meant to be on probation and mandated to a supervised residential facility included learning to cope with intensive supervision. She was encouraged to accept this reality as a temporary condition, with emphasis on how she would become free of such intensive supervision over time, depending upon her behavior. Ms.

F. W. readily understood what this meant and was able to clearly express her intentions in this regard. "I know what I have to do. I have to submit clean urine. I have to make all my scheduled appointments. I can't do anything I'm not supposed to do. I have to get permission for everything I want to do. I have to follow all the rules at the residence. I have to follow all the rules at this program. I have to follow all the rules my probation officer gives me. I have to do everything I have to do to get my children back. And I have to be patient."

Again, in response to her long list of things she was both doing and had to continue to do, Ms. F. W. received reinforcement in the form of my verbal comments of support. I stated as follows: "You're doing a really great job. I'm very proud of you. I believe you can do it." In this manner, I was also fostering optimistic thinking in her by role modeling such thinking (*Incorporating Contemporary Trends in Psychology: Multiculturalism, Positive Psychology, the Strengths-Based Approach, and Optimistic Thinking/Learned Optimism*).

There was also the issue of Ms. F. W.'s deep emotional pain over missing her two children. She cried freely at one point in the individual session when she arrived at this issue. Ms. F. W. reiterated what she had already shared in the mental-health group, repeating, "Once I get them back, I am never going through anything like this again. I won't do anything to risk losing them." And, just as she did in the mental-health group, she received empathy and support from me: "It's going to get better. It takes time and it's not easy. But you will get your children back if you continue doing what you're doing." Again, I role modeled and sought to foster her optimistic thinking, and I offered a positive prophecy I hoped she would fulfill.

GAINS MADE THROUGH THE INDIVIDUAL SESSION

Thus, this individual psychotherapy session provided an opportunity to further strengthen the therapeutic alliance, following a *Special Focus on Building a Strong Therapeutic Alliance/Social-Support Network (TASS)*. I responded with genuine empathy to her pain and frustration, especially with regard to issues that were easier to share in the privacy of an individual session. But, just as in the mental-health-group sessions, Ms. F. W. received positive reinforcement for both talking honestly and openly about her feelings, and for engaging in change talk, as occurs with *Motivational Interviewing/Motivational Enhancement Therapy (MET)/Brief Interventions*, specifically motivational interviewing. And she also received a reflection of her strengths, as well as my optimistic appraisal and sharing of positive prophecy for her future (*Incorporating Contemporary Trends in Psychology: Multiculturalism, Positive Psychology, the Strengths-Based Approach, and Optimistic Thinking/Learned Optimism*).

SESSION 3 IN THE MENTAL-HEALTH GROUP

On yet another occasion in the third mental-health group she attended, Ms. F. W. talked about her determination to maintain her behavioral changes even after she reunites with her husband, who is serving time in prison for charges related to his involvement in drug distribution. It seemed as though she was continuing a conversation started somewhere else, maybe in another group; this is quite common when clients are part of a program following *The Matrix Model—Or, a Day-Treatment Approach, or an IEC Outpatient Model That Is* I *for Intensive (4–5 days per week),* E *for Extensive (6–12 months), and* C *for Comprehensive (TASS, CBT/RP, IDC, GDC, drug testing, etc.).* In this manner, material recently stimulated within a client in one individual drug-counseling or group session may be further processed in yet another one across several days of the same week.

In this regard, perhaps, she had heard a woman in another group in our program talk about relapsing once her husband came home from prison, or about how a peer's husband had begun using drugs or selling drugs once he returned from incarceration. Or, perhaps she had merely begun to think about these issues on her own. Whatever the origin, Ms. F. W. was appropriately anticipating the most critical issue facing families and communities in contemporary society: what to do and how to cope once a husband returns from incarceration. Ms. F. W. had arrived at her personal answer and was able to share it with great conviction, emphatically stating, "I love my husband, but I don't know if he is going to get himself together. We have been together a long time, and he loves me. But, I will let him go in a minute if he gets involved with drugs when he gets out of prison."

It was both a bit surprising and amazingly refreshing to hear a woman in her situation arrive at such firm conviction. Ms. F. W. was sounding like a pillar of strength with unbending determination born of the suffering and misery of intensely missing her two toddlers while she was incarcerated. Her ability to engage in adaptive cognitive coping, specifically problem-solving skills, consequential thinking, and exercise of good judgment and reality testing, seemed to be fully crystallizing now that she was free from the marijuana haze that had once daily engulfed her. Although Ms. F. W. could not know her husband's mind or what he was thinking and planning, she clearly knew her own mind and what she was thinking and planning.

Ms. F. W. was essentially following a key tenet of relapse prevention: to anticipate high-risk situations for one's own relapse and to plan in advance how one will cope. Ms. F. W. was clearly doing that, and it was quite impressive. To the extent that she had been exposed to *Cognitive-Behavioral Therapy (CBT)/Relapse Prevention (RP)/Social-Skills Training (SST)*, likely in many different settings in the outpatient program (both individual and group), she was successfully generalizing and applying this information.

As I sat and listened to Ms. F. W., I felt so happy and pleased that she was able to serve as such an excellent role model for how to engage in adaptive cognitive, affective, and behavioral coping responses in front of the other group members. Sitting there so very impressed and amazed, I had to prod myself to speak up and deliver positive verbal reinforcement in response to her production of change talk. I stated, "You are really using excellent judgment. You've made a really good decision. What you've decided to do is not easy. But it is a great decision. I only wish that more women would make the decision that you are making. I'm really proud of you."

SESSION 4 IN THE MENTAL-HEALTH GROUP

However, there were still very hard tests that Ms. F. W. faced. In the fourth mental-health group she attended, Ms. F. W. cried openly, sharing her pain that she would miss out on a celebration for one of her children, given the residential program's rules and restrictions. She shared how other women in the residential facility who knew of her pain were starting to avoid talking in front of her about their children and the special events coming up in their lives, trying to protect her feelings. Ms. F. W. described how she told them not to do this. Reflecting great strength and resilience, she did not want to detract from or interfere with the joy of other mothers, despite her own pain. She explained, "If it means I have to cry, then I just have to cry." She then privately processed her own pain in the residential facility. But, here in the mental-health group, she could openly share that pain and cry.

She described how she did her very best to not cry when it was time for a supervised visit with her children to come to an end. It was so very painful to leave them. But she reflected upon and reminded herself of the negative consequences that would follow if she violated the strict guidelines for when, where, and for how long she could spend time with her children. In this manner, she evidenced, once again, excellent adaptive cognitive coping, specifically consequential thinking. Ms. F. W. described how deeply she cried after the visit was over and her children were gone.

Those of us in the group sat with her in silence, allowing her to fully cry, empathizing with her pain, for there are times in life when things are so painful that it is an adaptive coping response to simply cry. I thought of the many women who had not successfully gotten to the point where they cried and adaptively processed their pain. Instead, they repeatedly acted out violently, aggressively verbally abused others, or relapsed to chemical use after experiencing the classic pain of a childcare visit's coming to an untimely end. In contrast, Ms. F. W. was in that moment a powerful role model for the kind of adaptive coping responses that would avert such negative outcomes, and she was also verbally processing her pain.

Apparently, Ms. F. W. had successfully learned across the earlier sessions in the mental-health group (and likely had been reinforced during many other varied treatment experiences in other settings) how openly crying was much preferable to stuffing her feelings and potentially acting them out via a relapse to marijuana use or violence.

DELIVERING VITAL POSITIVE REINFORCEMENT IN MENTAL-HEALTH GROUP 4

After a long moment of silence in what we created as the safe holding environment of the group—a temporary space where she could release her pain, and those of us there could feel it, hold it, and accept it—Ms. F. W. was positively reinforced for adapting to reality, accepting the strict limits upon her, and coping with them the best she possibly could. I offered, "That's the way it is. You have to accept it. And you're doing a really good job dealing with it. I know it wasn't easy to wait until your children were gone to cry. But you did a great job, sparing them from seeing you cry. . . . You were a strong woman and good mother to do that. . . . And it's OK to cry. . . . It's good to cry here. . . . It's going to get better. . . . It's OK. . . . You're going to get them back in your custody."

This intervention served as more than just positive reinforcement for how Ms. F. W. had even further successfully generalized adaptive coping responses to an especially hard test in the real world. Ms. F. W. was clearly demonstrating that she knew how, when, where, and with whom to share and express her feelings. This was evidence of a major accomplishment, involving both generalization of her adaptive coping responses to varied situations, as well as growing sophistication in coping as she discerned which coping response was most appropriate for certain kinds of situations. This suggests a process occurring over time with regard to the establishment of adaptive coping responses. But, *Incorporating Contemporary Trends in Psychology: Multiculturalism, Positive Psychology, the Strengths-Based Approach, and Optimistic Thinking/Learned Optimism*, the intervention also sought to give her hope, helping her to appreciate her own strengths and good qualities, as well as the possibility of her fulfilling the positive prophecy of reunification with her children, given my positive expectations for her (again, see chapter 5 or Wallace, 1996a, for a fuller discussion).

As it turned out, Ms. F. W. had both bad news and good news to share in this fourth mental-health group. She wiped away her tears, appeared hopeful, and felt comforted by what those of us in the group said to her. She moved on to the good news. In fact, she also role modeled for the group the benefits of a good cry. She appeared to feel better and was able to move on to something new: the good news. It turned out she had good reason for hope and to be optimistic, beyond the optimistic prophecy I had just offered.

And she had more proof that she had strengths and good qualities, coming from another objective source—the judge overseeing her case in drug court.

MORE VITAL POSITIVE REINFORCEMENT
FROM THE JUDGE IN DRUG COURT

Ms. F. W. had gone before the judge handling her case for the third time a few days earlier. She was especially proud to share the story of this recent court scene and the judge's comments. Ms. F. W. had evolved into someone who was so motivated to change, and indeed *was* changing so rapidly, that this female judge had commented upon Ms. F. W.'s tremendous growth and transformation. The judge complimented her and encouraged her to keep up the excellent work in treatment.

Sharing this story with the group, Ms. F. W. smiled with pride. In fact, all of us in the group were now smiling. Ms. F. W. actually seemed as amazed as the judge with her progress over the three snapshot interactions she had had with the judge—from the time of her sentencing nearly ten months ago, to her release from jail and her mandate into the residence and addiction treatment two months ago, up to the present time, now having a little over two months in community-based addiction treatment in the real world.

Ms. F. W. talked about how things had been ten months ago: "I did what I wanted to do. Nobody told me what to do. You couldn't. Not with the way I was." Ms. F. W. was, in this manner, also able to reflect upon the progress she had made and her tremendous strides in developing a new identity as one who adaptively coped in response to stress. She was now bringing new adaptive coping responses to the occasional extremely hard tests she faced: these typically involved having staff at probation, her residence, and at the child-protection agency constantly telling her what to do, often talking down to her in the process. She was coping well with the stress involved in interacting regularly with varied authority figures who were potentially having negative countertransference reactions to her, even intermittently displaying affects of disdain, stigmatizing her, or discriminating against her.

Ms. F. W. had not sought to change these individuals in positions of authority; she obeyed their rules, complied with their demands, avoided the delivery of negative graduated sanctions, and instead changed what she could: herself. Patterns of adaptive affective, behavioral, and cognitive coping were now the hallmark feature of Ms. F. W. She even passed the hardest test of all and impressed the one authority with the most power to deliver the very worst graduated sanctions against her: the drug-court judge. In this manner, her case even included the use of elements of the *Community Reinforcement Approach (CRA)/Vouchers: Contingency Management (CM)*, as listed in table 6.1, insofar as she could have received negative graduated sanctions for positive urine-test results under probation, for returning late with her children from unsupervised visits to the child-protection agency, or for failing to meet the specifications of the judge.

A SPECIAL FORM OF POSITIVE REINFORCEMENT

Finally, given her progress, Ms. F. W. received much praise and reinforcement from both her peers and me in reaction to the good news she shared in the mental-health group. The members of the group clapped and cheered, following my lead. This clapping and cheering served as a special form of positive reinforcement that was reserved for such extraordinary moments in the group. We were celebrating a miracle! The miracle involved the rather rapid, indeed radical, transformation of Ms. F. W.

FINAL COMMENTARY ON THE CASE OF MS. F. W.

The case covers the first two months of Ms. F. W.'s being in outpatient community-based addiction treatment, describing her participation in four mental-health-group sessions and an individual psychotherapy session during this period. In sum, Ms. F. W. was a powerful role model in the mental-health group with regard to how an individual could rapidly change, even amazing herself, given her response to the external pressure coming from the criminal justice system, the supervising authorities in her residential facility, and the child-protection authorities. Her own internal motivation to change emerged as so enhanced and so fundamentally strengthened that she successfully coped with those stressful challenges she encountered in the early phase of her treatment/action stage, actively changing her addictive and violent behavior in the real world once released from jail. Most importantly, she role modeled for others in the group how to engage in adaptive affective, behavioral, and cognitive coping responses to the challenges inherent in recovery; how to cope with the stress of being stigmatized, disdained, and discriminated against by corrections officers in jail, as well as by a program director once out of jail; and even how to cope with being talked down to in a harsh, disrespectful, denigrating manner.

The case shows how practitioner deployment of techniques common to the evidence-based *Motivational Interviewing/Motivation Enhancement Therapy (MET)/Brief Interventions* served to enhance her internal motivation to change, even to the extent that it came to replace a largely external motivation to change coming from external pressures from probation, the judge, and child-protection authorities. Specifically, this accomplishment both occurred spontaneously within her and was also further enhanced and strengthened via frequent use of the motivational-interviewing technique of reinforcing her for engaging in change talk and for manifesting actual concrete behavioral changes. Other verbal positive reinforcement and the delivery of brief education on the goals of treatment, specific social skills, and skills for coping with interpersonal and general life stress served to help Ms. F. W. further shape, refine, and generalize to varied real-world situations her new adaptive affective, behavioral, and cognitive coping responses. This work was consistent with practitioner deployment of techniques common to the evidence-based *Cognitive-Behavioral Therapy (CBT)/ Relapse Prevention (RP)/Social-Skills Training (SST)*.

In addition, the case of Ms. F. W. shows how practitioners may also draw upon recommended state-of-the-art practices, as summarized in table 6.1. For example, the case shows the process by which Ms. F. W. successfully acquired in treatment and deployed in the real world new adaptive affective, behavioral, and cognitive responses to the stress of being intensively supervised by criminal-justice-system personnel, other contracted residential supervisors, and child-protection-agency staff; this followed the recommended state-of-the-art practice of fostering *Acquisition of Affective, Behavioral, and Cognitive Coping Skills—or the Learning of New ABCs.*

Finally, the case of Ms. F. W. is highlighted by her success in displaying her new social skills in front of a judge. Meanwhile, her record of clean urines, the positive report from her residential program, the positive report from her community-based addiction-treatment program, and the positive report from child-protection authorities were all shared with the judge.

In this manner, Ms. F. W. emerges—as early as ten months since her arrest, and two months since her release from jail and entrance into mandated community-based addiction treatment—as a client who is well on her way toward the establishment of a new identity as one who adaptively affectively, behaviorally, and cognitively copes with reality. This replaces her former identity as one who smoked marijuana, readily dominated others through expressions of anger and aggression, and thereby did what she wanted to do. This reflects at least partial use of what is a state-of-the-art practice involving *Integration of Motivational Interviewing, Stages of Change, and Identity Development Theory for a Diverse Identity Involving Race, Sexual Orientation, and/or Disability*, but in this case for an identity as one who copes adaptively with stress without resorting to violence and marijuana use. This included the stress of interacting with individuals in positions of authority who might be having negative countertransference reactions to her as a stigmatized "drug addict" and "bad mother."

The case also illustrates the manner in which use of the seven evidence-based interventions effectively creates a unified model that guides practitioners in delivering treatment. And the case shows how use of five recommended state-of-the-art practices effectively allows for a unified theory to guide practitioners in delivering treatment. Together, the unified model and theory serves to provide practitioners with a framework for use in service delivery.

CONCLUSION

This chapter presented the case of Ms. F. W. across two months of outpatient community-based addiction treatment, along with detailed commentary highlighting the many kinds of negative countertransference reactions a practitioner may have toward a contemporary client. Also presented was the goal that practitioners attain adaptive cognitive, affective, and behavioral responses so as to avoid negative countertransference. Table 6.2 summarizes key elements of this process for practitioners. A parallel process involving clients was also discussed, illustrating for practitioners how they can help their clients learn to cope with the stress of encountering negative countertransference reactions toward them as a client. A common example of this stress involves clients being talked down to by authorities in the criminal justice system, as well as in the addiction-treatment community. As a consequence, the chapter demonstrated how practitioners may help clients in the acquisition of new adaptive cognitive, affective, and behavioral responses to this stress and other more general life stress. Perhaps most importantly, the chapter illustrated in table 6.1 how twelve of the fourteen items on the menu of options were integrated and adapted for use, allowing for a unified model and theory to guide the treatment process.

Hopefully, practitioners will follow what has been suggested in this chapter, for the authoritarianism of those placed in the role of conducting intensive supervision of clients within the criminal justice system and/or of enforcing criminal sanctions may mean that they are not easily or readily effective in motivating clients (Ginsburg et al., 2002). Criminal-justice-system personnel may have the leverage and authority to apply external pressure and enhance extrinsic motivation to participate in treatment, but they may not necessarily be the best natural candidates for enhancing internal motivation to change and for fostering enduring behavioral change that is maintained over time. Going beyond what those in the criminal justice system can provide through their intensive supervision, drug-testing surveillance, and graduated sanctions, contemporary practitioners are being called upon to bring a compassionate approach informed by the perspective presented in this chapter.

However, all readers, including criminal-justice-system personnel and diverse professionals, paraprofessionals, and community members, may potentially learn how to make mandated addiction treatment work by enhancing internal motivation to change. Members of clients' social-support networks may play an invaluable role in providing clients with positive reinforcement, specifically positive feedback, encouragement, and praise ("Good. Excellent. I see a difference. You're doing very well. I'm proud of you. Keep it up!"). This may provide clients with some of the most pertinent information and stories that they may bring back into individual and group sessions for sharing with their practitioners and peers. The case of Ms. F. W.

illustrated the powerful role of the judge in being a source of such positive verbal reinforcement.

As suggested by the case of Ms. F. W., clients would benefit greatly by having practitioners, program directors, criminal-justice-system personnel, and judges who could all consistently respond to clients in a way that makes it easier for them to deploy the new adaptive affective, behavioral, and cognitive coping responses that they are learning within community-based addiction treatment. But, all too often, many of us, as societal members, fail to truly reach our potential for being viable sources of social support, due to our exposure to negative social conditioning and our resulting potential for stigmatizing and discrimination.

By virtue of the training provided in this chapter with regard to the task of replacing maladaptive responses with adaptive ones, a practitioner may move toward the establishment of what will hopefully prove to be enduring affective, behavioral, and cognitive coping responses that are part of a new corresponding identity as one who adaptively responds to contemporary clients in community-based addiction treatment. Ideally, the result will also be attainment of an identity as one supportive of a growing collective effort to promote the ascension of a new era of rationalism and compassion, an era that values rehabilitation and mandates to addiction treatment. But, most importantly, practitioners and all readers may now have a better understanding of what it means to deliver interventions from a rational and compassionate state of being, one reflecting liberation from common socially conditioned negative countertransference reactions of stigmatization, disdain, and discrimination against clients with addictive and criminal behaviors. Practitioner fidelity and flexibility in delivering evidence-based interventions may follow from such a state of liberation. Meanwhile, clients may benefit from assistance in learning to cope more effectively with the stress attendant to ongoing life-context factors, including the common stigmatization in the social context of those involved with drugs and criminality.

7

Conducting the Initial
Psychological Assessment
and Psychiatric Screening

Practitioners need a practical guide as to how to conduct a brief psychological assessment and psychiatric screening so as to uncover key client characteristics and needs. The correct timing for this brief psychological assessment and psychiatric screening is at the time of intake into a community-based addiction-treatment program, or as soon as possible after a client makes contact with the program. In this manner, the assessment/screening should occur as one of the very first steps to be taken in the early phase of treatment. While the time of program intake is ideal, the brief psychological assessment and psychiatric screening may occur at any point when the client is encountered, whether by special referral or as part of some program routine.

There may be findings that direct client-to-intervention and client-to-treatment-modality matching strategies. Assessment findings can reveal whether or not a client needs to be matched to a specific treatment intervention such as anger management, rape counseling, domestic-violence counseling, counseling services for being a victim of a crime, couples counseling, HIV/AIDS counseling, or mental-health services for comorbidity. Results of the psychiatric screening determine the need for referral for psychiatric treatment. And the assessment/screening may also constitute a brief intervention within itself; such a brief intervention aims to enhance a client's internal motivation to pursue whatever emerges as a clearly needed intervention or treatment modality. A practitioner taking the time to discuss assessment findings with a client may also produce a powerful moment that leads clients to move across stages of change, from precontemplation (not thinking about changing), to contemplation (ambivalent, but thinking about change), to preparation (feeling prepared to pursue change), to action (actually taking action toward change); this suggests the potential of a brief intervention (Miller & Rollnick, 1991, 2002; Miller, Wilbourne, & Hettema, 2003) such as the evidence-based *Motivational Interviewing/Motivation Enhancement Therapy (MET)/Brief Intervention.*

The findings from the psychological assessment and psychiatric screening may also bring to light a need for contingency contracting. Contingency contracting can also enhance client motivation to change (Higgins & Silverman, 1999). And contingency contracts are also ideally made at the time of intake or earliest contact with a client. This underscores the value of using to some extent the evidence-based *Community Reinforcement Approach (CRA)/Vouchers: Contingency Management (CM).*

Hence, motivational interviewing and contingency management are both evidence-based interventions with a body of supportive research (Higgins & Abbott, 2001; Higgins & Silverman, 1999; Miller & Rollnick, 2002; Miller, Wilbourne, & Hettema, 2003) and having an important role to play within the context of the brief psychological assessment/psychiatric screening. And at all times and in all cases, there is an important role for a *Special Focus on Building a Strong Therapeutic Alliance/Social-Support Network (TASS).*

This chapter will provide training to practitioners for conducting the initial psychological assessment and psychiatric screening of clients in community-based addiction treatment. The purpose of and questions encompassing the brief psychological assessment/psychiatric screening will be presented in this chapter. The chapter reflects changes in my own work with regard to how to conduct a thorough clinical interview (Wallace, 1991b), including careful probing for past experiences of trauma (Wallace, 1996a), given managed-care dictates to transform assessments/screening to as brief a period as thirty minutes. However, practitioners may benefit, nonetheless, by familiarizing themselves with how to conduct a thorough clinical interview (Wallace, 1991b), as well as how to assess clients for trauma (Wallace, 1996a). The importance that assessment be an ongoing process that continues across phases of treatment and recovery has also been highlighted (Wallace, 1991b, 1996a), a point to be underscored repeatedly in this book, as well.

However, following the guidelines for assessment/screening put forth in this chapter, merely carefully screening for mood and anxiety disorders typically leads to the unveiling of pertinent traumas. Yet it may be argued, as in chapter 4, that all clients with any evidence of post-traumatic stress disorder should be thoroughly screened for trauma, and that trauma should be properly addressed in treatment along with the addictive disorder. The case chosen for discussion in this chapter (that of Mr. F. T.) illustrates such unveiling of past pertinent trauma in the assessment/screening.

The case of Mr. F. T. also effectively illustrates the role of motivational interviewing, contingency contracting at the time of initial assessment, and the importance of building a strong therapeutic alliance. Also, the case of Mr. F. T. allows for extensive illustration of the role of many additional evidence-based interventions and state-of-the-art practices. Of note, the case of Mr. F. T. presents the worst-case scenario a practitioner may encounter during performance of the assessment/screening, as a compelling training tool. And, to further illustrate the importance of what happens within the assessment/screening, the case is followed for key events up to eight weeks after the day of assessment/screening, as well as during the first three months in outpatient community-based addiction treatment, spanning a total of five months, or most of an early phase of treatment/action stage. The case will also illustrate the role of key variables (e.g., psychiatric symptoms/comorbidity) in directing client-treatment matching strategies in which care is tailored for an individual client.

THE BRIEF PSYCHOLOGICAL
ASSESSMENT/PSYCHIATRIC SCREENING

Given the constraints of time and the imperatives of managed care to conduct brief assessments, ideally within the span of thirty-to-sixty-minute time slots but using professional judgment to spend time with clients as needed, several assessment questions are deemed essential in the community-based addiction-treatment setting. Ideally, the practitioner asking these questions has training as a psychologist, social worker, or psychiatrist. This assessment may be distinguished from that of the intake worker who is doing one kind of initial assessment, that of a substance-abuse counselor who is conducting a complete psychosocial assessment, as well as that of the physician who is conducting a complete medical assessment.

The brief psychological assessment/psychiatric screening serves several key functions. These include the establishment of client appropriateness for the current level of care. An appropriate level of care may include a brief five-to-seven-day inpatient detoxification; a longer, twenty-eight-to-forty-five-day inpatient rehabilitation; an outpatient program; or a residential therapeutic community (TC) as the community-based addiction-treatment option. The assessment/screening also brings to light important client characteristics and determines additional client needs. A determination may also be made about potential risks for the client or potential risks to other clients and staff in the facility, including those risks related to suicidality, homicidality, and violence. In addition, findings may result in a range of referrals for mental-health treatment and to address other client characteristics and needs. The possibilities include referral to outpatient psychiatric care, inpatient psychiatric hospitalization, a residential or outpatient program for mentally ill chemical abusers (MICAs), or even crisis intervention. On occasion, crisis intervention may include calling emergency medical services (EMS) and/or the police to come immediately to the facility to assist with client disposition and referral for more intensive crisis intervention. The underlying purpose

**Table 7.1.   The Underlying Purpose of the Brief Psychological
Assessment/Psychiatric Screening**

1. Is this client appropriate for treatment in this community-based addiction-treatment setting?
2. Does this community-based addiction-treatment setting constitute the right level of care, or is referral to another level of care indicated by assessment findings?
3. Are there psychiatric symptoms (comorbidity) that suggest that the client must receive mental-health or psychiatric treatment?
4. Are there any potential risks for the client, other clients, or for staff, given a client's psychiatric symptoms (comorbidity)?
5. What referrals are needed in order for the client to be either admitted into the program, retained in treatment, or for the client to be able to function adequately, successfully, and without risk to self or others in the community-based addiction-treatment setting?
6. What client-to-intervention and client-to-treatment-modality matching strategies need to be followed, given assessment findings?
7. Given assessment findings, what kind of contingency contracts need to ideally be made with clients in advance of admission?

of the brief psychological assessment/psychiatric screening may be summarized through the questions listed in table 7.1. Vital decisions follow from the assessment/screening, as the questions in table 7.1 suggest.

QUESTIONS WITHIN THE BRIEF PSYCHOLOGICAL ASSESSMENT/PSYCHIATRIC SCREENING

The actual questions posed by practitioners appear in table 7.2. Some general questions serve the purpose of establishing rapport with clients. Other questions serve the purpose of actually uncovering psychiatric symptoms, related behavior, and key characteristics and needs of clients.

Initial Rapport-Building Questions

General initial rapport-building questions allow practitioners during the assessment/screening to understand the overall social context for client's lives and their entrance into community-based addiction treatment at this point in time. With regard to the client, these questions allow the practitioner to get a sense of who clients are, how their life course has been going, and where they are at this point in time. Some questions are always asked. Other questions may not necessarily be asked, depending upon the initial answers received and other factors, such as the practitioner's having initial clues that the client actually does have an extensive psychiatric background that will require careful probing. It is also helpful for the practitioner to know the client's level of education, any history of special education, and something about the ability of the client to comprehend and respond to questions. This

Table 7.2. Practitioners' Initial Assessment/Screening Questions

Initial rapport-building questions: What is your name? How old are you? What is your date of birth? Who referred you to our program? How did you find out about our program? When were you arrested? What were you arrested for? What was your sentence, and how much time did you serve? When were you released? When is your period of probation/parole over? When did you last get high? What did you use, and how much did you use? At the height of your addiction, what was your pattern of drug and alcohol use in terms of dose and frequency? Who are you living with now? Are you in a relationship now? Do you have any children? Who is caring for your children? Are you in contact with them? How far did you go in school? Were you in special education? What kind of training do you have? Are you working now? What kind of work have you done in the past? What was your longest job? What kind of medical problems do you have? Are you taking medication for any medical conditions?

Nine core areas of psychological assessment/psychiatric screening and related questions
  1. Auditory hallucinations: Have you ever had auditory hallucinations? . . .
  2. Visual hallucinations: Have you ever had visual hallucinations? . . .
  3. Paranoia and delusions: Do you feel like anyone is out to get you, is trying to hurt you, is after you, or is following you? Do you have any special powers? Do you have any beliefs that are causing problems for you? . . .
  4. Depression and suicidality: Are you depressed at this time? How is your sleeping pattern? . . . How is your appetite? Do you have a history of serious depression? Are you feeling suicidal now? Do you wish you were dead? . . .
  5. Anxiety: Are you experiencing anxiety/nervousness/shakiness at this time? Do you have a history of experiencing anxiety/nervousness/shakiness? . . .
  6. Homicidality: Are you feeling homicidal? Is there anyone that you want to hurt or kill now? Do you have a plan? . . .
  7. Risk of violence: Have you ever been arrested for assault? When was the last time you had a physical fight? . . .
  8. Psychiatric treatment history: Have you ever been an inpatient in a psychiatric hospital? Have you ever seen a psychiatrist in an outpatient setting? Have you ever seen a psychiatrist in any other setting? . . .
  9. Motivational enhancement and increasing internal motivation for change: What are your concerns? What do you feel you need help with? What are your goals? What's the next step for you? What options are you considering?

has implications for the subsequent exploration of a client's psychiatric symptoms and other issues. The rapport building questions are presented at the top of table 7.2.

The Nine Core Areas of Assessment/Screening and Related Questions

These nine core psychological-assessment/psychiatric-screening questions should be considered as involving a kind of decision tree. An initial answer of "no" allows the practitioner to skip all the subsequent questions under that heading and to go to the next heading. The practitioner can often move very quickly through all nine of the core areas of assessment, perhaps in as short a period of time as two to three minutes. This is especially the case when the initial question under each heading is usually a closed-ended question requiring a yes-or-no answer. But an answer of "yes" leads to many open-ended questions that require clients to tell a story or to elaborate on what happened and what they did, opening the door for much more time to be taken up in the session. In some cases, the period of questioning may extend to twenty to fifty minutes, or even to over an hour in rare instances. Indeed, it can be a painstaking task to obtain all the details to explain that "yes." In general, a client's degree and extent of current and past psychiatric symptoms and whether or not they were ever treated determines the length of the brief psychological assessment/psychiatric screening and whether or not it is indeed brief, or quite long.

It is important to take the requisite time needed, as the implications of a symptom—for example, feeling homicidal—will only become clear, in terms of the ramifications for placing program staff and other clients at risk, if many other questions are asked. These may include asking whether the client has been arrested for assault, asking when the last time was that the client was violent or had a physical fight, and asking whether the client tends to dissociate during violence and not recall what happened. What may be a painstaking task is pursued for excellent reason, given the need to determine the appropriate level of care for a client, any necessary referrals, essential client-to-intervention and client-to-treatment-modality matching strategies, and which contingency contracts are deemed as essential.

The client's level of education and ability to comprehend will determine whether more technical or less complicated language is used, for example, asking about visual hallucinations versus seeing things, insomnia versus having trouble sleeping, being suicidal versus wanting to kill oneself, having anxiety versus nervousness or shakiness, or being homicidal versus wanting to kill someone. Thus, not every one of the recommended/listed questions in table 7.2 (and later in this chapter) are asked of any one client, but they serve to indicate the phrasing used when the client can comprehend technical terms, as well as alternative language used when clients require a more simple rephrasing of questions.

By the end of the brief psychiatric screening, and at the end of the interview as a whole, the final task is to very briefly enhance the client's internal motivation to engage in and pursue treatment. This means adapting motivational interviewing (Miller & Rollnick, 1991, 2002) to the context of the last three to five minutes of the brief psychological assessment/psychiatric screening, asking clients questions about their concerns and goals and the next steps they see themselves taking. By eliciting concerns and goals and the next steps clients see themselves taking, clients end up engaging in change talk, consistent with motivational interviewing (Miller & Rollnick, 2002). The production of change talk is then very briefly positively reinforced with simple practitioner comments, such as "Good," "Excellent," or "That sounds like a good plan." Both the production of change talk in clients and the receipt of positive reinforcement from a practitioner may serve to decrease any client resistance and enhance internal motivation to change. Given that a client's referral source may be probation, parole, a child-protection agency, or welfare—suggesting external pressure to change and extrinsic motivation to do so—enhancing a client's internal motivation to change at this early point in treatment is important.

If the practitioner has time, meaning the assessment did not take a great deal of time, the practitioner may also choose to deliver a summary reflection, also consistent with motivational interviewing (Miller & Rollnick, 2002). For example, the practitioner might say, "So, you want to focus on making sure you don't go back to jail, that you get training, and that you get a good job so you can stay with your family and watch your children grow up." This summary reflection would also be accompanied by the delivery of positive reinforcement in the form of a broad smile or a comment such as "Excellent," "Sounds good," or "Perhaps this could all be a blessing in disguise, including this mandate." This reinforcement of a client for having produced change talk may increase the chances that the client produces yet more change talk in the future, perhaps with other practitioners in the treatment program, following principles of operant conditioning and the function of positive reinforcement within the motivational interviewing techniques of Miller and Rollnick (2002).

The final thirty-second-to-two-minute closing of the psychiatric screening also provides an opportunity to engage in some brief cognitive reframing of addiction treatment as a reward in and of itself, and as involving many rewards. This may effectively move clients away from any negative cognitive conditioning or negative thoughts with regard to the current course of treatment they are about to begin. Perhaps clients who are mandated or coerced (or even voluntary) are thinking of treatment as a punishment or as a waste of their time. Cognitive reframing may be accomplished by merely stating several positive features about the treatment facility, whether this covers recent renovations to the physical plant, the availability of a free nutritious lunch, the variety of groups available, access to vocational and educational opportunities, or the positive attributes of program staff. These brief comments can help to define access to treatment in the facility as a positive reward, potentially further enhancing clients' internal motivation to attend the program and change their behavior, whether they arrived at the treatment door because of a mandate or not.

Thus, this brief (thirty minutes to one hour) psychological assessment/psychiatric screening represents a very important initial experience that can build a strong therapeutic alliance to not only the practitioner, but also to the overall social and therapeutic milieu of the treatment program that is there to support the client. By building this therapeutic alliance to the overall social-support system inherent within the addiction-treatment program, starting

from the very beginning of treatment, indeed in the opening assessment/
screening, a stronger therapeutic alliance is built that may produce better retention in treatment, more disclosure of client problems, and better treatment
outcome. This follows the recommendations of Lebow et al. (2002).

Having explained the overall function of the nine core areas of questions
that make up the psychological assessment/brief psychiatric screening, they
may now be presented below, expanding on what appears in table 7.2.

1. Auditory Hallucinations

Have you ever had auditory hallucinations? Have you ever heard voices of
people that you could not see? Are you hearing voices now? What are the
voices saying? What kinds of things have they said to you in the past? Do the
voices ever tell you to hurt yourself or anyone else? Have you followed what
the voices have told you to do? What kinds of things have you done? (Ask standard follow-up questions about the client's history of treatment for symptoms,
as described below.)

Practitioners' Standard Follow-Up Questions about Client History of Treatment of a Symptom

If there is an affirmative answer with regard to area 1 or any of those questions under areas 2 through 6, practitioners should ask several follow-up
questions listed below:

Tell me about the first time, all the other times, and the last time that you had
that experience, as well as what happened and what you did. More specifically,
what kind of treatment did you receive? Specifically, did you receive emergency-
room treatment, inpatient psychiatric treatment, outpatient psychiatric treatment, or psychiatric medication? Are you taking any psychiatric medication
now? What are you taking? Do you take it regularly? Does the medication seem
to be helping? How is it helping?

2. Visual Hallucinations

Have you ever had visual hallucinations? Have you ever had the experience of seeing things that other people could not see? Are you having visual hallucinations/
seeing things now? What are you seeing? What kinds of visual hallucinations have
you had/kinds of things have you seen in the past? (Ask standard follow-up questions about client's history of treatment for symptoms.)

3. Paranoia and Delusions

Do you feel like anyone is out to get you, is trying to hurt you, is after you, or is
following you? Is there anyone that you feel particularly suspicious of or who
has a plot against you? Do you have any special powers? Do you have any

beliefs that are causing problems for you? (Ask standard follow-up questions about client's history of treatment for symptoms.)

4. Depression and Suicidality

Are you depressed at this time? How is your sleeping pattern? Are you having trouble sleeping (insomnia), having trouble oversleeping (hypersomnia), finding it hard to fall asleep, having disturbed/fitful/interrupted sleep, or waking up early in the morning? How is your appetite? Has it changed in any way? Have you lost weight or gained weight without intending to? Do you have a history of serious depression? Are you feeling suicidal now? Do you wish you were dead? Do you have a plan? What is your plan? Do you have access to what it takes to carry out your plan? Do you think you will act on that plan? (Ask standard follow-up questions about client's history of treatment for symptoms.)

5. Anxiety

Are you experiencing anxiety/nervousness/shakiness at this time? Do you have a history of experiencing anxiety/nervousness/shakiness? Have you ever had a panic attack, felt like you couldn't breathe, felt like you were going to have a heart attack, or been afraid you might die? Do you ever have flashbacks or nightmares from traumas you have experienced? (Ask standard follow-up questions about client's history of treatment for symptoms.)

6. Homicidality

Are you feeling homicidal? Is there anyone that you want to hurt or kill now? Do you have a plan? What is your plan? Do you have access to what it takes to carry out your plan? Do you think you will act on that plan? What would it take for you to act on your plan, or to kill someone? (Ask standard follow-up questions about client's history of treatment for symptoms.) Perhaps add: Have you actually killed someone or seriously injured someone? Tell me the story about what you did and what happened. Were you caught, charged, arrested, or incarcerated?

7. Risk of Violence

When is the last time you had a physical fight? What happened? Were any weapons involved, and was anyone seriously injured? Have you been arrested for assault? What was the outcome? Have you been arrested for domestic violence? What was the outcome? Have you ever been violent but did not remember what you did, being told about it later, because you somehow dissociated/lost awareness of what you were doing? Do you think there is a chance that you will be violent in this treatment setting? What would it take for you to be violent in this setting? What would someone have to do or say for you to become violent?

8. Psychiatric Treatment History

Have you ever been an inpatient in a psychiatric hospital? Have you ever seen a psychiatrist in an outpatient setting? Have you ever seen a psychiatrist in any other setting? Have you ever been treated by a psychiatrist in an emergency room? Have you ever been prescribed or taken psychiatric medication?

9. Motivational Enhancement and Increasing Internal Motivation for Change

What are your concerns? What are your goals? What's the next step for you? What options are you considering?

Table 7.2 summarizes all of the questions that make up the brief psychological assessment/psychiatric screening, including the initial rapport-building questions. Since they were presented in the text, the complete set of questions that follow from the nine main core areas of inquiry do not appear in table 7.2, as the ellipses suggest.

Psychiatric Referral Options Based on Client Answers to the Nine Questions

What are clinicians to do immediately upon uncovering psychiatric symptoms or pertinent psychiatric histories, or as a consequence of discovering the hidden population of clients with comorbid conditions? For to know means to act, especially if no one else knows and no one else has ever acted. This may be the case, since some clients are just now finally abstinent and newly released from incarceration. Such clients may have just had their first clear picture taken of their psychiatric symptoms within the snapshot obtained during the assessment/screening. There are a few options for clients to receive psychiatric treatment and different ways of getting the client there.

The goal is to provide clients with an experience wherein the delivery of their substance-abuse and psychiatric treatment is integrated. However, there is ideal integration in a conceptual world, and real-world integration of treatment. And often, because the client has been uncovered within a community-based addiction-treatment program, the first step toward this goal is to have the client make contact with psychiatric treatment in the community. Ideally, a community-based addiction-treatment program has a psychiatrist working at least part-time on staff. However, if this is not the case, options include the following: (1) client receipt of psychiatric treatment through an emergency room, with possible inpatient psychiatric hospitalization; (2) outpatient psychiatric treatment in a community-based mental-health clinic that may be attached to a hospital or free-standing in the community; (3) psychiatric treatment within a MICA program for mentally ill chemical abusers that also provides substance-abuse counseling, whether an inpatient rehabilitation program, residential program, day-treatment program, or outpatient program.

Again, motivational interviewing may come in to play in getting the client there, or in getting the client to feel prepared to accept a necessary referral for psychiatric treatment. For example, there are some clients who actually need treatment but may refuse the idea of going to or being escorted to an emergency room in order to be considered for inpatient psychiatric hospitalization. They will need a brief motivational interviewing intervention exploring their concerns about their psychiatric symptoms or other aspects of their life, with a directive form of motivational interviewing being deployed (Miller & Rollnick, 2002) that seeks the outcome of their psychiatric hospitalization or their gaining immediate access to psychiatric medication. In some cases it seems clear from the outset of the referral that there are medications that the client has tried before that brought about rather quick stabilization, and only an injection of the appropriate psychiatric medication— for example, Prolixin or Haldol—in the emergency room is needed in order to avert further psychiatric deterioration.

In other cases, it seems clear from the outset that the person needs the protected, safe environment of the inpatient hospital setting; a psychiatric evaluation to determine which medications may be best for the client; and what may be a process of trial and error in stabilizing the client on a psychiatric medication to which the client responds, perhaps over one to several weeks, especially if the client has multiple psychiatric symptoms. There is also the reality with regard to how to get clients to that inpatient psychiatric treatment. One option is for clients to go voluntarily and sit on their own for hours in an emergency room. There are those clients who are, especially after receipt of brief motivational interviewing, very motivated to obtain psychiatric care and medication on their own. For example, a client who is stable and free of auditory and visual hallucinations for several years but experiences multiple stressors and has a relapse to psychotic symptoms may only need hear his own concerns reflected back to him in order to have sufficient motivation to go to an emergency room on his own. Clients may also benefit from having reflected back to them their own recollections of how they responded to different medications in the past, effectively recalling and embracing what may work for them now.

Another option is for clients to be escorted by a staff member, such as a counselor, who sits with them in the emergency room. In some cases, it is imperative to call EMS and the police to make sure that the client receives emergency psychiatric treatment despite her lack of cooperation, given the need to ensure the client's and/or the public's safety.

There are also those clients who need to begin outpatient psychiatric treatment. The wait for an appointment at an outpatient mental-health clinic for psychiatric treatment may involve (1) no delay, given a walk-in clinic for psychiatric treatment or (2) a delay of anywhere from one day to up to one to three weeks or even longer. Some clients need rather immediate relief of psychiatric symptoms through prescription of psychiatric medication. Such cases can potentially create a quandary for a referring practitioner if there is a delay in the client's gaining an appointment, seeing a psychiatrist, being prescribed appropriate psychiatric medication, and undergoing a process of achieving stability on psychiatric medication.

In some cases, clients may only be appropriate for admission to and retention in a community-based addiction-treatment program if they are actually stable on appropriate psychiatric medication. Other clients may be appropriate for admission to community-based addiction treatment while they are still waiting to see a psychiatrist in order to go through the process of being prescribed and stabilized on psychiatric medication. However, for those clients for whom stabilization on psychiatric medication appears to be a prerequisite for admission to and retention in the community-based addiction-treatment program, there will be a necessary delay in a client's gaining admission to or starting to regularly attend and participate in the program. For example, the treatment of depression and severe insomnia might not preclude admission to the community-based addiction-treatment program; however, the treatment of outbursts of anger characterized by dissociation and lack of recall of what happened would definitely delay admission. Case consultation with other staff, especially medical staff and those supervising the work of counselors and practitioners, can play a vital role in making such decisions.

CONTINGENCY CONTRACTING AT THE END OF THE BRIEF PSYCHOLOGICAL ASSESSMENT/PSYCHIATRIC SCREENING

Many times it is important to engage in oral contingency contracting with clients around what has been recommended with regard to the receipt of additional psychiatric treatment. The goal is to use the power of the current mandate for addiction treatment under which clients are currently experiencing external pressure to gain admission to the outpatient community-based addiction-treatment program. The power of this mandate may be seen in how it operates to compel clients to cooperate with the psychological assessment/psychiatric screening and overall intake process. Given such a point in time when the power of the external pressure of the mandate is quite great upon them, clients may be told that their behavior of oral consent to a contingency contract is the act that can secure their admission into the program, or that their failing to agree to the oral contract can mean that they cannot be admitted to the program. The oral contingency contracts that result are varied and depend upon what has been uncovered in the assessment/screening.

These oral contracts make clear both those kinds of behaviors that are necessary requirements for clients' admission to and continuing participation in the outpatient addiction-treatment program, and/or those kinds of behaviors that are not recommended/not acceptable within the program and could prevent clients' admission to and ongoing participation within the program.

What Is the Reward in the Contingency Contract?

Admission to and ongoing participation in the community-based addiction-treatment program are considered valued rewards. This is especially the case when a client has been mandated to an addiction-treatment program, must satisfy the requirement to gain admission for parole, and must maintain admission for the specified mandated period in order to avoid being violated by parole and reincarcerated. The rewards of admission and ongoing participation are therefore valued for their ability to meet criminal-justice-system requirements. However, there is also an inherent cognitive reframing that is suggested for a client in this process, insofar as there are also rewards associated with program participation. Conceptualizing the program as a reward that permits access to many other rewards (e.g., vocational/job training, certificates, special holiday dinners, picnics, graduation) likely introduces a new set of cognitions that are very different from those associated with thinking one is being sent someplace against one's will as punishment or as a requirement, not to mention personal cognitions like "I resent this imposition on my time" or "this is a waste of my time." Thus, the task of reframing these initial cognitions toward new cognitions wherein treatment is seen both as being a reward and as permitting access to many other rewards represents an important step in the initial phase of community-based addiction treatment.

What Is Receipt of the Reward of Program Admission/Participation Contingent Upon?

In order to access the reward of program admission/participation and all the rewards that come with program participation, the behavior that is under the client's control and determines the client's personal success involves the act of agreeing to the oral contingency contract at the end of the brief psychological-assessment/psychiatric-screening session. This includes a client's verbally stating aloud his or her understanding of the oral contract and clearly consenting to the agreement.

What Are the Sanctions for Behavior Not Permitted under the Contingency Contract?

Subsequent behavior that is under the client's control is stipulated in the oral contingency contract, as well as are the consequences that will follow if the client fails to engage in those specified behaviors. There are also clearly specified consequences for client behavior that constitutes noncompliance with the contract. These consequences are usually graduated in severity and are made in staff case consultation, and the delivery of these consequences is ideally swift, with the nature of the sanctions being appropriate for any individual case. For example, sanctions include things such as being asked to accept a referral to a more intensive intervention, such as a five-to-seven-day inpatient detoxification, a twenty-eight-day rehabilitation, or a longer-term residential therapeutic-community setting. Or, sanctions may include being referred elsewhere for additional treatment (e.g., to a mental-health clinic, to a psychiatrist, to domestic-violence counseling, or to grief counseling); being placed on probation/suspension from the program until the client is compliant with the referral; or the more graduated sanction of being asked to leave the program. In sum, sanctions include a treatment-team decision to refer a client elsewhere for sessions, suspending a client from treatment for a period of time, or discharging a client from the program. This is in keeping with the principle of contingency contracting put forth in chapter 4.

What Are Examples of Contingency Contracts?

Five standard contingency contracts typically executed at the end of the brief psychological assessment/psychiatric screening follow directly from findings of psychiatric symptoms that require psychiatric treatment or pose a risk to the clients or to staff and peers in the program. These may also be thought of as the five instances in which admission to a community-based addiction-treatment program should be made contingent upon the client's agreeing to perform certain clearly specified behaviors.

In all cases involving the five types of contract specified in table 7.3, after a presentation of the contingency contract, clients should be asked if they feel able to make the oral contract and to verbally repeat aloud that which they are agreeing to do. Meanwhile, it is recommended that the behavioral act of a client's agreeing to the oral contract(s) and repeating the contract(s) in his or her own words lead to the reward of admission. Five recommended contingency contracts are presented in table 7.3 and are described below.

Contract 1: Admission Contingent on Documenting Current Psychiatric Care

Some clients may need to enter into a contract specifying how the reward of admission is contingent on their documenting psychiatric care, given that they are already under the care of a psychiatrist and are taking psychiatric medication. The contract specifies how they must also continue to see their psychiatrist and take medication, or jeopardize their continuation in the program.

Other related standard policy includes clients' signing a release that allows for communication between the program staff and clients' psychiatrist. It is also worth mentioning that, ideally, the sanctions for discontinuing psychiatric treatment, discontinuing medication, or preventing communication

Table 7.3. Five Recommended Oral Contingency Contracts: What Practitioners Actually Say to Clients

Contract 1. Admission contingent on documenting current psychiatric care: In order for you to be accepted into this program for admission, bring a letter from your psychiatrist indicating your diagnoses and the medication that you are taking. In addition, you will have to continue psychiatric treatment and take prescribed medication. If you stop these behaviors, staff will review your case and make a decision regarding what seems best for you at that time, including transfer to another program. Are you able to make this oral contract? Please repeat what you have to do.

Contract 2. Admission contingent on obtaining psychiatric care: In order for you to be accepted into this program, (1) start seeing a psychiatrist, (2) start taking any medication prescribed for you, and (3) bring a letter from your psychiatrist indicating the medications you are taking and your diagnoses. In addition, you will have to continue psychiatric treatment and taking prescribed medication. If you stop these behaviors, staff will review your case and make a decision regarding what seems best for you at that time, including transfer to another program. Are you able to make this oral contract? Please repeat what you have to do.

Contract 3. Admission contingent on obtaining psychiatric care and achieving stability: In order for you to be accepted into this program, (1) start seeing a psychiatrist, (2) take any medication prescribed for you, (3) wait until you are stable on medication before you return to the program, and (4) bring a letter to the program from your psychiatrist indicating the medications you are taking, your diagnoses, and stating that you are stable on that medication. This process may take several weeks, delaying admission to our program. Once you are admitted into the program, you will have to continue psychiatric treatment and taking prescribed medication. If you stop these behaviors, staff will review your case and make a decision regarding what seems best for you at that time, including transfer to another program. Are you able to make this oral contract? Please repeat what you have to do. I can write it all down for you.

Contract 4. Admission contingent on making a contract for suicidality: If you start feeling suicidal, you must inform staff, telling your counselor, the psychologist, or any available staff member. Staff will make a decision with regard to the next steps that are best for you, talking to you and including you in this process. If you become suicidal in the evening or over the weekend, go to the emergency room. Inform our program staff about any emergency psychiatric treatment you receive as soon as you can. Are you able to make this oral contract? Please repeat what you have to do.

Contract 5. Admission contingent on making a contract for homicidality/violence: Walk away before you become verbally or physically aggressive. You have permission to walk out of groups, the cafeteria, or the building. Once you walk away, do not return to the program until you feel calm again, whether this takes ten minutes or three days. Once you return to the program, you must inform staff about the incident. A decision will be made with regard to the next steps that are best for you, including transfer to another program. Are you able to make this oral contract? Please repeat what you have to do.

between program staff and psychiatric staff are graduated, and the delivery of sanctions follows staff case consultation. Case consultation implies that the delivery of graduated sanctions is based on a collective decision by a team, potentially avoiding a client's directing anger and resentment about the delivery of sanctions toward any one individual. Possible sanctions include clients' being referred elsewhere for additional treatment, being placed on probation/suspension from the program until they are compliant with the oral contingency contract, or being asked to leave the program. However, there are some cases where the risk of a client's returning to certain more problematic psychiatric symptoms—such as command hallucinations, suicidality, or homicidality/violence—necessitates less flexibility and certain discharge when contracts are broken.

Contract 2: Admission Contingent on Obtaining Psychiatric Care

In other cases, the reward of admission is made contingent on clients accepting a referral and seeking psychiatric care. Such individuals may be admitted to the outpatient addiction-treatment program with the understanding that it is within the next few weeks that they should have attained the status of being under the care of a psychiatrist, especially since an immediate referral is typically made. Similarly, program participation would be jeopardized if clients were to discontinue psychiatric treatment and medication adherence.

Contract 3: Admission Contingent on Obtaining Psychiatric Care and Achieving Stability

In much more rare instances, program admission is delayed until clients are actually successfully stabilized on an appropriate psychiatric medication, given the serious nature of their psychiatric symptoms. Thus, the reward of program admission is made contingent on clients' attaining psychiatric stability. This type of contract means that admission to the program has not been granted and will not be granted until a process of attaining psychiatric stability has occurred over a period of time. Because there is a hidden population of those with severe psychiatric disturbance who have never been diagnosed or treated, and because the criminal justice system may mandate them to community-based addiction treatment, such a contract has found a place, even if it is rarely offered to clients. Nonetheless, this kind of contract can be explained with great empathy and care. Motivational interviewing may play an important role in enhancing client motivation to comply.

Contract 4: Admission Contingent on Making a Contract for Suicidality

The reward of admission to a community-based addiction-treatment program may be made contingent upon clients' behavior of agreeing to an oral contract with regard to the risk of suicidality, a common dimension of clients' ongoing struggles with depression. Clients must agree to inform available program staff in the event that they begin to feel suicidal, also accepting that appropriate decisions will be made regarding their care at that time. The limits of community-based addiction-treatment programs that cannot monitor clients' behavior in the evening and on weekends necessitate that clients agree to going to an emergency room when feeling suicidal at such times of program closure. Ideally, such clients are also under the care of a psychiatrist, and this type of contract is merely an additional precaution.

Contract 5: Admission Contingent on Making a Contract
for Homicidality/Violence

The reward of admission to a community-based addiction-treatment program may also be made contingent upon clients' behavior of agreeing to an oral contract with regard to the risk of homicidality and violent acting-out behavior. The client behavior of walking away is specified, including being granted permission to walk out of groups and the building facility as needed. Clients are urged to return to the program only after they feel calm, whether this takes anywhere from ten minutes outside the facility to three days. And, upon their return, they are to inform an available staff member regarding what happened and their response, understanding that appropriate decisions will be made at that time, including the possibility of transfer to another program or discharge, given what they share.

The act of clients' signing a list of program rules with another program worker (intake worker or counselor), which specifies how violence and threats of violence can be grounds for discharge, compliments this oral contract. The oral contingency contract that makes admission contingent upon a contract for homicidality/violence serves to provide a means by which this outcome of discharge or other negative consequences of violence can be avoided. The contract specifies for clients a clear set of behaviors (walking away, waiting to be calm, returning and informing staff) that can be performed and are under client control so that violence can be avoided at all costs.

◄───

CASE EXAMPLE: MR. F. T.

The case of Mr. F. T. is presented in order to illustrate the kind of information that is generated when the questions in table 7.2 are asked of clients within the psychological assessment/psychiatric screening. The case demonstrates the process of executing contingency contracts and the use of evidence-based interventions and state-of-the-art practices marked with an X in table 7.4.

The Initial Psychological Assessment/Psychiatric Screening of Mr. F. T.

Mr. F. T. is a thirty-five-year-old male presenting cocaine dependence in full sustained remission, cannabis dependence in partial remission, and alcohol

**Table 7.4.   Options from the Menu Used (X) in the Case of Mr. F. T.
in a Ninety-Minute Assessment/Screening and Early Phase of Treatment**

Selections (X) for Mr. F. T. from category 1: Evidence-based addiction treatments
   X * Special focus on building a strong therapeutic alliance/social-support network (TASS)
   X * Motivational interviewing/motivational enhancement therapy (MET)/brief
       interventions
   X * Cognitive-behavioral therapy (CBT)/relapse prevention (RP)/social-skills training (SST)
   X * Twelve-step facilitation (TSF)/guidance using Alcoholics and/or Narcotics
       Anonymous
   X * Individual drug counseling (IDC) and/or supportive-expressive psychotherapy (SEP)
   X * Community reinforcement approach (CRA)/vouchers: Contingency management
       (CM)
   X * The Matrix Model—or, a day-treatment approach, or an IEC outpatient model that
       is *I* for intensive (4–5 days per week), *E* for extensive (6–12 months), and *C* for
       comprehensive (TASS, CBT/RP, IDC, group drug counseling [GDC], drug testing,
       etc.)
Selections (X) for Mr. F. T. from category 2: Recommended state-of-the-art practices
   X * Integration of motivational interviewing and stages of change
   X * Integration of stages of change and phases of treatment and recovery
     * Integration of harm reduction, moderation approaches, and abstinence models
   X * Integration of psychoanalytic and cognitive-behavioral theories and techniques
   X * Acquisition of affective, behavioral, and cognitive coping skills—learning new ABCs
   X * Integration of motivational interviewing, stages of change, and identity development
       theory for a diverse identity involving race, sexual orientation, and/or disability
   X * Incorporating contemporary trends in psychology: Multiculturalism, positive
       psychology, the strengths-based approach, and optimistic thinking/learned optimism

dependence in partial remission. He is very tall and of large stature, and he sat slumped in the chair during the interview, opening up, to his surprise, and honestly disclosing the many dimensions of his psychiatric condition. Such open disclosure rather readily begins to occur when practitioners are free of negative countertransference reactions and display adaptive affective, behavioral, and cognitive coping responses to clients and their characteristics (see chapter 6 and table 6.2).

As Mr. F. T. proceeded to open up and honestly share, he could not recall with certainty any of the diagnoses that several different psychiatrists had given him, or the names of all of the medications he had been given. However, Mr. F. T. clearly explained how he had just been released from prison one week ago and had been referred by the prison psychiatrist to our outpatient community-based addiction-treatment program. He had been under the prison psychiatrist's care throughout his incarceration for sale of a controlled substance. The client had, however, refused to take his psychiatric medication for the last two months of his incarceration, leading to his prison release without any prescriptions for psychiatric medication. The client had apparently been taking a powerful antipsychotic medication—one used for sedation—as well as an antidepressant and one other nightly medication for his insomnia. "I got tired of walking around like a zombie," he explained, so he had refused all medication for the past two months.

Of note, the client was not on parole. He had been violated and reincarcerated to complete his prison sentence; this was in response to his having police contact and being taken to a psychiatric emergency room where he was kept for several days as a psychiatric inpatient. This inpatient psychiatric stay was the first red flag to be raised in his brief psychological assessment/psychiatric screening, serving as an indicator that his psychiatric status would have to be explored in great detail and that this was beginning to look like a long versus a brief assessment/screening session.

Mr. F. T. was next asked about the last time he got high. He explained that he last used marijuana and drank beer "last night" so that he could induce sleep. Without the benefit of the psychiatric medication he had refused in prison for the past two months, the client was now experiencing the reoccurrence of insomnia. The client was proud of the manner in which he no longer engaged in "daily, all day long, heavy" consumption of marijuana, and no longer averaged a six-pack of beer per day, in addition to abandoning weekend crack-cocaine smoking and intranasal use of cocaine.

However, using a key technique in motivational interviewing (see *Motivational Interviewing/Motivational Enhancement Therapy (MET)/Brief Interventions* in table 7.4), I asked him the following: "Do you have any concerns about smoking marijuana again?" The client responded that he did not. Inquiring further, I asked if he had any concerns about having to purchase marijuana, given his just recently becoming free of criminal-justice-system supervision and incarceration. Mr. F. T. responded, "No, I wouldn't have to go back to jail for marijuana. It's a misdemeanor. Plus, I'm off of parole." In this manner, my attempted use of motivational interviewing was not effective at this early point in the session. Ideally, following motivational-interviewing techniques, Mr. F. T. would have been able to respond to my question about concerns and talk about fears/concerns of rearrest and incarceration. Perhaps he was more concerned about being able to sleep and saw self-medication with marijuana as a solution. In any event, I needed to move on, given my knowledge that this was going to be a rather lengthy assessment/screening.

The decision was made to proceed to general rapport-building questions that would allow me to get a sense of the larger context for Mr. F. T.'s life as one newly released from incarceration, uncovering some revealing information. Mr. F. T. was now living with his father and another male relative and was not yet working, but he was looking forward to getting a job within the coming month, given his past employment history. As a father to adolescent sons ages sixteen and fourteen, Mr. F. T. was excited about resuming their physically active relationship involving bicycle riding, basketball, and fishing trips, already having visited with them several days over the past week since his release from prison. He had no hope of reconciling with their mother and was not in a relationship at this time.

Mr. F. T. had no history of visual or auditory hallucinations. Nor was there any evidence of a thought disorder. The client was not depressed. In fact, he reported that he had never been depressed, even though several psychiatrists told him that he suffered from depression and had prescribed him antidepressant medication. Thus, he had never been suicidal and had never had any passing thoughts of suicide at any point in his lifetime. However, he did feel that he suffered from anxiety at times, but he was not able to link his recurrent moments of anxiety to anything in particular.

DISCUSSION OF ANXIETY SYMPTOMS
UNCOVERS POST-TRAUMATIC STRESS DISORDER

Exploration of pertinent past trauma and possible symptoms of post-traumatic stress disorder led to an adolescent incident in which he had felt "deceived and duped" by his father. Indeed, they had only reconciled in recent years, after being estranged from each other for nearly eighteen years, given the stance taken by Mr. F. T. toward his father. The client reported having recurrent memories of the incident wherein he felt "deceived and duped by my dad. It was a really big explosion. Things were never the same between us. We physically fought." Thus, it seemed that the client responded to stimuli reminiscent of this trauma—feeling "deceived and duped"—with the defense of splitting and dissociation and the behavior of acting out violence compulsively without recollection of the violence in which he engaged.

EVIDENCE OF COMPULSIVELY COMMITTING
VIOLENCE IN STATES OF SPLITTING WITHOUT RECALL

It was with regard to being homicidal that Mr. F. T. became most animated and forthcoming. He explained, "I have never been homicidal. But sometimes I just go there. I go to this place where somebody else living inside of me gets violent. Now, that person is definitely homicidal." Mr. F. T. did not feel able to take responsibility for what transpired in moments of splitting/dissociation in which, at some point, "I loose it," and no recall of what happened was possible. Mr. F. T. explained further, "I get angry really fast. And whatever you do, don't deceive me or try to dupe me." The consequences of such treatment were further elaborated upon: "Actually, I don't get angry. Let me take that back. I go into this blind rage. Then I don't remember what happens. But usually I end up arrested or in a psychiatric institution."

Mr. F. T. was asked about the last time he had such an experience, which took us directly to the earlier red flag raised with regard to his prior recollection of police contact and his subsequent stay in an inpatient psychiatric unit. The client described having this incident two and a half years ago with a friend, where he felt "deceived and duped. I lost it. I destroyed my friend's car, breaking all of his headlights, the windshield, the windows, and everything. The police came, and I fought them, too. They took me to an emergency room where they shot me up, sedated me. They kept me there for a few days, drugged like a zombie." Mr. F. T. explained how he had obtained an excellent lawyer, leading to his avoiding serving time for charges related to assault of those police officers who arrived at the scene.

It turned out that Mr. F. T. had had two other similar incidents over the past decade, each spaced approximately two and a half years apart. Thus, this explained Mr. F. T.'s being under the care of a psychiatrist throughout his prison stay, during which the psychiatrist also sought to drug him "like a zombie." However, he had not been able to establish any meaningful long-term outpatient psychiatric-treatment regime, given his violation of parole and reincarceration for having police contact.

EXPLORING RESUMPTION OF
PSYCHIATRIC TREATMENT/MEDICATION

When the client was asked about his intent with regard to reestablishing contact with a psychiatrist and resuming the taking of psychiatric medication, he explained how he did not plan to pursue such a course of action. Instead, he planned to use a strategy of "smoking a little marijuana and drinking a couple of beers every night to go to sleep." In addition, he planned to keep to himself, except for spending time with his sons and going back to work as soon as possible. He felt that this strategy allowed him to avoid situations where he might feel "deceived and duped," leading to his "losing it."

However, upon my inquiry, Mr. F. T. admitted that this strategy of keeping to himself did not always work, as he had been nearly violent just less than two months ago within the prison setting. "Luckily a friend of mine, this really big guy, just held me until I snapped back into reality. That other person inside of me became homicidal. Luckily, my friend was strong enough to hold me. I lost it." This encompassed the period during which he had begun refusing to take his psychiatric medication.

Drawing toward the end of the assessment/screening session, I explained my concern to the client with regard to how he could only be admitted to our program if he could make two oral contracts. I honestly shared that I was not sure if he would agree to the first oral contract, given what he had told me thus far: he had stopped taking medication in the prison setting over the past two months and therefore had been released without medication or prescriptions for medication. As a result, we now faced an obstacle to his admission to our outpatient treatment program. With regard to seeing a psychiatrist and resuming the taking of psychiatric medication, Mr. F. T. quickly stated that he did not intend to do such a thing. His eyes swelled up with tears, and he stated his deep heartfelt desire. "I need this program. I want to come here. I opened up to you and told you everything. Now you're telling me that I wasted my time."

Clearly, even without a mandate from parole, given how he had completed his prison sentence and was no longer on parole, Mr. F. T. perceived admission to our program as a highly valued and personally meaningful reward. It was not clear what the prison psychiatrist had told him or what he had come to learn about our program in the short span of his three hours on the premises, but his desire for admission was clearly deeply heartfelt.

Mr. F. T.'s emotional state and my new knowledge of his potential for violence led me to be as honest as possible as early as possible in the interview, for I had to be very careful not to "deceive and dupe" him, given my new knowledge of his idiosyncratic triggers for violence and "losing it." Being honest, I proceeded to explain that I did not have concerns about *him* potentially becoming violent, but it was "the other person living inside" of him who had a potential for violence that was of concern. Reflecting back to the client his very own words (even using direct quotes) is a highly effective technique that helps to avoid client resistance, and I used it for this reason.

I then emphasized that I was currently treating other clients in the outpatient program who also had problems with becoming violent and having no memory of what they did when they were violent; however, they were all taking psychiatric medication and were under the care of a psychiatrist in an outpatient mental-health clinic. And, if he agreed to engage in the same type of outpatient psychiatric care, then I would be able to work with him within our outpatient treatment program. In fact, I expressed my belief that I could help him, but this was only possible if he agreed to see a psychiatrist and to take prescribed medication. In this manner, I once again expressed my optimism and offered a positive prophecy (*Incorporating Contemporary Trends in Psychology: Multiculturalism, Positive Psychology, the Strengths-Based Approach, and Optimistic Thinking/Learned Optimism*). In fact, I truly believed this.

An effort was made to reassure him that he could metaphorically go shopping for a psychiatrist and seek to find one with whom he felt comfortable, and that it was possible to take medications that would not "make him like a zombie" but would address his risk for violent acting-out behavior.

Unfortunately, Mr. F. T. continued to refuse any psychiatric medication, but he stated his willingness to see a psychiatrist. I responded that medication was an important part of his being properly and ethically treated, given his symptoms. However, another client knocked on the door, interrupting our lengthy session. I asked Mr. F. T. how that interruption made him feel. He said, "angry." I pointed out that these were the kinds of things that happened in our outpatient setting, underscoring my concerns for him and my perception that he needed psychiatric medication. Another client similarly knocked on the door, given that our "brief" session was now running well over an hour. Suddenly, progress was made. Mr. F. T. stated that he was willing to see an outpatient psychiatrist. Being as honest as possible, I empathized with his concern about wanting to avoid being overly sedated "like a zombie," suggesting that alternative medications could be prescribed and that he could adjust to them. We talked about the pros and cons of several psychiatric medications.

EXPLORING TERMINATION OF MARIJUANA AND ALCOHOL USE

Wanting to avoid his feeling "deceived and duped" at any future point in the treatment process, I went on to gently express my other concerns about his case. I explained that he would likely receive pressure once in our program to terminate his marijuana and alcohol use, something he engaged in to help him sleep at night. His refusal to terminate his marijuana and alcohol use could also create problems down the road, given the pressure that he would face from program counselors and peers. This might be taken as another possible indication that our program was not appropriate for him, given his desire to continue to smoke marijuana and drink alcohol in order to be able to fall asleep. Thus, the option of Mr. F. T.'s taking psychiatric medication to help him sleep was raised once again, citing this as preferable to the risk of criminal involvement and potential arrest when purchasing marijuana. In this manner, the pros and cons of continued marijuana and alcohol use to address his insomnia were effectively reviewed.

OFFERING A MENU OF OPTIONS

It became clear that there were several next steps that he could take, selecting from a menu of available options in the social context, and, consistent with motivational-interviewing techniques (*Motivational Interviewing/ Motivational Enhancement Therapy (MET)/Brief Interventions*), these were reviewed with him. These potential next steps and available options included his leaving our assessment/screening session and searching for another program, or his searching for a psychiatrist with whom he felt comfortable and taking an appropriate psychiatric medication (an option that would allow him to return to our program), as well as his abandoning marijuana and alcohol use, or his continuing marijuana and alcohol use.

SUDDEN MOVEMENT ACROSS STAGES OF CHANGE

To my surprise, but consistent with the typical results of deploying motivational-interviewing techniques, the client suddenly agreed to see a psychiatrist and to take "only one medication, but nothing that makes me feel like a zombie." My honesty and empathy and use of the motivation enhancement technique of motivational interviewing seemed to have helped to move Mr. F. T. across stages of change, from not even thinking about taking psychiatric medication once again (precontemplation stage/ relapse stage), to contemplation, to a preparation stage in which he made a determination to take action on a referral to a psychiatrist and cooperate in taking prescribed medication. Moreover, he similarly seemed to have moved from not even thinking about terminating his marijuana smoking and beer drinking to at least a contemplation stage where he was also thinking about terminating this chemical use.

I declared the progress and movement made in our session thus far a miracle. This represented one concrete way in which I provided reinforcement for Mr. F. T.'s freely engaging in change talk covering his plan to follow through with my recommendations.

OTHER CONCERNS ARE REITERATED

Yet, I went on to share my own concerns with regard to how we might still face the eventual problem of needing sleep medication to replace his use of marijuana and beer in order to fall asleep at night. This was necessary, given how my earlier attempt to use motivational interviewing and elicit Mr. F. T.'s own personal concerns about marijuana use, marijuana purchases, and the risk of arrest and reincarceration had failed. Moreover, thus far, he was agreeing to take only one medication. So, after expressing my own concerns (versus a harsh confrontation telling him what he should or must do), I suggested he remain open to the possibility that sleep medication would come to play an important role in his treatment plan.

GOOD JUDGMENT AND PROGRESS ON THE PART OF MR. F. T.

Reflecting excellent judgment and preempting my personal offer, Mr. F. T. wisely asked for a letter of referral to a psychiatrist. He explained, "I opened up and told you everything. I don't want to have to do that again." Thus, Mr. F. T. was reassured that he would be given such a letter containing a detailed summary of his psychiatric history. And his request for such a letter suggested the likelihood that he would follow through and see a psychiatrist.

In this manner, progress was made in moving Mr. F. T. out of a state of denial with regard to his need for psychiatric medication, his need for psychiatric care, and the overall reality that he had a mental disability. He had begun to take a step forward in accepting and establishing an identity as one with a mental disability (reflecting use of an *Integration of Motivational Interviewing, Stages of Change, and Identity Development Theory for a Diverse Identity Involving Race, Sexual Orientation, and/or Disability*, from table 7.4).

EXECUTING ORAL CONTINGENCY CONTRACTS

His case necessitated an oral contract specifying that his admission to the program was contingent on his first seeing a psychiatrist; developing an ongoing relationship with the psychiatrist in an outpatient mental-health treatment setting; taking prescribed medication; and bringing a letter from his psychiatrist stating his diagnoses, medication prescribed, and that Mr. F. T. was stable on that medication. Also, Mr. F. T.'s admission to the program and continued participation would be contingent on his agreeing to continue to take his medication and remain under a psychiatrist's care throughout his stay in the program. And his admission would be contingent on his agreeing to an oral contract wherein he would walk away from all situations in which he felt he was about to become argumentative, be verbally aggressive, or might engage in physical violence. He was granted permission under his contract to literally walk out of any individual sessions, group sessions, the cafeteria, or off the premises, as needed. Also, under this contract for homicidality, anger, and violence, Mr. F. T. was told that he would not return to the program until he felt calm, whether this took ten minutes or three days to achieve. Finally, he would report to a staff member as soon as he returned to the program facility, explaining what transpired that made him angry or upset, as well as the actions he took. Possible consequences included his transfer to another program.

In this manner, what was executed with Mr. F. T. was the most restrictive contingency contract requiring the very most of clients (contract 3 in table 7.3), and the one that if not executed (contract 5 in table 7.3) could leave program staff and other clients in great danger. The need to execute these two oral contracts underscored the severity of the risk inherent in the admission of Mr. F. T.

Suggesting his strength and resiliency (something I saw because of *Incorporating Contemporary Trends in Psychology: Multiculturalism, Positive Psychology, the Strengths-Based Approach, and Optimistic Thinking/Learned Optimism*), Mr. F. T. calmly stated that he would follow through with seeing a psychiatrist and agree to all three contracts so that he could gain admission to our program. He was told that, once admitted to the program, he would also likely see me in individual psychotherapy at least once per week, and as needed depending upon what he was going through.

PROGRAM ADMISSION EIGHT WEEKS LATER

To my surprise, one day approximately eight weeks after his initial assessment/screening, Mr. F. T. showed up, requesting to see me. He had a letter in hand from a psychiatrist, indicating that he was taking 1,500 mg of Depakote a day. He even had a recent medical report indicating his Depakote blood level. In this manner, he had met the key conditions upon which his admission to the program was contingent.

Mr. F. T. sat and imitated the foreign accent of the psychiatrist he had been seeing since the day after his assessment/screening session with me. "She kept asking me if I was going back to the program. 'Are you going back to the program? Are you going back?'" He sat comfortably, laughing as he mocked his psychiatrist's accent. As he smiled and laughed in a relaxed manner, this stood in great contrast to the angry, tense, and sarcastic man I had assessed/screened eight weeks earlier; clearly his psychiatric care and medication were helping. He also had in hand the letter I had given him, specifying all the conditions of his admission. Mr. F. T. indicated his willingness to meet those remaining conditions. This included agreeing to continue to see his psychiatrist and take his medication, as well as agreeing to walk away from any potential violent situations in the program. In addition, he was willing to see me in weekly individual psychotherapy sessions.

He was asked about his marijuana smoking and beer drinking. Mr. F. T. indicated that he stopped smoking marijuana and drinking beer the day he saw me, for the next day he saw the psychiatrist, and she indicated that the prescribed Depakote medication should not be combined with marijuana smoking, and she asked him to stop. He also indicated that he took all of his medication at once at night and was able to sleep through the night. Hence, he now had two months since his last marijuana/alcohol use, being in an early phase of treatment/action stage.

Mr. F. T. was fully admitted into the program. This meant, in essence, that he was gaining exposure to what was akin to *The Matrix Model—Or, a Day-Treatment Approach, or an IEC Outpatient Model That Is I for Intensive (4–5 days per week), E for Extensive (6–12 months), and C for Comprehensive (TASS, CBT/RP, IDC, GDC, drug testing, etc.),* as shown in table 7.4. Our program included exposure to many pertinent elements, such as groups, permitting exposure to *Cognitive-Behavioral Therapy (CBT)/Relapse Prevention (RP)/Social-Skills Training (SST)* as well as *Twelve-Step Facilitation (TSF)/Guidance Using Alcoholics and/or Narcotics Anonymous.* And, his primary substance-abuse counselor would be delivering *Individual Drug Counseling (IDC) and/or Supportive-Expressive Psychotherapy (SEP)* (see table 7.4).

SUMMARY OF MR. F. T.'S FIRST THREE MONTHS IN TREATMENT

Mr. F. T. began a course of individual psychotherapy under my care, following use of *Individual Drug Counseling (IDC) and/or Supportive-Expressive Psychotherapy (SEP)*, in particular, SEP, which at various points in time included an *Integration of Psychoanalytic and Cognitive-Behavioral Theories and Techniques* (see table 7.4). He was seen once per week. He also voluntarily attended several mental-health group sessions I conducted. Some of the work done in this group served to further foster his identity development as a person with a mental disability (reflecting *Integration of Motivational Interviewing, Stages of Change, and Identity Development Theory for a Diverse Identity Involving Race, Sexual Orientation, and/or Disability*).

Over the course of the first three months in treatment, Mr. F. T. made considerable progress. He had no violent incidents. He regularly took his medication and demonstrated learning how to walk away from potentially violent incidents.

ANGER AS A DEFENSE AGAINST PAIN: RULING OUT HOMICIDALITY

At one point, about a month into his outpatient treatment at our program, a pattern was established wherein he would have a stressful experience in the real world and would sit and ventilate about his intention to go back to that setting and "hurt people." It seemed that it was becoming routine for me to thoroughly explore and assess him for homicidality, needing to rule out his being at risk for actually committing homicide or hurting people. Frankly, I was getting tired of repeatedly ruling out homicidal risk and began to wonder if he was actually inappropriate for our community-based addiction-treatment program. I wondered if I had made a mistake in admitting him to the program.

As I sat frustrated and silent, listening to him and searching for a solution, I had a sudden insight. It seemed as though this pattern of talking about wanting to hurt people was just an overlearned habit pattern, from a cognitive-behavioral perspective, or an ego defense, from a psychoanalytic perspective. I realized it was potentially a defense against his feeling hurt inside. I offered him an interpretation: "You tend to start talking about wanting to hurt people when your feelings have been hurt; and your feelings are hurt very easily because you are extremely sensitive and intelligent. Talking about your hurt feelings doesn't make you feel strong." The intervention included explaining to the client a resultant new treatment goal: for him to learn how to talk about his feelings when they were hurt, instead of falling into a habit pattern of making statements about wanting to hurt people. He was told how "anger is a defense against pain. You have to learn to talk about your pain."

Mr. F. T. was also given straightforward education about how every time he talked about wanting to hurt people, I was forced to assess him for homicidality and make a decision about whether he was appropriate for our outpatient program, or whether he needed to be placed in a psychiatric hospital. I also informed him of my responsibility to inform both the police and the person he intended to harm if I heard him making statements about his intent to kill people or do them serious bodily harm. This intervention also served to enhance his reality testing and judgment.

After this intervention, I escorted him to his primary substance-abuse counselor's office and informed her of our new treatment goal for him to learn to talk about his feelings when they were hurt, and the nature of my interpretation/intervention. She shook her head affirmatively as I closed the door and left the two of them in private, trusting she would further reinforce the need for this new treatment goal. In this manner, I was also ensuring that a social network of program staff was working together to help him achieve a positive treatment outcome, consistent with a *Special Focus on Building a Strong Therapeutic Alliance/Social-Support Network (TASS)*.

LEARNING TO PROCESS PAINFUL AFFECTS: ACQUISITION OF ADAPTIVE COPING SKILLS

As a result of that key interpretation/critical intervention, the client began to make progress in sessions in talking about his feelings and even opening up to the point of crying about things that created stress or hurt his feelings. He began learning, thereby, much more about adaptive coping responses, involving how to process his feelings of hurt and not resort to the defense of anger and verbally making statements of wanting to "hurt people" as a maladaptive cognitive coping strategy.

The short-term goal of acquiring adaptive coping responses, a stronger ego, and enhanced ego functions would have important implications for achieving other long-term treatment goals, such as being able to effectively cope with any impending crises, typical life stress, avoiding relapse, and so on. This analysis was in keeping with an *Integration of Stages of Change and Phases of Treatment and Recovery*, which provided a guide for the correct timing of the delivery of interventions in order to achieve short-term goals in this early phase of treatment/action stage.

This short-term goal of achieving mental and emotional stability involved a process of his ego undergoing systematic strengthening and surrendering old defensive patterns, as well as his learning new adaptive affective, behavioral, and cognitive coping responses, which was supported by *Integration of Psychoanalytic and Cognitive-Behavioral Theories and Techniques* and a focus on *Acquisition of Affective, Behavioral, and Cognitive Coping Skills—Learning New ABCs*.

The hope was that by learning to process painful affects that arose within him when his feelings were hurt, and by talking in sessions and in groups about this pain, the client's ego would undergo a strengthening process and would learn to tolerate his inner self experiencing painful affects without resorting to the defense of angry ventilation or violent acting out, and that adaptive ego functions of good judgment and reality testing, including consequential thinking, might gain in prominence. The capacity of his ego to engage in self-observation was also being cultivated, allowing him to observe the moment when painful affects arose within his self. He could then enact an alternative to a defense, or adaptive coping, and he could report back in counseling sessions the results of self-observation/self-monitoring. This kind of work and short-term goal is best suited for the early phase of treatment/ action stage, when a client is spending his first six months in treatment in the real world, outside of a correctional or confinement setting.

Because of the success he was having in adaptively coping and processing his painful affect without resorting to old ego defenses, it was anticipated that Mr. F. T. would continue to remain stable and free from violent acting out. This positive expectation was supported by the manner in which he was also regularly taking his Depakote. This positive expectation of success was in keeping with *Incorporating Contemporary Trends in Psychology: Multiculturalism, Positive Psychology, the Strengths-Based Approach, and Optimistic Thinking/Learned Optimism.*

GOOD JUDGMENT: DECISION TO MOVE INTO A HOMELESS SHELTER

At home, Mr. F. T. was coping with a hostile male relative who was harassing him and refusing to speak to or interact with him, making Mr. F. T. feel as though he was back in prison, enduring the punishment of isolation in the hole for some violence he had typically committed in prison. This made him feel rather sad, and he demonstrated his growing ability to talk about his feelings. However, he was also able to report in sessions the results of his self-observation/self-monitoring while at home with this male relative: feelings of aggression and thoughts about doing bodily harm to this man were being evoked within him. His home had now become a high-risk situation for relapse to serious violence.

Mr. F. T. decided on his own to move out of the apartment where this male relative lived, showing good judgment and wisely choosing homelessness over the risk of being violent against this relative. "I didn't want to throw him out the window, so I had to leave. He would stand there and yell at me. The Depakote made me just stand there. Now there is some kind of delay thing going on. I just listened to him. Before, I would have thrown him out the window." Again, Mr. F. T. was demonstrating the ideal situation in which a client has successfully learned to self-observe/self-monitor his experiences in reality.

Mr. F. T. entered the shelter system, reporting this after the fact in one of his sessions. And, within the shelter system, he dealt very well with "hostile and poorly trained" security guards who "harassed" him, taking away his psychiatric medication bottle when they searched his bags upon his return to the shelter. Mr. F. T. used our sessions to ventilate his anger about how he was being treated, even as the reality of what it meant to be a person with a mental disability and to be a stigmatized homeless man became apparent to him through these experiences. A great deal of stress was involved in these interactions with the security guards, constituting a high-risk situation for relapse to violence. As a result of our discussions in session, he began to call upon security supervisors to negotiate his conflicts with problematic security guards, finding relief from harassment through this strategy. In this manner, benefiting from my role modeling assertive verbal responses, my coaching, and his rehearsal in sessions, Mr. F. T. was able to engage in higher-order adaptive coping responses involving the delivery of positive, assertive verbal responses with security guards and their supervisors. It got to the point where all understood his condition, he could talk about it calmly, and he felt he was being treated with respect. This was a radical change from his initial angry exchanges of shouting, cursing, and inviting security guards to go outside and fight with him.

What emerges is how clients must learn over time how and when to deploy avoidant coping strategies (such as standing in silence and then walking away from his male relative and leaving that home), versus active coping strategies (positive, assertive verbal responses such as "May I speak to your supervisor?" or "I have a mental condition and take prescribed medication. That is my bottle of medication"). Work with regard to Mr. F. T.'s coping responses, as he deployed them in the real world, only proceeded so well because he was able to self-observe/self-monitor and bring into sessions accurate reports of what had transpired. Meanwhile, his interactions with security guards at the shelter where he had to negotiate the search process upon his return each and every night may have represented important training ground for Mr. F. T.'s learning how to refine his adaptive coping strategies. He was able to use this training ground to self-observe/self-monitor as he became angry, even enraged, and was poised to become violent, yet he was able to interrupt/stop himself from responding to this trigger with the response of violence. He was able to then use this high-risk situation to advance in his ability to deploy active coping responses involving verbal exchanges, especially as he could not always just walk away and avoid interactions with the security guards.

ENTRANCE INTO A MICA SHELTER

I informed Mr. F. T. of some of the advantages of being in a MICA shelter (for mentally ill chemical abusers), in terms of his receiving more assistance with getting housing in a more rapid fashion. So he quickly found a MICA shelter and entered it, also going to another MICA advocacy agency and obtaining a caseworker to help him with applying for Social Security disability. This again reflected his possession of great strengths and resiliency, something I had readily perceived (*Incorporating Contemporary Trends in Psychol-*

ogy: Multiculturalism, Positive Psychology, the Strengths-Based Approach, and Optimistic Thinking/Learned Optimism, from table 7.4).

According to Mr. F. T., the MICA shelter meant adjusting to a "dirty, smelly place with schizophrenics who talk out loud. I have to get used to the nurse giving me my medication after waiting in this long, winding line. And the bathroom and shower are horrible. At least in the other shelter people were working together to keep it clean." All of his concerns were listened to and reflected back to him, and he was reinforced for change talk that he would persevere in order to receive needed housing and benefits. He responded well to all interventions and continued to take action on these goals, further developing an identity as a person with a mental disability, consistent with an *Integration of Motivational Interviewing, Stages of Change, and Identity Development Theory for a Diverse Identity Involving Race, Sexual Orientation, and/or Disability*.

ADJUSTING TO MILD MEDICATION SIDE EFFECTS

Additional evidence was brought into sessions with regard to how Mr. F. T. was learning to engage in positive, assertive verbal responses in a range of situations. This involved a potential high-risk situation for violence, as he stared at others on the subway. He readily explained to strangers on the subway that he was on medication and was not staring at them in a provocative manner, effectively diffusing a couple of potentially tense situations. He forged this active coping verbal strategy on his own, again suggesting the tremendous strengths he possessed, and that I readily perceived (*Incorporating Contemporary Trends in Psychology: Multiculturalism, Positive Psychology, the Strengths-Based Approach, and Optimistic Thinking/Learned Optimism*). He had no disturbing or unusual side effects from his medication that created problems he could not manage. He did not feel like "a zombie," most importantly.

A REQUEST TO ADDRESS TRAUMA
AT THE END OF MONTH THREE IN TREATMENT

By the end of the first three months of treatment, Mr. F. T. took the initiative and expressed his own inner sense that he needed to start talking about his traumatic past. He had achieved by this point in time a full five months since his last marijuana/alcohol use. Thus, our individual session followed Mr. F. T.'s lead in what he chose to focus upon, and he went on to talk about some adolescent trauma involving the blowup with his father when he felt "duped."

Most importantly, he had learned how to self-observe/self-monitor and to interrupt/stop (with the help of the Depakote medication) moments of

being triggered by cues for relapse, replacing this with adaptive coping responses. For example, he was now regularly processing his painful affects
and performing adaptive coping responses instead of resorting to verbal aggression and violent acting out.

In fact, his case illustrates how once the ego has been strengthened and is
able to tolerate painful affects arising within the self, that same client ego exercises good judgment and reality testing and deems it the correct time to finally allow other painful affects to arise, such as within the process of talking about past trauma. In this manner, clients tend to have an inner sense
and are able to communicate when they are indeed ready to talk about
trauma; some clients are correct, while others are not. Only proceeding cau-
tiously in treatment leads to an answer. The exercise of caution includes delaying, until the middle-to-late phase of treatment/maintenance stage (more
than six months into taking action to change), trauma resolution work involving working through and integration of traumatic memories with the
processing of painful affects, describing and fully feeling what happened in
moments of trauma. This is consistent with the guide for the correct timing
of interventions for trauma survivors presented in chapter 5 and table 5.2,
also reflecting an *Integration of Stages of Change and Phases of Treatment and Recovery*. However, in the case of Mr. F. T., an individual assessment of where
he was and what he preferred allowed discussion of his trauma to proceed.

THE VALUE OF A COGNITIVE AND INTELLECTUAL FRAMEWORK FOR UNDERSTANDING TRAUMA

The value in allowing Mr. F. T. to talk (with just five months since his last
marijuana and alcohol use) about underlying trauma that was incurred during his adolescence involved the possibility that this work would further reduce his risk of using ego defenses that stemmed from this trauma, such as
using anger as a defense against pain. But, the sessions were still largely educational in nature, without any deep releases of painful affect, and the
client listened to the education I delivered on the possible impact of this
trauma upon him, fostering a cognitive and intellectual understanding of
what had happened to him. Proceeding with this level and quality of trauma
work reflected my consideration of his stability on Depakote, his active involvement in psychiatric treatment, his good therapeutic alliance with me in
individual psychotherapy, and my overall individualized assessment of how
his learning to adaptively process painful affect had considerably strengthened his ego and replaced prior patterns of using the ego defenses of verbally ventilating aggression and/or behaviorally acting out violence. Thus,
the client was deemed appropriate for this largely educational approach to
his past trauma, emphasizing coping.

By providing him with a cognitive and intellectual framework for understanding his past trauma, Mr. F. T. was taught the following, taken from Wallace (1996a): "If you know the trauma you can figure out the drama." Thus, he could interpret the impact of trauma upon himself in terms of interpersonal patterns of behavior or dramas that might tend to be repeated in his adult life with different people. This included a tendency to think people might be out to dupe him, something he could now see as maladaptive cognitive coping (stemming from his trauma of feeling duped by his father in adolescence) that could be replaced with more adaptive cognitive coping strategies. For example, it was suggested to him that he might think in the future, "I have to separate what happened to me as a teenager from what is going on now in my relationship with this male authority figure." The goal was for him to engage in such cognitive coping, a level of coping that would also reflect his attainment of a considerably strengthened ego and enhanced ego functioning involving good judgment and reality testing. Mr. F. T. seemed well on his way to being able to engage in such cognitive reframing of what transpired during his interpersonal interactions.

CASE CONCLUSION

In sum, being stable on Depakote, the client was a pleasant individual who readily smiled and laughed and apparently absolutely enjoyed participation in the treatment program. Indeed, he responded well to my observation that he "loved coming to the program," as it was ever so apparent. He was working hard in individual psychotherapy, was appropriate in the mental-health group when he attended, and especially enjoyed his relationship with his substance-abuse counselor and many, many peers in the program. His urines were all negative for marijuana use, as well as all other illicit substances.

Even though he applied for Social Security disability, he was aware of the possibility that he might be rejected, and he was also moving forward with paperwork that would support his vocational training for future employment. Mr. F. T. was also enjoying regular contact with his sons, several members of his family, and a new girlfriend, thus benefiting from a social-support network that was helping to enhance his chances of a successful positive long-term recovery.

COMMENTARY ON THE CASE OF MR. F. T.

Practitioners may learn a great deal from the case of Mr. F. T., as it involves one of the very worst case scenarios in terms of what can arise from the initial psychological assessment/psychiatric screening. Going back to the underlying purpose of the brief psychological assessment/psychiatric screening summarized in table 7.1, each of the critical questions posed in that table produced absolutely alarming answers that required clear action.

When asking, "Is this client appropriate for treatment in this community-based addiction-treatment setting?" the initial answer was no. For "Does this community-based addiction-treatment setting constitute the right level of care, or is referral to another level of care indicated by assessment findings?" the answer was that outpatient care was the correct level, but immediate referral to a psychiatrist in an outpatient setting was crucial. Regarding "Are there psychiatric symptoms (comorbidity) that suggest that the client must receive mental-health or psychiatric treatment?" the answer was a resounding yes. Most importantly, for "Are there any potential risks for the client, other clients, or for staff, given a client's psychiatric symptoms (comorbidity)?" the answer was also yes. With regard to "What referrals are needed in order for the client to be either admitted into the program; retained in treatment; or for the client to be able to function adequately, successfully, and without risk to self or others in the community-based addiction-treatment setting?" the answer was long-term outpatient psychiatric care with stabilization on medication specifically geared to controlling violent impulses. In response to "What client-to-intervention and client-to-treatment-modality matching strategies need to be followed, given assessment findings?" the answer was long-term outpatient mental-health care with both a psychiatrist providing once-per-month medication monitoring and a psychologist providing once-per-week individual psychotherapy.

Finally, "Given assessment findings, what kind of contingency contracts need to ideally be made with clients in advance of admission?" led to several answers; his admission was made contingent on his obtaining psychiatric care and achieving stability on psychiatric medication that would reduce his risk of violent acting out, on his continuing that psychiatric care and the taking of his medication throughout the duration of his participation in our outpatient program, as well as on his making a contract for homicidality/violence. Thus, his case served to also illustrate the most challenging kind of scenario wherein what is meant to be a brief psychological-assessment and psychiatric-screening process actually ends up taking one and a half hours.

The case of Mr. F. T. makes clear the underlying purpose of the brief psychological assessment/psychiatric screening, the value of the assessment/screening questions posed in table 7.1, and the important role of the contingency contracts presented in table 7.3. Mr. F. T.'s case also serves to reveal the manner in which the initial psychological assessment/psychiatric screening may also serve as a brief intervention in and of itself. Indeed, the use of motivational interviewing, as a brief intervention, can effectively move a client across stages of change for more than one problem behavior (e.g., psychiatric-medication noncompliance and marijuana/alcohol use). The case illustrates the ideal scenario wherein motivational interviewing successfully serves to move a client across stages of change in a very brief period of time, even within the expanse of just one ninety-minute session with a practitioner.

Since the client returned to treatment after achieving stabilization on Depakote under the care of his new psychiatrist, the case also illustrates the use of several other evidence-based interventions and recommended state-of-the-art practices, indeed a full thirteen of the total of fourteen options on the recommended menu in table 7.4. And the case powerfully illustrates the role of key variables (e.g., psychiatric symptoms/comorbidity) in client-treatment matching to psychiatric treatment and medication, as treatment was tailored for Mr. F. T.

CONCLUSION

This chapter provided training to practitioners in how to conduct the initial psychological assessment/psychiatric screening of clients in community-based addiction treatment. An important table, table 7.1, presented the underlying purpose of the brief psychological assessment/psychiatric screening. Another table, table 7.2, summarized the questions that compose the assessment/screening, covering rapport-building questions and the nine core areas of assessment/screening and an array of related questions. Table 7.3 presented the five kinds of oral contingency contracts typically made with clients at the conclusion of the assessment/screening, literally offering to practitioners what they may say and do, providing a vital guide. The chapter provided practitioners with important training with regard to how the brief psychological assessment/psychiatric screening may serve as a powerful vehicle for revealing where a client is and what the client needs, as well as what the client is willing to do and prefers to do at the time of admission to a community-based addiction-treatment program.

Once practitioners discover this information, there may still emerge certain imperatives; the oral contingency contracts introduced in this chapter represent a creative application of contingency-management procedures, serving to enhance client motivation to comply with treatment referrals/recommendations and likely contributing to a more positive treatment outcome. Another motivation-enhancement technique, motivational interviewing, as a brief intervention, may also play an important role within the assessment/screening, further increasing a client's internal motivation. The case of Mr. F. T. illustrated, in particular, the role of both motivational interviewing and contingency contracting in enhancing a client's internal motivation for change.

The case of Mr. F. T. went on to describe subsequent developments over five months (i.e., initial assessment/screening, entrance into outpatient psychiatric care across eight weeks before returning to our outpatient community-based addiction-treatment program, and three months of individual psychotherapy in our program under my care). This case effectively spanned most of the early phase of treatment/action stage; this allowed for discussion of the many other evidence-based interventions and state-of-the-art practices available for deployment with a challenging MICA client. Table 7.4 served to depict with a mark of X those items on the menu of options that were deployed in work with this client. In this manner, the case also illustrated how a resulting unified model of treatment (combining the use of numerous evidence-based interventions) and a unified theory (combining the use of numerous state-of-the-art practices) could provide a guiding framework for practitioners throughout service delivery.

Practitioners may now have a better sense of both how to conduct a brief psychological assessment/psychiatric screening, as well as how to select from the array of evidence-based options and recommended state-of-the-art practices, those best suited in work with some of the most challenging and difficult cases, integrating and tailoring treatment depending on what is being presented at any given point in time. What may generalize from the training is how to proceed with less difficult clients.

8

◆

Case Conceptualization: Short- and Long-Term Treatment Goals

Prior chapters served to reveal that which contemporary multiproblem clients are bringing into the treatment setting, as their characteristics, needs, and diversity (chapter 2), and how the practitioner should proceed in terms of correct timing, focusing on those matters to be urgently addressed immediately and those that can wait to be addressed until later, once the client has stabilized (chapter 5). In addition, a prior chapter (chapter 4) highlighted those evidence-based interventions and recommended state-of-the-art options available for deployment in community-based addiction treatment, as practitioners conceptualize the course of treatment for a client. And, the previous chapter (chapter 7) provided training in how to conduct a psychological assessment/psychiatric screening in order to bring to light pertinent client characteristics and needs.

This chapter will answer the following question: How do practitioners go about the task of prioritizing client issues needing immediate versus future attention and select from a menu of options interventions/practices to meet short- and long-term treatment goals? This chapter will offer a case example of a multiproblem client in order to provide practitioners with training in case conceptualization to identify short- and long-term treatment goals, given the approach being put forth in this book for making mandated addiction treatment work.

◆

CASE CONCEPTUALIZATION FOR MS. M. T.

The case of Ms. M. T. covers her initial engagement in treatment, spanning her intake into treatment, including my conducting a psychological assessment/

psychiatric screening. Her case also covers the first three months she spent in outpatient community-based addiction treatment. As a multiproblem client, her case exemplifies important short-term goals deemed essential in what was an early phase of treatment/action stage for addressing her marijuana dependence. The case also illustrates the process of relegating certain treatment tasks to the middle-to-late phase of treatment/maintenance stage, as long-term goals.

THE PSYCHOLOGICAL ASSESSMENT/
PSYCHIATRIC SCREENING OF MS. M. T.

My performance of the recommended psychological assessment/psychiatric screening presented in the previous chapter, chapter 7, produced pertinent findings. Ms. M. T. was a twenty-seven-year-old mother of sons ages three and ten. Her probation officer mandated Ms. M. T. to outpatient addiction treatment after she tested positive just once for marijuana use while on probation for petty larceny. She had been caught writing bad checks, as she briefly explained. Her experience included several nights in jail. Ms. M. T. was given five years probation. She had private insurance from her employment, and she used it to access her mandated addiction treatment. The first community-based addiction-treatment program she attended expelled her after she missed just two sessions, despite her claiming difficulty finding a parking space downtown and "just going back home." She still had to comply with probation's mandate, as she soon discovered upon visiting her probation officer. Thus, she found another outpatient program, ours, and was seeking admission.

Her case reflected a common urgent contemporary need and characteristic of clients—the need for assistance from practitioners in addressing first things first in order to meet her intensive supervision requirements (see guide for correct timing of the delivery of interventions in chapter 5 and table 5.1, item I-A) as a vital short-term goal. Consistent with this short-term goal for the early phase of treatment/action stage, involving a need to comply with the mandate and avoid potential graduated sanctions she could face while under supervision with probation, Ms. M. T. was asked about her last marijuana use. She admitted to last using marijuana just one week ago. She reported a history of smoking marijuana "once in a while," mainly for stress relief and to help her sleep. Ms. M. T. understood both how long marijuana stayed in the system and how frequently (twice per week, randomly) she would be tested in our outpatient program.

Ms. M. T. denied feeling depressed at the time of assessment/screening. However, she indicated that she got depressed "at times," as she was missing her ten-year-old son attending a military boarding school. She attributed her stress as follows: "I raised myself on my own, now raising my own kids by myself, and working full time. At times I feel like breaking down from the pressure. But I have to cope." Ms. M. T. admitted to feeling suicidal at times but denied feeling suicidal at the time of assessment/screening.

She had a prior history of being suicidal. She explained how her mother, as an injection drug user with a history of incarceration, had abandoned the family, and her father (also an addict) had remained behind to raise her. The trauma of parental abandonment was most painful for her, especially since her father "then left me," dying from AIDS a few years ago. Of note, Ms. M. T. knew intimately about generational cycles of addiction, abuse, and trauma, and what it meant to have a history of parental separation (see chapter 5 and table 5.1, items II-A and II-B). However, consistent with the rough guide (table 5.1) for the correct timing for the delivery of interventions for a multiproblem client such as Ms. M. T., these were the types of issues to be dealt with in the middle-to-late phase of treatment/maintenance stage, after she had obtained a period greater than six months or longer of taking action on her marijuana dependence. To address such historical factors would serve to further reduce her risk of relapse and recidivism. However, the task of addressing these historical factors was deemed a long-term goal reserved for the middle-to-late phase of treatment/maintenance stage.

While this follows a rough guide for correct timing for the delivery of interventions with multiproblem clients (table 5.1), and some clients may benefit from discussing these historical issues earlier in treatment, perhaps as early as months one through six in treatment, the assessment/screening of Ms. M. T. suggested a more cautious approach. This was deemed especially so given the subsequent findings in the assessment/screening.

Ms. M. T. shared how, at one point, because of family dissolution, she ended up living in a shelter. Ms. M. T. experienced the stress of homelessness and lack of social support, given the loss of her parents. While living in the shelter, she was suicidal in response to this stress, but she never made a suicide attempt and never received psychiatric care at that or at any point in her life up to the time of the psychological assessment/psychiatric screening. Yet, on the bright side, she did find an apartment on her own and started her own family.

As part of her depression, Ms. M. T. reported that she did not sleep well, averaging two to three hours per night, and she also had little appetite; she thought she had lost weight. Her severe insomnia and lack of appetite were current ongoing symptoms.

Ms. M. T. denied feeling homicidal at the time of admission, but she admitted that in the past, "I felt like killing my babies' father because of the things he put me through—beating me up, not wanting to give me money. Sometimes I wish he were dead. I said if he put his hands on me I'd take his head off." She ended up cutting him with a knife on the arm several months ago. This domestic violence was the last time she was involved in a physical fight with anyone. She explained, "I blanked out and cut his arm. That last hit just tore it up."

Interestingly enough, the metaphor of something being torn up was reminiscent of what had likely happened to her psyche, as she now seemed to suffer from splitting and dissociation, having had a moment of enacting violence when she "blanked out." This release of her own aggression was likely a consequence of the trauma of protracted battering at the hands of this man, her "babies' father." Her batterer had his own struggles with alcohol and crack addiction, likely contributing to the violence he had instigated at home on a recurrent basis. The collective evidence of her depression, suicidality, homicidality, and capacity to "blank out" when violent suggested that stabilization on appropriate psychiatric medication was a vital short-term goal to be addressed in the early phase of treatment/action stage (first six months of her working on her marijuana dependence), as spelled out in the guidelines in chapter 5 (table 5.1, items I-B-1 and I-B-3).

Following her release of aggression upon her babies' father, this man left their home, and they are no longer together. But she continued to get "aggravated by him not meeting his responsibility," as he failed to send money for the care of his children. "But, I have to stay away from him. He makes me angry and stresses me out." Indeed, it seemed that only this man served as a trigger for her anger, aggression, and violent acting out behavior. Avoiding him reflected good judgment and reality testing on the part of her ego.

In addition to depression, she suffered from occasional anxiety, possibly from the combined traumas of being abandoned by her parents and especially from the experience of recurrent domestic violence over several years. At the time of the assessment/screening, upon inquiry, Ms. M. T. linked the times when she felt anxiety to "feeling things aren't going my way." Given this self-report, it was possible that anxiety was a signal to the ego that other potentially dangerous aggressive impulses were about to emerge or surface; support for her problems with the emergence of aggressive impulses (i.e., homicidality and suicidality) arose in later sessions, beyond the initial assessment/screening session.

ADDRESSING KEY ASSESSMENT/SCREENING FINDINGS: PSYCHIATRIC SYMPTOMS

By using the evidence-based *Special Focus on Building a Strong Therapeutic Alliance and Social-Support Network (TASS)* (see table 8.1), my empathy for her painful affective experiences allowed her to open up and share many details of her life. As is typical for many clients who experience such empathy, she found herself sharing details of her life she had not shared with anyone heretofore.

Building on this rapport, the end of the session also allowed me to ask Ms. M. T. about her concerns, allowing her to briefly reiterate her depression, anxiety, and insomnia. The use of a summary statement that reflected back

**Table 8.1.   Options from the Menu Used (*X*) in the Case of Ms. M. T. to Meet
Short- and Long-Term Treatment Goals**

Selections (*X*) for Ms. M. T. from category 1: Evidence-based addiction treatments
  X * Special focus on building a strong therapeutic alliance and social-support network
  X * Motivational interviewing/motivational enhancement therapy (MET)/brief interventions
  X * Cognitive-behavioral therapy (CBT)/relapse prevention (RP)/social-skills training (SST)
  X * Twelve-step facilitation (TSF)/guidance using Alcoholics and/or Narcotics
      Anonymous
  X * Individual drug counseling (IDC) and/or supportive-expressive psychotherapy (SEP)
  X * Community reinforcement approach (CRA)/vouchers: Contingency management (CM)
  X * The Matrix Model—or, a day-treatment approach, or an IEC outpatient model that is
      I for intensive (4–5 days per week), *E* for extensive (6–12 months), and *C* for
      comprehensive (TASS, CBT/RP, IDC, group drug counseling [GDC], drug testing, etc.)
Selections (*X*) for Ms. M. T. from category 2: Recommended state-of-the-art practices
  X * Integration of motivational interviewing and stages of change
  X * Integration of stages of change and phases of treatment and recovery
  X * Integration of harm reduction, moderation approaches, and abstinence models
  X * Integration of psychoanalytic and cognitive-behavioral theories and techniques
  X * Acquisition of affective, behavioral, and cognitive coping skills—learning new ABCs
  X * Integration of motivational interviewing, stages of change, and identity development
      theory for a diverse identity involving race, sexual orientation, and/or disability
  X * Incorporating contemporary trends in psychology: Multiculturalism, positive
      psychology, the strengths-based approach, and optimistic thinking/learned optimism

to her those concerns, as well as other things she had mentioned in the assessment/screening were consistent with use of the evidence-based *Motivational Interviewing/Motivational Enhancement Therapy (MET)/Brief Interventions* (see table 8.1). Continuing to use motivational interviewing techniques, Ms. M. T. was then offered a menu of options that included her coming to our program, her pursuing psychiatric treatment at an outpatient mental-health clinic, and the possibility that she could go to another MICA program for mentally ill chemical abusers. From this short list of options on the menu she was offered, Ms. M. T. was asked to choose what would be her next step. She chose the first option. She appeared willing and able to accept the goal of not only coming to our program, but also of obtaining psychiatric care, including taking psychiatric medication for her depression, anxiety, and insomnia. This was noteworthy, given that she had never before thought about seeing a psychiatrist or seeking out psychiatric medication. I positively reinforced her for this decision/selection, stating, "Excellent."

SUCCESSFUL MOVEMENT ACROSS STAGES OF CHANGE: ACCEPTANCE OF PSYCHIATRIC-TREATMENT REFERRAL

Ms. M. T. had rather quickly moved across stages of change from not having thought about seeing a psychiatrist and taking psychiatric medication (precontemplation) to contemplation, and then a preparation stage, making a determination to accept my referral. This conceptualization of what she had accomplished was in keeping with the *Integration of Motivational Interviewing and Stages of Change*, as listed in table 8.1; this example of her accepting change in the area of her mental health also supported my optimistic viewpoint with regard to her treatment (*Incorporating Contemporary Trends in Psychology: Multiculturalism, Positive Psychology, the Strengths-Based Approach, and Optimistic Thinking/Learned Optimism*, from table 8.1).

Discussion during the assessment/screening also served to initiate her into the process of accepting herself as one who needed psychiatric medication and care, and she exhibited good signs of acceptance. This initial acceptance was just the beginning of what would be an ongoing course of identity development as a person with a mental disability. In this manner, her case conceptualization and the interventions deployed with her also reflected *Integration of Motivational Interviewing, Stages of Change, and Identity Development Theory for a Diverse Identity Involving Race, Sexual Orientation, and/or Disability* (see table 8.1). Only ongoing progress in fully accepting this new identity as a person with a mental disability over time would ensure long-term medication compliance and appropriate engagement with psychiatric treatment.

FOSTERING OPTIMISM AND A FOCUS ON STRENGTHS

My comments served to provide Ms. M. T. with some hope and optimism that things might improve for her once she started taking psychiatric medication. This reflected my *Incorporating Contemporary Trends in Psychology: Multiculturalism, Positive Psychology, the Strengths-Based Approach, and Optimistic Thinking/Learned Optimism*. In addition to fostering her optimistic thinking, and role modeling such thinking, I then mentioned her strengths and resilience in being able to find an apartment on her own and take care of her children despite her painful experiences. The goal was for the client to feel positive, optimistic, strong, resilient, and as empowered as possible to move forward, despite any challenges.

ORAL CONTINGENCY CONTRACT: ADMISSION CONTINGENT ON OBTAINING PSYCHIATRIC CARE

By the end of the session, a telephone call to an outpatient mental-health clinic was made, and an appointment was scheduled for her in three weeks. The appointment date seemed acceptable at that time. An oral contract was made with Ms. M. T., specifically, *Contract 2—Admission Contingent on Obtaining Psychiatric Care*, as discussed in chapter 7; this suggested some partial use of the *Community Reinforcement Approach (CRA)/Vouchers: Contingency Management (CM)* (see table 8.1) via use of this oral contract.

She agreed to see the psychiatrist, remain under psychiatric care, and continue to take prescribed medication throughout the duration of her participation in our program. She repeated the essence of this contract back to me in her own words, also understanding that any decision to not follow through with what the oral contract specified could lead to her transfer to another program or discharge. Without an established identity as a person with a mental disability and the deep acceptance of her condition that would come with such an identity, the oral contract also played a vital function in ensuring her compliance with psychiatric treatment. The use of such a contingency contract (i.e., admission contingent on obtaining psychiatric care) was also viewed as a motivation enhancing intervention.

Of note, this level of contract (contract 2) would allow her to begin outpatient treatment in our program while we waited three weeks for her psychiatric treatment to begin. To some extent, such a decision reflected a certain amount of optimism and rested on my perception that she possessed the strength to be responsible and follow through with this plan, again following *Incorporating Contemporary Trends in Psychology: Multiculturalism, Positive Psychology, the Strengths-Based Approach, and Optimistic Thinking/Learned Optimism.*

ACCEPTANCE INTO OUTPATIENT COMMUNITY-BASED ADDICTION TREATMENT: KEY EVENTS

Given execution of the oral contract, Ms. M. T. was deemed fully admitted into our program. Soon thereafter, Ms. M. T. stopped working and began coming to our program for the day. This meant, in effect, that Ms. M. T. was now exposed to all of the elements of a program such as *The Matrix Model— Or, a Day-Treatment Approach or an IEC Outpatient Model That Is* I *for Intensive (4–5 days per week),* E *for Extensive (6–12 months), and* C *for Comprehensive (TASS, CBT/RP, IDC, GDC, drug testing, etc.),* as listed in table 8.1

Once she became involved in our outpatient program, Ms. M. T. discontinued her use of marijuana for stress relief, understanding our use of random drug testing and how her probation officer would be able to access the results. The possibility of facing graduated sanctions for positive drug-test results reflected elements of the *Community Reinforcement Approach (CRA)/ Vouchers: Contingency Management (CM).*

As several weeks passed by, it became clear to her counselor that Ms. M. T. could rather easily articulate suicidal and homicidal thoughts in response to stress. Perhaps marijuana was no longer being used for a self-medication function that had assisted her in attaining states of calm. Or, in addition, following a referral by her substance-abuse counselor to domestic-violence counseling, merely talking at length about her domestic-violence experiences (something stimulated by attendance at this program) apparently triggered such intense affect and aggression that she would become homicidal and suicidal.

CRISIS-INTERVENTION WORK IN INDIVIDUAL SESSIONS

Ms. M. T.'s substance-abuse counselor aptly observed how her psychiatric symptoms of recurrent homicidality and suicidality began to complicate the challenge of treating her marijuana dependence in individual drug counseling (IDC). Without delay, she executed a referral back to me for crisis-intervention work in intensive individual psychotherapy; the client was seen twice per week. This crisis intervention occurred within *Individual Drug Counseling (IDC) and/or Supportive-Expressive Psychotherapy (SEP)*, in particular, SEP, also including an *Integration of Psychoanalytic and Cognitive-Behavioral Theories and Techniques* (see table 8.1). This work included my having to continually rule out the need for emergency inpatient hospitalization, given her homicidal and suicidal ideation.

Within crisis-intervention/individual psychotherapy sessions, Ms. M. T. initially ventilated readily and loudly about wanting to commit violence. She would cycle back and forth from talking about how "I want to die" and "I want to kill him." It became an urgent matter to foster her *Acquisition of Affective, Behavioral, and Cognitive Coping Skills—Learning New ABCs* (see table 8.1). The self-talk/self-calming exercise "I am calm, centered, and balanced," was role modeled for her and practiced along with her in session. She was also given the repetition and rehearsal of this self-talk/self-calming exercise as homework to do alone at home and as needed whenever she became stressed, angry, or agitated. This exercise represented an adaptive coping response with affective, behavioral, and cognitive components.

Of note, it was a challenge to sit and listen to her ventilating her feelings of anger and her desire to "kill him." While other family members and friends were distancing themselves from her because of her loud and angry displays, the goal was for her to feel accepted for where she was, as well as to feel my empathy for her affective experience. This was justified by the evidence-based *Special Focus on Building a Strong Therapeutic Alliance and Social-Support Network (TASS)*. The goal was to build the kind of strong therapeutic alliance with her that would allow for the production of positive treatment outcomes, especially the short-term goal of attaining mental and emotional stability.

ACHIEVING THE SHORT-TERM GOAL OF STABILIZATION AND LEARNING ADAPTIVE COPING

But, there was a clear obstacle to this short-term goal. It was clear that her freely and loudly ventilating her anger was maladaptive, as it served to agitate her, even leading to homicidality and/or suicidality. This showed how her freely and loudly talking needed to simply end at such times, and the maladaptive behavior of verbal aggressiveness needed to be replaced with the adaptive coping response of engaging in the self-talk/self-calming exercise "*I am calm, centered, and balanced.*"

I would interrupt her ventilating, and we would literally sit and practice this self-talk/self-calming exercise in sessions together. (Because of the stress involved in working with her at such times, I, too, benefited.) She was also asked to observe the moment she became stressed at home and was repeatedly reminded of her homework to then perform this self-talk/self-calming exercise at such moments. The goal of strengthening her ego and teaching her ego to engage in self-observation/self-monitoring was pursued in this manner as vital work in this early phase of treatment/action stage.

Detailed discussion and processing of painful affects with regard to what her babies' father said or did, given how it was part of a series of traumas involving domestic violence, was not deemed productive or helpful. This kind of work with regard to her trauma was not appropriate, given the short-term goal of mental and emotional stabilization.

As part of the stabilization process, Ms. M. T. was taught the technique of *thought stopping*. She was given instructions to pay attention to the thoughts that she was having, like watching the clouds pass by, or like watching the thoughts merely crossing her mental space. If any were negative (about her babies' father), then she was to take her hand and hit the nearest table or surface and say "stop" aloud. Next, she was directed to repeat the self-talk/self-calming exercise.

The goal was for the combined use of thought stopping and the self-talk/self-calming exercise to prevent relapses to homicidality and suicidality, especially while at home. She was also given very practical advice to avoid all talk of her babies' father. In this manner, she was being taught that the trigger of her own thoughts or any conversation on the topic of her babies' father could lead to a relapse to homicidality/suicidality or states of agitation/aggression. This application of relapse prevention (*Cognitive-Behavioral Therapy (CBT)/Relapse Prevention (RP)/Social-Skills Training (SST)* in table 8.1) was building upon that which she had begun to receive in varied groups in the program. Technically, she was being taught an avoidant coping strategy; she needed to avoid all conversation and thoughts in regard to her babies' father. Consistent with relapse prevention and skills training, clients are typically taught to avoid triggers for relapse, especially in an early phase of treatment/action stage.

Of note, engagement in the recommended self-talk/self-calming exercise actually served an additional purpose. This strategy served to both calm her and distract her ego from disturbing material about her babies' father after such material had spontaneously emerged or had been triggered in her and she become agitated (homicidal and suicidal) by talking about it. In this manner, during this period of crisis intervention/individual psychotherapy, the conceptualization of her case reflected the state-of-the-art practice of *Integration of Psychoanalytic and Cognitive-Behavioral Theories and Techniques* (see table 8.1). Most importantly, the interventions deployed with her allowed for a very different picture of Ms. M. T. to emerge by the end of each session. She was calm and polite so that, by the end of each such session, she could calmly verbalize, "Thank you. When will I see you again?" She was also able to calmly drive herself home.

AN EPISODE OF ALCOHOL USE AND
REJECTION FROM A MENTAL-HEALTH CLINIC

By our fifth individual session, Ms. M. T. described going to a friend's house and being offered alcohol. She drank to the point of a blackout from alcohol. But, before that blackout, she recalls becoming angry, agitated, and ranting and raving about her babies' father in her intoxicated state, even attempting to call this man so she could berate him. Her friend became very annoyed, describing this drunken behavior the next day. In discussing this incident, the client presented herself as "rarely drinking" and as not having a problem with alcohol. However, the incident raised the issue of Ms. M. T.'s needing to abstain from alcohol, especially given the short-term goal of attaining mental and emotional stability, and given how alcohol exacerbated her difficulty regulating her anger and aggressive impulses. All of this education was totally new to her, and she had to now think about what she would do in terms of her drinking, especially as she had never considered it a problem before and it was a very rare event for her to drink.

Although in this early phase of treatment/action stage, Ms. M. T. was feeling overwhelmed with child-care issues and needed to avoid excess external stimulation, given how easily she became stressed out and agitated. Once she stabilized further, a host of practitioners (her substance-abuse counselor, other group counselors, and myself) would intensify their efforts to deliver interventions suggestive of *Twelve-Step Facilitation (TSF)/Guidance Using Alcoholics and/or Narcotics Anonymous* (under category 1). It may not be until she achieves the more immediate goal of mental and emotional stability that she will be able to become more involved in Narcotics Anonymous (NA)/Alcoholics Anonymous (AA). Exposure to NA/AA may help her to appreciate the manner in which her drinking alcohol to the point of blackout was problematic.

A portion of the session required the delivery of brief education on harm reduction and moderate drinking versus total abstinence, as well as motivational interviewing to enhance her immediate motivation to remain abstinent from alcohol for now as she thought about her long-term options. In this manner, an *Integration of Harm Reduction, Moderation Approaches, and Abstinence Models* and *Motivational Interviewing/Motivational Enhancement Therapy (MET)/Brief Interventions* (see table 8.1) were used.

Using motivational interviewing, I asked whether she had any concerns about what happened when she drank alcohol at her friend's house. Ms.

M. T. spoke about not wanting to lose the few friends she had. Also, discrepancy was created between her behavior and a valued goal. I offered, "On the one hand you say you want to keep your friends, but on the other hand you drank alcohol to the point of agitation and annoying your friend. What do you think about that? What do you think you need to do?" Ms. M. T. responded that she needed to not "drink like that." She also felt like it really didn't matter anyway, as she rarely drank alcohol. But she seemed motivated to want to avoid becoming agitated again and further alienating one of the few friends she had, given such a small social-support network and absence of any parental support. She finally agreed to stop drinking "for now."

Interventions with Ms. M. T. also emphasized just how important it was to maintain and cultivate a social-support network to increase the chances of successful long-term recovery. She was open to this education and responsive to keeping her friends and avoiding exposing them to her angry and agitated state that also tended to occur over the telephone when covering the topic of her babies' father. She was urged, once again, to not talk about him with her friends and family, as it both made her angry and agitated and alienated other people from her. Also, once again, she was reminded that talking about her babies' father was a trigger for her relapse to homicidality and suicidality, as the drinking episode further underscored. Except, this time, her friend's response to her served to mirror back and reflect to her just how undesirable she became in this state of anger/agitation, especially when combined with alcohol intoxication.

REJECTION FROM AN OUTPATIENT MENTAL-HEALTH CLINIC

Soon thereafter, Ms. M. T. came to a session sharing a letter of rejection from the mental-health outpatient program. They rejected Ms. M. T., feeling she posed too great a risk and needed inpatient hospitalization and/or residential drug-and-alcohol rehabilitation, being concerned about their ability to effectively treat her. Obviously, she had ventilated readily and loudly about her suicidal and homicidal thoughts at intake with them as well. She also told them about her night of drinking alcohol to the point of blackout, making them feel she needed a twenty-eight day inpatient drug-and-alcohol rehabilitation.

Ms. M. T. repeated how she rarely drank alcohol and had not used marijuana since joining our program. The emergent consensus at our outpatient program was that she could remain under our care.

ALTERNATIVE ARRANGEMENTS TO FOSTER STABILIZATION

Fortunately, Ms. M. T.'s private physician responded to her lamentations about insomnia, anxiety, and depression. This physician took the initiative in prescribing psychiatric medication for Ms. M. T. that began to assist her while ongoing attempts were made at our outpatient program to stabilize Ms. M. T. This included pursuing, once again, the short-term goal of having Ms. M. T. attend another outpatient mental-health clinic for receipt of appropriate ongoing psychiatric care. Her willingness to deploy the adaptive cognitive coping skills and self-talk/self-calming exercise she was taught in our individual sessions helped considerably in the process of stabilizing Ms. M. T. so that by the end of her first three months in outpatient community-based addiction treatment, considerable progress had been made.

However, she still had to wait several more weeks for another intake appointment at another mental-health clinic. However, the chances appeared much better that she would be accepted for admission to the new mental-health clinic. To her benefit, she was also acquiring substantial time abstinent from marijuana—three months—often a requirement for admission to such mental-health clinics. She seemed unlikely to drink alcohol again in the near future, based on her verbalizations. Because her private physician had prescribed her medication, she was able to wait for this appointment instead of pursuing the option of going through a walk-in clinic attached to a hospital for access to more emergency psychiatric care.

———◆———

COMMENTARY ON THE CASE OF MS. M. T.

The case of Ms. M. T. illustrates the process of putting it all together as practitioners engage in case conceptualization. This process specifically involves consideration of the following: (1) a client's characteristics, needs, and diversity; (2) the correct timing for the delivery of different interventions, given client characteristics and needs, as well as the client's stage of change and phase of treatment and recovery; and (3) the practitioner's actually formulating short- and long-term treatment goals and pursuing these by selecting interventions from the menu of options containing effective alternatives and recommended state-of-the-art practices, as summarized in table 8.1.

Key Client Characteristics and Needs

Ms. M. T. is a good example of the hidden population having serious psychiatric problems that are uncovered for the first time at the initial assessment/screening for entrance into a community-based addiction-treatment program. The case illustrates the role of generational cycles of addiction, a history of childhood parental abandonment by an injection drug user, and the death of the remaining parent from AIDS. This kind of history and emergent psychiatric disturbance are ever so common in our contemporary era. Ms. M. T. has also had the resultant all-too-common experiences of homelessness and living in a shelter with one's family. Yet, despite this, her strength and resilience are such that she has attained education, housing, employment, and a car. However, she also became criminally involved, writing bad checks, perhaps given compromised judgment from her own marijuana dependence. Her marijuana use likely reflects a self-medication strategy for the effects of trauma. Collectively, her childhood, adolescent, and young-adult trauma created a mood disorder (depression), as well as generalized anxiety, specifically, post-traumatic stress disorder, and there are also particularly pronounced problems in self-regulation of affects of anger and aggressive impulses. These problems in self-regulation are reflected in cutting her babies' father's arm and in becoming homicidal and suicidal.

Issues to Be Addressed in the Early Phase of Treatment/Action Stage

Thus, in light of the characteristics Ms. M. T. was presenting, there were clear indications for the correct timing of the delivery of addiction-treatment interventions. The uncovering of her psychiatric symptoms requires that, in an early phase of treatment/action stage, Ms. M. T. receive rather urgent psychiatric treatment in order to achieve the short-term goal of her mental and emotional stabilization. In this manner, the case shows how key variables (e.g., psychiatric symptoms) guide client-treatment matching to specific interventions, as treatment is tailored for a client. Her case shows how frequently an extended assessment period serves to best reveal the nature and extent of clients' psychiatric symptoms, especially when they have never been diagnosed or treated before and when termination of self-medication strategies with marijuana permits the full emergence of psychiatric symptoms. A typical recommendation is to allow four weeks to pass within an extended assessment period in order to allow for a more accurate determination of a client's actual mental disorders and psychiatric symptoms separate and apart from any symptoms in a withdrawal phase (see chapter 4 discussion and Wallace, 1996a).

Ms. M. T.'s psychiatric symptoms also had implications for that which needed to be selected from the menu of evidence-based addiction treatment options and recommended state-of-the-art practices. Her case required a response to what manifested as rather urgent psychiatric needs. This led to the delivery of crisis intervention in the form of intensive twice-per-week individual psychotherapy. Individual psychotherapy focused on teaching her more adaptive coping skills to produce a state of calm, being designed to replace her poor self-regulation of angry affects and aggressive impulses. This meant a focus on Ms. M. T.'s rapid acquisition of specific adaptive affective, behavioral, and cognitive coping responses to stress intended to reduce the risk that aggressive impulses would be directed against others (homicide against her babies' father) or against herself (suicide). This also involved strengthening her ego and fostering the capacity of her ego to engage in self-observation/self-monitoring of the moment when angry affects and aggressive impulses arose within the self. She then learned how to replace maladaptive coping responses with more adaptive ones, practicing the self-talk/self-calming exercise both in the sessions and at home. The deployment of selected interventions designed to strengthen her ego and enhance her coping in order to avoid a relapse to the release of anger and aggression, was in keeping with guidelines for how to manage survivors of trauma in an early phase of treatment/action stage (see chapter 5 and table 5.2). Thus, an important short-term goal involved her stabilizing so that she did not act out her aggression, versus any detailed verbal description of her past trauma or encouragement to process her painful affects. The early phase of treatment/action stage included the short-term goal of having her receive psychiatric treatment and psychiatric medication (see chapter 5 and table 5.1) even though there were problems in securing such care for her. And, all of the interventions she received during this phase would also further reduce the risk of relapse to marijuana use.

In the early phase of treatment/action stage, taking a cautious approach, the intent is to avoid any risk of potentially overstimulating the client by having her talk in detail about her past traumas; such overstimulation might provoke a relapse to violent acting out or relapse to marijuana use. In effect, this is what happened via referral to domestic-violence counseling by her substance-abuse counselor. Discussion of domestic-violence episodes led to states of overstimulation and verbal discharge of aggression, with homicidal impulses toward her batterer; this, in turn, led to suicidal ideation. Such detailed discussion of past trauma is actually contraindicated for survivors of trauma who are also presenting the kind of mood disorder and generalized anxiety disorder with poor regulation of anger and aggression that Ms. M. T. did, at least in an early phase of treatment/action stage.

It is possible (but not likely) that in the coming months, still in an early phase of treatment/action stage, specifically in months four, five, or six in treatment, Ms. M. T. might begin to feel ready to talk in greater depth about her trauma. And she might indeed emerge able to do so without relapsing to recurrent states of homicidality/suicidality and without experiencing overstimulation from anger and aggression arising with her. If this were the case, it would only be because of the hard-won victory of her first successfully stabilizing across months two and three in treatment. In particular, this victory involved the following: systematic strengthening of Ms. M. T.'s ego; learning self-observation/self-monitoring of the moment anger/aggression arose within; learning how to interrupt/stop moments of being triggered (by her own earlier conversation about her babies' father) to release anger and aggression; and learning how to replace maladaptive responses with adaptive coping responses, especially via the self-talk/self-calming exercise.

Issues to Be Addressed in the Maintenance Stage

Ms. M. T. brought to treatment characteristics involving generational cycles of addiction in her family, the trauma of childhood parental abandonment, and her rather contemporary adult trauma involving domestic violence. It would only be much later in treatment, after Ms. M. T. entered a middle-to-late phase of treatment/maintenance stage for her taking action in ending marijuana use and violence, that any working through and integration of her traumatic memories would be recommended as a process of trauma resolution (see chapter 4 and Wallace, 1996a).

No details with regard to this trauma (with release of painful affect) should be discussed in detail within trauma resolution until Ms. M. T. is in a middle-to-late phase of treatment/maintenance stage for both her marijuana use and violence. Although things might change in her course of treatment as she attains more than three months in outpatient community-based addiction treatment, the hard-won gain of her stabilizing (no longer angrily ventilating and threatening release of aggressive impulses) needs to be fully appreciated. The gain of stability after the crisis of recurrent states of homicidality and suicidality was only attained because Ms. M. T. was systematically directed to avoid such detailed discussion of what her babies' father did in our individual psychotherapy sessions in an early phase of treatment/action stage.

A cautious case conceptualization is to plan to relegate all detailed discussion (and processing of painful affect, that is, working through and integration of traumatic memories) of matters relating to her experiences of trauma to a middle-to-late phase of treatment/maintenance stage. This would be after she had greater than six months abstinent from marijuana and free from the release of aggressive impulses. And, as maintenance is a lifelong stage, only a thorough individualized assessment would determine the correct timing for any trauma-resolution work in this maintenance stage—whether, specifically, at seven months, thirteen months, twenty-four months, or perhaps not at all—if this work threatened to destabilize her and place her at risk of relapse. Thus, the case of Ms. M. T. is helpful in showing the value of a case conceptualization that is cautious and follows the rough guide for correct timing of the delivery of interventions across phases of treatment and stages of change, following discussion in chapter 5 and what is summarized in tables 5.1 and 5.2.

Selected Evidence-Based Interventions and Recommended State-of-the-Art Practices

Given the menu of evidence-based options and recommended state-of-the-art practices presented in chapter 4, the case of Ms. M. T. is also ideal insofar as it demonstrates the use of literally every intervention shown in table 8.1, with each intervention used demarcated with the mark of an X. Not all cases would call for the use of so many of the recommended state-of-the-art practices, such as the following: *Integration of Harm Reduction, Moderation Approaches, and Abstinence Models* and *Integration of Motivational Interviewing, Stages of Change, and Identity Development Theory for a Diverse Identity Involving Race, Sexual Orientation, and/or Disability*. Yet her case utilizes these—as well as every other evidence-based intervention and recommended state-of-the-art practice listed on the menu of options—at some point in time in just her first three months in treatment. In this manner, the case shows how the evidence-based interventions begin to constitute a unified model, while the state-of-the-art practices begin to constitute a unified theory, and both provide a framework for practitioners by guiding the treatment process.

CONCLUSION

This chapter answered the following question: How do practitioners go about the task of prioritizing client issues needing immediate versus future attention and select from a menu of options interventions/practices to meet short- and long-term treatment goals? Using the case example of Ms. M. T., the process was shown to include ascertaining client characteristics via assessment/screening, prioritizing client characteristics requiring immediate versus future attention, and conceptualizing the course of treatment by selecting from a menu of options those interventions and practices for both immediate and future deployment. Indeed, the case of Ms. M. T. was unusual in allowing for the use of literally all of the evidence-based addiction-treatment interventions and recommended state-of-the-art practices shown in table 8.1.

What emerges from this chapter is the manner in which practitioners in contemporary community-based addiction treatment may pioneer the adaptation of evidence-based interventions and practices with multiproblem clients in the real world. Ms. M. T. is clearly the kind of client who would not have met the strict exclusion/inclusion criteria in many empirical investigations such as Project MATCH. Her homicidality, suicidality, and probationary status would have deemed her inappropriate for participation. However, she is exactly the kind of mandated and multiproblem client practitioners are encountering in the real world of contemporary community-based addiction treatment. Such clients are challenging practitioners to exercise both fidelity to that which is embodied in evidence-based interventions, as well as flexibility in terms of when to adapt, integrate, and tailor treatment to individual client needs, while also drawing upon the use of recommended state-of-the-art practices.

In terms of short-term goals to be accomplished as soon as possible in the early phase of treatment/action stage, the case of Ms. M. T. illustrates the following: it is important to foster the acquisition of adaptive affective, behavioral, and cognitive coping responses; to focus on relapse prevention to mal-adaptive coping responses; as well as to strengthen the ego, replacing habit-ual defensive strategies (ventilation of aggression and violent acting out, as well as marijuana use for self-medication) with enhanced ego functions. The successful accomplishment of such short-term goals increases the chances that clients will be able to accomplish future long-term goals in a middle-to-late phase of treatment/maintenance stage, such as the following adap-tive coping in response to ongoing events in their life, especially with regard to constructively processing any painful affects that may arise. Painful affec-tive states may arise merely within the course of negotiating a stressful life as a single parent or from multiproblem clients' current, recent, or past trauma. A host of different evidence-based interventions/state-of-the-art practices for deployment in the early phase of treatment/action stage, as well as in the middle-to-late phase of treatment/maintenance stage play a vital role in ensuring client's long-term successful coping with stress and painful affects. For example, failure to successfully build a strong therapeu-tic alliance or engage a client in an intensive/extensive/comprehensive (IEC) outpatient program or psychiatric care, as important short-term goals to be accomplished in an early phase of treatment/action stage, could pre-vent success in attaining other long-term goals in a middle-to-late phase of treatment/maintenance stage, such as protracted freedom from relapses and avoidance of graduated sanctions on probation.

9

◆

Creating Positive Long-Term Treatment Outcomes

The ultimate goal for practitioners is to forge positive long-term treatment outcomes for clients, despite their clients' being multiproblem, having ever-so-challenging characteristics and needs. What happens in the early phase of treatment/action stage may determine what happens in a middle-to-late phase of treatment/maintenance stage, as well as overall long-term treatment outcome. Once a practitioner overcomes any negative counter-transference reactions to clients (chapter 6) with addictive and criminal be-haviors, there is the task of acquiring vital information in assessment/screening (chapter 7). And what must be underscored is the absolute impor-tance of learning how to develop the kind of therapeutic alliance that is as-sociated with positive long-term treatment outcome. The early phase of treatment is also a time to strengthen clients' social-support networks, as these, too, positively impact long-term treatment outcome.

This chapter uses a case example (Mr. K. X.) and provides training in cre-ating positive long-term treatment outcomes, placing a special focus on building a strong therapeutic alliance and social-support network, as well as on how to integrate and adapt evidence-based and state-of-the-art practices to meet individual client characteristics and needs, tailoring treatment for that client. The case of Mr. K. X. spans a fourteen-month period, effectively illustrating how a practitioner who successfully builds a strong therapeutic alliance and successfully encourages a client to cultivate and remain in-volved with a social-support network, in particular, will likely help to pro-duce positive treatment outcomes. However, as the case of Mr. K. X. will also reveal, many contemporary clients have characteristics and needs that make a course of treatment a winding, steep, rocky road to travel. But, such is the nature of community-based addiction treatment in the real world, as the case of Mr. K. X. demonstrates.

SESSION 1, WEEK 1

Mr. K. X. was referred to see me for completion of paperwork for Social Security disability. Upon first meeting Mr. K. X., he appeared guarded, distant, irritated, and annoyed, bordering on angry. At age thirty-three, he was currently involved in a nine-to-twelve-month residential program. Initially standing, Mr. K. X. appeared to be over six feet tall and very thin in stature, but posing to emphasize his strength. I asked him to have a seat. He pulled his chair very close to me, up to the edge of the desk. Mr. K. X. was told, "Please move your chair back." Not a very empathic beginning, admittedly, yet this maintained my own level of comfort, as well as important boundaries, reestablishing the preexisting seating arrangement. Or, perhaps his moving his chair so close to me was an act of intimidation, and I was correct to defend my territory. Maybe on some intuitive level I sensed the anger seething beneath his surface, and I wisely established a protective boundary or zone across which he could not readily reach. In any event, I felt comfortable again once he moved his chair back.

Perusing his paperwork, it became evident that his counselor had already completed pertinent portions. Mr. K. X. was asked who else was submitting paperwork for him. He told me that he had a psychiatrist he was seeing at a local hospital currently prescribing his medication—Depakote. The psychiatrist had already submitted paperwork for him.

The assessment proceeded. Mr. K. X. presented alcohol and marijuana dependence in partial remission, for which he was being treated in the residential facility. He also presented bipolar disorder, post-traumatic stress disorder, and antisocial personality disorder.

During the assessment, he was treated with all the formalities and respect due a gentleman, being called "Mr.," thus establishing his feeling respected as a crucial first step in our building a working therapeutic alliance; this is essential with a potentially angry or violent client. His taking Depakote was the first red flag, suggesting a potential for violence, justifying my showing the highest level of respect. However, this respect was just part of the essential affective state of empathy, respect, acceptance, and optimism that I hoped to genuinely convey in the very first assessment/screening session. This was in keeping with the evidence-based *Special Focus on Building a Strong Therapeutic Alliance/Social Support Network (TASS)* and *Incorporating Contemporary Trends in Psychology: Multiculturalism, Positive Psychology, the Strengths-Based Approach, and Optimistic Thinking/Learned Optimism*, and it also displayed multicultural sensitivity and competence in accepting him as a person with a mental disability (see table 9.1).

Table 9.1. Options from the Menu Used (X) in the Case of Mr. K. X. Striving to Create Positive Long-Term Treatment Outcomes

Selections (X) for Mr. K. X. from category 1: Evidence-based addiction treatments

X * Special focus on building a strong therapeutic alliance/social-support network (TASS)

X * Motivational interviewing/motivational enhancement therapy (MET)/brief interventions

X * Cognitive-behavioral therapy (CBT)/relapse prevention (RP)/social-skills training (SST)

X * Twelve-step facilitation (TSF)/guidance using Alcoholics and/or Narcotics Anonymous

X * Individual drug counseling (IDC) and/or supportive-expressive psychotherapy (SEP)

X * Community reinforcement approach (CRA)/vouchers: Contingency management (CM)

X * The Matrix Model—or, a day-treatment approach, or an IEC outpatient model that is *I* for intensive (4–5 days per week), *E* for extensive (6–12 months), and *C* for comprehensive (TASS, CBT/RP, IDC, group drug counseling [GDC], drug testing, etc.)

Selections (X) for Mr. K. X. from category 2: Recommended state-of-the-art practices

X * Integration of motivational interviewing and stages of change

X * Integration of stages of change and phases of treatment and recovery

  * Integration of harm reduction, moderation approaches, and abstinence models

X * Integration of psychoanalytic and cognitive-behavioral theories and techniques

X * Acquisition of affective, behavioral, and cognitive coping skills—learning new ABCs

X * Integration of motivational interviewing, stages of change, and identity development theory for a diverse identity involving race, sexual orientation, and/or disability

X * Incorporating contemporary trends in psychology: Multiculturalism, positive psychology, the strengths-based approach, and optimistic thinking/learned optimism

A History of Violence and Risk of Violent Acting Out

Mr. K. X.'s history was obtained, and I found cause for alarm as well as for initiating a course of therapy with him. He had a considerable history of violence and recurrent homicidal ideation, making him a risk to others. Crisis-intervention work immediately began in order to stabilize Mr. K. X. and reduce his risk for violently acting out. He admitted to thinking about hurting peers in the residential facility, but to having no plan or specific intent to kill them when angered.

A Missed Opportunity to Execute a Contingency Contract at Program Admission

It turned out that Mr. K. X. had been admitted to the residential community-based addiction-treatment facility after signing a contingency contract specifying how violence or threats of violence could lead to discharge from the residential program. Ideally, given his diagnoses and history, he should have seen me at time of intake, and an additional oral contract should have been executed specifying how he should walk away from potential violent encounters in order for him to be able to remain in the facility. Also, in retrospect, an oral contract should have been executed specifying that he remain under psychiatric care and take his medication regularly throughout the program in order to remain in the residence. The use of all such contracts is supported (see the *Community Reinforcement Approach (CRA)/Vouchers: Contingency Management (CM)* in table 9.1).

Acknowledging the missed opportunity to execute other contingency contracts at time of program admission, my attention turned to his risk of violence/homicidality. This was my main concern, justifying beginning work immediately on the short-term goal of Mr. K. X.'s attaining mental and emotional stability with reduced risk of violently acting out and assaulting other peers in the residential facility.

Crisis Intervention Work Begins to Stabilize Mr. K. X.

To meet this short-term goal of mental and emotional stabilization, a crisis-intervention plan was established, seeing Mr. K. X. in twice-per-week intensive individual psychotherapy (see *Individual Drug Counseling (IDC) and/or Supportive-Expressive Psychotherapy (SEP)* particularly, SEP, including an *Integration of Psychoanalytic and Cognitive-Behavioral Theories and Techniques* in table 9.1).

My approach followed recommended guidelines for the correct timing of interventions with multiproblem clients, such as Mr. K. X. (see chapter 5 and table 5.1, items I-A-1, I-A-2, II-B-1, II-B-2, and II-B-3). Mr. K. X. had urgent contemporary needs and characteristics, suggesting first things first; he needed assistance complying with the one contingency contract that had been executed with him at time of program admission, having to avoid violent acting out in the residence to prevent sudden discharge. This was especially important, as he would likely end up homeless again, something he had experienced for the prior six months, and having to hustle, deal drugs, and engage in violence to survive on the streets. And, if he returned to that lifestyle, it would include a relapse to heavy marijuana and alcohol use. Mr. K. X. also had an urgent need for individual sessions to augment the benefits of psychiatric medication for control of aggressive impulses. What he vitally needed was then urgently delivered.

Uncovering the Link between Past Trauma and His Current Risk of Violence

At the time of initial history taking in our very first session, Mr. K. X. told me about an early childhood trauma at age seven, suggesting likely roots for his psychiatric disorder and violent acting out. This age-seven trauma involved Mr. K. X.'s witnessing the horrific murder of his father by repeated stabbing during an alcohol-induced brawl with a neighbor over an ongoing land dispute. "I saw everything," he stated frankly. To make matters worse, Mr. K. X. was extremely close to his father as the only son in the family, having four sisters. His mother's ensuing depression and attempts to find solace in alcohol led to her inability to parent her five children, with Mr. K. X. being the next to youngest. Fortunately, while being raised by other family members, Mr. K. X. was still able to remain with his three older sisters who provided him with a great deal of affection and doting. His youngest sister, still an infant, went to yet another relative's home.

Current family ties included his sisters and a fifteen-year-old daughter with whom he was seeking to develop a closer relationship after spending fourteen years in and out of correctional settings for drug dealing and assaults. Underlying this history was a preoccupation with knives and machetes and a history of stabbing people.

Teaching Self-Calming/Anger Management to Enhance Coping

In the very first session, I taught Mr. K. X. the anger-management/self-calming technique of repeating both aloud and then silently within, "*I am calm, centered, and balanced.*" I also taught him to visualize himself sitting in a safe place. Mr. K. X. was told to practice this self-calming technique twice a day and whenever he felt angry or stressed out. Also, ideally, he would walk away from any potential argument or violent confrontation and go sit in his room where he was to silently repeat the self-talk/self-calming exercise. He was to repeat this self-talk/self-calming exercise at least nine times in an emergency, but ideally as a five-to-ten-minute meditation twice a day. He was given the suggestion that he would be in certain situations where he was getting upset and that this self-talk would automatically begin, and he would be able to notice himself repeating it silently within and actually calming down. Theoretically, such a development harkens the establishment of a significantly strengthened ego with the capacity to engage in self-observation/self-monitoring. However, in order to get to that point, he had to practice repeating this self-talk for five to ten minutes twice a day, and especially whenever he got upset.

This intervention represented an important first step in Mr. K. X.'s learning adaptive coping responses (see *Acquisition of Affective, Behavioral, and Cognitive Coping Skills—Learning New ABCs* in table 9.1). Collectively, he was learning to perform an adaptive cognitive coping response of repeating internal self-talk, an adaptive behavioral coping response of walking away and sitting in his room, and an adaptive affective coping response of inner calmness (versus violently acting out). Or, quite simply, he was learning adaptive coping responses.

An Oral Contract Specifying What to Do to Avoid Potential Violence

Most importantly, as part of a program of anger management to which I introduced him, Mr. K. X. agreed to an oral contract specifying that he walk away from all situations involving potential violence. This included permission to walk out of groups if he felt that was necessary in order to contain aggressive impulses. He was able to repeat back to me, quite simply, "walk away, go to my room, sit down, and calm myself." This was adding a further specification to the prior oral contract he had made at the residence, specifying a risk of discharge for violence and threats of violence. With this specification of what to do when at risk of angry displays or acts of violence, Mr. K. X. might be able to avoid the most graduated sanction of program discharge.

The emphasis on walking away highlighted the importance of teaching what may be considered an avoidant coping response, at least initially, in an early phase of treatment/action stage. Ideally, clients eventually learn to deploy the ideal active coping response of delivering a positive, assertive verbal response. However, to walk away is preferable and relatively adaptive when contrasted to the clearly maladaptive behavior of engaging in verbal aggression or physical violence. These considerations were consistent with a focus on *Integration of Stages of Change and Phases of Treatment and Recovery* (see table 9.1).

Exploring the Client's Concerns

Toward the end of this first session, the client was given an opportunity to talk freely by being asked, "Do you have any concerns?" Asking about concerns is common within motivational interviewing (see *Motivational Interviewing/Motivational Enhancement Therapy (MET)/Brief Interventions* in table 9.1). Mr. K. X. spoke about certain behaviors on the part of two of his family members, leading him to condemn them, especially the older woman, his sister. He was planning to cut off ties with both relatives. Yet he also mentioned an upcoming family reunion in two months that would bring everyone together.

I used motivational interviewing to create dissonance. I pointed out the discrepancy between his planned behavior of cutting off ties and the goal of going to a family reunion where he planned to have a good time. I asked Mr. K. X. what he thought he should do. He seemed rigid in still wanting to judge and condemn these two relatives.

I tried another approach to foster his abandonment of a position that seemed rigid, harsh, and judgmental. So I asked Mr. K. X. what his sister had done for him while he was incarcerated. "She sent me money orders," he replied. I asked, "Did anyone else send you anything?" He responded dryly, "No." I pondered aloud, "So, she has never held it against you that you have gone to jail or seem to repeatedly stab or cut people." He acknowledged, "No." I further inquired, "And if something goes wrong and you had to leave this residential facility, she would let you sleep on her sofa in an emergency?" Mr. K. X. had to acknowledge, "Yes." I explained my rationale for the question I was about to ask, stating, "A lot of clients in the residential facility only have one place to visit on their passes." I then asked, "Is this one of the few places you have to visit when you have a pass from the facility?"

Mr. K. X. replied as follows: "Yes, the main place I would visit. Maybe I could visit one of my other sisters."

I then went on to suggest that if his sister had not rejected him for his behavior, then maybe he should accept her despite her behavior, even if it was a political decision, meaning he might need something from her in the future. Hence, the decision to cut off ties could lead to negative consequences for him in the future. He could lose access to a vital source of social support he might need in future emergencies and from which he had benefited in the past. Also, resolution of this conflict and bringing about an end to his condemnation of this sister and another family member was the only way to ensure that he felt comfortable at this upcoming family reunion.

In this manner, our dialogue illustrates when confrontation is a gentle but direct process of bringing a client in touch with the reality of a situation, but without harsh confrontation being used, as in motivational interviewing. In this form of confrontation, the delivery of brief education is often used, serving to reframe cognitions, as in explaining a political decision. This intervention was also serving to role model consequential thinking and decision making in an effort to strengthen his ego so that he could better perform, in the future, critical ego functions such as good reality testing and judgment. I also role modeled acceptance and compassion, as a contrast to Mr. K. X.'s tendencies toward being rigid, harsh, and judgmental. This kind of rigidity typically signals how a client is engaged in the overuse of defenses. This possibility was not surprising, given the strength of the aggressive impulses against which Mr. K. X. seemed to be defending when not merely unleashing aggressive impulses in violent acting out. Hence, elements of an *Integration of Psychoanalytic and Cognitive-Behavioral Theories and Techniques* (table 9.1) provided a rationale for the intervention delivered.

My ego demonstrated performance of reality testing and judgment, something his ego seemed to not be able to do at this early point in his treatment given his presentation of ever-so-common ego deficits in this early phase of treatment/action stage. What I did not tell Mr. K. X. was how having a supportive social network, especially including supportive family members, would increase his chances of successful recovery. And, for this, I had a rationale (*Special Focus on Building a Strong Therapeutic Alliance/Social Support Network, TASS*).

At the end of this first session, Mr. K. X. was given an appointment to return in two days. This reflected my decision to see him twice per week, initially, as crisis intervention.

SESSION 2, WEEK 1

By the second session, Mr. K. X. was an enthusiast of therapy. He talked about having had several incidents in the residence where he struggled with his aggressive impulses, wanting to assault other residents. In fact, he had followed my permission and walked out of a group. He talked about how hard it was to contain his urges to be violent in the residential treatment setting.

Evidence of Adaptive Coping

He described the genuine pain and strain inherent in containing aggressive impulses as he nonetheless successfully walked away, went to his room, sat down, and practiced anger management/self-calming as specified in our oral contract. Mr. K. X. elaborated on his predicament. "These guys in the facility don't know what they are dealing with. They could never have made it where I was." Mr. K. X. was referring to those violent skills he had refined in the streets and in prison that other residential clients lacked, being quite facile with a knife or with anything he fashioned to use as a weapon. An incident he had the night before in the residence, during the airing of an important sports game, was the most critical of all the incidents he reported. Mr. K. X. had to leave the residential community room and could not see the remainder of the game being televised, for he had strong aggressive urges toward one resident in particular. "This big guy kept blocking the television; I was going to beat him over the head with a chair. So I had to leave the room. I went up to my room and calmed myself. They don't know that my specialty is taking down really big guys."

Use of Empathy and Positive Reinforcement

Feeling empathy for his predicament and his pain in restraining aggressive impulses he normally freely unleashed upon others, I reflected back to him, "It's hard for you to do that, to walk away. But you did it. That's what you're going to have to do. Excellent." The delivery of positive reinforcement via the verbal comment of "Excellent" was intended to increase the likelihood that he would perform again in the future adaptive coping responses (i.e., walking away, going to his room, sitting down, and verbally repeating the anger-management/self-calming exercise). The intent was to also strengthen behavior on the part of his ego; this involved his ego's observing/self-monitoring his self getting angry; its engaging in good judgment and reality testing; its deciding not to execute the old and familiar defensive behavior of acting out aggressively; and, instead, its directing him to walk away, go to his room, sit down, and repeat, "I am calm, centered, and balanced." Given that he reported doing this several times in just the past two days since our last session, the result was the systematic strengthening of his ego, the cultivation of the capacity for self-observation/self-monitoring, and the practice of adaptive coping responses (reflecting *Integration of Psychoanalytic and Cognitive-Behavioral Theories and Techniques*). And, though he was being taught what might be considered avoidant coping strategies, such coping was more adaptive than the clearly maladaptive response of verbal aggressiveness/ physical violence. Nonetheless, the goal was for Mr. K. X. to eventually learn the higher-order (active) adaptive coping response of delivering positive, assertive verbal responses.

A Cause for Optimism

Given what Mr. K. X. reported in session two, there was cause for optimistic thinking in regard to his case. His ability to adhere to the oral contract and follow my instructions suggested that he had strengths, including intelligence, good memory, and a spirit of cooperation. I consciously acknowledged these strengths (*Incorporating Contemporary Trends in Psychology: Multiculturalism, Positive Psychology, the Strengths-Based Approach, and Optimistic Thinking/Learned Optimism*, from table 9.1).

SESSION 3, WEEK 2

By the third session, Mr. K. X. returned talking about how much therapy was helping him and how well things went when he visited his older sister over the weekend. This was the same sister that had been the focus of our discussion in session 1. While at her home, he also ran into the other family member against whom he had also been taking a rigid, harsh, judgmental stance. He reported getting along well with both of them. Our therapeutic alliance was also evolving and getting stronger, especially as Mr. K. X. was receiving rewards in the real world, benefiting from the intervention he received in session 1. This intervention was allowing Mr. K. X. to experience the positive rewards inherent in having a social-support network that included family such as his sister, this being key to a positive long-term treatment outcome. Mr. K. X. appeared to have found in our session a safe space in which to talk about his concerns with positive results.

Impact of Fourteen Years of Incarceration

Feeling safe, Mr. K. X. opened up further. He spoke eloquently about what it was like to be institutionalized, given fourteen years of incarceration. He explained how he was typically only out of jail for ninety days to six months before the next incarceration. He described himself and his violence in greater detail, perhaps because of feeling safe in sessions and the empathic responses he received from me when he opened up and talked about his aggressive impulses in the past. He freely shared incidents in which he had stabbed or cut people on the streets, and how quickly he tended to get caught, soon thereafter facing reincarceration. Once incarcerated, he continued to fight frequently.

A Prison Institutionalization Syndrome

Mr. K. X. also talked about how he was not a social person. His thinking reflected a prison institutionalization syndrome (see chapter 5), having an unconscious tendency to repeat and re-create the conditions of social isolation common during incarceration, especially for one such as Mr. K. X., who was frequently punished for violence by being placed in isolation for a prescribed period, whether thirty days, sixty days, or several months. Of note, now that he was no longer incarcerated, his goal was to live in a room all by himself, describing in great detail the studio apartment he wanted to call his own following what he anticipated to be a year in residential treatment. Each time he repeated this theme of isolation, I wondered if it was the legacy of having spent months in isolation/solitary confinement. I offered a positive expectation that he might fulfill as prophecy: "I think you can find someone to be with." He then spoke of women he had dated, but also of how repeated incarceration became an obstacle to maintaining any long-term relationship. Yet he appeared to want to believe the prophecy I offered.

Also, when Mr. K. X. asserted that he was not a social person, I pointed out the contrasting reality. I identified the friends he had made in the residence, actually forging relationships with men who became the newly found brothers he never had. Next, I spoke of the people he was spending time with, such as his older sister, and the people he could plan to spend even more time with, including his fifteen-year-old daughter. She loved him and always responded positively to him on the telephone, despite separation due to his incarceration.

The delivery of brief education and an interpretation about the impact of the trauma of imprisonment was delivered. I explained how this trauma might have produced certain negative cognitions and well-hidden fears, establishing the expectation that he was destined for isolation. It was also possible that through his behavior he was unconsciously re-creating isolation experiences, thereby attempting to master his past trauma of repeated solitary confinement. The concept of a prison institutionalization syndrome was also discussed with him.

If You Know the Trauma, You Can Figure Out the Drama

Mr. K. X. received brief education on the impact of trauma, as I explained how, "If you know the trauma, you can figure out the drama" (see Wallace, 1996a). I explained how human beings tended to create dramas that followed from the original trauma. Also, the positive expectation of his success in creating and maintaining social ties with his sister, other family members, daughter, and newly found brothers in residential treatment was offered; contemporary evidence to support this positive expectation was thereby underscored. The goal was for the positive expectation to support new behaviors of connecting with his social-support network, replacing the recurrent drama of his re-created isolation experience that stemmed from his traumas in the hole during solitary confinement.

Of note, this kind of trauma resolution work performed in an early phase of treatment/action stage (less than six months of working on violence) was largely educational and geared toward enhancement of his coping skills. The short-term goal was to give his ego a cognitive and intellectual framework for understanding what happened to him during trauma. Specifically, he was being taught more adaptive cognitive coping strategies to replace old maladaptive coping responses (e.g., replacing the maladaptive "I always end up alone and in pain" with the more adaptive "I am a social person and have valued connections with others"). This adaptive cognitive coping might also become an expectation or prophecy fulfilled in the future.

Traumatic Contact with the Ku Klux Klan

Mr. K. X. opened up further, wanting me to understand the magnitude of this prison-isolation trauma. He shared the story of being placed in the hole, in solitary confinement, in a prison in a border southern state. The prison guards said to him, "Nigger, you're going to die in here." As he calmly reflected on that experience, he finally stated quietly, "I didn't die."

He explained how this prison was in Ku Klux Klan territory. He went to this border southern state after completing a New York "bid" in order to "get away and live with my uncle." Unfortunately his eventual return to alcohol, marijuana, and violence led to a new "bid" in this state. He first learned what it meant to live in that region of the country the day there was a Ku Klux Klan rally in broad daylight. Mr. K. X. described standing on the lawn of his uncle's home as the Ku Klux Klan paraded by, headed toward their rally. "They were calling us niggers and spitting on us. My uncle held my arm and told me there are some things we just can't do anything about. I was crying. I was bawling. Tears were running down my face. I wanted to go and get the biggest machete I could find and wipe them all out."

With the reality of the situation made clear to him, as his uncle had done, demonstrating excellent judgment and reality testing, Mr. K. X.'s ego was able to contain his anger and aggression, but with great difficulty. I sought confirmation for what I sensed was his inner affective state and the meaning of his experience as I grasped it with empathy. I asked, "You were crying because you couldn't attack them?" And Mr. K. X. said, "Yes."

In opening up further, it seemed his ego was responding to finding a safe place to share his most painful stories of trauma. He was also anticipating receiving more help in moving toward more adaptive coping responses.

SESSION 4, WEEK 2

In a fourth session, Mr. K. X. was able to talk further about this struggle involving containing his aggressive impulses, given that it was a daily affair in the residential treatment facility. He explained, "I'm sitting there, and

I'm seeing the whole thing happen. I see myself hurting people. Dr. Wallace, I'm so tired of it. I'm so tired of thinking about hurting people. I don't want to go back to prison." Having heard about his traumatic experiences of repeated incarceration and isolation in the hole in prison, I believed him. And I was also coming to understand how Mr. K. X. also often became flooded with images of doing violence against others. Yet, as Mr. K. X. spoke, I also heard the melody of hope and a tremendous motivation to change, even as his was also a desperate cry for help. I could feel his desperation and pain in feeling compelled to repeat over and over again the same maladaptive behavioral responses of releasing aggression, with the same unsatisfactory outcome. Empathizing with him, and finding cause for optimism in his intense inner motivation to change, my own commitment to assist him was enhanced.

Prior History of Homicidal Ideation toward a Treatment Staff Member

However, Mr. K. X. went on to have a confession type of session that served to temper my growing enthusiasm to work with him. He spoke of his fears that he might fail in controlling his violent impulses, given negative experiences he had in another treatment program. As is typical of so many clients, Mr. K. X. was technically a treatment failure in other settings. Most telling was how he had been in an outpatient treatment program about seven months ago and had a humiliating incident with a counselor who deployed harsh confrontation with him. The counselor talked down to Mr. K. X. in front of a group of people in a public setting. This humiliating experience resulted in Mr. K. X.'s decision to return the next day to the treatment program with a knife, being determined to stab this counselor. Mr. K. X. never verbalized his plan, but other clients in the program who knew Mr. K. X. (seemingly better than the treatment providers) shared concerns about pending violence with staff.

Mr. K. X. explained how when he returned to the treatment program the next day the counselor had wisely decided to stay home from work. Staff called the police as soon as Mr. K. X. showed up at the facility. He explained, "I was able to run away and dump my knife before the police got me," potentially finding him in possession of a weapon and arresting him. Other devastating consequences involving a relapse to drug dealing, the street life, homelessness, and drug/alcohol use followed from his sudden departure from treatment.

Mr. K. X. was no longer feeling homicidal toward this counselor, or toward anyone else, at this point in time during this session. But the memory he shared dramatically underscored his fear of failing to control his aggressive impulses and losing a placement in another drug-treatment program—this time a residential program.

Cause for Reality Testing, Caution, and Reevaluation

Now I had to engage in reality testing and exercise the best possible judgment, assessing the risks inherent in working with a client who had a history of intent to stab a treatment provider. Even though this prior treatment provider had erred and used very poor judgment in humiliating Mr. K. X., I had to consider several things. One consideration involved the potential risks to my own physical safety in electing to work with him. Another was the potential risk to the safety of other staff, including counselors who might unwittingly make an unprofessional error similar to that of the counselor in the prior program. On the other hand, there was the potential benefit to society and reduction of the public-health threat posed by Mr. K. X.'s violence if the present course of treatment was successful. This consideration was always a powerful tool in holding at bay negative countertransference reactions toward a client.

As I processed these considerations, instead of having affects of fear, I had to objectively cognitively cope with the situation. This included obtaining peer supervision by telephone. It was also important to clearly differentiate myself and what I did as a practitioner in individual psychotherapy sessions from that which Mr. K. X. had experienced with the prior counselor he had intended to cut with a knife. After careful thought, I decided to proceed with treatment. In addition, I actively sought to inform program staff in case conferences of the risks inherent in treating Mr. K. X., sharing what he was capable of doing in terms of violence, and the importance of managing this risk appropriately.

Optimism and Cognitive Reframing—Making Miracles Happen

My optimism and ability to see Mr. K. X.'s strengths were important in the decision to continue to work with him, consistent with *Incorporating Contemporary Trends in Psychology: Multiculturalism, Positive Psychology, the Strengths-Based Approach, and Optimistic Thinking/Learned Optimism.* I still needed to avoid any negative countertransference reaction that might include projecting negative and low expectations upon Mr. K. X., perhaps thinking he was destined for recidivism, relapse, or treatment failure again. Especially helpful in this regard is the powerful cognitive reframing in the concept of *making miracles happen.* My work with Mr. K. X. included verbally conveying how he could become a miracle, changing despite great odds having historically been stacked against him. By providing Mr. K. X. with this powerful positive cognitive reframing, both he and I could draw on the hope that he could become a miracle and not relapse to violence and lose another opportunity for treatment in a program. Optimistic thinking replaced both his fears and my concerns.

SESSION 5, WEEK 3

Following a weeklong vacation I took around the Fourth of July, Mr. K. X. spoke about the impact of therapy: "Dr. Wallace, I have to be real with you. This is really working. I know I'll never end up homeless again or in a situation where I won't reach out for help." I sought clarity, asking, "Because of therapy?" He responded, "Yes, because of therapy. This is really helping me." The seeds of optimism, planted in the prior session in the cognitive reframing that he could become a miracle, had sprouted and grown.

Traumatic Memories Surface and Observation by the Ego

He proceeded to talk about memories that had surfaced within him in recent days. This development was consistent with what follows from placing a focus upon the *Acquisition of Affective, Behavioral, and Cognitive Coping Skills— Learning New ABCs* in an early phase of treatment/action stage as a vital short-term treatment goal, reflecting a consideration of *Integration of Stages of Change and Phases of Treatment and Recovery*. In fact, after just two weeks of practicing adaptive affective, behavioral, and cognitive coping responses (i.e., walking away from stressful interpersonal interactions; sitting in his room; and repeating, "I am calm, centered, and balanced"), Mr. K. X. was evidencing a considerably strengthened ego that could now self-observe/ self-monitor and report in sessions what was arising within the self. Instead of this being the mere recurrence of flashbacks from past trauma, consistent with his post-traumatic stress disorder, the manner in which he was able to both observe and then report these memories in session suggested the strengthening of his ego and his learning of adaptive coping skills. His ego could thereby attain further assistance in coping upon reporting his observations in the safe place of our sessions.

Two memories had been surfacing recently. One memory was possibly his earliest and involved looking out of the window and watching his father running in a state of fear. He dated this memory to possibly as early as age three. He then spoke about another trauma wherein one of his older sisters had intentionally cut his body; he thought he was age four at the time. He was rather straightforward in describing these incidents, presenting little affect. And, unfortunately, the nature of the outpatient treatment setting meant that another impulsive client knocked on the door and inquired about a session, interrupting the moment.

SESSION 6, WEEK 3

Two days later, we returned to his traumatic memories, with my bringing it up. I provided brief education on the impact of his trauma, emphasizing the short-term goal of enhancing his coping. The goal was to give Mr. K. X. a cognitive and intellectual framework with which to understand his past trauma and what was happening to him; this would permit more adaptive cognitive coping as he thought about the legacy of what he had survived.

Delivering Psychoeducation on Trauma as Moments of Severe Overstimulation

I drew a schematic diagram depicting three key moments of trauma/over-stimulation as three spiked peaks on a timeline of his early life: (1) seeing his father run in fear at age three, (2) having his body cut by his sister at age four, and (3) witnessing the murder of his father at age seven (see figure 9.1). I explained how, as a result of these traumas, especially witnessing the murder of his father, he had subsequently experienced the spontaneous emergence of states of excitation, drawing another schematic diagram similar to the one in figure 9.2.

I also explained how, as human beings, "We do what we learn. We do what we see." I sought to explain the process of identification with the aggressor and Mr. K. X.'s subsequent pattern of being violent against others. Hence, it was no surprise that Mr. K. X. tended to cut or stab people, given his conditioning from two prior traumas. I further explained how his use of alcohol/marijuana might be an attempt at self-medicating/ameliorating states of physiological and emotional arousal (i.e., states of heightened aggression, fear, and sadness) that were the legacy of his experiences of traumatic overstimulation, pointing to the peaks in figure 9.2.

It was also my hope that this education I provided via the schematic diagram might help him to understand why he got high when he did in the past, and why he had gotten violent when he did in the past. There was more to it than just being provoked or finding cause for provocation in the real world. Instead, there were states that arose within him when he felt particularly prone to violence (e.g., states of heightened aggression, fear, and sadness); these were the spiked peaks in figure 9.2, suggesting the spontaneous reemergence of inner states of heightened aggression, fear, and sadness as the legacy of his childhood traumas, contributing to his perceiving a cause for being violent at that point in time.

An inner dynamic established by his early experiences of trauma (shown in figure 9.1) was serving to propel him to act out compulsively with violence, or to use alcohol/marijuana, especially at certain points in time (shown in figure 9.2) when some people in reality may have unwittingly been serving as triggers to provoke Mr. K. X.'s compulsive enactment of violence/relapse. At other times men, especially, could become triggers reminiscent of potential assaulters, leading Mr. K. X. to attack first. He was told he needed to be on guard for unconsciously expecting to be assaulted as he had seen his father assaulted and as his sister had attacked him out of the

Figure 9.1. The Early Life Trauma of Mr. K. X. Depicted as Three Moments of Severe Overstimulation

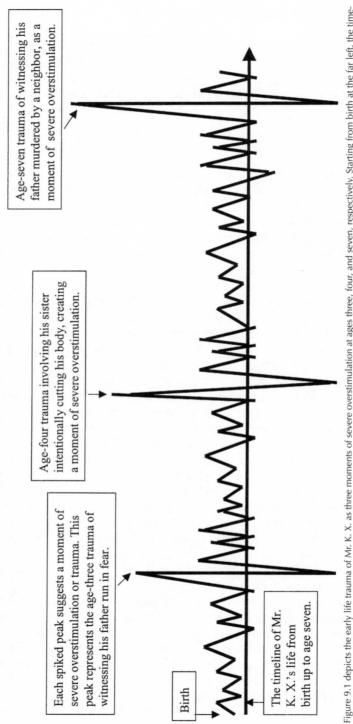

Age-seven trauma of witnessing his father murdered by a neighbor, as a moment of severe overstimulation.

Age-four trauma involving his sister intentionally cutting his body, creating a moment of severe overstimulation.

Each spiked peak suggests a moment of severe overstimulation or trauma. This peak represents the age-three trauma of witnessing his father run in fear.

Birth

The timeline of Mr. K. X.'s life from birth up to age seven.

Figure 9.1 depicts the early life trauma of Mr. K. X. as three moments of severe overstimulation at ages three, four, and seven, respectively. Starting from birth at the far left, the timeline of Mr. K. X.'s life reflects, initially, normal moments of frustration in life, perhaps as delays in caretakers' responding with sources of nutrition and nurturing, or separation anxiety. However, the first spiked peak represents his first significant trauma in life at age three. Moving further along in life, other normal frustrations occur. But, by age four, there is another trauma represented by a second spiked peak. Life proceeds with other normal experiences of frustration, until there is a third major trauma at age seven, symbolized by the third highest spiked peak. Each spiked peak represents an instance of overstimulation involving a state of heightened arousal wherein Mr. K. X. experienced within his self the most power affects (fear, sadness, anger) and impulses (aggression) ever to occur at such points in his life. A basic template was encoded in his psyche involving images of the trauma, as well as the affects and impulses mobilized within his self.

Figure 9.2.   The Legacy of Early Life Trauma for Mr. K. X.: Recurrent, Spontaneous States of Heightened Arousal

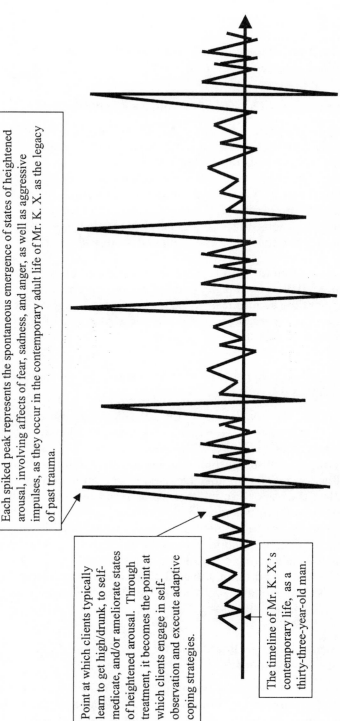

Each spiked peak represents the spontaneous emergence of states of heightened arousal, involving affects of fear, sadness, and anger, as well as aggressive impulses, as they occur in the contemporary adult life of Mr. K. X. as the legacy of past trauma.

Point at which clients typically learn to get high/drunk, to self-medicate, and/or ameliorate states of heightened arousal. Through treatment, it becomes the point at which clients engage in self-observation and execute adaptive coping strategies.

The timeline of Mr. K. X.'s contemporary life, as a thirty-three-year-old man.

Figure 9.2 depicts how Mr. K. X. suffers as an adult from recurrent states of heightened arousal represented by the peaks. Some peaks represent the spontaneous emergence of memories of past trauma, while others represent the moment of being triggered to respond with compulsive acting out of behavioral dramas derived from past exposure to trauma. In the case of Mr. K. X., this involves violent acting out, usually cutting people with knives. With the onset of a recurrent state of heightened arousal, clients typically learn to self-medicate/ameliorate distressing affects and overwhelming impulses with chemicals. The goal is to teach clients to execute adaptive coping responses (e.g., walking away, sitting down, repeating self-talk/self-calming exercise) at the moment wherein they self-medicated or acted out in the past, so that adaptive coping replaces past maladaptive coping. This goal is only reached if clients have attained a strengthened ego with the capacity to engage in self-observation/self-monitoring and interrupt/stop the moment of being triggered/spontaneous emergence of heightened states of arousal—just before the peak in the figure. Providing hope for his future, Mr. K. X. successfully accomplished the goal.

blue. Such expectations of assault could serve as a powerful prophecy, justi-fying any preemptive strike by Mr. K. X.

Insight into the Origins of a Lack of Feeling Safe and Secure

Also, one could see the earliest origins of his lack of feeling any safety or se-curity in the world, through his experience of seeing his father feeling vul-nerable and running in a state of fear, through his sister intentionally physi-cally injuring him, and especially in the murder of his father by a neighbor. Mr. K. X.'s experiences in therapy were reparative, helping him to believe that he could be safe in the world. If he found places to feel safe, such as in individual therapy sessions, this might generalize to other relationships and reduce his tendency to enter states of heightened arousal and expect violence to occur.

Mr. K. X. listened intently and seemed to understand. Only time would tell how and in what manner this new understanding might serve him. Ide-ally, this understanding would lead to new cognitions—such as "I can feel safe. I do not need to expect violence. I do not need to attack others first"—to replace those rooted in trauma.

The Goal of Engaging in Self-Calming in Response to Recurrent States of Heightened Arousal

My hope for Mr. K. X. was that the use of the self-talk/self-calming exercise "I am calm, centered, and balanced"—which he had come to diligently use as his main anger-management tool, along with walking away from situations—had the potential to replace self-medication and violent acting-out strategies. The goal was for this, essentially an affective, behavioral, and cognitive coping strategy, to replace the use of alcohol/marijuana to self-medicate/ameliorate the recurrent states of physiological and emotional arousal (i.e., states of heightened aggression, fear, and sadness) that originated from his early expe-riences of traumatic overstimulation. The goal was for this coping strategy to replace his compulsively acting out violence as a state of splitting. This goal was explained to him. In addition, the goal of his eventually learning to de-cide when he was calm enough to deliver a positive, assertive verbal response in some situations was also discussed.

The Goal of Initial Use of Avoidant Coping to Be Replaced Later by Positive Assertive Responses

Hence, the goal was to initially encourage what might be classified as avoidant coping (walking away from stressful interpersonal interactions; sit-ting in his room; and repeating, "I am calm, centered, and balanced"). How-ever, eventually this kind of avoidant coping would be replaced with active forms of coping in actual high-risk situations for a relapse to violence. This would include Mr. K. X.'s delivering positive, assertive verbal responses such as, "Man, let's just forget about it. It's not worth arguing about." He and another resident might even shake hands and move beyond the incident. But, initially, what might be classified as avoidant coping (walking away from stressful interpersonal interactions; sitting in his room; and repeating, "I am calm, centered, and balanced") was actually adaptive, whereas the release of anger and violent acting out was maladaptive.

SESSION 7, WEEK 4

In the seventh session, I was amazed at how calm Mr. K. X. appeared and how well he seemed to be doing. Perhaps he was starting to generalize a feeling of safety beyond our sessions and starting to believe he did not have to be in a state of hypervigilance, expecting violence and being ever ready for a preemptive strike against potential assaulters.

I asked Mr. K. X. about whether or not there had been any incidents in the residence. He spoke of one incident in which he had asked for a special privilege in the kitchen but was denied by the resident working that day. Mr. K. X. had responded to this fellow resident by saying, "I want what I want, and you can't give it to me. That's OK. Don't worry about it. I'll work out another solution." In fact, the other resident was a bit anxious and apologetic, as he expected Mr. K. X. to get angry and start a confrontation. However, Mr. K. X. was able to display a higher-order form of adaptive coping that might be considered active coping (as opposed to avoidance and walking away); he delivered a verbal response that was positive and assertive.

I positively reinforced Mr. K. X. in the session for how he had coped in this situation, stating "Excellent! You dealt really well with that situation." I pointed out how the goal was for him to be able to say how he felt in a variety of situations, including groups. Ideally, this was the best solution. But he still had to decide for himself whether or not he was calm enough to remain in the situation and attempt to talk, versus sensing that he was in danger of verbal abuse or violence and needed to walk away; sit in his room; and repeat, "I am calm, centered, and balanced."

Mr. K. X. indicated that he understood. He then volunteered how he had already started doing this. If anything in a group session in the residence upset him, he would merely sit in silence, appear to be paying attention, and repeat his self-talk/self-calming exercise silently within. Eventually, he was fully present in the group again, absorbing the material being discussed/ presented. In some groups, he was speaking up at such times and saying what he felt.

In another incident in a group in which the counselor saw that Mr. K. X. appeared tense and asked him what was going on, Mr. K. X. explained, "I'm not comfortable with everything going on in this room (an indirect reference to another male resident who was serving as a trigger for Mr. K. X.), but I'm all right. I can sit here and listen." Again, I delivered positive reinforcement, encouraging Mr. K. X. to continue to expand his repertoire of coping responses to common situations in the residence. What was emphasized was the most important thing: to not respond with verbal aggression, threats of violence, or actual violence, given the range of negative consequences and negative sanctions he could face. Mr. K. X. spoke of also using consequential thinking in such situations, reminding himself of what could happen and how he did not want to end up homeless or back in prison. In this manner, Mr. K. X. was making progress toward the goal of eventually replacing what might be considered avoidant coping (leaving high-risk situations before a relapse to violence) with active forms of coping while remaining in the actual high-risk situation.

Mr. K. X. also mentioned in passing that he had stopped smoking cigarettes and that this was his ninth day cigarette free, offering that he was wearing the patch. Based on my observations of many clients in the process of giving up cigarettes within residential treatment, I offered to him that he was doing extremely well and seemed to lack some of the irritability that was very common. He stated, "Believe me, Dr. Wallace, I get irritable." Yet it seemed important to repeat my observation, "Let me tell you, you are doing extremely well."

This brief interaction highlights the extent to which it is also important to reflect and mirror back to clients their strengths, evidence of resilience, and examples of actively and adaptively coping well on their own, as well as to reinforce them and support them, allowing the ego to gain further strength. This session also reflected the extent to which he had achieved stability and had successfully weathered the prior period of crisis when he was at risk of relapse to violence.

Treatment in Months Two through Seven

Mr. K. X. was reduced to once-per-week treatment, given that he was much improved after four weeks of intensive twice-per-week treatment that allowed him to reduce his risk of violent acting out. Success was attained with regard to the short-term goals of helping Mr. K. X. to achieve mental and emotional stability, deploy adaptive coping responses, avoid relapse to violence, and avoid sanctions in the residence from violent acting out, including the most severe sanction of discharge. Moreover, his adaptive coping responses were generalizing to a variety of situations, as well as undergoing greater sophistication. For example, positive, assertive verbal responses were starting to replace what he was initially taught to do—walk away, as an avoidant form of coping.

Microanalysis of a Relapse Episode

After I returned in early September from a four-week August vacation, Mr. K. X. shared that he had had a lapse to marijuana use on one occasion. This lapse allowed for the microanalysis of this incident for antecedents and determinants (see *Cognitive-Behavioral Therapy (CBT)/Relapse Prevention (RP)/Social-Skills Training (SST)* in table 9.1). The determinants of the relapse episode were identified, and a plan for how he would cope differently with these triggers in the future was formulated. The goal was to use the lapse as an opportunity to learn and plan a strategy for how he would cope differently in the future to prevent another lapse from occurring. A connection was found between his discontinuation of psychiatric medication; an increase in depression; not having individual sessions in which to talk about his depression, perhaps given my vacation; and his onetime use of marijuana. This resonated with our prior discussion of the role of the recurrence of states of heightened arousal—specifically aggression, fear, and sadness—in creating high-risk situations for relapse to both violence and alcohol/marijuana use. Beyond the figures we had examined together (see figures 9.1 and 9.2), this lapse made the point tangible for Mr. K. X. in reality, allowing this lapse to be transformed into an opportunity to learn about determinants of relapse and the relapse process, as well as how it might be avoided in the future.

Emphasis was placed on the importance of avoiding an initial relapse to medication noncompliance, as well as having a sponsor with whom he could talk. He admitted to secretly experimenting with discontinuation of his psychiatric medication and to how he never called and rarely saw his sponsor in Narcotics Anonymous.

Need for Progressive Development of an Identity as a Person with a Mental Disability

The relapse to medication noncompliance, depression, and then to marijuana use also reflected a bigger issue that needed to be addressed in treatment: Mr. K. X.'s need to make progress in accepting his mental disability and in developing an identity as a person with a disability. Appropriate interventions were delivered (*Integration of Motivational Interviewing, Stages of Change, and Identity Development Theory for a Diverse Identity Involving Race, Sexual Orientation, and/or Disability* in table 9.1).

Once-per-week sessions began to involve ongoing monitoring of his medication regime. We also discussed his concerns about medication side effects. A plan for medication monitoring was set up in the residential drug program. In addition to listening to these concerns, motivational interviewing sought to elicit other concerns about the possibilities of getting arrested and reincarcerated, being prematurely discharged from the residential program, and becoming homeless once again.

Dissonance was created, also, as I pointed out the discrepancy between his behavior and his valued goals. I stated, "On the one hand you want to avoid becoming homeless, getting arrested, and being reincarcerated, but on the other hand you still are not taking your Depakote correctly." I asked him, "What do you think you need to do?" He replied, "I guess, take my medication." But some ambivalence remained. Still, his internal motivation to take his medication and accept his mental disability was enhanced to some extent, in this manner. He was also encouraged to talk about medication side effects with his psychiatrist. The reality of his having to accept some initial degree of sedation from his medication was also discussed in our sessions; it was actually something from which he might benefit, helping to further reduce his risk of violent acting out.

Microanalysis of an Episode of Relapse to Alcohol Use

In October, one month later, Mr. K. X. had a lapse to one night of alcohol use at a party. "I was getting my groove on, Dr. Wallace," he explained, smiling, indeed beaming and waving his arms in the air. He was momentarily reliving dancing with a woman and hoping it might lead to sexual intimacy, something he had not had for the nearly six months he had been in the residential program. As was the routine in such instances, discussion proceeded to a microanalysis of this relapse episode, searching for the determinants. It became apparent that this second lapse to alcohol drinking involved the high-risk situation of a party where there was easy access to alcohol and desire for sexual intimacy. Parties with alcohol needed to be avoided. His decision to attend the party contrasted with the decision of one of the men in the residence who was like a newly found brother to him; this man had refused to attend the party, reflecting a better decision-making strategy.

Also discussed was how Mr. K. X. would have to learn how to be sexually intimate without the use of marijuana and alcohol. He had to learn to anticipate and cope in situations that might lead to sexual intimacy without the use of chemicals. The importance of learning to talk about one's feelings with a potential partner was emphasized, and I role modeled the kind of conversation that might precede sexual intimacy. The goal was to use interventions (*Cognitive-Behavioral Therapy (CBT)/Relapse Prevention (RP)/Social-Skills Training (SST)*) that would ensure that he had better interpersonal skills in the future, consistent with the goal of eventual successful pursuit of sexual intimacy. Also discussed were the recommendations from Alcoholics Anonymous/Narcotics Anonymous with regard to waiting until one has one year of abstinence before pursuing a relationship, and how he still needed to follow up with the task of finding a sponsor with whom he actually shared communication. It was unclear how soon Mr. K. X. would obtain a new sponsor, preferring instead to talk to his newly found brothers in recovery who lived in the residential facility with him.

This lapse also made clear how once a client is in a high-risk situation, having decided to not use avoidant coping (i.e., not go to the party), active forms of coping, including the deployment of socially appropriate verbal skills, are needed. Whether drink-refusal skills or verbal skills conducive to eventual sexual intimacy, Mr. K. X. still needed to learn, practice, and generalize to a variety of situations to appropriate positive, assertive verbal responses. Ideally, a male sponsor, who would be in his life for a long period of time, would be an additional person to whom Mr. K. X. could turn when he needed to devise positive, assertive verbal coping responses for active use in high-risk situations. However, Mr. K. X. still resisted my suggestion to obtain a real sponsor, repetitively referring to his newly found brothers in recovery.

A Case Conference Decision to Transfer Mr. K. X. to a MICA Residential Program

Despite the manner in which the two lapses of Mr. K. X. were used in our sessions as opportunities for learning about determinants and fostering more adaptive coping on his part, the treatment team felt it was time to take action and deliver more graduated sanctions. A staff member in the residence reported a recent increase in Mr. K. X.'s engaging in angry outbursts. The staff acknowledged how he had made much progress. He had a period of successfully walking away from potentially violent incidents, as well as of displaying the ability to talk to his peers and diffuse potentially violent situations. But there had also been recent deterioration in his functioning. This seemed to further substantiate my report about his relapse to medication noncompliance. The team felt compelled to recommend transfer to another eighteen-month residential program, one specifically for MICA clients.

Fostering Acceptance of His Disability and Transfer to a MICA Residence

It was very difficult to convince Mr. K. X. that he needed to enter a MICA residential program, requiring deployment of appropriate interventions (*Integration of Motivational Interviewing, Stages of Change, and Identity Development Theory for a Diverse Identity Involving Race, Sexual Orientation, and/or Disability*). He needed yet more assistance accepting his mental disability and further resolving his ambivalence about the reality of his condition. Also, other interventions (*An Integration of Motivational Interviewing and Stages of Change*) sought to help Mr. K. X. progress through stages of change from precontemplation—not even thinking about going into another residential program—to contemplation, preparation, and action stages, resulting in his finally taking action on this plan. But, ultimately, the strength of our therapeutic alliance and his trust in me and my judgment led to his agreeing to enter a

MICA program. This reflected gains in treatment by placing a *Special Focus on Building a Strong Therapeutic Alliance/Social Support Network (TASS).*

Phone calls were made, paperwork was completed, and interviews were arranged. Throughout the nearly month-long transfer process, Mr. K. X. stated repeatedly, "Only because you say so, Dr. Wallace." He complied with the intake interview, did nothing to sabotage it, and gained entrance into the residential MICA program. His brothers in recovery within his current residential program also supported this course of action, recommending that he pursue it. We all consistently explained to Mr. K. X. how, without such a program, he was in danger of relapsing to active addiction and violence; homelessness; and incarceration for drug possession, assault, or murder.

TREATMENT FROM MONTHS THIRTEEN TO FOURTEEN

Mr. K. X. was briefly seen in a series of five individual sessions approximately one year after he had first started treatment under my care. In fact, he went to great lengths to arrange his own referral. This reflected his use of positive, assertive verbal responses and active coping with events in his current life as he successfully negotiated gaining access to sessions with me. He was still in the MICA residential program, but was going through some stress associated with the departure of the primary counselor he had across his first five months in the residence; this was part of the rationale he used in negotiating access to sessions with me. Mr. K. X. managed to come with an escort to see me in the outpatient program. He came once per week, rescheduling twice because of time conflicts, having a total of seven sessions. I was able to get a clear picture of his progress up to that point in time.

The fact that his mental disorders (bipolar disorder, post-traumatic stress disorder, antisocial personality disorder) allowed him to function at a higher level than most of the schizophrenics in the MICA program led to Mr. K. X.'s moving up into leadership roles in the facility, boosting his self-esteem and self-efficacy. Staff became reliant upon him to be the responsible one in many situations. However, while seeing me, there was one relapse to verbal aggressiveness in response to the threatening provocation of a paranoid schizophrenic. Staff expected him to walk away in total silence and report such incidents to them, yet a one-line aggressive comment was delivered instead, and the other client reported it to staff. Mr. K. X. accepted his punishment in the MICA program. This, too, was analyzed in our individual session as a lapse to aggressiveness and was analyzed for determinants. He spoke of feeling repetitively annoyed by this woman across several incidents and wanting to intimidate her, actually thinking it was funny. The good news was that it was a lapse to verbal aggressiveness but not actual physical violence. However, Mr. K. X. autonomously engaged in consequential thinking and admitted that he did not want to risk losing the opportunity to obtain housing at the end of his MICA residential treatment stay. He received positive reinforcement for such thinking, as I stated, "Good. Please keep that in mind."

It turned out that Mr. K. X. was still in contact with his older sister, his adolescent daughter, and one of his newly found brothers from his prior residential facility. He and this "brother" enjoyed a warm friendship and shared a silly sense of humor. But, perhaps most importantly, Mr. K. X. was determined to continue to stay in the MICA residential facility, patiently waiting for the treatment outcome of his own newly renovated apartment for independent living. His fourteen-year cycle of repeated incarceration and risk of homicidal acting-out behavior seemed to be nearly broken, while he now had a fourteen-month period marked by two several-hour lapses, one to marijuana and one to alcohol. Over these fourteen months, he experienced a few lapses to verbal aggressiveness, but without violent acting-out behavior. This was an especially major victory.

My final assessment of Mr. K. X. was that he was evidencing good signs of medication adherence, accepting current side effects of weight gain, coping with interpersonal stress without acting out violently, and adaptively coping with living in a facility with clients who seemed to him to be much more ill than he, most of them having schizophrenia. His identity development was progressing well as one with a mental disability who needed to comply with his psychiatric-medication regime. This represented tremendous progress. But his main intrinsic motivation for remaining in the residential MICA program was to avoid ever going back to a correctional setting and to avoid the homelessness and street activities that would likely lead to reincarceration. Also, he was waiting to receive independent housing so that he could avoid homelessness upon leaving the residential setting.

Figure 9.3 summarizes the course of his treatment. The figure depicts what is also a typical course of treatment for clients in general. Adaptive coping comes to predominate, replacing prior maladaptive coping, even where a few lapses occur to addictive/problem behavior. This includes progress in replacing avoidant coping with active forms of coping, ideally involving positive, assertive verbal responses to ongoing stress in the social context.

◄►

COMMENTARY ON THE CASE OF MR. K. X.

The case of Mr. K. X. effectively illustrates the value in practitioners' placing a special focus on building a strong therapeutic alliance and social-support network, following the work of Lebow et al. (2002). Specifically, the strong therapeutic alliance established with Mr. K. X. seemed to be related to his successfully remaining in the residential treatment program and even entering a second MICA residential facility when good cause for a transfer arose. In addition, the strength of the therapeutic alliance seemed directly related

Figure 9.3. Timeline of Mr. K. X.'s Fourteen Months in Treatment: Enhanced Coping Over Time

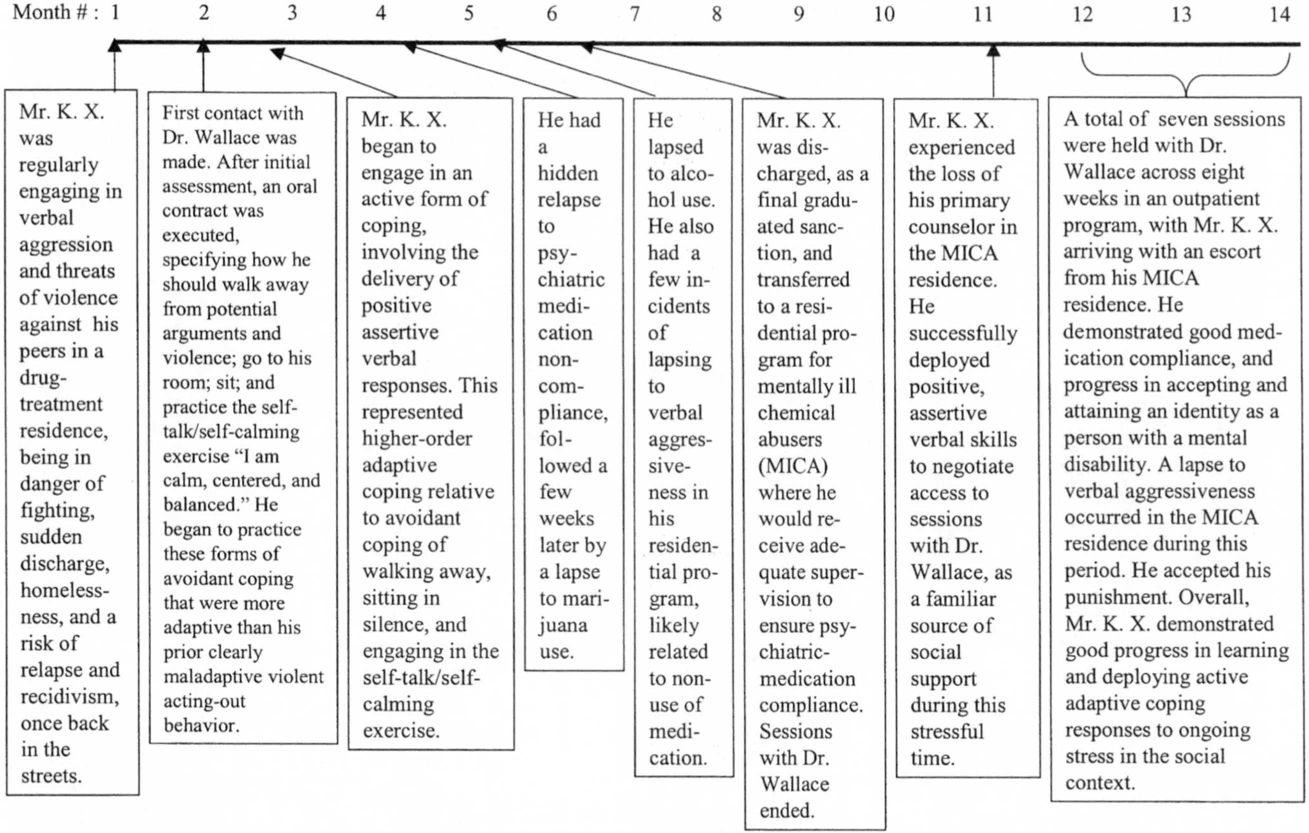

Month #: 1 2 3 4 5 6 7 8 9 10 11 12 13 14

Month 1:
Mr. K. X. was regularly engaging in verbal aggression and threats of violence against his peers in a drug-treatment residence, being in danger of fighting, sudden discharge, homelessness, and a risk of relapse and recidivism, once back in the streets.

Months 2–3:
First contact with Dr. Wallace was made. After initial assessment, an oral contract was executed, specifying how he should walk away from potential arguments and violence; go to his room; sit; and practice the self-talk/self-calming exercise "I am calm, centered, and balanced." He began to practice these forms of avoidant coping that were more adaptive than his prior clearly maladaptive violent acting-out behavior.

Months 4–5:
Mr. K. X. began to engage in an active form of coping, involving the delivery of positive assertive verbal responses. This represented higher-order adaptive coping relative to avoidant coping of walking away, sitting in silence, and engaging in the self-talk/self-calming exercise.

Months 6–8:
He had a hidden relapse to psychiatric medication noncompliance, followed a few weeks later by a lapse to marijuana use. He lapsed to alcohol use. He also had a few incidents of lapsing to verbal aggressiveness in his residential program, likely related to nonuse of medication.

Months 9–10:
Mr. K. X. was discharged, as a final graduated sanction, and transferred to a residential program for mentally ill chemical abusers (MICA) where he would receive adequate supervision to ensure psychiatric-medication compliance. Sessions with Dr. Wallace ended.

Month 11:
Mr. K. X. experienced the loss of his primary counselor in the MICA residence. He successfully deployed positive, assertive verbal skills to negotiate access to sessions with Dr. Wallace, as a familiar source of social support during this stressful time.

Months 12–14:
A total of seven sessions were held with Dr. Wallace across eight weeks in an outpatient program, with Mr. K. X. arriving with an escort from his MICA residence. He demonstrated good medication compliance, and progress in accepting and attaining an identity as a person with a mental disability. A lapse to verbal aggressiveness occurred in the MICA residence during this period. He accepted his punishment. Overall, Mr. K. X. demonstrated good progress in learning and deploying active adaptive coping responses to ongoing stress in the social context.

Figure 9.2 illustrates the typical process of clients' replacing maladaptive coping responses with adaptive ones, in addition to a few lapses. Despite these lapses, overall adaptive coping responses predominated, suggesting a positive long-term treatment outcome, even as Mr. K. X.'s characteristics will necessitate matching him to ongoing psychiatric care for many years to come.

to Mr. K. X.'s willingness to explore problems in treatment. His prior experience with a counselor who humiliated him supports the finding by Lebow et al. (2002) that when the therapist is more confrontational, the client is more likely to show negative in-treatment behavior; this is consistent with Mr. K. X.'s going so far as to secure a knife and plan to stab this counselor, and then having to run from police and discontinue that treatment episode.

The case of Mr. K. X. also follows the findings of Lebow et al. (2002) in showing how, when a stronger alliance is established, the client tends to experience less distress and more pleasant moods during treatment, as the sessions we shared became a place where Mr. K. X. was quite comfortable and relaxed, opening up to share what was going on with him. They also became something he enjoyed and toward which he looked forward. Sessions felt like a safe place. In sessions, he could receive assistance with stress related to events in his overall life context. Even though Mr. K. X. experienced two brief lapses to marijuana and alcohol, the case also supports the finding by Lebow et al. (2002) suggesting that when the therapist establishes a stronger alliance with the client, the client is more likely to abstain from alcohol and drugs during treatment and to show more improvement in patterns of use of other substances. Mr. K. X. even had a cigarette cessation attempt during treatment.

Lebow et al. (2002) also found a relationship between the treatment alliance and longer-term outcome. Consistent with this, the case of Mr. K. X. reflected how when the therapist establishes a stronger alliance with the client, the client tends to experience better outcomes related to substance use, given that he was followed up to month fourteen of his time in residential treatment placements and only had two brief lapses. The case also supports the finding that a strong treatment alliance may have an especially beneficial influence on specific subgroups of clients, such as those who have an antisocial personality or high levels of anger. Indeed, the case of Mr. K. X. makes this point as perhaps no other case could, given the extent of his history of violence and the strength of his aggressive impulses pressing for release.

However, important relationship factors include those in the broader treatment context, as Lebow et al. (2002) emphasize. The case of Mr. K. X. also supports the finding by Lebow et al. (2002) that when treatment programs create a stronger alliance with clients (i.e., are involving, supportive, and expressive), patients are more likely to remain in treatment and to have better in-program outcomes. The team present at case conferences seemed to reflect these elements that also seemed to permeate the residential program.

In addition, the case of Mr. K. X. seems to support the finding with regard to the following: when treatment programs create a stronger alliance with clients (that is, are involving, supportive, and expressive), clients are more likely to have more positive discharge and postprogram outcomes. This is certainly the case insofar as once Mr. K. X.'s transfer to a MICA program seemed necessary, the staff worked hard and found an appropriate MICA slot for him in a new modern residential facility. The staff kept Mr. K. X. in residence until the bed for him in the MICA residence was available, indeed keeping him for approximately another five weeks. He in no way could feel abandoned or kicked out. In this manner, Mr. K. X. was able to benefit from being in a treatment program that sensitively recognized the dynamic interplay between his psychiatric diagnoses, angry outbursts in the facility, depression, relapses to marijuana/alcohol, risk of recurrent homelessness, and risk of recidivism/reincarceration, showing support for him and involvement in his case in many ways.

While Lebow et al. (2002) emphasize that a good therapeutic alliance is a fundamental quality underlying effective treatment and has considerable impact on treatment engagement, treatment completion, and both short- and long-term outcome, they conclude that clients with social systems supportive of treatment are more likely to enter and complete treatment and achieve better outcomes. And, when family members are constructively engaged in treatment, client engagement and outcomes are also likely to be improved (Lebow et al., 2002). Thus, Lebow et al. (2002) highlight the role of the client's relationships with family and peers. From the very beginning of treatment, as the practitioner I worked with Mr. K. X. toward the goal of cultivating a social-support network, including his sister, other family, his daughter, and male peers in the facility. This is consistent with the finding of Lebow et al. (2002) that clients who indicate they receive general social support and support for reduced substance use during the time of treatment experience better treatment outcomes, while family involvement in treatment may help produce better outcomes. The role of his "brothers" in the program was also important in his recovery and was consistent with the finding that involving a supportive sponsor peer in treatment results in better outcomes. However, Moos (2003) asserts that there is no compelling reason to distinguish between the influence of informal (e.g., family, friend, spouse, AA sponsor) and formal (e.g., counselor, therapist) help.

Also pertinent is how both I, as the practitioner, and residential-program staff made extensive efforts to have Mr. K. X. obtain a new sponsor in either AA or NA—one with whom he had more regular contact. Yet he resisted complying fully with this recommendation. Again, he had come to rely on his "brothers" in the program. Yet the rationale for these efforts to foster meaningful connection with an AA or NA sponsor can be seen in the work of Lebow et al. (2002).

Beyond the manner in which the case of Mr. K. X. demonstrates the importance of practitioners' placing a special focus on building a strong therapeutic alliance and promoting client cultivation of a social-support network, yet more emerges. In sum, the case demonstrates the use of nearly all of the interventions taken from the menu of options, as shown in table 9.1, as well as the correct timing for their deployment across phases of treatment and recovery and stages of change. In this manner, what emerges is the role of a unified model—combining a multitude of evidence-based interventions—in ensuring that practitioners pay adequate attention to ongoing life-context factors impacting a client's life. Also, the role of a unified theory in providing a rationale for that which practitioners say and do emerges from the case, illustrating the role of numerous state-of-the-art practices that integrate theory. The result is a powerful framework that practically guides practitioners in devising client-treatment matching to varied interventions as treatment is tailored to meet individual client needs.

CONCLUSION

This chapter provided important training for practitioners, covering the creation of a strong therapeutic alliance and production of positive treatment outcomes. A case showed how practitioner attainment of genuine empathy, respect, and acceptance are a part of forging a strong therapeutic alliance. The case of Mr. K. X. served to illustrate the process of building the therapeutic alliance as it occurs in the real world with very difficult and challenging clients. The case also served to demonstrate the important role of a strong therapeutic alliance, family support, and a social-support network in helping to produce a favorable treatment outcome. The work of Lebow et al. (2002) was very helpful in establishing what constitutes an evidence-based approach for building a therapeutic alliance, as well as for developing the kind of social support that may contribute to a more positive treatment outcome. Practitioner assistance in helping a client cope with ongoing life-context factors, especially involving negotiating relationships with others, also emerged as vital in treatment. The unified model and theory also effectively led practitioner attention to ongoing life-context factors, resulting in the delivery of specific interventions.

The importance of practitioners' adapting the use of a number of evidence-based addiction-treatment interventions and recommended state-of-the-art practices in producing a positive treatment outcome, at least by month fourteen in a residential treatment setting, was also illustrated via the case of Mr. K. X. Finally, a table (table 9.1) summarized all the interventions used in his treatment, suggesting the manner in which a unified model and theory provided practitioners with a framework to guide service delivery.

It might be asserted that the case of Mr. K. X. is not an ideal one for demonstrating long-term positive treatment outcome, for he went from one residential treatment setting where he had two very brief relapses to another specialized MICA program where he attained fourteen months under my care in intermittent individual psychotherapy. Yet that is in essence what this book on making mandated addiction treatment work is all about—the real versus the ideal, and how to forge successful outcomes across the lifespan of

clients when reality dictates their becoming lost to follow-up. Instead, clients
have treatment careers. Clients in the real world are so very different from
those in research studies such as Project MATCH who are frequently selected according to strict criteria so that they would not have Mr. K. X.'s com-
plication of marijuana use in addition to his alcohol problem and homicidal
tendencies, and a great risk of reinvolvement in the criminal justice system
and rearrest. And, when evidence-based addiction treatments and recommended state-of-the art practices are deployed with clients such as Mr. K. X.
in the real world, sometimes the best that practitioners can do is overcome
obstacles so as to work with clients for *as much* or *as little* as fourteen months,
depending upon one's perspective.

   But, wherever Mr. K. X. may be, hopefully he knows that he represents the
"miracle" of recovery from a chronic pattern of recidivism and criminal behavior; violence; alcohol/marijuana dependence; and, to some extent, from
trauma. And hopefully he still believes that he will never become homeless
again and that he can always reach out for help, given what we shared as a
strong therapeutic alliance born of genuine empathy, respect, acceptance,
optimism, and the positive expectation that he need never again be alone,
stuck in the isolation of a hole in a prison setting.

10

◆

The Rationale for
Recommendations Put Forth
and What We Need to Know

As this book has established, community-based addiction treatment represents a national frontier for pioneering on the front lines and in the trenches the adaptation of evidence-based addiction treatment interventions with multiproblem clients who are diverse across a multitude of dimensions. This book provides practical guidance to practitioners with regard to how evidence-based interventions may be integrated, adapted, and tailored, given client backgrounds involving not only addiction, but also incarceration, ongoing criminal-justice-system supervision, performance of risky behaviors, histories of trauma across the lifespan, engagement in violence, psychiatric comorbidity, and a high risk of recidivism and relapse to more than one problem behavior. A distinction was made between those clients who enter treatment as either mandated, coerced, or concerned—those fearing negative consequences to drug/alcohol use and criminal involvement.

Not only practitioners, but all who come in contact with such clients within community-based addiction treatment have been given a guide for overcoming negative countertransference reactions toward clients, given the prevailing social conditioning within our current conservative, moralistic, intolerant era, which stigmatizes those involved with drugs. The book also plays an important role in moving society away from the current era that promoted criminal sanctions and zero tolerance, and in fostering the dawning and ascendance of a new era of rational and compassionate drug policy that restores the value of rehabilitation for drug offenders and relies upon mandates to evidence-based addiction treatment. Diverse readers within varied professions may find through this book a way to overcome social conditioning for intolerance and stigmatization, attaining to greater empathy for clients. This prepares readers for becoming more effective members of clients' social-support networks; and a strong social-support network is key to forging long-term positive treatment outcomes.

What is promoted through this book is the ideal of an integrated approach that combines criminal-justice supervision and involvement in community-based addiction treatment, effectively addressing concerns about both public safety and public health. Most importantly, within the recommended integrated model, there is an important role for contemporary practitioners within community-based addiction treatment who deliver services. A central feature of this book is the presentation of a menu of options containing a variety of treatment interventions having empirical support. The selections on the recommended menu of options have also been described as effective alternatives or effective psychosocial modalities derived from diverse ideologies. The evidence-based options share in common a very practical focus upon enhancing clients' competence in coping with daily life, developing clients' social skills, improving the match between clients' abilities and environmental demands, and altering reinforcement patterns in clients' community settings. However, in recognition of the role of expert practitioners in contributing the results of naturalistic longitudinal observations over the course of their work with clients, a recommended list of state-of-the-art practices was also added to the menu. The recommended state-of-the-art practices also reflect the extent to which practitioners find a rationale for that which they say and do with clients within integrated theory. Together, the evidence-based interventions and state-of-the-art practices move the field of addiction toward a unified model and theory to guide service delivery.

In demonstrating the process of adapting evidence-based interventions in the real world with multiproblem clients, and of drawing upon recommended state-of-the-art practices, I used a casebook approach. I drew, in particular, upon my experiences over the past six years, striving to implement with fidelity the most recent evidence-based addiction-treatment interventions. Multiple examples of what practitioners should actually say and do were thereby offered. In sum, the result of what has been presented constitutes a timely, essential, and practical guide to making mandated addiction treatment work at a time when no issue in the field of addiction treatment is more relevant than the one this book seeks to address: the management and disposition of those clients convicted of drug-related crimes who are flooding jails, prisons, probation/parole departments, and community-based addiction-treatment centers across the United States in historically unprecedented numbers—as McLellan (2003a) so characterized our current predicament.

RATIONALE FOR APPROACH TAKEN IN THIS BOOK

This book is absolutely unique in demonstrating the integration of so many evidence-based interventions and state-of-the-art practices, reflecting movement toward a unified model and theory as meaningful progress within the field of addiction treatment. A practitioner following what is offered in this book may risk the characterization, at worse, of being an "uninformed and undisciplined eclectic therapist" (Miller & Hester, 2003, p. 1). Or, at best, such a practitioner may benefit from the characterization of being adequately prepared for the heterogeneity of clients in the real world who are entering contemporary community-based addiction treatment in record numbers. To counter the risk of a practitioner's being characterized as an "uninformed and undisciplined eclectic therapist" (Miller & Hester, 2003), this book takes great care in rooting all that was recommended for practitioners to say and do in both evidence-based interventions and state-of-the-art practices.

In support of the contention that this book provides practitioners with adequate preparation, so that they are both informed and disciplined, Miller, Wilbourne, and Hettema (2003) point out the following: there "does not seem to be any one treatment approach adequate to the task of treating all individuals with alcohol problems" (p. 41), and hope arises in focusing on a menu of effective alternatives and selecting what seems most appropriate in order to meet individual client needs, characteristics, and preference. This includes assembling from the choices on the menu of effective alternatives, appropriate combinations of elements for each individual client. The resulting process of selecting combinations of treatments in service delivery— whether using specific interventions in whole or in part—results in clients' receiving integrated treatment interventions. Finally, the resulting integrated treatment must be tailored for individual clients in light of ongoing assessment findings ascertained over time.

A Rationale for Practitioners' Exercising Both Fidelity and Flexibility

Also underscored throughout the book is the critical role of practitioners in exercising both fidelity and flexibility, following Moos (2002). There are many reasons for this requisite fidelity and flexibility. This includes fidelity to what is recommended, given findings of what treatments are empirically supported, as well as flexibility in light of most practitioners' lacking the kind of resources available to those conducting grant-funded empirical research. Another reason for exercising flexibility includes the need to integrate and tailor treatment to meet an individual client's distinct pattern of presenting multiple problems, characteristics, and needs, including how they change over time. Practitioner flexibility is also required in order to accommodate clients' preferences, or what they are willing to do. Practitioner flexibility also reflects discovering what works or seems to work with clients who differ demographically from those clients in empirical trials of treatment interventions who tend to be homogenous, following from the strict inclusion and exclusion criteria common to such investigations.

Given the essential role of the social context and extratreatment factors in the recovery process, practitioners may also exercise critical flexibility in adapting treatment interventions over time in light of such factors. Instead of viewing such contextual variables as error variance or nuisance factors, as they might be viewed in randomized clinical trials of treatment interventions (Tucker, 1999), practitioners must exercise flexibility in adapting treatment for clients as extratreatment factors change and influence clients over time. The casebook approach used in this book effectively demonstrates this. This is very different from practitioners in the field of addiction merely following the medical model's use of the randomized clinical trial as the gold standard for efficacy research, as Tucker (1999) has pointed out. Instead, as the cases in this book show, practitioners have to respond to the reality that behavior "change is a process, not a discrete event, that typically unfolds over time and depends to a large degree on the surrounding context" (Tucker, 1999, p. 23).

Thus, this book also emphasizes the importance of performing ongoing individualized assessments of clients, searching for the influence of extratreatment factors, as well as how clients themselves are changing and have different needs, concerns, preferences, and characteristics at various points in time. The result is an emphasis on practitioners' having to consider clients' phases of treatment and stages of change, or where they are, as well as the correct timing for the delivery of interventions. This involved practitioner consideration of when to do what, or what should be addressed immediately versus later. In other words, practitioners have to consider whether to address what seems to be most urgent and most pressing or essential to address immediately in order to stabilize the client and increase the chances of forging a successful, positive long-term treatment outcome for a particular client, versus what seems to be less urgent and less pressing and may be delayed until later when the client is more stable or does not seem at risk of immediate relapse/recidivism. As discussion in this book underscores, the result is that practitioners have to follow a standard of care, actively considering when to do what given where the client is, what the client needs, and what the client is willing to do or prefers to do when in a particular phase of treatment/stage of change.

Rationale for Integrating Interventions

The practitioner task of making mandated addiction treatment work involves exercising both fidelity and flexibility and following the recommended standard of care; this is a delicate task. What must be kept in mind is the manner in which those who have pioneered evidence-based addiction-treatment interventions have also recommended that their approaches be integrated with other interventions, either in whole or in part. For example, Miller and Rollnick (2002) invited practitioners to integrate motivational interviewing with other interventions, perhaps using it as a prelude to another intervention, as a permeating counseling/communication style, or as a fallback option. Similarly, Marlatt (2001) suggested the benefits of integrating relapse prevention and contingency management, speculating that contingency management could be further enhanced if clients are provided with coping-skills training for relapse prevention, in light of research findings that cognitive and behavioral coping-skills training enhances long-term maintenance. And, the Matrix Model is a prime example of a scientifically supported integrated-treatment approach (NIDA, 1999; Rawson, Shoptaw, et al. 1995), combining a variety of interventions (i.e., individual sessions with a trained therapist, and involvement with a variety of groups such as early-recovery skills-training groups, social-support/weekend-leisure planning groups, relapse-prevention groups, and twelve-step groups).

There is support for the approach taken in this book, emphasizing not only the integration of evidence-based interventions, but also the value of intensiveness and extensiveness in treatment. For example, Hubbard, Craddock, and Anderson (2003) used one-year and five-year follow-up results from DATOS, discovering that there was a relationship between experiencing longer treatment durations—specifically six months or more in long-term residential and outpatient drug-free treatment—and positive treatment outcomes. Moos (2003) identified research supporting an emphasis on the importance that treatment be extensive, covering a substantial period of time. But there is also research evidence on how intensive treatment "with a range of components" may be required to retain some clients in treatment, such as those with serious mental illness, severe cocaine/crack use, or criminal involvement that increases the likelihood of clients' dropping out of treatment (NIDA, 1999, p. 17). And, as the cases used in this book illustrate, these are exactly the kinds of clients entering contemporary community-based addiction treatment in historically unprecedented numbers. Hence, there is a strong rationale for what is put forth in this book for making mandated addiction treatment work, recommending and illustrating via case examples the importance of integrating a range of components, specifically a number of evidence-based interventions and state-of-the-art practices, and doing so over an extended period of time.

When conceptualizing and executing service delivery for contemporary multiproblem clients—including when to do what given where the client is, what the client needs, and what the client is willing to do or prefers to do when in a particular phase of treatment/stage of change—an integrated treatment can easily draw upon nearly all of the items on the menu of evidence-based options and state-of-the-art practices put forth in this chapter. This is especially so because extratreatment factors change, and clients also change over time. On the other hand, there is a strong rationale in offering to clients every evidence-based intervention and state-of-the-art practice in order to maximize the chances of a positive treatment outcome, especially if the concepts of both intensiveness of treatment and extensiveness are adhered to in designing treatment.

For example, none can deny the importance of placing a *Special Focus on Building a Strong Therapeutic Alliance/Social-Support Network (TASS)*. However, this book makes a new contribution to the field of addiction treatment by raising TASS to the level of an evidence-based intervention, following the work of Lebow et al. (2002). What is also new in this book is a focus on practitioners' learning adaptive affective responses to the potential stress of working with the stigmatized population of criminal offenders with drug involvement. New guiding definitions were offered for respect and acceptance as adaptive affective responses, adding to the long-standing emphasis on attaining a genuine empathy for clients. The manner in which TASS, as conceived in this book, was used in every case is consistent with what is recommended for all practitioners in all interactions with clients, especially given the social climate of conservativism, moralism, intolerance, and resulting stigmatization of the client population. A special focus on TASS is absolutely essential, therefore, in making mandated addiction treatment work.

The evidence-based intervention *Motivational Interviewing/Motivational Enhancement Therapy (MET)/Brief Interventions* similarly emphasizes practitioner empathy (Miller & Rollnick, 1991, 2002) and deserves to be a part of the treatment of every potential client in community-based addiction treatment. This is especially so given the options of using motivational interviewing as a prelude to the delivery of interventions, of integrating it with other interventions, or of using it as a permeating counseling/communication style or as a potential fallback option. However, what is new in this book is placing a special emphasis on how motivational interviewing plays a central role in work with clients who are mandated or coerced into treatment. In particular, extrinsic motivation from external pressure to enter and remain in treatment should be augmented with and/or eventually replaced by intrinsic motivation to change, something for which motivational interviewing is uniquely suited. Cases in this book serve to illustrate this use of motivational interviewing as a brief intervention (see the cases of Ms. F. W. in chapter 6 and Mr. F. T. in chapter 7). Moreover, at any point in treatment when ambivalence arises in a client, the fallback option of motivational interviewing becomes a vital tool to help the client move beyond it, renew commitment to change, and foster an enhanced internal motivation for pursuing further change (see cases of Ms. M. T. in chapter 8 and Mr. K. X. in chapter 9).

Similarly, it almost seems unethical at this point in time within the field of addiction treatment to deliver services within community-based addiction treatment and not include *Cognitive-Behavioral Therapy (CBT)/Relapse Prevention (RP)/Social-Skills Training (SST)*. Practitioners face an imperative to teach clients how to anticipate high-risk situations for relapse in advance, as well as to foster the ability to effectively and successfully cope when and if those situations are encountered. Thus, it is inconceivable that any viable addiction treatment would not integrate elements of CBT/RP/SST at some point in treatment (ideally, relatively early on), given the need to prevent relapse (often to more than one addictive/problem behavior), as well as recidivism. If one practitioner delivering individual sessions is not focusing on teaching CBT/RP/SST, another practitioner, perhaps within a group format, must be delivering CBT/RP/SST. However, even the practitioner in individual sessions has an obligation to draw upon and link the client's growing knowledge base to specific incidents that arise in session, carefully ensuring that the client is adequately prepared to prevent relapse/recidivism. And, if a relapse does occur, it is ideally the practitioner conducting individual sessions who may have the time to carefully review what happened in order to identify the determinants of the lapse/relapse and to help the client devise a strategy for coping with that high-risk situation again in the future. But, when such a microanalysis of the relapse episode, or review of the episode in search for determinants, does occur in a group setting, it represents an opportunity for all group members to learn. Thus, every case in this book included the use of CBT/RP/SST.

Many practitioners acknowledge with regard to each individual client what the client needs and what the client is willing to do or prefers to do, often leading to modifications to the recommendation for practitioners to deploy some form of *Twelve-Step Facilitation (TSF)/Guidance Using Alcoholics and/or Narcotics Anonymous*. Some clients do not like references to God or a higher power, as is common in Alcoholics Anonymous (AA) and Narcotics Anonymous (NA), rejecting this item on the menu of evidence-based options. Perhaps most importantly, practitioners must adjust their own thinking with regard to AA/NA and appreciate the evidence that participation can contribute to a positive treatment outcome, especially if clients receive guidance and support in how to utilize this resource. However, it is now a standard practice within community-based addiction treatment to provide such guidance and support to clients, even including some AA/NA meetings on the actual site of the treatment program, facilitating for clients great ease in introduction to this valuable community resource. Every case presented in this book includes encouragement and guidance with regard to participation in AA/NA.

As evidence-based interventions, *Individual Drug Counseling (IDC) and/or Supportive-Expressive Psychotherapy (SEP)* also find a valuable role in contemporary community-based addiction treatment as absolutely essential elements. Literally all clients should have at least once-per-week IDC with a practitioner, if not twice-per-week sessions, particularly if clients have had a recent relapse or are still actively using drugs/alcohol. Clients presenting comorbidity, problems with recurrent relapse/recidivism or histories of trauma may also need once-per-week SEP, and possibly twice-per-week SEP when negotiating a serious crisis. Through receipt of SEP, clients receive support in talking about their personal experiences, such as the details of what happened before and during a painful relapse; assistance in improving the regulation of their interpersonal behavior, especially in valued relationships; and help in improving the regulation of their affects, including having a safe space in which to process painful affects. Many contemporary multiproblem clients present sufficient comorbidity or problems in self-regulation of affects, impulses, and interpersonal behavior to justify adding SEP to their receipt of IDC. Thus, it is hard to imagine not deploying IDC with every client, while many multiproblem clients, especially those with comorbidity, need SEP.

With regard to the *Community Reinforcement Approach (CRA)/Vouchers: Contingency Management (CM)*, it is no surprise that practitioners are not routinely expected to be able to adapt in full the use of the evidence-based CRA (with vouchers) in light of insufficient resources and the difficulty of im-plementing such an approach within most community-based addiction-treatment programs. However, given the recommended ideal of an integrated model that combines community-based addiction treatment with criminal-justice-system supervision, it will be routine for probation/parole officers and others supervising clients (e.g., judges) to be in a position to apply graduated sanctions; this suggests the reality that contingency management is typically a routine part of treatment in an integrated model. This book also codifies as four principles a guide for how to best execute and manage contingency contracting. And this book takes a novel approach in introducing five recommended oral contingency contracts for execution at the time of intake into community-based addiction treatment in order to enhance the motivation of clients to comply with common directives for clients presenting comorbidity or dangerous psychiatric symptoms. Creative adaptations of contingency management seem essential to effective community-based addiction treatment, specifically in order to make mandated addiction treatment work. Every case in this book illustrates the varied uses of contingency contracting and how graduated sanctions could potentially be applied in the lives of clients.

Perhaps the case for integrating different treatment interventions is made in the most compelling manner via the recommendation that all clients in community-based addiction treatment need to participate in a program that to some degree approaches an evidence-based gold standard: *The Matrix Model—Or, a Day-Treatment Approach, or an IEC Outpatient Model That Is I for Intensive (4–5 days per week), E for Extensive (6–12 months), and C for Comprehensive (TASS, CBT/RP, IDC, GDC, drug testing, etc.).* The Matrix Model provides the strongest justification for practitioners' doing their very best to make sure clients receive a treatment package that combines multiple elements. Every case in the book illustrated how clients, whether outpatient or residential, were participating in an IEC program akin to the Matrix Model.

Integrated Theory Provides a Rationale
for What Practitioners Say and Do

This book makes a novel contribution in illustrating how practitioners find a rationale in integrated theory for that which they say and do in community-based addiction treatment. Practitioners need to follow a standard in which at any given moment they can articulate the theory in which any intervention delivered at any point in time is based. This follows a standard articulated by others (Pine, 1990; Wallace, 1996a) and followed in this book. Imagine sitting as a practitioner when a supervisor enters a group or individual session and taps you on the shoulder intermittently, asking, "What is the rationale for the intervention you just delivered? In what theory do you find a rationale for what you just said and did with this client?" It takes a great deal of discipline to be able to function in such a way that a practitioner always knows in which theory a rationale for interventions delivered may be found. And each time the practitioner is tapped on the shoulder and asked such questions, the answer may vary, given the multitude of theories available for drawing upon in devising a rationale for the delivery of interventions. To be able to function in this way would be the opposite of being an "uninformed and undisciplined eclectic therapist" (Miller & Hester, 2003, p. 1).

A unique strength of this book involves a casebook approach, including a lengthy presentation of several cases and discussion showing at which points in time I, as the practitioner, had in mind a particular theory that provided a rationale for what I said and did in delivering a specific evidence-based intervention. This serves to powerfully illustrate the role of multiple theories in providing a rationale for the selection and delivery of varied interventions designed specifically to address multiproblem clients' needs, characteristics, diversity, and preferences as they manifest and change over time.

And, precisely because contemporary clients are so very diverse, presenting multiple problems as well as complex needs and characteristics, including comorbidity, and having more than one addictive/problem behavior, multiple theories have been integrated and drawn upon in this book in order to accomplish positive long-term treatment outcome: *Integration of Motivational Interviewing and Stages of Change; Integration of Stages of Change and Phases of Treatment and Recovery; Integration of Harm Reduction, Moderation Approaches, and Abstinence Models; Integration of Psychoanalytic and Cognitive-Behavioral Theories and Techniques; Acquisition of Affective, Behavioral, and Cognitive Coping Skills—Learning New ABCs; Integration of Motivational Interviewing, Stages of Change, and Identity Development Theory for a Diverse Identity Involving Race, Sexual Orientation, and/or Disability;* and *Incorporating Contemporary Trends in Psychology: Multiculturalism, Positive Psychology, the Strengths-Based Approach, and Optimistic Thinking/Learned Optimism.* Moreover, the integrated theories drawn upon in providing a rationale for what practitioners should say and do during service delivery are also recommended state-of-the-art practices.

WHAT DO WE NEED TO KNOW?

Moos (2003) acknowledges that, despite substantial progress over the past thirty years of research, there are things that we do not know about (1) the structure and process of treatment, (2) the content of treatment, (3) treatment outcome, and (4) the context of addictive disorders. Moos (2003) refers to these as "seven puzzles" requiring attention in future research. The seven puzzles are presented in table 10.1.

As shown in this table, the unresolved puzzles involve the following: puzzle 1—how can we best conceptualize and examine service episodes and treatment careers?; puzzle 2—what is the role of the health-care work environment in treatment process and outcomes and in enhancing clinicians' morale and openness to innovations in treatment delivery?; puzzle 3—how can we better understand the connections among the theory, process, and outcome of treatment?; puzzle 4—how can we identify effective patient-treatment-matching strategies?; puzzle 5—how should we organize and sequence treatment for patients with dual disorders, such as patients with substance-use disorders and major depression or post-traumatic stress disorder?; puzzle 6—how can we integrate formal substance-abuse treatment and patients' involvement and participation in self-help groups?; and puzzle 7—how can we develop more unified models of the role of life-context factors, and formal and informal care, in the recovery process? These puzzles are worth considering in preparing practitioners for the task before them in delivering services in community-based addiction treatment. Practitioners pioneering across this nation the adaptation of evidence-based interventions on the front lines and in the trenches with contemporary challenging multi-problem clients may provide invaluable insight in the resolution of these puzzles, leading to important future directions in research.

This book assists practitioners in understanding how service episodes and treatment careers operate, as illustrated in the cases of Ms. M. T. and Mr. K. X., who experienced sequential treatment in different program settings. In terms of the connections between the theory and the process of treatment, this book is unique in using a casebook approach and literally pointing out at which points in the process of delivering treatment a rationale for what I said and did as the practitioner was rooted in theory (i.e., one of the seven state-of-the-art practices). With regard to the ongoing search for effective client-treatment-matching strategies, this book has contributed the understanding that the practitioner's performance of an ongoing assessment across phases of treatment/stages of change guides the process of matching clients to specific treatment interventions. Thus, even as Project MATCH (1997a, 1997b, 1998a, 1998b, 2001) may not have provided clear answers about client matching in the real world, practitioners must continue to use ongoing assessment findings in order to select specific interventions for delivery to clients. And, as the cases in this book powerfully illustrate, in the

Table 10.1. Moos's (2003) Seven Puzzles: What Do We Need to Know?

Puzzle 1: How can we best conceptualize and examine service episodes and treatment careers? Comparative studies of outcome typically consider only one segment of care (e.g., a specific course of residential or outpatient treatment), but almost all clients obtain packages of services (both substance-abuse and psychiatric care), or have episodes of care (greater than nine months) that encompass more than one setting (inpatient/residential and outpatient), modality (individual, group, and day treatment), and orientation. Over time, multiple service episodes merge and become treatment careers.

Puzzle 2: What is the role of the health-care work environment in treatment process and outcomes and in enhancing clinicians' morale and openness to innovations in treatment delivery? The work environment impacts provider satisfaction and performance, but little is known about how these, including providers' beliefs, relate to quality of treatment for clients, nor about the best way to alter problematic aspects of the work milieu. Staff members in supportive and goal-directed work environments were more likely to espouse disease-model beliefs/twelve-step orientation, and their clients received more services, were more involved in self-help groups, were more satisfied with treatment, improved more during treatment, and were more likely to participate in continuing care.

Puzzle 3: How can we better understand the connections among the theory, process, and outcome of treatment? Comparative evaluations of effectiveness neglect processes underlying the effects of different modalities, rarely providing information about how treatment works, for whom it works or does not work, or how it can work better, etc. Outcomes may be a function of common conditions across treatments (e.g., a factor in both twelve-step and CBT). There is a need to focus on and develop theories about common aspects of treatment (e.g., the alliance, goals, duration of care) and how specific combinations of conditions work.

Puzzle 4: How can we identify effective patient-treatment matching strategies? Key variables in client-treatment matching have eluded researchers, but promise is shown in the following: matching strategies based on clients' cognitive and psychosocial functioning (e.g., the functionally able versus the impaired); targeting services to address clients' specific problems; and problem-service matching that focuses on clients' life contexts (e.g., influence of peers).

Puzzle 5: How should we organize and sequence treatment for patients with dual disorders, such as patients with substance-use disorders and major depression or post-traumatic stress disorder? Dual disorder clients have poorer overall outcomes, and less is known about effective treatment for this group. Integrated care (combined substance-abuse and psychiatric care tailored for clients with comorbid disorders) seems most effective. But, what are the critical components? Can a single practitioner handle both disorders? And, if not, how can we best coordinate care?

Puzzle 6: How can we integrate formal substance-abuse treatment and patients' involvement and participation in self-help groups? Recovery-focused self-help groups and twelve-step facilitation (which encouraged self-help group involvement) produce positive outcomes, but AA participation may not add benefit to behavioral treatment. Also, is intensity (e.g., ninety meetings in ninety days), duration of participation, or the strength of relationship with a sponsor (a common factor) more important? And, what about the risk of subservience or isolation?

Puzzle 7: How can we develop more unified models of the role of life-context factors, and formal and informal care, in the recovery process? Ongoing life-context factors, formal treatment, and self-help groups need to be placed in a unified model to understand these apparently disparate contexts in terms of their underlying dimensions and dynamics—that is, the domains of (1) quality of interpersonal relationships, (2) person growth goals, and (3) level of structure; and the power of anything falling under one of these three domains depends on the relative emphasis on the others. We need to learn more about how formal treatment and self-help groups substitute for, amplify, or diminish the influence of other contexts.

real world, where the treatment process involves a multitude of discrete points in time, practitioners typically end up matching clients to different treatment interventions at different points in time, tailoring treatment for clients. This is because clients' characteristics and needs change over time, and some needs may require immediate attention, while others are less urgent and may be addressed later. This critical finding of what is needed when, depending upon where the client is, reflects how practitioners may contribute much from naturalistic longitudinal observations of the treatment process. This suggests a far more complex and fluid treatment process in the real world—one that may be very hard to scientifically evaluate and substantiate in a randomized clinical trial likely to exclude the kinds of multiproblem clients described in this book.

This book has also contributed to resolving the puzzle of how treatment should be organized and sequenced for clients with dual disorders/comorbidity. The case examples illustrate what was recommended, emphasizing how an important short-term goal is to stabilize clients emotionally and mentally, securing appropriate psychiatric treatment and medication, even executing oral contingency contracts with clients to enhance motivation to seek and remain under psychiatric care. Thus a very novel approach is taken with regard to ensuring that clients understand the importance of their both securing and remaining under the care of a psychiatrist across the course of their involvement in a community-based addiction-treatment program. Thus, addressing dual disorders/comorbidity is prioritized as vital to successful long-term recovery, and great care is taken by practitioners in supporting clients in learning how to adjust to their mental disorder(s), even facilitating progress in establishing an identity as a person with a mental disability. This focus on fostering identity development for those with a disability is also novel within the field of addiction treatment.

The cases in this book all illustrate how I, as the practitioner, sought to coordinate care for clients in light of clients' dual disorders/comorbidity, while individual assessment findings were key in determining how to organize and sequence care. The case of Mr. F. T., for example, illustrated when receipt of psychiatric care and stabilization on appropriate psychiatric medication absolutely needed to precede entrance into outpatient community-based addiction treatment. Once Mr. F. T. was stable on psychiatric medication, it was then safe to allow him to follow his preference for receipt of outpatient addiction treatment in a setting of his choice. On the other hand, the case of Ms. M. T. illustrated how greater practitioner flexibility was exercised and a parallel, simultaneous process was envisioned; the goal was for the simultaneous parallel receipt of both outpatient community-based addiction treatment and psychiatric treatment. However, there were unfortunate delays in Ms. M. T.'s securing psychiatric treatment.

The case of Mr. K. X. also showed how the goal was for parallel receipt of psychiatric and addiction treatment. Also, problems with ensuring psychiatric-medication compliance and difficulty in the client's accepting a new identity as a person with a mental disability were illustrated. Finally, the case of Mr. K. X. served to underscore how some clients with dual disorders need to be placed in a specialized program for mentally ill chemical abusers, where all services are delivered in an integrated fashion in one setting.

The cases also allow readers to witness the decision-making process of a practitioner, with regard to addressing clients' past experiences of trauma, following individual assessment findings. Specific guidelines for the correct timing for delivery of interventions to survivors of trauma were also offered. The importance of initially delivering educational and coping-skills interventions to enhance clients' coping is underscored, while simultaneously putting forward addressing trauma and addiction in an integrated model, being consistent with standard recommendations in the field. However, the individual cases show the critical role of a client's individual assessment findings, as practitioners exercised flexibility and tailored the approach to a client's past trauma as seen fit.

Toward a Unified Theory and Model Encompassing Life-Context Factors

In terms of the goal of developing a unified model and theory that can encompass both life-context factors and treatment within a common framework, this book makes an invaluable contribution. First, this book moves toward a unified model by creating an integrated treatment that draws upon the evidence-based interventions available in the social context. Second, this book advances the field toward a unified theory by identifying state-of-the-art practices that provide a rationale for each and every intervention delivered in a course of treatment. Third, the book's menu of evidence-based options and state-of-the-art practices effectively directs practitioners to attend to life-context factors and the treatment process across phases of treatment/stages of change, all within a common framework. The framework that this book provides for practitioners systematically considers both life context and treatment, especially as per discussion in chapter 5 and the material summarized in table 5.1. In fact, practitioners are urged to assist clients in regard to enhancing their coping skills in relation to specific tasks they face in the social context (e.g., developing and maintaining successful relationships with parole/probation officers, judges, family and community members, children, AA/NA sponsors, and psychiatrists).

Finally, part of what we need to know is whether or not there is value in what has been put forth in this book, in terms of treatment outcome for clients who are treated by practitioners using the unified model and theory. The imperative to provide a meaningful response to the current rise in mandated, coerced, and concerned clients entering community-based addiction treatment suggests a vital need for what has been put forth in this book.

Only time and the experiences of a multitude of practitioners on the front lines and in the trenches of community-based addiction treatment who systematically collect naturalistic longitudinal observations and provide feedback to researchers will help to determine the value of what this unique book contributes with regard to the task of making mandated addiction treatment work.

References

Acierno, R., Coffey, S. F., & Resnick, H. S. (2003). Introduction to the special issue: Interpersonal violence and substance use problems. *Addictive Behaviors, 28*, 1529–32.

Adler, J. L., Richter, S. S., Lorenz, A. R., & Hochhausen, N. M. (2002, August 25). *Designing a comprehensive and empirically sound chemical dependency treatment system.* Symposium presented at the 110th convention of the American Psychological Association, McCormick Place, Lakeside Center, Chicago, IL.

American Psychiatric Association. (2000). *Diagnostic and statistical manual of mental disorders* (4th ed., text rev.). Washington, DC: Author.

American University. (2000). *Drug court activity update: Summary.* Washington, DC: U.S. Department of Justice, Office of Justice Programs, Drug Court Clearinghouse.

Anderson, B. K., & Larimer, M. E. (2002). Problem drinking and the workplace: An individualized approach to prevention. *Psychology of Addictive Behaviors, 16*(3), 243–51.

Anglin, M. D. (1988). The efficacy of civil commitment in treating narcotic addiction. In C. G. Leukefeld & F. M. Tims (Eds.), *Compulsory treatment of drug abuse: Research and clinical practice* (pp. 8–34). Bethesda, MD: National Institute on Drug Abuse.

Anglin, M. D., & Hser, Y. (1990). Treatment of drug abuse. In M. H. Tonry and J. Wilson (Vol. Eds.), *Crime and justice: A review of research: Vol. 13. Drugs and crime* (pp. 393–460). Chicago: University of Chicago Press.

Anglin, D. M., Longshore, D., & Turner, S. (1999). Treatment alternatives to street crime. *Criminal Justice and Behavior, 26*, 168–95.

Anglin, M. D., Longshore, D., Turner, S., McBride, D., Inciardi, J., & Prendergast, M. (1996). *Studies of the functioning and effectiveness of treatment alternatives to street crime (TASC) programs* (Final report). Los Angeles: UCLA Drug Abuse Research Center.

Aspinwall, L. G., & Staudinger, U. M. (Eds.). (2003). *A psychology of human strengths: fundamental questions and future directions for a positive psychology.* Washington, DC: American Psychological Association.

Aubrey, L. L. (1998). *Motivational interviewing with adolescents presenting for outpatient substance abuse treatment.* Unpublished doctoral dissertation, University of New Mexico.

Auerhahn, K. (2002). Selective incapacitation, three strikes, and the problem of the aging prison populations: Using simulation modeling to see the future. *Criminology and Public Policy, 1*(3), 353–88.

Austin, J., Clark, J., Hardyman, P., & Henry, A. D. (1999). The impact of 'three strikes and you're out.' *Punishment and Society, 1*(2), 131–62.

Back, S., Dansky, B. S., Carroll, K., Foa, E. B., & Brady, K. T. (2001). Exposure therapy in the treatment of PTSD among cocaine dependent individuals: Description of procedures. *Journal of Substance Abuse Treatment, 21,* 35–45.

Baker, A., Boggs, T. G., & Lewin, T. J. (2001). Randomized controlled trial of brief cognitive-behavioral interventions among regular drug users of amphetamine. *Addiction, 96,* 1279–87.

Ball, J. C., & Ross, A. (1991). *The effectiveness of methadone maintenance treatment.* New York: Springer-Verlag.

Bandura, A. (1997). *Self-efficacy: The exercise of control.* New York: W. H. Freeman Company.

Barrowclough, C., Haddock, G., Tarrier, N., Lewis, S. W., Moring, J., O'Brien, R., Schofield, N., & McGovern, J. (2001). Randomized controlled trial of motivational interviewing, cognitive behavior therapy, and family intervention for patients with comorbid schizophrenia and substance use disorders. *American Journal of Psychiatry, 158,* 1706–13.

Bates, M. E., Labouvie, E. W., & Voelbel, G. T. (2002). Individual differences in latent neuropsychological abilities at addictions treatment entry. *Psychology of Addictive Behaviors, 16*(1), 35–46.

Battjes, R. J., & Carswell, S. B. (2002). Federal drug-abuse treatment research priorities. In C. J. Leukefeld, F. Tims, & D. Farabee (Eds.), *Treatment of drug offenders: Policies and issues* (pp. 348–61). New York: Springer.

Battle, C. L., Zlotnick, C., Najavits, L. M., Gutierrez, M., & Winsor, C. (2003). Post-traumatic stress disorder and substance use disorder among incarcerated women. In P. Ouimette & P. J. Brown (Eds.), *Trauma and substance abuse: Causes, consequences, and treatment of comorbid disorders* (pp. 209–26). Washington, DC: American Psychological Association.

Belenko, S. (1999). Research on drug courts: A critical review: 1999 update. *National Drug Court Institute Review, 2*(2), 1–58.

Belenko, S. (2002). Drug courts. In C. J. Leukefeld, F. Tims, & D. Farabee (Eds.), *Treatment of drug offenders: Policies and issues* (pp. 301–18). New York: Springer.

Belenko, S., & Logan, T. K. (2003). Delivering more effective treatment to adolescents: Improving the juvenile drug court model. *Journal of Substance Abuse Treatment, 25,* 189–211.

Benda, B. B. (2001). Factors that discriminate between recidivists, parole violators, and nonrecidivists in a 3-year follow-up of boot camp graduates. *International Journal of Offender Therapy and Comparative Criminology, 45*(6), 711–29.

Benda, B. B., Corwyn, R. F., & Rodell, D. E. (2001). Alcohol and violence among youth in boot camps for non-violent offenders. *Alcoholism Treatment Quarterly, 19*(1), 37–55.

Benda, B. B., Toombs, N. J., & Peacock, M. (2002). Ecological factors in recidivism: A survival analysis of boot camp graduates after three years. *Journal of Offender Rehabilitation, 35*(1), 63–85.

Bien, T. H., Miller, W. R., & Boroughs, J. M. (1993). Motivational interviewing with alcohol outpatients, *Behavioral Psychotherapy, 21,* 347–56.

Bigelow, G. E., & Silverman, K. (1999). Theoretical and empirical foundations of contingency management treatments for drug abuse. In S. T. Higgins & K. Silverman (Eds.), *Motivating behavior change among illicit-drug abusers: Research on contingency management interventions* (pp. 15–31). Washington, DC: American Psychological Association.

Botvin, G. J., Scheier, L. M., & Griffin, K. W. (2002). Preventing the onset and developmental progression of adolescent drug use: Implications for the gateway hypothesis. In D. B. Kandel (Ed.), *Stages and pathways of drug involvement: Examining the gateway hypothesis* (pp. 115–38). New York: Cambridge University Press.

Brecht, M. L., Anglin, M. D., & Wang, J. C. (1993). Treatment effectiveness for legally coerced versus voluntary methadone maintenance clients. *American Journal of Drug and Alcohol Abuse, 18,* 89–106.

Brecht, M. L., O'Brien, A., von Mayrhauser, C., & Anglin, M. D. (2004). Methamphetamine use behaviors and gender differences. *Addictive Behaviors, 29,* 89–106.

Breslin, J. J., & Skinner, H. (1999). Critical perspectives on the transtheoretical model and stages of change. In J. A. Tucker, D. M. Donovan, & G. A. Marlatt (Eds.), *Changing addictive behavior: Bridging clinical and public health strategies* (pp. 160–90). New York: Guilford Press.

Broner, N., Borum, R., & Gawley, K. (2002). Criminal justice diversion of individuals with co-occurring mental illness and substance use disorders: An overview. In. G. Landsberg, M. Rock, L. K. W. Berg, & A. Smiley (Eds.), *Serving mentally ill offenders: Challenges and opportunities for mental health professionals* (pp. 83–106). New York: Springer.

Broner, N., Borum, R., Whitmire, L., & Gawley, K. (2002). A review of screening instruments for co-occurring mental illness and substance use in criminal justice programs. In G. Landsberg, M. Rock, L. K. W. Berg, & A. Smiley (Eds.), *Serving mentally ill offenders: Challenges and opportunities for mental health professionals* (pp. 289–337). New York: Springer.

Bronstein, P., & Quina, K. (Eds.). (2003). *Teaching gender and multicultural awareness: Resources for the psychology classroom.* Washington, DC: American Psychological Association.

Brown, J. M., & Miller, W. R. (1993). Impact of motivational interviewing on participation and outcome in residential alcoholism treatment. *Psychology of Addictive Behaviors, 7,* 211–18.

Brown, P. J., Read, J. P., & Kahler, C. W. (2003). Comorbid posttraumatic stress disorder and substance use disorders: Treatment outcomes and the role of coping. In P. Ouimette & P. J. Brown (Eds.), *Trauma and substance abuse: Causes, consequences, and treatment of comorbid disorders* (pp. 171–90). Washington, DC: American Psychological Association.

Brown, P. J., Stout, R. L., & Mueller, T. (1999). Substance use disorder and posttraumatic stress disorder comorbidity: Addiction and psychiatric treatment rates. *Psychology of Addictive Behaviors, 13*(2), 115–22.

Brownstein, H. H., & Goldstein, P. J. (1990). Research and the development of public policy: The case of drugs and violent crime. *Journal of Applied Sociology, 7,* 77–92.

Budney, A. J., & Higgins, S. T. (1998). A community reinforcement plus vouchers approach: Treating cocaine addiction. (National Institute on Drug Abuse: Therapy Manuals for Drug Addiction, Manual 2; NIH Publication No. 98:4309.) Rockville, MD: National Institute on Drug Abuse.

Bureau of Justice Statistics. (2000). *Special report: Drug use, testing, and treatment in jails.* Washington, DC: U.S. Department of Justice.

Burke, B. L., Arkowitz, H., & Dunn, C. (2002). The efficacy of motivational interviewing and its adaptations. In W. R. Miller & S. Rollnick (Eds.), *Motivational interviewing: Preparing people for change* (2nd ed., pp. 217–50). New York: Guilford Press.

Burke, B. L., Vassilev, G., Kantchelov, A., & Zweben, A. (2002). Motivational interviewing with couples. In W. R. Miller & S. Rollnick (Eds.), *Motivational interviewing: Preparing people for change* (2nd ed., pp. 347–61). New York: Guilford Press.

Carey, M. P., Braaten, L. S., Maisto, S. A., Gleason, J. R., Forsyth, A. D., Durant, L. E., & Jaoworski, B. C. (2000). Using information, motivation enhancement, and skills training to reduce the risk of HIV infection for low-income urban women: A second randomized clinical trial. *Health Psychology, 19*, 3–11.

Carey, M. P., Maisto, S. A., Kalichman, S. C., Forsyth, A. D., Wright, E. M., & Johnson, B. T. (1997). Enhancing motivation to reduce the risk of HIV infection for economically disadvantaged urban women. *Journal of Consulting and Clinical Psychology, 65*, 531–41.

Carroll, K. M. (1997). Relapse prevention as a psychosocial treatment: A review of controlled clinical trials. In G. A. Marlatt & G. R. VandenBos (Eds.), *Addictive behaviors: Readings on etiology, prevention, and treatment* (pp. 697–717). Washington, DC: American Psychological Association.

Carroll, K. M. (1998). *A cognitive-behavioral approach: Treatment of cocaine addiction.* Therapy Manuals for Drug Addiction. Rockville, MD: National Institute on Drug Abuse.

Carroll, K. M. (2001). Combined treatments for substance dependence. In M. T. Sammons & N. B. Schmidt (Eds.), *Combined treatments for mental disorders: A guide to psychological and pharmacological intervention* (pp. 215–37). Washington, DC: American Psychological Association.

Carter, R. T. (Ed.). (2000). *Addressing cultural issues in organizations: Beyond the corporate context.* Newbury Park, CA: Sage.

Caulkins, J. P., Rydell, C. P., Schwabe, W. L., & Chiesa, J. (1997). *Mandatory minimum drug sentences: Throwing away the key or the taxpayer's money?* Santa Monica, CA: RAND.

Chang, E. C. (Ed.). (2001). *Optimism and pessimism: Implications for theory, research, and practice.* Washington, DC: American Psychological Association.

Chesney-Lind, M. (2002). Imprisoning women: The unintended victims of mass imprisonment. In M. Mauer & M. Chesney-Lind (Eds.), *Invisible punishment: The collateral consequences of mass imprisonment* (pp. 79–94). New York: New Press.

Clark, C., & Kellam, L. (2001). These boots are made for women. *Corrections Today, 63*(1), 50–54.

Clark, D. B., Wood, D. S., Cornelius, J. R., Bukstein, O. G., & Martin, C. S. (2003). Clinical practices in the pharmacological treatment of comorbid psychopathology in adolescents with alcohol use disorders. *Journal of Substance Abuse Treatment, 25*, 293–95.

Cimmarusti, R. A. (1992). Family preservation practice based upon a multisystems approach. *Child Welfare, 71*(3), 214–56.

Coffey, S. F., Dansky, B. S., & Brady, K. T. (2003). Exposure-based, trauma-focused therapy for comorbid posttraumatic stress disorder-substance use disorder. In. P. Ouimette & P. J. Brown (Eds.), *Trauma and substance abuse: Causes, consequences, and treatment of comorbid disorders* (pp. 127–46). Washington, DC: American Psychological Association.

Colledge, D., & Gerber, J. (2002). Rethinking the assumptions about boot camps. In W. R. Palacios, P. F. Cromwell, & R. G. Dunham (Eds.), *Crime and justice in America: Present realities and future prospects* (pp. 382–93). Upper Saddle River, NJ: Prentice-Hall.

Compton, P. (2002, August 23). *Epidemiology of prescription opiod abuse—The problem as seen from different perspectives.* Paper presented within a symposium entitled "Prescription opiod abuse: The problem as seen from different perspectives," at the 110th annual convention of the American Psychological Association, McCormick Place, Lakeside Center, Chicago, IL.

Connors, G. J., Donovan, D. M., & DiClemente, C. C. (2001). *Substance abuse and the states of change: Selecting and planning intervention.* New York: Guilford Press.

Cook, F. (2002). Treatment accountability for safer communities: Linking the criminal justice and treatment systems. In C. J. Leukefeld, F. Tims, & D. Farabee (Eds.), *Treatment of drug offenders: Policies and issues* (pp. 105–10). New York: Springer.

Courtright, D. T. (2002). The roads to H: The emergence of the American heroin complex, 1898–1956. In D. F. Musto (Ed.), *One hundred years of heroin* (pp. 3–19). Westport, CT: Auburn House.

Crits-Christoph, P., Siqueland, L., Blaine, J., Frank, A., Luborsky, L., Onken, L. S., Muenz, L. R., Thase, M. E., Weiss, R. D., Gastfriend, D. R., Woody, G. E., Barber, J. P., Butler, S. F., Daley, D., Salloum, I., Bishop, S., Najavits, L. M., Lis, J., Mercer, D., Griffin, M. L., Moras, K., & Beck, A. T. (1999). Psychosocial treatment for cocaine dependence: National Institute on Drug Abuse Collaborative Cocaine Treatment Study. *Archives of General Psychiatry, 56*(6), 493–502.

Cromwell, P. (2002). Evolving role of parole in the criminal justice system. In W. R. Palacios, P. F. Cromwell, & R. G. Dunham (Eds.), *Crime and justice in America: Present realities and future prospects* (2nd ed., pp. 405–12). Upper Saddle River, NJ: Prentice-Hall.

Cropsey, K., Eldridge, G. D., & Ladner, T. (2004). Smoking among female prisoners: An ignored public health problem. *Addictive Behaviors, 29,* 425–31.

Cullen, E., Jones, L., & Woodward, R. (Eds.). (1997). *Therapeutic communities in prison.* New York: Wiley.

Daley, D. C., & Mercer, D. (2002). *Drug counseling for cocaine addiction: The collaborative cocaine treatment study model.* National Institute on Drug Abuse, U.S. Department of Health and Human Services (NIH Publication No. 02-4381). Bethesda, MD: National Institute on Drug Abuse.

Daley, D. C., Salloum, I. M., Zuckoff, A., Kirisci, L., & Thase, M. E. (1998). Increasing treatment adherence among outpatients with depression and cocaine dependence: Results of a pilot study. *American Journal of Psychiatry, 155,* 1611–13.

Daley, D. C., & Zuckoff, A. (1998). Improving compliance with the initial outpatient session among discharged inpatient dual diagnosis clients, *Social Work, 43,* 470–73.

DeCou, K., & Van Wright, S. (2002). A gender-specific intervention model for incarcerated women: Women's V.O.I.C.E.S (Validation Opportunity Inspiration Community Empowerment Safety). In G. Landsberg, M. Rock, L. K. W. Berg, & A. Smiley (Eds.), *Serving mentally ill offenders: Challenges and opportunities for mental health professionals* (pp. 172–90). New York: Springer.

Deitch, D. A., Carleton, S., Koustsenok, I. B., & Marsolais, K. (2002). Therapeutic community treatment in prisons. In C. J. Leukefeld, F. Tims, & D. Farabee (Eds.), *Treatment of drug offenders: Policies and issues* (pp. 127–37). New York: Springer.

De Leon, G. (1984). *The therapeutic community: Study of effectiveness* (NIDA Treatment Research Monograph 84-1286). Rockville, MD: U.S. Government Printing Office.

De Leon, G. (1988). Legal pressure in therapeutic communities. *Journal of Drug Issues, 18*, 625–40.

De Leon, G. (2000). *The therapeutic community: Theory, model & method.* New York: Springer.

De Leon, G., Melnick, G., & Tims, F. M. (2001). The role of motivation and readiness in treatment and recovery. In F. M. Tims, C. G. Leukefeld, & J. J. Platt (Eds.), *Relapse and recovery in addictions* (pp. 143–71). New Haven, CT: Yale University Press.

De Leon, G., Sacks, S., & Wexler, H. K. (2002). Modified prison therapeutic communities for the dual- and multiple-diagnosed offender. In C. J. Leukefeld, F. Tims, & D. Farabee (Eds.), *Treatment of drug offenders: Policies and issues* (pp. 138–48). New York: Springer.

Dembo, R., Livingston, S., & Schmeidler, J. (2001). Treatment for drug-involved youth in the juvenile justice system. In C. J. Leukefeld, F. Tims, & D. Farabee (Eds.), *Treatment of drug offenders: Policies and issues* (pp. 226–39). New York: Springer.

Denning, P. (2001). Strategies for implementation of harm reduction in treatment settings. *Journal of Psychoactive Drugs, 33*, 23–26.

Dennis, M. L. (2002, August 23). *Long-term outcome after the cannabis youth treatment (CYT) experiment.* Paper presented within a symposium entitled "Persistent effects of adolescent substance abuse treatment," at the 110th annual convention of the American Psychological Association, McCormick Place, Lakeside Center, Chicago, IL.

Department of Health and Human Services (2000). *The AFCARS Report.* Washington, DC: Department of Health and Human Services.

Derby, K. (1992a). The role of 12-step self-help groups in the treatment of the chemically dependent. In B. C. Wallace (Ed.), *The chemically dependent: Phases of treatment and recovery* (pp. 159–70). New York: Brunner/Mazel.

Derby, K. (1992b). Some difficulties in the treatment of character-disordered addicts. In B. C. Wallace (Ed.) *The chemically dependent: Phases of treatment and recovery* (pp. 115–24). New York: Brunner/Mazel.

Des Jarlais, D. C. (1995). Harm reduction: A framework for incorporating science into drug policy (editorial). *American Journal of Public Health, 85*, 10–12.

DiClemente, C., & Velasquez, M. M. (2002). Motivational interviewing and the stages of change. In W. R. Miller and S. Rollnick (Eds.), *Motivational interviewing: Preparing people for change* (2nd ed., pp. 201–16). New York: Guilford Press.

Dodes, L. M., & Khantzian, E. J. (1998). Individual psychodynamic psychotherapy. In R. J. Frances & S. I. Miller (Eds.), *Clinical textbook of addictive disorders* (2nd ed., pp. 479–95). New York: Guilford Press.

Donovan, B., Padin-Rivera, E., & Kowaliw, S. (2001). Transcend: Initial outcomes from a posttraumatic stress disorder/substance abuse treatment program. *Journal of Traumatic Stress, 14*, 757–72.

Donovan, D. M. (1998). Continuing care: Promoting the maintenance of change. In W. R. Miller & N. Heather (Eds.), *Treating Addictive Behaviors* (2nd ed., pp. 317–36). New York: Plenum Press.

Donovan, D. M. (1999). Assessment strategies and measures in addictive behaviors. In B. S. McCrady & E. E. Epstein (Eds.), *Addiction: A comprehensive guidebook* (pp. 187–215). New York: Oxford University Press.

Donovan, D. M., & Rosengren, D. B. (1999). Motivation for behavior change and treatment among substance abusers. In J. A. Tucker, D. M. Donovan, & G. A. Marlatt (Eds.), *Changing addictive behavior: Bridging clinical and public health strategies* (pp. 127–59). New York: Guilford Press.

Drieschner, K. H., Lammers, S. M. M., & van der Staak, C. P. F. (2004). Treatment motivation: An attempt for clarification of an ambiguous concept. *Clinical Psychology Reviews, 23*, 1115–37.

Earleywine, M. (2002). *Understanding Marijuana: A new look at the scientific evidence.* New York: Oxford University Press.

Ellison, R. (1952). *Invisible man.* New York: Random House.

Evans, K., & Sullivan, M. (1994). *Treating trauma and addiction.* New York: Guilford Press.

Fals-Stewart, W., Golden, J., & Schumacher, J. A. (2003). Intimate partner violence and substance use: A longitudinal day-to-day examination. *Addictive Behaviors, 28*, 1555–74.

Farabee, D., & Leukefeld, C. G. (2001). Recovery and the criminal justice system. In F. M. Tims, C. G. Leukefeld, & J. J. Platt (Eds.), *Relapse and recovery in addictions* (pp. 40–59). New Haven, CT: Yale University Press.

Farabee, D., & Leukefeld, C. G. (2002). HIV and AIDS prevention strategies. In C. J. Leukefeld, F. Tims, & D. Farabee (Eds.), *Treatment of drug offenders: Policies and issues* (pp. 172–85). New York: Springer.

Farabee, D., Prendergast, M., & Anglin, M. D. (1998). The effectiveness of coerced treatment for drug-abusing offenders. *Federal Probation, 62*(1), 3–10.

Farmer, P. (2002). The house of the dead: Tuberculosis and incarceration. In M. Mauer and M. Chesney-Lind (Eds.), *Invisible punishment: The collateral consequences of mass imprisonment* (pp. 239–57). New York: New Press.

Federal Bureau of Investigation. (1997). *Crime in the United States, 1996, FBI uniform crime report.* Washington, DC: U.S. Government Printing Office.

Fenwick, M. E. (2002). Maxing out: Imprisonment in an era of crime control. In W. R. Palacious, P. F. Cromwell, & R. G. Dunham (Eds.), *Crime and justice in America: Present realities and future prospects* (2nd ed., pp. 423–30). Upper Saddle River, NJ: Prentice-Hall.

Fletcher, B. W., Broome, K. M., Delany, P. J., Shields, J., & Flynn, P. M. (2003). Patient and program factors in obtaining supportive services in DATOS. *Journal of Substance Abuse Treatment, 25*(3), 165–75.

Flynn, P. M., Joe, G. W., Broome, K. M., Simpson, D. D., & Brown, B. S. (2003). Recovery from opiod addiction in DATOS. *Journal of Substance Abuse Treatment, 25*(3), 177–86.

Frances, R. J., & Miller, S. I. (1998). *Clinical textbook of addictive disorders* (2nd ed.). New York: Guilford Press.

Franklin, A. J. (2004). *From brotherhood to manhood: How black men rescue their relationships and dreams from the invisibility syndrome.* Hoboken, NJ: Wiley.

Freese, T., Miotto, K., & Reback, C. J. (2002). The effects and consequences of selected club drugs. *Journal of Substance Abuse Treatment, 23*(2), 151–56.

Frese, F. J., Stanley, J., Kress, K., & Vogel-Scibilia, S. (2001). Integrating evidence-based practices and the recovery model. *Psychiatric Services, 52*, 1462–68.

Freudenberg, N. (2001). Jails, prisons, and the health of urban populations: A review of the impact of the correctional system on community health. *Journal of Urban Health: Bulletin of the New York Academy of Medicine, 78*(2), 214–35.

Gerstein, D., & Harwood, H. (Eds.). (1990). *Treating drug problems* (Vol. 1). Washington, DC: National Academy Press.

Ginsburg, J. I., Mann, R. E., Rotgers, F., & Weekes, J. R. (2002). Motivational interviewing with criminal justice populations. In W. R. Miller & S. Rollnick (Eds.), *Motivational interviewing: Preparing people for change* (2nd ed., pp. 333–46). New York: Guilford Press.

Glater, J. D. (2002, August 15). Most companies meet deadline for certifying results. *New York Times*, C3.

Glaze, L. E. (2002, August). Probation and parole in the United States, 2002. *Bureau of Statistics Bulletin*. (U.S. Department of Justice, NCJ 195669)

Goddard, P. (2003). Changing attitudes towards harm reduction among treatment professionals: A report from the American Midwest. *International Journal of Drug Policy, 14*, 257–60.

Goldfried, M. R., & Wolfe, B. E. (1996). Psychotherapy practice and research: Repairing a strained alliance. *American Psychologist, 51*, 1007–16.

Goldstein, P. J. (1985). The drug/violence nexus: A tripartite conceptual framework. *Journal of Drug Issues, 15*, 493–506.

Gottfredson, D. C., & Exum, M. L. (2002). The Baltimore City drug court: One-year results from a randomized study. *Journal of Research on Crime and Delinquency, 39*, 337–56.

Greenberg, D. F. (2002). Striking out in democracy. *Punishment and Society, 4(2)*, 237–52.

Greenwood, P., Rydell, C., Abrahamse, A., Caulkins, J., Chiesa, J., Model, K. E., & Klein, S. P. (1994). *Three strikes and you're out: Estimated benefits and costs of California's new mandatory sentencing law (MR-509-RC)*. Santa Monica, CA: RAND.

Greenwood, P., Rydell, C., Abrahamse, A., Caulkins, J., Chiesa, J., Model, K. E., & Klein, S. P. (1996). Estimated benefits and costs of California's new mandatory-sentencing law. In D. Shichor & D. K. Sechrest (Eds.), *Three strikes and you're out: Vengeance as public policy*. Thousand Oaks, CA: Sage.

Gregoire, T. K., & Burke, A. C. (2004). The relationship of legal coercion to readiness to change among adults with alcohol and other drug problems. *Journal of Substance Abuse Treatment, 26*, 35–41.

Grella, C. E., Hser, Y., & Hsieh, S. (2003). Predictors of drug treatment re-entry following relapse to cocaine use in DATOS. *Journal of Substance Abuse Treatment, 25(3)*, 145–54.

Grella, C. E., Joshi, V., & Hser, Y. (2003). Follow-up of cocaine-dependent men and women with antisocial personality disorder. *Journal of Substance Abuse Treatment, 25(3)*, 155–64.

Gusfield, J. R. (1967). Moral passage: The symbolic process in public designations of deviance. *Social Problems, 15*, 175–88.

Haas, A. L. (2002, August 23). *What makes treatment effective: Participant factors.* Paper presented within a symposium entitled "Beyond the treatment manual: Key ingredients in effective alcohol and drug treatment," at the 110th annual meeting of the American Psychological Association, McCormick Place, Lakeside Center, Chicago, IL.

Halpern, J. H., Sholar, M. B., Glowacki, J., Mello, N. K., Mendelson, J. H., & Siegel, A. J. (2003). Diminished interleukin-6 response to proinflammatory challenge in men and women after intravenous cocaine administration. *Journal of Clinical Endocrinology and Metabolism, 88*(3), 1188–93.

Handmaker, N., Packard, M., & Conforti, K. (2002). Motivational interviewing in the treatment of dual disorders. In W. R. Miller & S. Rollnick (Eds.), *Motivational interviewing: Preparing people for change* (2nd ed., pp. 362–76). New York: Guilford Press.

Haney, C., & Zimbardo, P. (1998). The past and future of U.S. prison policy: Twenty-five years after the Stanford prison experiment. *American Psychologist, 53*(7), 709–27.

Harlow, C. W. (2003, January). Education and correctional populations. *Bureau of Justice Statistics Special Report*. U.S. Department of Justice. (Office of Justice Programs, NCJ 195670.)

Harm Reduction Coalition (HRC). (1996). *Mission and principles of harm reduction.* [Brochure]. Oakland, CA: Author.

Harrell, A., & Kleiman, M. (2002). Drug testing in criminal justice settings. In C. J. Leukefeld, F. Tims, & D. Farabee (Eds.), *Treatment of Drug Offenders: Policies and Issues* (pp. 149–71). New York: Springer.

Harrison, P. M., & Beck, A. J. (2003). *Prisoners in 2002*. Washington, DC: U.S. Department of Justice.

Hegamin, A., Longshore, D., & Monahan, G. (2002). Health services in correctional settings: Emerging issues and model strategies. In C. J. Leukefeld, F. Tims, & D. Farabee (Eds.), *Treatment of drug offenders: Policies and issues* (pp. 335–47). New York: Springer.

Herrell, J. M. (2002, August 23). *Overview of CSAT's methamphetamine treatment project: Rationale and methods.* Paper presented within a symposium entitled "Understanding and treating abuse of methamphetamine and club drugs," at the 110th annual convention of the American Psychological Association, McCormick Place, Lakeside Center, Chicago, IL.

Hester, R. K., & Miller, W. R. (Eds.). (2003). *Handbook of alcoholism treatment approaches: Effective elternatives* (3rd ed.). Boston, MA: Allyn & Bacon.

Higgins, S. T. (1999). Potential contributions of the community reinforcement approach and contingency management to broadening the base of substance abuse treatment. In J. A. Tucker, D. M. Donovan, & G. A. Marlatt (Eds.), *Changing addictive behavior: Bridging clinical and public health strategies* (pp. 283–306). New York: Guilford Press.

Higgins, S. T., & Abbott, P. J. (2001). CRA and treatment of cocaine and opiod dependence. In R. J. Meyers & W. R. Miller (Eds.), *A community reinforcement approach to addiction treatment* (pp. 123–46). New York: Cambridge University Press.

Higgins, S. T., & Silverman, K. (1999). *Motivating behavior change among illicit-drug abusers: Research on contingency management interventions.* Washington, DC: American Psychological Association.

Hill, C. (2002). Prison populations. *Corrections Compendium, 27*(6), 10–23.

Hiller, M. L., Knight, K., Broome, K. M., & Simpson, D. D. (1998). Legal pressure and treatment retention in a national sample of long-term residential programs. *Criminal Justice and Behavior, 25*(4), 463–81.

Hiller, M. L., Knight, K., Rao, S. R., & Simpson, D. D. (2002). Assessing and evaluating mandated correctional substance-abuse treatment. In C. J. Leukefeld, F. Tims, & D. Farabee (Eds.), *Treatment of drug offenders: Policies and issues* (pp. 41–56). New York: Springer.

Hoaken, P. N. S., & Stewart, S. H. (2003). Drugs of abuse and the elicitation of human aggressive behavior. *Addictive Behaviors, 28*, 1533–54.

Howard, D. L. (2003). Culturally competent of African American clients among a national sample of outpatient substance abuse treatment units. *Journal of Substance Abuse Treatment, 24*, 89–102.

Hubbard, R. L., & Marsden, M. E. (1986). Relapse to use of heroin, cocain, and other drugs in the first year after treatment. *Relapse and recovery in drug abuse* (NIDA Research Monograph 72, pp. 247–53). Rockville, MD: U.S. Government Printing Office.

Hubbard, R. L., Marsden, M. E., Rachal, J. V., Harwood, H. J., Cavanaugh, E. R., & Ginzberg, H. M. (1989). *Drug abuse treatment: A national study of effectiveness.* Chapel Hill: University of North Carolina Press.

Hubbard, R. L., Rachal, J. V., Craddock, S. G., & Cavanaugh, E. R. (1984). Treatment outcome prospective study (TOPS): Client characteristics and behaviors before, during, and after treatment. In F. M. Tims & J. P. Ludford (Eds.), *Drug abuse treatment evaluation: Strategies, progress, and prospects* (NIDA Research Monograph 51, pp. 42–68). Rockville, MD: National Institute on Drug Abuse.

Hughes, T. A., Wilson, D. J., & Beck, A. J. (2002). Trends in state parole: The more things change, the more they stay the same. *Perspectives, 26*(3), 26–33.

Humphreys, K., & Weisner, C. (2000). Use of exclusion criteria in selecting research subjects and its effect on generalizability of alcohol treatment outcome studies. *American Journal of Psychiatry, 157*, 588–94.

Ignatius, A. (2002, December 30–January 6). Wall Street's Top Cop. *Time*, 65–79.

Inciardi, J., Surratt, H. L., Martin, S. S., & Hooper, R. M. (2002) The importance of aftercare in a corrections-based treatment continuum. In C. J. Leukefeld, F. Tims, & D. Farabee (Eds.), *Treatment of drug offenders: Policies and issues* (pp. 204–15). New York: Springer.

Institute of Medicine, National Academy of Sciences. (1990). *Broadening the base of treatment for alcohol problems.* Washington, DC: National Academy Press.

Isralowitz, R. (2002). *Drug use, policy, and management* (2nd ed.). Westport, CT: Auburn House.

Jainchill, N. (2002, August 23). *Discussant.* Paper presented within a symposium entitled "Persistent effects of adolescent substance abuse treatment," at the 110th annual convention of the American Psychological Association, McCormick Place, Lakeside Center, Chicago, IL.

Joe, G., Simpson, D., & Broome, K. (1999). Retention and patient engagement models of different treatment modalities in DATOS. *Drug and Alcohol Dependence, 57*, 113–25.

Johnson, B. D., & Golub, A. (2002). Generational trends in heroin use and injection in New York City. In D. F. Musto (Ed.), *One hundred years of heroin* (pp. 91–128). Westport, CT: Auburn House.

Johnson, M. E., Yep, M. J., Brems, C., Theno, S. A., & Fisher, D. G. (2002). Relationship among gender, depression, and needle sharing in a sample of injection drug users. *Psychology of Addictive Behaviors, 16*(4), 338–42.

Johnson, S. (2002, September 7, 2002). Personal Communication.

Jones, E. E., Farina, A., Hastorf, A. H., Markus, H., Miller, D. T., & Scott, R. A. (1983). *Social stigma: The psychology of marked relationships.* New York: Freeman.

Jones, J. M. (1997). *Prejudice and racism* (2nd ed.). New York: McGraw-Hill.

Joseph, J., Breslin, C., & Skinner, H. (1999). Critical perspectives on the transtheoretical model and stages of change. In J. A. Tucker, D. M. Donovan, & G. A. Marlatt (Eds.), *Changing addictive behavior: Bridging clinical and public health strategies* (pp. 160–90). New York: Guilford Press.

Kagee, A. (2003). Political torture in South Africa: Psychological considerations in the assessment, diagnosis, and treatment of survivors. In B. C. Wallace & R. T. Carter (Eds.), *Understanding and dealing with violence: A multicultural approach* (pp. 271–90). Thousand Oaks, CA: Sage.

Kandel, D. B. (Ed.). (2002). *Stages and pathways of drug involvement: Examining the gateway hypothesis.* New York: Cambridge University Press.

Kauffman, K. (2002). Prison nurseries: New beginnings and second chances. *Women, Girls and Criminal Justice, 3*(1), 1–2, 14–15.

Kelly, A. B., Halford, W. K., & Young, R. M. (2002). Couple communication and female problem drinking: A behavioral observation study. *Psychology of Addictive Behaviors, 16*(3), 269–71.

Kellogg, S. H. (2003). On "gradualism" and the building of the harm reduction-abstinence continuum. *Journal of Substance Abuse Treatment, 25,* 241–47.

Khantzian, E., Halliday, K. S., & McAuliffe, W. E. (1990). *Addiction and the vulnerable self: Modified dynamic group therapy for substance abusers.* New York: Guilford Press.

King, A. (1993). The impact of incarceration on African American families: Implications for practice. *Families in Society: Journal of Contemporary Human Services, 74,* 145–53.

King, R. S., & Mauer, M. (2002). State sentencing and corrections policy in an era of fiscal restraint, Sentencing Project, National Institute of Justice/NCJRS: Rockville, MD.

Kinlock, T. W., & Hanlon, T. E. (2002). Probation and parole interventions. In C. J. Leukefeld, F. Tims, & D. Farabee (Eds.), *Treatment of drug offenders: Policies and issues* (pp. 243–58). New York: Springer.

Kirby, K. C., Amass, L., & McLellan, A. T. (1999). Disseminating contingency management research to drug abuse treatment practitioners. In S. T. Higgins & K. Silverman (Eds.), *Motivating behavior change among illicit-drug abusers: Research on contingency management interventions* (pp. 327–44). Washington, DC: American Psychological Association.

Kirby, K. C., Marlowe, D. B., Festinger, D. S., Garvey, K. A., & La Monaca, V. (1999). Community reinforcement training for family and significant others of drug abusers: A unilateral intervention to increase treatment entry of drug abusers. *Drug and Alcohol Dependence, 56,* 85–96.

Knight, K., Simpson, D. D., & Hiller, M. L. (1999). Three-year reincarceration outcomes for in-prison therapeutic community treatment in Texas. *Prison Journal, 70*(3), 337–51.

Koob, G. F. (2002). Neurobiology of drug addiction. In D. B. Kandel (Ed.), *Stages and pathways of drug involvement: Examining the gateway hypothesis* (pp. 337–61). New York: Cambridge University Press.

Ladd, G. T., & Petry, N. M. (2002). Disordered gambling among university-based medical and dental patients: A focus on internet gambling. *Psychology of Addictive Behaviors, 16*(1), 76–79.

La Greca, A. M., Silverman, W. K., Vernberg, E. M., & Roberts, M. C. (Eds.). (2002). *Helping children cope with disasters and terrorism.* Washington, DC: American Psychological Association.

Landsberg, G., Rock, M., Berg, L. K. W., & Smiley, A. (Eds.). (2002) *Serving mentally ill offenders: Challenges and opportunities for mental health professionals.* New York: Springer.

Lange, J. E. (2002). Alcohol's effect on aggression identification: A two-channel theory. *Psychology of Addictive Behaviors, 16*(1), 47–55.

Larimer, M. E. (2002, August 25). *Discussant remarks.* Paper presented within a symposium entitled "Designing a comprehensive and empirically sound chemical dependency treatment system," at the 110th convention of the American Psychological Association, McCormick Place, Lakeside Center, Chicago, IL.

Lazar Institute. (1976). *Phase I report, treatment alternatives to street crime (TASC) national evaluation program.* Washington, DC: Law Enforcement Assistance Administration.

Lebow, J., Moos, R., Kelly, J., & Knobloch-Fedders, A. L. (2002, August 23). *Beyond the treatment manual: Key ingredients in effective alcohol and drug treatment.* Paper presented within a symposium entitled "Beyond the treatment manual: Key ingredients in effective alcohol and drug treatment," at the 110th annual convention of the American Psychological Association, McCormick Place, Lakeside Center, Chicago, IL.

Leshner, A. I. (1998). Addiction is a brain disease—and it matters. *National Institute of Justice Journal, 237,* 2–6.

Leshner, A. I. (2002). Foreword. In D. B. Kandel (Ed.), *Stages and pathways of drug involvement: Examining the gateway hypothesis* (pp. xiii–xiv). New York: Cambridge University Press.

Leukefeld, C. G., Farabee, D., & Tims, F. (2002). Clinical and policy opportunities. In C. G. Leukefeld, F. Tims, & D. Farabee (Eds.), *Treatment of drug offenders: Policies and issues* (pp. 3–8). New York: Springer.

Leukefeld, C. G., Tims, F. M., & Platt, J. J. (2001). Future directions in substance abuse relapse and recovery. In F. M. Tims, C. G. Leukefeld, & J. J. Platt (Eds.), *Relapse and recovery in addictions* (pp. 401–13). New Haven, CT: Yale University Press.

Levin, J. D. (1999). *Primer for treating substance abusers.* Northvale, NJ: Jason Aronson.

Levin, J. D. (2001). *Therapeutic strategies for treating addiction: From slavery to Freedom.* Northvale, NJ: Jason Aronson.

Linton, S. (1998). *Claiming disability: Knowledge and identity.* New York: New York University Press.

Lincourt, P., Kuettel, T. J., & Bombardier, C. H. (2002). Motivational interviewing in a group setting with mandated clients: A pilot study. *Addictive Behaviors, 27,* 381–91.

Lipton, D., & Wexler, H. K. (1988). The drug-crime connection: Rehabilitation shows promise. *Corrections Today, 50,* 144–47.

Lloyd, J. (2002). *Rohypnol.* Rockville, MD: ONDCP Drug Policy Information Clearinghouse.

Locke, T. F., & Newcomb, M. D. (2003). Childhood maltreatment, parental alcohol/drug-related problems, and global parental dysfunction. *Professional Psychology: Research and Practice, 34*(1), 73–79.

Longshore, D., Grills, C., & Annon, K. (1999). Effects of a culturally congruent intervention on cognitive factors related to drug use recovery. *Substance Use and Misuse, 34,* 1223–41.

Longshore, D., Turner, S., & Anglin, M. D. (1998). Effects of case management on drug user's risky sex. *Prison Journal, 78*(1), 6–30.

Lopez, S. J., & Snyder, C. R. (Eds.). (2003). *Positive psychological assessment: A handbook of models and measures.* Washington, DC: American Psychological Association.

Luborsky, L. (1984). *Principles of psychoanalytic psychotherapy: A manual for supportive-expressive treatment.* New York: Basic Books.

Lutze, F. E. (2001). Influence of shock incarceration programs on inmate adjustment and attitudinal change. *Journal of Criminal Justice, 29*(3), 255–67.

MacKenzie, D. L., Wilson, D. B., & Kider, S. B. (2001). Effects of corrections boot camps on offending. In D. P. Farrington & B. C. Welsh (Eds.), *Annals of the American Academy of Political and Social Science* (Vol. 578, pp. 126–43). Thousand Oaks, CA: Sage Publications.

Majoor, B., & Rivera, J. (2003). SACHR: An example of an integrated, harm reduction drug treatment program. *Journal of Substance Abuse, 25,* 257–62.

Margolis, R. D., & Zweben, J. E. (1998). *Treating patients with alcohol and drug problems: An integrated approach.* Washington, DC: American Psychological Association.

Mark, F. O. (1988). Does coercion work? The role of referral source in motivating alcoholics in treatment. *Alcoholism Treatment Quarterly, 5,* 5–22.

Marlatt, G. A. (1997). Introduction. In G. A. Marlatt & G. R. VandenBos (Eds.), *Addictive behaviors: Readings in etiology, prevention, and treatment* (pp. xi–xxv). Washington, DC: American Psychological Association.

Marlatt, G. A. (Ed.). (1998a). *Harm reduction: Pragmatic strategies for managing high risk behaviors.* New York: Guilford Press.

Marlatt, G. A. (1998b). Highlights of harm reduction: A personal report from the first National Harm Reduction Conference in the United States. In G. A. Marlatt (Ed.), *Harm reduction: Pragmatic strategies for managing high risk behaviors* (pp. 3–29). New York: Guilford Press.

Marlatt, G. A. (1998c). Harm reduction and public policy. In G. A. Marlatt (Ed.), *Harm reduction: Pragmatic strategies for managing high-risk behaviors* (pp. 353–78). New York: Guilford Press.

Marlatt, G. A. (1999). From hindsight to foresight: A commentary on Project MATCH. In J. A. Tucker, D. M. Donovan, & G. A. Marlatt (Eds.), *Changing addictive behavior: Bridging clinical and public health strategies* (pp. 45–66). New York: Guilford Press.

Marlatt, G. A. (2001). Integrating contingency management with relapse prevention skills: Comment on Silverman et al. *Experimental and Clinical Psychopharmacology, 9*(1), 33–34.

Marlatt, G. A., Blume, A. W., & Parks, G. A. (2001). Integrating harm reduction therapy and traditional substance abuse treatment. *Journal of Psychoactive Drugs, 33,* 13–21.

Marlatt, G. C., & Gordon, J. R. (1985). *Relapse prevention: Maintenance strategies in the treatment of addictive behaviors.* New York: Guilford Press.

Marlatt, G. A., Tucker, J. A., Donovan, D. M., & Vuchinich, R. E. (1997). Help-seeking by substance abusers: The role of harm reduction and behavioral-economic approaches to facilitate treatment entry and retention. In L. S. Onken, J. D. Blaine, & J. J. Boren (Eds.), *Beyond the therapeutic alliance: Keeping the drug dependent individual in treatment* (NIDA Research Monograph, No. 165, pp. 44–84). Rockville, MD: U.S. Department of Health and Human Services, Public Health Services, National Institutes of Health.

Marlatt, G. A., & VandenBos, G. R. (Eds.). (1997). *Addictive behaviors: Readings on etiology, prevention, and treatment.* Washington, DC: American Psychological Association.

Marlatt, G. A., & Witkiewitz, K. (2002). Harm reduction approaches to alcohol use: Health promotion, prevention, and treatment. *Addictive Behaviors, 27,* 867–86.

Marlowe, D. B. (2003). Integrating substance abuse treatment and criminal justice supervision. *Science & Practice Perspectives, 2*(1), 4–14.

Marlowe, D. B., Elwork, A., Festinger, D. S., & McLellan, A. T. (2003). Drug policy by popular referendum: This, too, shall pass. *Journal of Substance Abuse Treatment, 25,* 213–21.

Marlowe, D. B., Glass, D. J., Merikle, E. P., Festinger, D. S., DeMatteo, D. C., Marczyk, G. R., & Platt, J. J. (2001). Efficacy of coercion in substance abuse treatment. In F. M. Tims, C. G. Leukefeld, & J. J. Platt (Eds.), *Relapse and recovery in addictions* (pp. 208–27). New Haven, CT: Yale University Press.

Marlowe, D. B., Merikle, E. P., Kirby, K. C., Festinger, D. S., & McLellan, A. T. (2001). Multidimensional assessment of perceived treatment-entry pressures among substance abusers. *Psychology of Addictive Behaviors, 15*(2), 97–108.

Marques, A. C., & Fourmigoni, M. L. (2001). Comparison of individual and group cognitive-behavioral therapy for alcohol and/or drug dependent patients. *Addiction, 96,* 836–46.

Marshall, W. L., Hudson, S. M., & Ward, T. (1992). Sexual deviance. In P. H. Wilson (Ed.), *Principles and practice of relapse prevention* (pp. 235–54). New York: Guilford Press.

Martino, S., Carroll, K. M., O'Malley, S. S., & Rounsaville, B. J. (2000). Motivational interviewing with psychiatrically ill substance abusing patients. *American Journal of Addictions, 9,* 88–91.

Mauer, M., & Chesney-Lind, M. (2002). Introduction. In M. Mauer & M. Chesney-Lind (Eds.), *Invisible punishment: The collateral consequences of mass imprisonment.* New York: New Press.

Maxwell, S. R. (2000). Sanction threats in court-ordered programs: Examining their effects on offenders mandated into drug treatment. *Crime & Delinquency, 46*(4), 542–63.

McBride, D. C., VanderWaal, C. J., Pacula, R. L., Terry-McElrath, Y., & Chriqui, J. F. (2002). Mandatory minimum sentencing and drug-law violations: Effects on the criminal justice system. In C. G. Leukefeld, F. Tims, & D. Farabee (Eds.), *Treatment of drug offenders: Policies and issues* (pp. 319–34). New York: Springer.

McFarlin, S. K., & Fals-Stewart, W. (2002). Workplace absenteeism and alcohol use: A sequential analysis. *Psychology of Addictive Behaviors, 16*(1), 17–31.

McLaughlin, B. (1997). Jail San Diego style. *Law Enforcement Quarterly, 26,* 3, 20–26, 38.

McLellan, A. T. (2003a). Crime and punishment and treatment: Latest findings in the treatment of drug-related offenders. *Journal of Substance Abuse Treatment, 25,* 187–88.

McLellan, A. T. (2003b). What's the harm in discussing harm reduction: An introduction to a three-paper series. *Journal of Substance Abuse Treatment, 25,* 239–40.

McLellan, A. T., Alterman, A. I., Metzger, D. S., Grissom, G. R., Woody, G. E., Luborsky, L., & O'Brien, C. P. (1997). Similarity of outcome predictors across opiate, cocaine, and alcohol treatments: Role of treatment services. In G. A. Marlatt & G. R. VandenBos (Eds.), *Addictive Behaviors: Readings on etiology, prevention, and treatment* (pp. 718–58). Washington, DC: American Psychological Association.

McLellan, A. T., Arndt, L., Metzger, D. S., Woody, G. E., & O'Brien, C. P. (1993). The effects of psychosocial services in substance abuse treatment. *Journal of the American Medical Association, 269*(15), 1953–59.

McLellan, A. T., Luborsky, L., Woody, G. E., & O'Brien, C. P. (1982). Is treatment for substance abuse effective? *Journal of the American Medical Association, 247*, 1423–27.

Meehan, K. E. (2000). California's three-strikes law: The first six years. *Corrections Management Quarterly, 4*(4), 22–33.

Mercer, D. E., & Woody, G. E. (1999). *Individual drug counseling*, National Institute on Drug Abuse, U.S. Department of Health and Human Services, National Institutes of Health Publication No. 99-4380. Rockville, MD: National Institute on Drug Abuse.

Meyers, R. J., & Smith, J. E. (1995). *Clinical guide to alcohol treatment: The community reinforcement approach.* New York: Guilford Press.

Meyers, R. J., & Miller, W. R. (Eds.). (2001). *A community reinforcement approach to addiction treatment.* Cambridge: Cambridge University Press.

Milby, J. B., Schumacher, J. E., Raczynski, J. M., Caldwell, E., Engle, M., Michael, M., & Carr, J. (1996). Sufficient conditions for effective treatment of substance abusing homeless. *Drug and Alcohol Dependence, 43*, 39–47.

Miller, E. J. (2001). Practice and promise: The Azrin studies. In R. J. Meyers & W. R. Miller (Eds.), *A community reinforcement approach to addiction treatment* (pp. 8–27). New York: Cambridge University Press.

Miller, W. R., Andrews, N. R., Wilbourne, P., & Bennett, M. E. (1998). A wealth of alternatives: Effective treatments for alcohol problems. In W. R. Miller & N. Heather (Eds.), *Treating addictive behaviors* (2nd ed., pp. 203–16). New York: Plenum Press.

Miller, W. R., Brown, J. M., Simpson, T. L., Handmaker, N. S., Bien, T. H., Luckie, L. F., Montgomery, H. A., Hester, R. K., & Tonigan, J. S. (1995). What works? A methodological analysis of the alcohol treatment outcome literature. In R. K. Hester & W. R. Miller (Eds.), *Handbook of alcoholism treatment approaches* (2nd ed., pp. 12–44). Boston, MA: Allyn & Bacon.

Miller, W. R., & Heather, N. (Eds.). (1998). *Treating addictive behaviors* (2nd ed.). New York: Plenum Press.

Miller, W. R., & Hester, R. K. (1986). The effectiveness of alcoholism treatment: What research reveals. In W. R. Miller & N. Heather (Eds.), *Treating addictive behaviors: Processes of change* (pp. 121–74). New York: Plenum Press.

Miller, W. R., & Hester, R. K. (2003). Treating alcohol problems: Toward an informed eclecticism. In R. K. Hester & W. R. Miller (Eds.), *Handbook of alcoholism treatment approaches: Effective alternatives* (3rd ed., pp. 1–12). Boston, MA: Allyn & Bacon.

Miller, W. R., & Meyers, R. J. (2001). Summary and reflections. In R. J. Meyers & W. R. Miller (Eds.), *A Community reinforcement approach to addiction treatment* (pp. 161–70). New York: Cambridge University Press.

Miller, W. R., & Rollnick, S. (Eds.). (1991). *Motivational interviewing: Preparing people to change addictive behaviors* (1st ed.). New York: Guilford Press.

Miller, W. R., & Rollnick, S. (Eds.) (2002). *Motivational interviewing: Preparing people for change* (2nd ed.). New York: Guilford Press.

Miller, W. R., Wilbourne, P. L., & Hettema, J. E. (2003). What works? A summary of alcohol treatment outcome research. In R. K. Hester & W. R. Miller (Eds.), *Handbook of alcoholism treatment approaches: Effective alternatives* (3rd ed., pp. 13–63). Boston, MA: Allyn & Bacon.

Miller, W. R., Yahne, C. E., & Tonigan, J. S. (2003). Motivational interviewing in drug abuse services: A randomized trial. *Journal of Consulting and Clinical Psychology, 71*(4), 754–63.

Molina, B. S. G., Bukstein, O. G., & Lynch, K. G. (2002). Attention-deficit/hyperactivity disorder and conduct disorder symptomatology in adolescents with alcohol use disorder. *Psychology of Addictive Behaviors, 16*(2), 161–64.

Moos, R. H. (2002, August 25). Addictive disorders in context: Principles and puzzles of effective treatment and recovery. Invited address at the 110th convention of the American Psychological Association, McCormick Place, Lakeside Center, Chicago, IL.

Moos, R. H. (2003). Addictive disorders in context: Principles and puzzles of effective treatment and recovery. *Psychology of Addictive Behaviors, 17*(1), 3–12.

Moos, R. H., & Moos, B. S. (2004). Long-term influence of duration and frequency of participation in alcoholics anonymous on individuals with alcohol use disorders. *Journal of Consulting and Clinical Psychology, 72*(1), 81–90.

Moyers, T. (2003). Motivational interviewing. In J. L. Sorenson, R. Rawson, J. Guydish, & J. E. Zweben (Eds.), *Drug abuse treatment through collaboration: Practice and research partnerships that work* (pp. 139–50). Washington, DC: American Psychological Association.

Musto, D. (1999). *The American disease: Origins of narcotic control.* New York: Oxford University Press.

Musto, D. F. (Ed.). (2002). *One hundred years of heroin.* Westport, CT: Auburn House.

Nadelman, E. A. (1998). Commonsense drug policy. *Foreign Affairs, 77,* 111–26.

Najavits, L. M. (2003). Seeking safety: A new psychotherapy for posttraumatic stress disorder and substance use disorder. In P. Ouimette & P. J. Brown (Eds.), *Trauma and substance abuse: Causes, consequences, and treatment of comorbid disorders.* Washington, DC: American Psychological Association.

National Institute on Drug Abuse (NIDA). (1999). *Principles of drug addiction treatment: A research-based guide,* U.S. Department of Health and Human Services, NIH Publication No. 99-4180, Bethesda, MD: National Institute on Drug Abuse.

National Institute on Drug Abuse. (2003). *Drug use among racial/ethnic minorities,* U.S. Department of Health and Human Services, NIH Publication No. 03-3888, Bethesda, MD: National Institute on Drug Abuse.

Neeley-Bertrand, D. (2001). Should camps get the boot? Could once-popular juvenile boot camps, now widely regarded as failed experiments, be made to succeed? *Children's Voice, 10*(2), 20–23.

Newman, C. F., Leahy, R. L., Beck, A. T., Reilly-Harrington, N. A., & Gyulai, L. (2002). *Bipolar disorder: A cognitive therapy approach.* Washington, DC: American Psychological Association.

New York City Department of Mental Health, Mental Retardation, and Alcoholism Services (NYCDMHMRAS). (1998). *New York City Plan Update for Alcoholism and Substance Abuse Services.* New York: Author.

Office of the National Drug Control Policy. (1997a). *National drug control strategy.* Washington, DC: Author.

Office of the National Drug Control Policy. (1997b). *State and local spending on drug control activities: Report from the national survey on local and state governments.* Washington, DC: Author.

Ouimette, P., & Brown, P. J. (Eds.). (2003). *Trauma and substance abuse: Causes, consequences, and treatment of comorbid disorders.* Washington, DC: American Psychological Association.

Ouimette, P., Moos, R. H., & Brown, P. J. (2003). Substance use disorder–posttraumatic stress disorder comorbidity: A survey of treatments and proposed guidelines. In P. Ouimette & P. J. Brown (Eds.), *Trauma and substance abuse: Causes, consequences, and treatment of comorbid disorders*. Washington, DC: American Psychological Association.

Ouimette, P., Moos, R. H., & Finney, J. W. (2003). PTSD treatment and 5-year remission among patients with substance use and posttraumatic stress disorder. *Journal of Consulting and Clinical Psychology, 71*(2), 410–14.

Palepu, A., Horton, N. J., Tibbetts, N., Dukes, K., Meli, S., & Samet, J. H. (2003). Substance abuse treatment and emergency department utilization among a cohort of HIV-infected persons with alcohol problems. *Journal of Substance Abuse Treatment, 25*, 37–42.

Panas, L., Caspi, Y., Fournier, E., & McCarty, D. (2003). Performance measures for outpatient substance abuse services: Group versus individual counseling. *Journal of Substance Abuse Treatment, 25*, 271–78.

Parrott, D. J., Drobes, D. J., Saladin, M. E., Coffey, S. F., & Dansky, B. S. (2003). Perpetration of partner violence: Effects of cocaine and alcohol dependence and posttraumatic stress disorder. *Addictive Behaviors, 28*, 1587–602.

Peters, R. H., & Matthews, C. O. (2002). Jail treatment for drug offenders. In C. J. Leukefeld, F. Tims, & D. Farabee (Eds.), *Treatment of drug offenders: Policies and issues* (pp. 186–203). New York: Springer.

Petersilia, J. (1999). Parole and prisoner reentry in the United States. In M. Tonry & J. Petersilia (Eds.), *Prisons* (pp. 479–529). Chicago: University of Chicago Press.

Pimlott, S., & Sarri, R. C. (2002). Forgotten group: Women in prisons and jails. In J. Figueira-McDonough and R. C. Sarri (Eds.), *Women at the margins: Neglect, punishment, and resistance* (pp. 55–86). Binghamton, NY: Hawthorn Press.

Pine, F. (1990). *Drive, ego, object, and self: A synthesis for clinical work*. New York: Basic Books.

Poussaint, A. F., & Alexander, A. (2000). *Lay my burden down: Unraveling suicide and the mental health crisis among African-Americans*. Boston, MA: Beacon Press.

Prendergast, M. L., & Burdon, W. M. (2002). Integrated systems of care for substance-abusing offenders. In C. J. Leukefeld, F. Tims, & D. Farabee (Eds.), *Treatment of drug offenders: Policies and issues* (pp. 111–26). New York: Springer.

Prochaska, J. O., & DiClemente, C. C. (1983). Stages and processes of self-change of cigarette smoking: Toward in integrative model of change. *Journal of Consulting and Clinical Psychology, 51*, 390–95.

Prochaska, J. O., & DiClemente, C. C. (1992). Stages of change in the modification of problem behaviors. *Progress in Behavior Modification, 28*, 183–218.

Prochaska, J. O., DiClemente, C. C., & Norcross, J. C. (1992). In search of how people change: Applications to addictive behaviors. *American Psychologist, 47*, 1102–14.

Project MATCH Research Group. (1997a). Matching alcoholism treatments to client heterogeneity: Project MATCH posttreatment drinking outcomes. *Journal of Studies on Alcohol, 58*, 7–29.

Project MATCH Research Group. (1997b). Project MATCH secondary a priori hypotheses. *Addiction, 92*, 1671–98.

Project MATCH Research Group. (1998a). Matching alcoholism treatments to client heterogeneity: Treatment main effects and matching effects on drinking during treatment. *Journal of Studies on Alcohol, 59*, 631–39.

Project MATCH Research Group. (1998b). Matching alcoholism treatment to client heterogeneity: Project MATCH three-year drinking outcomes. *Alcoholism: Clinical and Experimental Research, 22,* 1300–1311.

Project MATCH Research Group. (2001). *Project MATCH hypothesis: Results and causal chain analyses* (Monograph No. 8, NIH No. 01-4238). Bethesda, MD: National Institute on Alcohol Abuse and Alcoholism.

Quigley, B. M., Corbett, A. B., & Tedeschi, J. T. (2002). Desired image of power, alcohol expectancies, and alcohol-related aggression. *Psychology of Addictive Behavior, 16*(4), 318–24.

Rafee, J. (1995). California's "three strikes" law: An unconstitutional infringement upon the power of the judiciary? *San Diego Justice Journal, 3*(2), 535–49.

RAND Corporation. (1995). *Projecting future cocaine use and evaluating control strategies.* (Research Brief No. 6002). Santa Monica, CA: Rand Drug Policy Research Center.

Rawson, R. (2002a, August 23). *Methamphetamine treatment project: Rationale and methods.* Paper presented within a symposium entitled "Understanding and treating abuse of methamphetamine and club drugs," at the 110th annual convention of the American Psychological Association, McCormick Place, Lakeside Center, Chicago, IL.

Rawson, R. (2002b). Treatment of methamphetamine use disorders: An update. *Journal of Substance Abuse Treatment, 23*(2), 145–50.

Rawson, R., Huber, A., Brethen, P., Obert, J., Vikas, G., Shoptaw, S., & Ling, W. (2002). Status of methamphetamine users 2–5 years after outpatient treatment. *Journal of Addictive Diseases, 21,* 117–30.

Rawson, R., Shoptaw, S., Obert, J. L., McCann, M., Hasson, A., Marinelli-Casey, P., Brethen, P., & Ling, W. (1995). An intensive outpatient approach for cocaine abuse: The matrix model. *Journal of Substance Abuse Treatment, 12*(2), 117–27.

Read, J. P., Bollinger, A. R., & Sharkansky, E. (2003). Assessment of comorbid substance use disorder and posttraumatic stress disorder. In P. Ouimette & P. J. Brown (Eds.), *Trauma and substance abuse: Causes, consequences, and treatment of comorbid disorders* (pp. 111–25). Washington, DC: American Psychological Association.

Reback, C. (1997). *The social construction of a gay drug: Methamphetamine use among gay and bisexual males in Los Angeles.* Los Angeles: City of Los Angeles, AIDS Coordinator.

Resnicow, K., DiLorio, C., Soet, J. E., Borreli, B., Ernst, D., Hecht, J., & Thevos, A. K. (2002). Motivational interviewing in medical and public health settings. In W. R. Miller & S. Rollnick (Eds.), *Motivational interviewing: Preparing people for change* (2nd ed., pp. 251–69). New York: Guilford Press.

Riehman, K. S., Iguchi, M. Y., & Anglin, D. (2002). Depressive symptoms among amphetamine and cocaine users before and after substance abuse treatment. *Psychology of Addictive Behaviors, 16*(4), 333–37.

Riggs, D. S., Rukstalis, M., Volpicelli, J. R., Kalmanson, D., & Foa, E. B. (2003). Demographic and social adjustment characteristics of patients with comorbid posttraumatic stress disorder and alcohol dependence: Potential pitfalls to PTSD treatment. *Addictive Behaviors, 28,* 1717–30.

Ripley, A. (2002, December 30–January 6). The night detective. *Time,* 45–50.

Robert Wood Johnson Foundation. (1993). *Substance abuse: The nation's number one health problem: Key indicators for policy.* Princeton, NJ: Author.

Roche, T. (2000, November 13). The crisis in foster care. *Time,* 74–82.

Rogers, C. R. (1951). *Client-centered therapy: Its practice, implications and theory.* Boston, MA: Houghton Mifflin.

Rogers, D. (2002). Juvenile boot camps. *Law Enforcement Technology, 29*(6), 88–95.

Rollnick, S., Allison, J., Ballasiotes, S., Barth, T., Butler, C. C., Rose, G. S., & Rosengren, D. B. (2002). Variations on a theme: Motivational interviewing and its adaptations. In W. R. Miller & S. Rollnick (Eds.), *Motivational interviewing: Preparing people for change* (2nd ed., pp. 270–83). New York: Guilford Press.

Rollnick, S., & Bell, A. (1991). Brief motivational interviewing for use by the nonspecialist. In W. R. Miller & S. Rollnick (Eds.), *Motivational interviewing: Preparing people to change addictive behavior* (pp. 203–13). New York: Guilford Press.

Rosenberg, H., & Phillips, K. T. (2003). Acceptability and availability of harm-reduction interventions for drug abuse in American substance abuse treatment agencies. *Psychology of Addictive Behaviors, 17*(3), 203–10.

Rotgers, F., Kern, M. F., & Hoeltzel, R. (2002). *Responsible drinking: A moderation management approach for problem drinkers.* Oakland, CA: New Harbinger Publications.

Rothschild, D. E. (1992). Treating the substance abuser: Psychotherapy throughout the recovery process. In B. C. Wallace (Ed.), *The chemically dependent: Phases of treatment and recovery* (pp. 82–91). New York: Brunner/Mazel Inc.

Rounds-Bryant, J. L., Motivans, M. A., & Pelissier, B. (2003). Comparison of background characteristics and behaviors of African American, Hispanic, and white substance abusers treated in federal prison: Result from the TRIAD study. *Journal of Psychoactive Drugs, 25*(3), 333–41.

Rubinstein, G., & Mukamal, D. (2002). Welfare and housing: Denial of benefits to drug offenders. In M. Mauer & M. Chesney-Lind (Eds.), *Invisible punishment: The collateral consequences of mass imprisonment* (pp. 37–49). New York: New Press.

Salasin, S. (2002). Overview: Working with women in jails: Developing a gender-based network of services for strengthening women and their families. In G. Landsberg, M. Rock, L. K. W. Berg, & A. Smiley (Eds.), *Serving mentally ill offenders: Challenges and opportunities for mental health professionals* (pp. 159–64). New York: Springer.

Samenow, S. E. (1998). *Straight talk about criminals.* Northvale, NJ: Jason Aronson.

Sammons, M. T. (2001). Combined treatments for mental disorders: Clinical dilemmas. In M. T. Sammons & N. B. Schmidt (Eds.), *Combined treatments for mental disorders: A guide to psychological and pharmacological interventions* (pp. 11–32). Washington, DC: American Psychological Association.

Sammons, M. T., & Schmidt, N. B. (2001). *Combined treatments for mental disorders: A guide to psychological and pharmacological interventions.* Washington, DC: American Psychological Association.

Sanchirico, A., & Jablonka, K. (2000). Keeping foster children connected to their biological parents: The impact of foster parent training and support. *Child and Adolescent Social Work Journal, 17*, 185–203.

Satel, S. (2002). Is drug addiction a brain disease? In D. F. Musto (Ed.), *One hundred years of heroin* (pp. 55–63). Westport, CT: Auburn House.

Saunders, B., Wilkinson, C., & Phillips, M. (1995). The impact of a brief motivational intervention with opiate users attending a methadone programme. *Addiction, 90*, 415–24.

Saxe, L. D. (1983). *The effectiveness and costs of alcoholism treatment: Health technology case study 22.* Washington, DC: U.S. Government Printing Office.

Sayre, S. L., Evans, M., Hokanson, P. S., Schmitz, J. M., Stotts, A. L., Averill, P., & Grabowski, J. (2004). "Who gets in?": Recruitment and screening processes in outpatient substance abuse trials. *Addictive Behaviors, 29,* 389–98.

Schewe, P. A. (Ed.). (2002). *Preventing violence in relationships.* Washington, DC: American Psychological Association.

Schilling, R. F., El-Bassel, N., Serrano, Y., & Wallace, B. C. (1992). AIDS prevention strategies for Latino and African-American substance users. *Psychology of Addictive Behavior, 6*(2), 81–90.

Schneider, R. J., Casey, J., & Kohn, R. (2000). Motivational versus confrontational interviewing: A comparison of substance abuse assessment practices at employee assistance programs. *Journal of Behavioral Health Services and Research, 27,* 60–74.

Schuckit, M. A. (2000). *Drug and alcohol abuse: A clinical guide to diagnosis and treatment* (5th ed.). New York: Academic/Plenum Publishers.

Schuckit, M. A., Smith, T. L., Danko, G. P., Bucholz, K. K., & Reich, T. (2001). Five-year clinical course associated with DSM-IV alcohol abuse or dependence in a large group of men and women. *American Journal of Psychiatry, 158,* 1084–90.

Seinfeld, J. (2002). *A primer of handling the negative therapeutic reaction.* Northvale, NJ: Jason Aronson.

Seligman, M. E. P. (1998). *Learned optimism: How to change your mind and your life.* New York: Simon & Schuster.

Seligman, M. E. P. (2002). *Authentic happiness: Using the new positive psychology to realize your potential for lasting fulfillment.* New York: Free Press.

Seligman, M. E. P., & Csikszentmihalyi, M. (2000). Positive psychology: An introduction. *American Psychologist, 55*(1), 5–14.

Shane, P. (2002, August 23). *Long-term outcomes at adolescent treatment model (ATM) study sites.* Paper presented within a symposium entitled "Persistent effects of adolescent substance abuse treatment," at the 110th annual convention of the American Psychological Association, McCormick Place, Lakeside Center, Chicago, IL.

Shaner, A., Tucker, D. E., Roberts, L. S., & Eckman, T. A. (1999). Disability income, cocaine use, and contingency management among patients with cocaine dependence and schizophrenia. In S. T. Higgins & K. Silverman (Eds.), *Motivating behavior change among illicit-drug abusers: Research on contingency management interventions* (pp. 95–121). Washington, DC: American Psychological Association.

Sheldon, K. M., & King, L. (2001). Why positive psychology is necessary. *American Psychologist, 56*(3), 216–17.

Siegal, H. A., Rapp, R. C., & Li, L., & Saha, P. (2001). Case management in substance abuse treatment: Perspectives, impact, and use. In F. M. Tims, C. G. Leukefeld, & J. J. Platt (Eds.), *Relapse and recovery in addictions* (pp. 253–74). New Haven, CT: Yale University Press.

Siegel, D. J. (1999). *The developing mind: Toward a neurobiology of interpersonal experience.* New York: Guilford Press.

Silverman, K., Preston, K. L., Stitzer, M. L., & Schuster, C. R. (1999). Efficacy and versatility of voucher-based reinforcement in drug abuse treatment. In S. T. Higgins & K. Silverman (Eds.), *Motivating behavior change among illicit-drug abusers: Research on contingency management interventions* (pp. 163–82). Washington, DC: American Psychological Association.

Silverman, K., Wong, C. J., Umbritch-Schneiter, A., Montoya, I. D., Schuster, C. R., & Preston, K. L. (1998). Broad beneficial effects of reinforcement of cocaine abstinence in methadone patients. *Journal of Consulting and Clinical Psychology, 66,* 811–24.

Simpson, D. D. (2002). Investigating drug abuse treatment for correctional populations. *Research Roundup, 12*(3), 1–3.

Simpson, D. D. (2003). Introduction to 5-year follow-up treatment outcome studies. *Journal of Substance Abuse Treatment, 25*(3), 123–24.

Simpson, D. D., Joe, G. W., & Rowan-Szal, G. A. (1997). Drug abuse treatment retention and process effects on follow-up outcomes. *Drug and Alcohol Dependence, 47*, 227–35.

Simpson, D. D., & Savage, L. (1980). Drug abuse treatment readmissions and outcomes. *Archives of General Psychiatry, 37*, 896–901.

Simpson, D. D., & Sells, S. B. (1982). Effectiveness of treatment for drug abuse: An overview of the DARP research program. *Advances in Alcohol and Drug Abuse, 2*, 7–29.

Simpson, D. D., Wexler, H. K., & Inciardi, J. A. (1999). Introduction. *Prison Journal, 79*, 291–93.

Smith, H. (2003). Despair, resilience, and the meaning of family: Group therapy with French-speaking African survivors of torture. In B. C. Wallace & R. T. Carter (Eds.), *Understanding and dealing with violence: A multicultural approach* (pp. 291–316). Thousand Oaks, CA: Sage.

Sobell, M. B., & Sobell, L. C. (2002). Foreword. In F. Rotgers, M. F. Kern, & R. Hoeltzel (Eds.), *Responsible drinking: A moderation management approach for problem drinkers* (pp. vii–viii). Oakland, CA: New Harbinger Publications.

Sorenson, J. L., Guydish, J., Rawson, R., & Zweben, J. E. (Eds.). (2003). Introduction: The need for research-practice collaboration. In J. L. Sorenson, R. Rawson, J. Guydish, & J. E. Zweben (Eds.), *Drug abuse treatment through collaboration: Practice and research partnerships that work* (pp. 3–10). Washington, DC: American Psychological Association.

Sorenson, J. L., Rawson, R., Guydish, J., & Zweben, J. E. (Eds.). (2003). *Drug abuse treatment through collaboration: Practice and research partnerships that work.* Washington, DC: American Psychological Association.

Spiess, M. (2002, April). *MDMA (ecstasy).* Rockville, MD: ONDCP Drug Policy Information Clearinghouse.

Springer, D. W., McNeece, C. A., & Arnold, E. M. (2003). *Substance abuse treatment for criminal offenders: An evidence-based guide for practitioners.* Washington, DC: American Psychological Association.

Stark, M. (1994). *Working with resistance.* Northvale, NJ: Jason Aronson.

Staton, M., Leukefeld, C. G., & Logan, T. K. (2002). Clinical issues in treating substance-abusing women. In C. J. Leukefeld, F. Tims, & D. Farabee (Eds.), *Treatment of drug offenders: Policies and issues* (pp. 217–25). New York: Springer.

Steenberg, T. A., Meyers, A. W., May, R. K., & Whelan, J. P. (2002). Development and validation of the gamblers' belief questionnaire. *Psychology of Addictive Behaviors, 16*(2), 143–49.

Stephens, R. S., Roffman, R. A., & Curtin, L. (2000). Comparison of extended versus brief treatments for marijuana use. *Journal of Consulting and Clinical Psychology, 68*, 898–908.

Stewart, S. H., & Conrod, P. J. (2003). Psychosocial models of functional associations between posttraumatic stress disorder and substance use disorder. In P. Ouimette & P. J. Brown (Eds.), *Trauma and substance abuse: Causes, consequences, and treatment of comorbid disorders* (pp. 29–55). Washington, DC: American Psychological Association.

Stinchcomb, J. B., & Terry, W.C. (2001). Predicting the likelihood of rearrest among shock incarceration graduates: Moving beyond another nail in the boot camp coffin. *Crime and Delinquency, 47*(2), 221–42.

Stitzer, M. L., & McCaul, M. E. (1987). Criminal justice interventions with drug and alcohol abusers. In E. K. Morris & C. J. Braukmann (Eds.), *Behavioral approaches to crime and delinquency: A handbook of application, research, and concepts* (pp. 331–62). New York: Plenum Press.

Stolzenberg, L. (1999). "Three strikes and you're out": The impact of California's new mandatory sentencing law on serious crime rates. In L. Stolzenberg & S. J. D'Alessio (Eds.), *Criminal courts for the 21st century*. Paramus, NJ: Prentice Hall.

Stotts, A. M., Schmitz, J. M., Rhoades, H. M., & Grabowski, J. (2001). Motivational interviewing with cocaine-dependent patients: A pilot study. *Journal of Consulting and Clinical Psychology, 69*, 858–62.

Strathdee, S. A. (2003). Sexual HIV transmission in the context of injection drug use: Implications for interventions. *International Journal of Drug Policy, 14*, 79–81.

Strausner, S. L. A. (2001). Ethnocultural issues in substance abuse treatment. In. S. L. A. Strausner (Ed.), *Ethnocultural factors in substance abuse treatment* (pp. 3–28). New York: Guilford Press.

Stuart, G. L., Moore, T. M., Ramsey, S. E., & Kahler, C. W. (2003). Relationship aggression and substance use among women court-referred to domestic violence intervention programs. *Addictive Behaviors, 28*, 1603–10.

Sue, D. W. (2003). *Overcoming our racism: The journey to liberation*. New York: Wiley.

Sue, D. W., Carter, R. T., Casas, J. M., Fouad, N. A., Ivey, A. E., Jensen, M., LaFromboise, T., Manese, J. E., Ponterotto, J. G., & Vazquez-Nutall, E. (1998). *Multicultural counseling competencies: Individual and organizational development*. Thousand Oaks, CA: Sage.

Sue, D. W., & Sue, D. (2003). *Counseling the culturally diverse: Theory and practice* (4th ed.). New York: Wiley.

Suinn, R. M. (2001). The terrible twos: Anger and anxiety: Hazardous to your health. *American Psychologist, 56*(1), 27–36.

Sung, H., Belenko, S., Feng, L., & Tabachnick, C. (2004). Predicting treatment noncompliance among criminal justice–mandated clients: A theoretical and empirical exploration. *Journal of Substance Abuse Treatment, 26*, 13–26.

Swanson, A. J., Pantalon, M. V., & Cohen, K. R. (1999). Motivational interviewing and treatment adherence among psychiatric and dually diagnosed patients. *Journal of Nervous and Mental Disease, 187*, 630–35.

Tatarsky, A. (2002). *Harm reduction psychotherapy: A new treatment for drug and alcohol problems*. Northvale, NJ: Jason Aronson.

Tatarsky, A. (2003). Harm reduction psychotherapy: Extending the reach of traditional substance use treatment. *Journal of Substance Abuse Treatment, 25*, 249–56.

Tatarsky, A., & Washton, A. (1992). Intensive outpatient treatment: A psychological perspective. In B. C. Wallace (Ed.), *The chemically dependent: Phases of treatment and recovery* (pp. 28–38). New York: Brunner/Mazel.

Thompson, C. E., & Carter, R. T. (Eds.). (1997). *Racial identity theory: Applications to individual, group, and organizational interventions*. Mahwah, NJ: Erlbaum.

Timpson, S. C., Williams, M. L., Bowen, A. M., & Keel, K. B. (2003). Condom use behaviors in HIV-infected African American crack cocaine users. *Substance Abuse, 24*(4), 211–20.

Tonigan, J. S., & Tuscova, R. (1998). Mutual-help groups: Research and clinical implications. In W. R. Miller & N. Heather (Eds.), *Treating addictive behaviors* (2nd ed., pp. 285–98). New York: Plenum Press.

The TOPPS-II Interstate Cooperative Study Group. (2003). Drug treatment completion and post-discharge employment in the TOPPS-II interstate cooperative study. *Journal of Substance Abuse Treatment, 25*(1), 9–18.

Triffleman, E., Carroll, K., & Kellogg, S. (1999). Substance dependence posttraumatic stress disorder therapy: An integrated cognitive-behavioral approach. *Journal of Substance Abuse Treatment, 17,* 3–14.

Trulson, C., Triplett, R., & Snell, C. (2001). Social control in a school setting: Evaluating a school-based boot camp. *Crime and Delinquency, 47*(4), 573–609.

Tucker, J. A. (1999). Changing addictive behavior: Historical and contemporary perspectives. In J. A. Tucker, D. M. Donovan, & G. A. Marlatt (Eds.), *Changing addictive behavior: Bridging clinical and public health strategies* (pp. 3–44). New York: Guilford Press.

Turner, N. R., & Wilhelm, D. F. (2002). Are the politics of criminal justice changing? *Corrections Today, 64*(7), 74–76.

Tyler, T. R., & Boeckmann, R. J. (1997). "Three strikes and you are out, but why": The psychology of public support for punishing rule breakers. *Law and Society, 13*(2), 237–65.

van Wormer, K. (2001). *Counseling female offenders and victims: A strengths-restorative approach.* New York: Springer.

van Wormer, K., & Davis, D. R. (2003). *Addiction treatment: A strengths perspective.* Pacific Grove, CA: Brooks/Cole.

Vaughan, S. C. (2001). *Half empty, half full: Understanding the psychological roots of optimism.* New York: Harcourt.

Verebey, K., Buchan, B. J., & Turner, C. E. (1998). Laboratory testing. In R. J. Frances & S. I. Miller (Eds.), *Clinical textbook of addictive disorders* (2nd ed., pp. 71–88). New York: Guilford Press.

Vietello, M. (1997). Three strikes: Can we return to rationality? *Journal of Criminal Law and Criminology, 87*(2), 395–481.

Wallace, B. C. (1987). Cocaine dependence treatment on an inpatient detoxification unit. *Journal of Substance Abuse Treatment, 4*(2), 85–92.

Wallace, B. C. (1989a). Psychological and environmental determinants of relapse in crack cocaine smokers. *Journal of Substance Abuse Treatment, 6*(2), 95–106.

Wallace, B. C. (1989b). Relapse prevention in psychoeducational groups for crack cocaine smokers. *Journal of Substance Abuse Treatment, 6*(4), 229–39.

Wallace, B. C. (1990a). Crack addiction: Treatment and recovery issues. *Contemporary Drug Problems, 17*(1), 79–119.

Wallace, B. C. (1990b). Crack cocaine smokers as adult children of alcoholics: The dysfunctional family link. *Journal of Substance Abuse Treatment, 7*(2), 89–100.

Wallace, B. C. (1990c). Treating crack cocaine dependence: The critical role of relapse prevention. *Journal of Psychoactive Drugs, 22*(2), 149–58.

Wallace, B. C. (1991a). Chemical dependency treatment for pregnant addicts: Beyond the criminal sanctions perspective. *Psychology of Addictive Behaviors, 5,* 23–35.

Wallace, B. C. (1991b). *Crack cocaine: A practical treatment approach for the chemically dependent.* New York: Brunner/Mazel.

Wallace, B. C. (1991c). Crack cocaine: What constitutes state-of-the-art treatment? *Journal of Addictive Diseases, 11*(2), 83–102.

Wallace, B. C. (1992a). Conclusion: Future directions in chemical dependence treatment and the need to break silence on child abuse. In B. C. Wallace (Ed.), *The chemically dependent: Phases of treatment and recovery* (pp. 337–46). New York: Brunner/Mazel.

Wallace, B. C. (1992b). Inpatient treatment for the first phase of withdrawal. In B. C. Wallace (Ed.), *The chemically dependent: Phases of treatment and recovery* (pp. 15–27). New York: Brunner/Mazel.

Wallace, B. C. (1992c). Multidimensional relapse prevention from a biopsychosocial perspective across phases of recovery. In B. C. Wallace (Ed.), *The chemically dependent: Phases of treatment and recovery* (pp. 171–84). New York: Brunner/Mazel.

Wallace, B. C. (1992d). Relapse prevention for the cocaine and crack dependent: An essential treatment component. In R. R. Watson (Ed.), *Treatment of drug and alcohol abuse* (pp. 175–203). Clifton, NJ: Humana Press.

Wallace, B. C. (Ed.). (1992e). *The chemically dependent: Phases of treatment and recovery.* New York: Brunner/Mazel.

Wallace, B. C. (1992f). The therapeutic community as a treatment modality and the role of the professional consultant: Spotlight on Damon House. In B. C. Wallace (Ed.), *The chemically dependent: Phases of treatment and recovery* (pp. 39–58). New York: Brunner/Mazel.

Wallace, B. C. (1992g). Treating crack cocaine dependence: The critical role of relapse prevention. *Journal of Psychoactive Drugs, 24*(2), 213–22.

Wallace, B. C. (1992h). Treatment and recovery in an evolving field. In B. C. Wallace (Ed.), *The chemically dependent: Phases of treatment and recovery* (pp. 3–14). New York: Brunner/Mazel.

Wallace, B. C. (1992i). Toward effective treatment models for special groups: Criminal, pregnant, un-insured, adolescent, HIV positive, methadone-maintained, and homeless populations. In B. C. Wallace (Ed.), *The chemically dependent: Phases of treatment and recovery* (pp. 310–36). New York: Brunner/Mazel.

Wallace, B. C. (1993a). Cross-cultural counseling with the chemically dependent: Preparing for service delivery within our culture of violence. *Journal of Psychoactive Drugs, 24*(3), 9–20.

Wallace, B. C. (1993b). Drugs, alcohol, and the dysfunctional family: Male/female differences. In R. R. Watson (Ed.), *Addictive behaviors in women* (pp. 71–96). Clifton, NJ: Humana Press.

Wallace, B. C. (1995). Women and minorities in treatment. In A. M. Washton (Ed.), *Psychotherapy and substance abuse: A practitioner's handbook* (pp. 470–92). New York: Guilford Press.

Wallace, B. C. (1996a). *Adult children of dysfunctional families: Prevention, intervention, and treatment for community mental health promotion.* Westport, CT: Praeger.

Wallace, B. C. (1996b). Counseling the cocaine dependent client. *Directions in Substance Abuse Counseling, 4*(6), 3–6.

Wallace, B. C. (1996c, March 2). Treatment guidelines across phases of recovery. Paper presented at the Annual Addiction Symposium sponsored by Cambridge Hospital/Harvard Medical School, Boston, MA.

Wallace, B. C. (1997). *Let me tell you why: An educational learning tool about HIV/AIDS for children age 8 and above.* New York: Author.

Wallace, B. C. (2000a). A call for change in multicultural training at graduate schools of education: Educating to end oppression and for social justice. *Teachers College Record, 102*(6), 1086–111.

Wallace, B. C. (2000b). The influence of culture on the development of theory and practice in the field of mental health. In R. T. Carter (Ed.), *Addressing cultural issues in organizations.* Thousand Oaks, CA: Sage.

Wallace, B. C. (2002). The healing power of groups and the residential therapeutic community: The case of Ms. E—A study in success and mutual transformation. In A. Tatarsky (Ed.), *Harm reduction psychotherapy: A new treatment for drug and alcohol problems.* Northvale, NJ: Jason Aaronson.

Wallace, B. C. (2003). A multicultural approach to violence: Toward a psychology of oppression, liberation, and identity development. In B. C. Wallace & R. T. Carter (Eds.), *Understanding and dealing with violence: A multicultural approach* (pp. 3–40). Thousand Oaks, CA: Sage.

Wallace, B. C. (2005). A practical skills approach for racial-cultural skill acquisition. In R. T. Carter (Ed.), *Handbook of racial-cultural psychology and counseling: Vol. 2.* New York: Wiley.

Wallace, B. C., & Carter, R. T. (Eds.). (2003). *Understanding and dealing with violence: A multicultural approach.* Thousand Oaks, CA: Sage.

Wallace, B. C., Carter, R. T., Nanin, J., Keller, R., & Alleyne, V. (2003). Identity development for "diverse and different others": Integrating stages of change, motivational interviewing, and identity theories for race, people of color, sexual orientation, and disability. In B. C. Wallace & R. T. Carter (Eds.), *Understanding and dealing with violence: A multicultural approach* (pp. 41–92). Thousand Oaks, CA: Sage.

Watson, C. G., Brown, K., Tilleskjor, C., Jacobs, L., & Lucel, J. (1988). The comparative recidivism rates of voluntary- and coerced-admission male alcoholics. *Journal of Clinical Psychology, 44*(4), 573–81.

Weingart, K. R., & Marlatt, G. A. (1998). Harm reduction and public policy. In G. A. Marlatt (Ed.), *Harm reduction: Pragmatic strategies for managing high-risk behaviors* (pp. 353–78). New York: Guilford Press.

Weinstein, S. P., Gottheil, E., & Sterling, R. C. (1997). Randomized comparison of intensive outpatient vs. individual therapy for cocaine abusers. *Journal of Addictive Diseases, 16,* 41–56.

Wells-Parker, E. (1994). Mandated treatment: Lessons from research with drinking and driving offenders. *Alcohol Health and Research World, 18,* 302–6.

Wexler, H. K. (2003). The promise of prison-based treatment for dually diagnosed inmates. *Journal of Substance Abuse Treatment, 25*(3), 223–31.

Wexler, H. K., De Leon, G., Thomas, G., Kressel, D., & Peters, J. (1999). The Amity Prison TC evaluation: Reincarceration outcomes. *Criminal Justice and Behavior, 26,* 147–67.

Wexler, H. K., Falkin, G., & Lipton, D. (1990). Outcome evaluation of a prison therapeutic community for substance-abuse treatment. *Criminal Justice and Behavior, 17*(1), 71–92.

Wexler, H. K., & Williams, R. (1986). The stay'n out therapeutic community: Prison treatment for substance abusers. *Journal of Substance Abuse Treatment, 18*(3), 221–30.

Whitehead, J. T., & Braswell, M. C. (2000). Future of probation: Reintroducing the spiritual dimension into correctional practice. *Criminal Justice Review, 25*(2), 207–33.

Wilson, P. H. (Ed.). (1992). *Principles and practice of relapse prevention.* New York: Guilford Press.

Winters, K. C., Stinchfield, R. D., Botzet, A., & Anderson, N. (2002). A prospective study of youth gambling behaviors. *Psychology of Addictive Behaviors, 16*(1), 3–9.

Wiscot, R., Kopera-Frye, K., & Begovic, A. (2002). Binge drinking in later life: Comparing young-old and old-old social drinkers. *Psychology of Addictive Behaviors, 16*(3), 252–55.

Woody, G. E., Luborsky, L., McLellan, A. T., O'Brien, C. P., Beck, A. T., Blaine, J., Herman, I., & Hole, A. (1983). Psychotherapy for opiate addicts: Does it help? *Archives of General Psychiatry, 40,* 639–45.

Woody, G. E., McLellan, A. T., Luborsky, L., & O'Brien, C. P. (1987). Twelve-month follow-up of psychotherapy for opiate dependence. *American Journal of Psychiatry, 144,* 590–96.

Woody, G. E., McLellan, A. T., Luborsky, L., & O'Brien, C. P. (1995). Psychotherapy in community methadone programs: A validation study. *American Journal of Psychiatry, 152*(9), 1302–8.

Wurmser, L. (1992). Psychology of compulsive drug use. In. B. C. Wallace (Ed.), *The chemically dependent: Phases of treatment and recovery* (pp. 92–114). New York: Brunner/Mazel.

Yalisove, D. L. (1992). Survey of contemporary psychoanalytically oriented clinicians on the treatment of the addictions: A synthesis. In. B. C. Wallace (Ed.), *The chemically dependent: Phases of treatment and recovery* (pp. 61–81). New York: Brunner/Mazel.

Yalisove, D. L. (Ed.). (1997). *Essential papers on addiction.* New York: New York University Press.

Young, E. B. (1995). The role of incest in relapse and recovery. In A. M. Washton (Ed.), *Psychotherapy and substance abuse: A practitioner's handbook* (pp. 451–69). New York: Guilford Press.

Zarkin, G. A., Dunlap, L., Bray, J. W., & Wechsberg, W. M. (2002). The effect of treatment completion and length of stay on employment and crime in outpatient drug-free treatment. *Journal of Substance Abuse Treatment, 23*(4), 261–71.

Zweben, J. E. (1992). Issues in the treatment of the dual-diagnosis patient. In B. C. Wallace (Ed.), *The chemically dependent: Phases of treatment and recovery* (pp. 298–309). New York: Brunner/Mazel.

Index

291

treatment for, 197, 198, 199, 204–17
passim, 222, 238
Marlatt, G. A., 52, 53, 72, 83, 93–94, 134,
255
Marlowe, D. B., 10, 40, 41, 43, 44, 49–50
Matrix Model, 56, 66, 67, 84, 85, 255,
258; case study applications of, 136,
137–38, 159, 184, 192, 207, 209, 223
McLellan, A. T., 3, 87, 252
mentally ill chemical abusers (MICA), 5,
169, 176, 196, 243; as multiproblem
clients, 26, 33, 34, 106, 112, 113, 202,
207, 244–49 passim, 263
Mercer, D. E., 74, 76–77, 87
MET. *See* motivational enhancement
therapy
metamphetamine dependence, 21, 26,
29, 31, 84
methadone, 51, 57, 75, 77, 81
MICA. *See* mentally ill chemical abusers
Miller, W. R., 58, 70, 71, 86, 94, 173, 252,
254–55
mood disorders, 18, 19, 21, 26, 28, 33, 112
Moos, R. H., 41, 49–60 passim, 65, 66,
67, 74, 89, 91, 92, 101, 107, 248, 253,
255, 260, 261
motivational enhancement therapy
(MET), 56, 66, 67, 72, 105; case
studies illustrating, 136, 144, 150, 158,
163, 184, 185, 189–90, 207, 212–13,
223, 226; definition of, 69;
effectiveness of, 52, 53, 69, 74. *See also*
motivational interviewing
motivational interviewing, 55, 56, 67,
69, 70–71, 86, 97, 98, 105, 255, 256;
case studies involving, 136, 138–39,
140, 144, 150–58 passim, 163–64, 168,
172, 173, 177, 182, 184, 185, 190, 193,
207, 208, 218, 223, 226–27, 256;
internal motivation of clients and,
12, 14, 16, 142, 200–201, 256. *See also*
motivational enhancement therapy
(MET)
multiculturalism, xiv, 67, 98–99, 136,
147, 161, 184, 207, 223; practitioner
sensitivity to, 4, 98–99, 149, 150, 222
multiproblem clients: case studies of,
17–28 passim, 118, 135, 137–66

passim, 168–69, 183–202 passim,
203–18 passim, 221–50 passim, 256,
260, 262–63; characteristics of, xv, 17,
29; ego, strengthening of, 106, 113,
114, 120, 121; guilt feelings, 122–23,
141, 146; internal motivation to
change, 155–56, 163, 167, 172, 173,
176, 245; parental rights, loss of,
123–24, 137; prioritization of
treatment for ("first things first"),
105–29 passim, 203, 218;
readjustment disorders, 115–16;
reintegration into family and
community, 110–11; stability,
mental and emotional, 111–12;
stigmatization of, 4, 133, 134, 142,
146, 147–48, 149, 152–53, 163, 166,
251. *See also* coerced clients;
concerned clients; mandated clients;
mentally ill chemical abusers
(MICA)

NA. *See* Narcotics Anonymous
Najavits, L. M., 89, 90–91
Narcotics Anonymous (NA), 67, 73–74,
75, 84, 257, 263; case studies
involving, 136, 137, 138, 157, 184,
192, 212, 223, 241, 242, 248. *See also*
Alcoholics Anonymous (AA);
twelve-step facilitation (TSF)
National Institute on Drug Abuse
(NIDA), 47, 49, 50, 56, 57, 66, 69, 133
negative countertransference reactions,
165, 184, 233; case studies
illustrating, 137, 142, 143, 144, 152,
154, 233; overcoming of, xv, 135, 144,
166, 221, 251
neurocognitive deficits, 106, 125–26
New York City, xiv, 7, 112, 127, 128
New York State, 6, 112, 113
NIDA. *See* National Institute on Drug
Abuse

opiate dependence, 7, 79, 81, 84
optimistic thinking/learned optimism,
67, 99, 147; case studies involving,
136, 144, 154, 158, 161, 184, 188, 191,
195, 207, 208, 222, 223, 233;

About the Author

Barbara C. Wallace, PhD, is a New York State licensed psychologist and tenured associate professor of health education in the Department of Health and Behavior Studies at Teachers College, Columbia University. Dr. Wallace has been honored with the status of fellow in Division 50 on Addictive Behaviors within the American Psychological Association. Her books include the following: *Crack Cocaine: A Practical Treatment Approach for the Chemically Dependent* (1991), *The Chemically Dependent: Phases of Treatment and Recovery* (Editor, 1992), *Adult Children of Dysfunctional Families: Prevention, Intervention and Treatment for Community Mental Health Promotion* (1996), and *Understanding and Dealing with Violence: A Multicultural Approach* (with coeditor Robert T. Carter, PhD, 2003). In addition, she has published numerous journal articles and chapters in edited books.

Dr. Wallace is engaged in regional, national, and international work as a consulting psychologist. She also travels widely as a keynote speaker, conference presenter, and workshop leader, covering a range of topics—chemical dependence, relapse prevention for a range of addictive and problem behaviors, HIV/AIDS, violence prevention, trauma resolution for sexual abuse, physical abuse, and domestic violence, as well as multiculturalism/diversity. She also cofounded and codirects the Research Group on Disparities in Health within the Department of Health and Behavior Studies at Teachers College, Columbia University, supporting the work of graduate students, postdoctoral fellows, and colleagues.